THIRD EDITION

P9-ASH-285

Social Policy and Social Programs

A Method for the Practical Public Policy Analyst

Donald E. Chambers

University of Kansas

Allyn and Bacon

Boston ▪ London ▪ Toronto ▪ Sydney ▪ Tokyo ▪ Singapore

Property of the Library
Wilfrid Laurier University

Property of WLU
Social Work Library

DISCARD

Series Editor, Social Work and Family Therapy: *Judy Fifer*
Vice-President and Editor-in-Chief, Social Sciences: *Karen Hanson*
Series Editorial Assistant: *Julianna M. Cancio*
Executive Marketing Manager: *Lisa Kimball*
Marketing Manager: *Jackie Aaron*
Production Editor: *Christopher H. Rawlings*
Editorial-Production Service: *Omegatype Typography, Inc.*
Composition and Prepress Buyer: *Linda Cox*
Manufacturing Buyer: *Julie McNeill*
Cover Administrator: *Jennifer Hart*
Electronic Composition: *Omegatype Typography, Inc.*

Copyright © 2000, 1993 by Allyn & Bacon
A Pearson Education Company
Needham Heights, MA 02494

Internet: www.abacon.com

All rights reserved. No part of the material protected by this copyright notice may be
reproduced or utilized in any form or by any means, electronic or mechanical, including
photocopying, recording, or by any information storage and retrieval system, without written
permission from the copyright owner.

Library of Congress Cataloging-in-Publication Data

Chambers, Donald E.
    Social policy and social programs : a method for the practical
public policy analyst / Donald E. Chambers. — 3rd ed.
        p.   cm.
    Includes index.
    ISBN 0-205-29148-1 (alk. paper)
    1. Public welfare administration—United States.   2. Social
problems—United States.   3. United States—Social policy.   I. Title.
    HV91.C444 2000
    361.6'1'0973—ddc21   98-45316
                                                                                    CIP

Printed in the United States of America

10 9 8 7 6 5 4 3 2 1   04 03 02 01 00 99

CONTENTS

PREFACE

The General Approach of the Book

This book is about public social welfare policy, social welfare program designs, and the instruments through which they are expressed: governmental organizations, public departments, and welfare bureaus. The book is intended for use in courses that prepare students for practice in social work or in one of the many other human service fields. It is written with the young student-practitioner in mind, assuming little or no experience with social programs and nothing more than an ordinary citizen's exposure to social problems. No doubt there will be many readers who do not fit this description, readers with years of rich experience as paraprofessional human service workers. Instructors know that such students bring additional depth and flavor to the material; the text is written with a view toward facilitating that kind of enrichment.

Of course, writing a social policy text is a special challenge precisely because of the wide variability in the age, experience, and preparation of its audience. Although social policy texts have multiplied in the last decade, no single text has been totally successful. It is quite clear why success has been so long in coming: the task is simply too demanding. The text must be written with the simplicity and clarity appropriate for beginning-level practitioners, yet still deal with the extraordinary complexity of the world of public social policy and social programs. In a text for frontline practitioners, it is not appropriate to linger over the fine details of social policy abstractions or the more technical points at the heart of current academic debate. In addition, there is the distressing fact that the basic concepts in this field (by whatever name it is called—public policy, policy analysis, or public administration) are fundamentally vague and incomplete. Given all this, it would not be unreasonable to conclude that a textbook on this topic might be premature. That will be left to the tender mercies of those who can judge it best: the readers and instructors who use this book. The solution I have chosen is to present a general orientation to the topic and its major elements, to focus on its most basic structure, and to bring into sharp focus only the most central issues: social problems, programs, and policies. My criterion for identifying these issues was to focus on social problems, social policies, and programs that are the main concern of organizations in whose employ the students who use this textbook are likely to find themselves. The following social problems and program areas are representative in that way: child welfare, health, poverty, and mental illness. There are other good candidates for inclusion—corrections, substance abuse, aging, and physical disablement, for example—so they are referred to in the textual examples and exercises. Instructors will find source material listed and annotated at the end of chapters.

The general approach of this text is designed for social work and human service practitioners (including their immediate supervisors) functioning as frontline practitioners—staff members of an organization whose task it is to enact social policy in direct encounters with citizens.[1] Such a practitioner selects and packages services and benefits, counsels and gives advice, makes referrals, and is supportive, among other things. It pays to keep in mind that direct-service practitioners also take away benefits and services and deliver negative sanctions and other punitive measures that society deems appropriate under given circumstances. Of course, social practitioners do not deal in abstractions but with living, breathing people. For the conscientious and service-oriented practitioner, the consequence of a mistaken social policy or program design is not just an overstressed budget to be set right with an adroit accounting maneuver or a condition that can be dismissed with some statement like, "Well, we'll have to get that right in next year's legislature." The consequence is a hungry mother or child; a wronged, irate, and morally indignant citizen; a neighborhood terrorized by a violent psychotic; or a hospitalized child bruised, battered, and broken by an out-of-control parent. What street-level social practitioners need most to know about social policy and program design are those things that will increase their ability to extract resources and capacities from social programs that are necessary to alleviate or prevent any or all of the catalog of modern social horrors listed before. There are three general aspects here, and the major share of this book will be devoted to them.

First, orchestrating the resources and assets of a community so that they effectively serve needs requires a practitioner's clear-eyed grasp of the way a particular social problem is viewed by the program staff who control the money, goods, or services that clients need. The sophisticated frontline practitioner knows that it is not necessary to agree with that viewpoint, but whether a client gets benefits he or she needs may well depend on the practitioner's ability to present client needs in ways that are compatible with the perspectives of program staff or administrators. For example, the practitioner must understand what the staff member or administrator takes to be the concrete indicators of a problem—its causes and its consequences—that it is *really* important to relieve. The practitioner who understands and can use the method of analyzing social problems presented in Chapter 1 will be prepared to do that.

Second, working practitioners need to know some of the more important structural elements of particular social program designs: social program goals and objectives, service-delivery administrative-system characteristics, entitlement rules, and so on. For example, an understanding of eligibility rules permits an advance estimate of the extent to which staff members are allowed to use their own discretion in awarding benefits or services of various kinds. Alternatively, understanding eligibility rules can yield important predictions as to what administrative level must be contacted before discretion is possible. The chapter on entitlement rules and other chapters on various other structural features of social programs are intended to prepare practitioners with a method of analyzing social program features so that they can anticipate such things.

Third, practitioners need to understand the legal constraints on both policy makers who control program resources and on clients' use of them. Increasingly, an activist judiciary at all levels from the U.S. Supreme Court to state district courts makes and breaks social policies and both creates and withdraws important social services and benefits. Chapter 3 on the judiciary is intended to prepare students to be alert to and understand the practice constraints and freedoms created anew by the judiciary.

This approach helps the student-practitioner develop an understanding of how others view social problems and how their views affect the administration of social policies and social programs. This book does not take a detailed look at the legislative and political factors (policy as "process") that account for the *formation* of policy and social programs—no doubt a very important aspect, of course, and worthy of a textbook all its own. This choice results from my view of the typical social practitioner, to whom this book is addressed, as not primarily responsible for nor active in the legislative and political process. Although that might not conform to professional ideals, a good case can be made that it is an accurate description of the facts of the matter. My conclusion is that nothing is served by adding complexities to an already complex book.

Instructors who take exception to that choice, or who view it in a different way, will want to add material. This approach applauds the effort and involvement of practitioners in the political process and supports the notion that such efforts are an important professional obligation. Although neither this textbook nor the course for which it is intended adequately addresses those functions, students will be better informed on the subject for having read it and will be better able thereby to participate in such efforts when the occasion arises.

The main features of the approach taken by this book are matters of direct, practical importance to frontline practitioners. However, even though the chapter on social policy history serves practicality indirectly, this book will give it unbegrudged attention, welcoming it for its irreplaceable contribution to understanding. The historical development of social welfare programs and policies is part and parcel of a professional rather than a purely technical approach to this subject matter. That is the reason for Chapter 2, "Creating the Context for the Analysis of Social Policies," which addresses the broad-scale historical changes that occurred coincidentally with and following the Great Depression of the 1930s, and the civil rights struggle and the War on Poverty in the Johnson Administration in the 1960s. The proximate roots of so much of today's social policy innovation are to be found in those decades. Note, however, that the full attention historical background merits cannot be given in a single volume or in a single course.

Finally, my particular objective in writing this book was to put together a method of analysis that ensures that students are taught how to judge whether a social policy or program could be good or bad for their clients—and to provide them with particular and explicit criteria by which to generate those judgments. Thus, program designs and features can be judged *in advance* to have such serious design faults and side effects that they cannot possibly achieve their goals. These evaluative criteria are included in each chapter for each program or policy operating feature. Many, if not most, books on social policy lack them entirely or rely on the traditional concepts of adequacy, equity, and efficiency taken from the field of economics. These refer to quite arbitrary concepts of justice and cost-benefit/cost-effectiveness to give them substance. The term "adequacy" does not immediately imply "adequacy-for-what-purpose." This book will take some pains to illustrate how the social problem analysis underlying the social policy/program conception provides a concrete context for defining those abstractions and applying them to the pressing realities that practitioners deal with in everyday life.

The Organization of the Book

This book is organized around two major aspects: social problem analysis and social policy and program analysis. The book opens with a presentation of the central importance of social policy in the professional practice of social work and other human services. Because social policies both create and constrain the possibilities in any social practice, students must grasp the fact that understanding social policies is not a matter of choice. The major task of Part One of this book is to show students how social problems can be analyzed using four interrelated but different aspects: problem definition, ideology, causal explanation, and identification of gainers and losers.

The second chapter in Part One shows the reader the importance of historical context in the analysis of social problems (and social policies and programs as well) and demonstrates some methods for gathering the historical context into an analysis. This style of policy analysis asks the reader to back off from a purely practical perspective at one point in the analysis and to view social policies and programs from a historical perspective. This perspective describes how social policies and programs have changed over time; how competing political processes, agendas, and compromise form operating programs and policy; and how different the actual operating characteristics can be from the legislative, political, or even judicial intention. The objective here is to sensitize students to the importance of history in policy and program development and analysis. Analysis at this level is at some remove from the fundamental concerns of the practitioner, but it is essential in enabling intelligent participation in the public forum and the legislative process.

The third chapter in Part One demonstrates how judicial decisions create social policies and provide many constraints and freedoms for social programs and social practitioners. It also teaches students a short method of analyzing judicial decisions for their practice and for local policy implications. This chapter is also intended to sensitize readers to the legal rights of clients to public social services and benefits, a topic that is further elaborated in Chapter 8 on administrative and service-delivery systems.

Part Two introduces the reader to a straightforward method of analyzing a social policy or social program. The intention is to help the student quickly grasp the minimum fundamental elements involved in a program or policy. More complex or sophisticated policy and program issues can follow in later courses.[2] The following elements are used in this analytic scheme:

1. Policy and program *goals and objectives*
2. *Forms of public benefits*
3. *Eligibility rules* for receiving benefits or services
4. *Administrative service-delivery system* (including program design[s]) through which benefits or services are delivered to consumers)
5. The method of *financing* the program benefits or services
6. Identifying important *interactions* within and between the preceding elements

Chapters 4 through 10 are devoted to the study of these basic program elements. Sometimes, classification schemes are developed to help the reader cope with confusing variations, such as those for types of eligibility rules and for types of benefits and services. In each chapter, a unique set of evaluative criteria is presented; for example, clarity and measurability are two of the several criteria for goals and objectives, just as accountability and response time are criteria for the service-delivery system.

The use of the method of analysis is demonstrated in Part Three in which the example is a particular social problem—child abuse—and a particular social program intended to deal with it. Chapter 11 opens with an analysis of social problem viewpoints; a concise description of historical issues, former program and policy efforts, and competing political agendas; and a brief review of various judicial decisions that have shaped present policy and program efforts in this area. By using the analytic method, a particular program dealing with child abuse is described and shows how the evaluative criteria for assessing the merit of the program are to be applied.

Acknowledgments

Because I never was taught by nor even conversed with the three people who have had the greatest influence on forming my ideas of what should be in this book, this is probably the only occasion there will ever be for acknowledging their influence and delivering my thanks for their contribution. The intellectual ground from which this book is taken uses concepts that Richard Titmuss first set to paper during his years at the London School of Economics and uses an analytic approach that Evelyn Burns, an LSE product herself, used in her 1948 classic, *The American Social Security System.* If this book succeeds in its aim, it is simply because it applies some of their ideas to the contemporary U.S. social policy context, a very different world from that of Titmuss in the 1950s and 1960s and from that of Burns in the late 1940s. Finally, this book is indebted to Martin Rein whose marvelously clear essays on value-critical policy analysis enabled me to think in a quite different way in the 1990s about how to teach students to make clear, practical, and unashamed value-based judgments on whether social policies and social programs are good for the clients they are intended to serve.

Other ideas that framed this book are likely to have come from that extraordinary group of teachers with whom I have been blessed and who have been (under)paid to teach me at various times over the course of almost forty years and two careers. For the most part, they have been gifts to me out of the abundance of the universe.

There is Professor Claude Henry, who taught me the wonder of ideas in the great literary classics; Professor Maude Merrill; Professor Garnet Larsen, who introduced, with great patience and forbearance, the subject of social policy to a very young, impertinent graduate student; Elizabeth Ossorio, who taught me about perseverance and wisdom in the research process; and William E. Gordon, a scientist teaching social workers, and Richard Rudner, a philosopher teaching about science.

More immediately, I would like to acknowledge the help of those who read the manuscript in one or another of its four drafts. Their fair and generous criticism is sincerely appreciated: Bradford Sheafor, Colorado State University; Anne Weick, University of Kansas; Winifred Bell, Cleveland State University; Mary Ellen Elwell, Western

Maryland College; John M. Herrick, Michigan State University; Milton S. Rosner, Ohio State University; Mitchell A. Greene, University of Northern Iowa; Kenneth R. Wedel, University of Oklahoma; Arthur J. Cox, East Tennessee State University; Joseph Kuttler, Tabor College; Gary L. Shaffer, University of Illinois at Urbana-Champaign; Jane F. R. C. Bonk, Lutheran Family and Children's Services of Illinois; Charles Rapp, University of Kansas; Rebecca Lopez, California State University-Long Beach; Murray Gruber, Loyola University-Chicago; Sharon Eisen, Mott Community College; David Iacono-Harris, University of Texas-El Paso. For their comments and suggestions on the third edition, I would like to thank Michael Forster, University of Southern Mississippi; I. Sue Jackson, Bloomsburg University; and Donald G. Magel, University of North Alabama.

I want to extend very special thanks to my (former) doctoral student, now colleague, Mary Katherine Rodwell, Virginia Commonwealth University, for her careful reading and intellectual contributions to many of the chapters. In the same way, I am indebted to John Pierpont, teaching colleague at the University of Kansas, whose ideas about policy matters and experience in using this method of policy analysis shaped the second edition in quite important ways. And I am indebted to Richard Wintersteen of the University of Minnesota-Mankato in just the same way in regard to the third edition.

I would like to thank my former editors at Macmillan Publishing Company for their efforts in the making of previous editions of this book, particularly Linda James Scharp, editor; Steve Robb, production editor; and Loretta Faber, copy editor. I would also like to thank Allyn and Bacon editor Judy Fifer for her help on this edition.

Special thanks go to my late wife, Mary Anne, who taught me so much about life and law and to whom much of Chapter 3 is indebted. Also, special thanks to James Bonk, without whose helpful assistance while I was in Central America I could not have managed. And, finally, I would like to thank Marylee Brochmann, University of Kansas, for her patient reading, support, and judicious suggestions (and helpful argument) during the third edition revision.

D. E. C.

NOTES

1. Michael Lipsky, *Street Level Bureaucracy: The Dilemma of the Individual in Public Services* (New York: Russell Sage Foundation, 1980), pp. 4–10.

2. Notice that no great attention is paid here to the distinction between *policy* and *program*. Although that distinction can deserve much attention in some contexts, it is not taken to be crucial here in this book for frontline practitioners—other than to note that policies are taken to be general rules or guides for action, whereas programs are taken to be the general human and organizational apparatus, or the instruments, through which policies are implemented.

PART ONE

Creating the Context for Social Policy Analysis

The Social Problem— Historical and Judicial Contexts

A man said to the universe:
"Sir, I exist!"
"However," replied the universe,
"That fact has not created in me
a sense of obligation."

—Stephen Crane, *War Is Kind*

Introduction: The Problem of Policy for Practitioners

The objective of this book is to help readers develop skill in the critical analysis of modern social welfare policies and programs. The motive is to preserve the sanity and dedication of social practitioners who, on behalf of clients, must daily interpret, enforce, advocate, circumvent, or challenge those policies and programs. Much of the working life of professional practitioners is spent in the context of those policies and programs. If practitioners are not employed on the staff of an agency administering such programs, they serve clients whose lives are affected vitally and daily by those programs: the client whose child is detained in a local juvenile detention center or the client whose Social Security disability benefit is suspended because a judgment of work capacity has been changed. Without being concerned about such policies or being prepared to analyze the nature of their strengths and shortcomings, no social worker can aspire to a professional calling.

Social work is unique for its simultaneous focus on the client *and* the social environment. Like family, community, psychological, and work factors, social policies and programs are a critical feature of the clients' surroundings and demand every bit as much care and attention from the working professional. For better or worse, the lives of all private citizens are subject to serious and widespread invasions by governmental social policy. For those whom social workers serve, it poses a special stress because it affects lives already burdened with fearsome and demoralizing social problems: hunger, illness, physical or mental disablement, violence, or disease.

Stephen Crane's lines at the beginning of this chapter are a moving rendition of the idea that immense forces are at work in the world, forces that have no concern for their effect on the fates of particular individuals. Crane means to call our attention to the idea that an earthquake or a volcano does not consider the suffering it causes to individuals in the cataclysmic changes it wreaks—changes begun long before those individuals were born, changes whose effects will outlive human memory.

Crane's point can be extended to modern social welfare policies and programs. Public policies generally are not designed with the needs of *individuals* in mind, rather they are designed for *groups of people* who share a common social problem. It is of utmost importance for social work practitioners to understand that because of this feature, *social policies and programs will fail some individuals on some occasions*. This fact of life is a pervasive problem and a prominent part of the work of most program administrators. It also identifies an important area of social work practice for those who work with individual clients: finding ways to meet clients' urgent and unique needs that cannot, at first glance, be met through existing programs. Examples are not difficult to find:

John Samuelson is a construction worker. Every year for the past five years he has received notice from the county attorney's office that Mildred Singer has filed suit against him for nonsupport of a child she claims is theirs. Each time a suit is filed, John loses about five working days' pay because of the time it takes to talk to his Legal Aid attorney, give depositions, and appear in court. Each year he and his present wife spend hours patching up the hard feelings recalled by his former relationship with Mildred. Each year thus far, the local judge has dismissed the case for lack of evidence because John has denied paternity on the basis that the baby was born ten and one-half months after he left Mildred. Mildred has admitted that she lived with other men during the time her child could have been conceived but nevertheless has identified John as the father. John once received a letter from Mildred admitting that, contrary to her allegation, she believed another man to be the baby's father, but John's wife destroyed the letter in a fit of jealousy. John agreed to take a blood test that, with 97 percent accuracy, tells whether a specific man can be *excluded* as a child's father.[1] The test declared that John could very well be the father. The prevailing judicial policy is to consider the test accurate, despite a 3 percent margin of error. John now must pay $200 per month in child support until the child is eighteen. In fact, Mildred (now the mother of three) does not wish to press nonsupport charges against John (now the father of four), but federal policy requires applicants for AFDC (like Mildred) to press nonsupport charges as a condition for continuing to receive financial assistance.

Note that in this case, it would be a peculiar moral position to argue that it is somehow wrong to enforce a public policy that makes fathers financially responsible for their children, pursues fathers across state lines to do so, and makes an accurate paternity test available. The reason, in this instance, that these public policies come to grief is that they did not anticipate the incredible complexity that characterizes the lives of individual ordinary citizens. Legal procedures assume—reasonably in most instances—that people will present *all* evidence in which clearly it is in their self-interest to do so. A test that is 97 percent accurate makes very few mistakes indeed, the fact that it *might* have made a mistake in this instance must be viewed in the context of ninety-seven other cases. Most people would be willing to let stand the possible injustice done to John. Here is another example:

> Nancy Willard's arms were burned off below the elbow when she caught them in the corner of a plastic injection mold. (Hot plastic disintegrates flesh and bone instantly.) Nancy was a dependable and efficient worker who earned $12 per hour. The law in her state requires all employers of more than six people to carry Workers Compensation insurance to provide for just such accidents. Nancy is twenty-eight years old and the mother of two children. The plant she works in spends a lot of money to keep it accident-free and has a 99 percent success rate—only two other serious accidents in its ten-year history. State law specifies that Nancy must agree to a lump-sum settlement of $25,000 in compensation for the loss of both arms below the elbow. Nancy's average annual earnings were $25,000—$20,000 net after taxes. She also had $1,000 worth of fringe benefits per year (medical and life insurance, uniforms, and bonuses).

There is nothing intrinsically wrong with the idea of worker-injury compensation or with public policy that requires lump-sum settlements. The problems here are with equity and adequacy that flow from the individual attributes of Nancy Willard. Were she working at minimum wage ($10,700 per year) or were she sixty-four with one year to go before retirement, a $25,000 settlement would be handsome compensation for loss of one year's work. At the age of twenty-eight, however, she has lost thirty-seven years of wages earned at full working capacity, because with prostheses to replace her arms, she probably will work at only minimum wage. Furthermore, she will lose all her earnings for a one-year period—the time it will take for surgery, prosthetic fitting, and training. This period alone will cost her $20,000, or one year of net income. (Her employer's insurance company is required to pay her medical bills.) The $25,000 lump-sum settlement will replace only a small fraction of her long-term economic loss, *and that settlement assumes that rehabilitation will be successful and that she can return to work.*

It is clear from these examples that, despite a practitioner's best efforts and good policy and program design and administration, some clients' needs will go unmet. That knowledge will be the cause of much hard feeling, bad public relations, and personal distress on the part of the social worker. If a client goes hungry for a week, loses a child, or loses a job that required months of effort to obtain, simply because public policy could not deal with the unique circumstances of his or her life, it cannot be easily forgotten or suffered willingly—nor should it be.

Neither are clients' lives measurably improved by drawing sweeping conclusions that such instances are the result of inadequacy or corruptness of the welfare system or its personnel. Although some features of some welfare systems can be shown (on certain moral assumptions) to be corrupt—and surely there is evidence that some personnel are corrupt—it is neither useful nor accurate to generalize along those lines. What is intended to be shown by the preceding illustrations is that there are natural limits to the effectiveness of social policies and programs. The more unique a citizen's situation is, the less likely it is that policies and programs will meet his or her need.

Therefore, the question might arise, "If so much deprivation continues because social welfare programs and policies cannot take individual circumstances into account, then might it be better if all programs intended for groups of people were replaced with programs intended for, and consciously designed to meet, *individual* needs?" This solution might entail a social welfare system in which persons in need applied for any kind of assistance to one—and only one—social worker who had access to the resources of *all* available programs. If the client needed financial assistance, the social worker would decide not only whether but how much to give. If the client needed medical care, the social worker would tell the client where to get it and would pay the bill. In fact, this vision might be sufficiently detailed to suggest that all monies from all current programs be put into one big pot and allocated to each social worker in proportion to the number of clients he or she served. The key constraint on largesse would be that the social worker must ensure that the pot last long enough. The vision might even anticipate that because each package of services and benefits would be individually tailored, no general standards of need would be necessary. Further, no paperwork would be necessary because the social worker would be accountable only to the client (and to the fiscal officer, to ensure that all monies went to clients). The issue here is that this is a legitimate, even plausible, style for the delivery of social benefits. In fact, a widely used strategy called purchase-of-service contracting (POSC) bears some resemblance to the system envisioned.

Although it is intrinsically appealing, this extremely custom-tailored approach to social policy is not without its own problems. For example, every social worker will likely have different standards for determining how much money, medical care, housing, and so on is needed. That would result in noticeable differences in benefits among people similarly situated. That would be a natural enough effect, for treating people individually was the basic idea behind this way of doing things. Consequently, we have a dilemma here: If we construct our social welfare system to be adequate in the sense that it meets unique needs and circumstances, it will be inevitable that some will need and thus will get more than others. But if we construct it so that it is exactly equitable (everybody gets the same benefit no matter what), it will always be inadequate for those who need more. Equity and adequacy, discussed later, are two major criteria by which modern social welfare programs should be evaluated. A third criterion is efficiency.

No doubt there are ways in which these inherent conflicts among equity, adequacy, and efficiency could be overcome and still keep social programs sufficiently flexible to take unique client need into account. I would encourage the reader to think along those lines because that is the way better policy solutions are developed.

However, the search for better solutions also reveals the limits of social welfare program design and demonstrates an important principle about social policies and programs: Every policy or program that solves the social needs of one client or client group will create additional problems for another needy client or client group. Social policy and program solutions are inherently imperfect to some degree and are constantly in need of revision. Far from being the occasion for disillusionment, it is this very fact that creates the opportunity for service by dedicated professional practitioners to people in need. Social policies and programs left to their own devices are unguided missiles, guaranteed to harm the unwitting and unwary. That danger can be tempered only by frontline practitioners devoted to seeking humane and rational interpretations of social policies directed toward human needs. It is the practitioner's responsibility to know the policy system well enough to do that, and it is to that end that the following chapters are directed.

NOTE

1. Harry D. Krause, *Child Support in America: The Legal Perspective* (Charlottesville, VA: The Mitchie Co., 1981), pp. 213–222. Of course, there are now tests of genetic material to determine paternity and they are 99.9 percent accurate.

1 Analyzing the Social Problem Background of Social Policies and Social Programs

The Nature of Social Problems

Earlier, the point was made that social welfare programs are solutions to social problems. Notice that not all "problems" are social problems and that they are not all equally important. Some argue that the "importance" of a social problem depends on two things: (1) the power and social status of those who are defining the problem and urging the expenditure of resources toward a solution and (2) the sheer number of people affected. Thus, the more people affected and the greater the social power and status of those urging a solution, the more important the social problem.

Examples of "big" and "little" social problems abound. Social problems often arise as a consequence of rare diseases with strong social effects—retinitis pigmentosa, for example. A relatively rare congenital defect that prevents those afflicted from seeing in the dark, retinitis pigmentosa is a medical problem surely, but it is also a social problem because it creates serious social consequences: For all practical purposes, the sufferer is blind during more than half the hours in a day. The disease is a small problem to most people because the number affected is comparatively small. To those so afflicted, however, it is a very big problem indeed, and they can cite persons of great social stature who have the defect. To date no one with widespread credibility (power and status) has presented the problem to the public as a matter of concern, so that to the world at large, it will remain a minor problem until it either affects more people or is redefined as socially important by a public opinion maker.

Less exotic examples of major social problems include unemployment, because it affects so many people; health, because potentially it affects everyone; what used to be called mental retardation, because after Rose Kennedy (mother of a U.S. president) became a public advocate of the issue, federal appropriations for the problem increased magically.

Whereas not all problems are social problems, of course, many do have important social consequences: When someone loses a job, it is a *personal* problem only for that individual and his or her immediate family; when a machine operator loses a job because of modern standards of worker safety or product quality, it is a *technological* problem; when there is a declining market for the things the machine produced, it is a *business* problem; when consumers no longer have money to buy what the machine produces, it is an *economic* problem. When, as a result of any or all of the foregoing problems, many people lose jobs and are unemployed, or when people of power, wealth, and social status become concerned about the effects of these problems, such concern becomes a *social problem*. Usually, an existing policy or program solution to the problem will remain in place at least until the personal, technological, business, or economic problem that created the social problem is solved. The social program may continue past that time; for example, social programs such as unemployment compensation were created to meet human social problems that are created by first-order economic, business, or technological problems.

In summary, social problems are those concerns about the quality of life for large groups of people where the concern is held as a consensus populationwide, and/or the concern is voiced by the socially powerful or the economically privileged. In general, it is these types of problems that spawn social policies and programs as corrective measures. Although this account of social problems is certainly not the only one, it is arguably the one most relevant to those who must understand social problems as a prerequisite of understanding social programs operated by the social welfare institution.

The purpose of this book is to help readers understand social programs and policies, and that understanding cannot be complete without ability to analyze the social problem for which the program or policy is intended to correct. This next section demonstrates how attention to four specific aspects of social problem viewpoints or statements will yield that basic understanding.

Social Problem Analysis

Understanding a social problem is not quite the same thing as understanding the truth of "how things really are." It is not quite the same thing as understanding how highways are built or trees grow. *To understand a social problem is to understand how and what another person (or group) thinks and believes about the social events being defined as a problem.* When you do that, you are doing an *analysis* of a social problem. A central aspect of social problems is that, although the events that identify or define them may be the same no matter who views them, the way in which those events are interpreted is likely to vary considerably. That a family of four has, say, $12,000 annual (gross) income is, on the face of it, an unambiguous fact but one bound to be interpreted differently by different observers. Whether the fact is interpreted as a social problem depends on the value bias and ideology used to render that judgment. For example, a person might believe that a car is vital or that no more than two persons should share a bedroom. In that case, then, $12,000 per year is unlikely to provide for those minimum standards for four people, and the straightforward conclusion is that a $12,000 annual income is an indicator of the presence of a social problem called poverty. However, notice that these standards clearly are value-biased; they are founded on cultural preferences; most people outside North America survive on far less.[1]

Note also how the reason for the existence of the social problem can vary with the viewer. Based on one kind of idea about how the economy and labor markets work, one person might say that this low income was the result of the skill this worker offered to an employer, the employer's need for it (how good business was), how good a worker the person was (productivity), and how many other people offered the same skill and effort (competition). Another person might say that the low income that creates this social problem is caused by the tradition among employers to pay workers according to the social status and prestige of the work they do and the families from which they come. The point in the initial stage of social problem analysis is not to decide whether the viewpoint presented is right, but to sort out what is being offered by way of explanation.

It should be clear from the preceding examples that the way social problems are understood is highly variable and depends on the viewer. On that account, there is no such thing as the "right" or the "only true" social problem viewpoint. Social problem viewpoints may be factual or not, clear or muddled, complete or incomplete, logical or illogical, or even useful or useless, but they are not right or wrong in some absolute sense. An unemployed person who has seen savings wither to nothing, while debts mount and children go hungry, will view the general problem of unemployment as excruciating, whereas those who believe they are paying high taxes so that the unemployed can loaf will not view it that way. Those who are outraged at a society that permits unemployment will view the problem differently from those for whom unemployment is merely a newspaper item. Unemployed persons stress food for children, whereas taxpayers stress the cost of that food and current events followers stress the difference between this year's and last year's unemployment figures. No one is wrong in any absolute sense here, and the basic issue for the person who wishes to understand social policies and programs is the viewpoint under every social policy and program.

The social problem analysis does *not* begin by judging whether something is right or wrong, rather it must await a clear understanding of the social problem viewpoint itself. The final thing to do in a social problem analysis is to make moral judgments about the argument; the first thing to do is to specify what the viewpoint is and how it differs from others. The reason for bearing down so hard on this idea is twofold: (1) Social problem analysis is a demanding task, and (2) at the end of the chapter, you will do analyses of the social problem viewpoints of other persons. In doing the exercises, another caution for the beginner is *to be sure to hold your own views very much apart while doing each social problem analysis.* Your own views are very important, but you will find that initially it takes some discipline to avoid letting them get in the way of the viewpoints of the writers whose materials you will analyze.

The remainder of this chapter is taken up with a discussion of the four dimensions to consider in doing a social problem analysis:

1. Identify the way the problem is defined.
2. Identify the cause(s) to which the problem is attributed (its antecedents) and its most serious consequences.

3. Identify the ideology—the values, that is—that makes the events of concern come to be defined as a problem.
4. Identify who benefits (gains) and who suffers (loses) from the existence of the problem.[2]

There are other aspects of social problems, of course (history and legal status, for example), and they will be discussed in later chapters.

Problem Definition

It is essential to begin a social problem analysis by determining its distinguishing marks or identifiers, that is, to state the *concrete observable signs by which its existence is to be known*. A social problem can be identified in a wide variety of ways. For example, one way to identify the problem of drug abuse is by noting the use, intentional exposure to, or ingestion of *any illegal chemical substances* in a nonmedical way (not prescribed by a physician). Thus, the nonmedically prescribed use of an illegal substance identifies this social problem. Another way is by defining drug abuse as an addiction; for example, defining drug abuse as occurring when most daily life affairs and social encounters are organized around the problems and pleasures of obtaining and using a chemical substance. Here the indicator of the existence of a social problem is determined not by the use or the legality of the chemical, but by its preeminence and the amount of time devoted to it in the user's life. The indicator here is an observer's judgment of the prominence of drug use in daily life.

Obviously, it makes an enormous difference whether the former or latter definition of the problem is chosen. For example, the first definition includes the occasional marijuana smoker and the long-haul trucker's use of amphetamines. The latter definition does not include such instances but *does* include all alcoholics and many tobacco smokers. Not only would conclusions about the qualitative nature and the number of people affected differ in each case, but conclusions about what kinds of people comprise the social problem group would differ radically. Clearly, it can be seen how different social programs would be depending on which view of the social problem is adopted. Table 1.1 presents examples of how two social problems may be defined differently. Each definition in the table was chosen precisely because it was used recently as a basis for distributing sizable cash and material benefits to real people. Each definition is said to define poverty or physical disablement, yet each definition refers to different kinds of people, different circumstances, and, certainly, different group sizes.

Even though social programs and policies are usually designed to solve social problems, sometimes (as noted earlier) *the social program creates social problems of its own*. This fact immediately creates interesting complications for the analysis of social problems. For example, in the material that follows, the U.S. minimum wage law (considered here as an example of a social policy and program) is said to *create* unemployment because, it is argued, the law reduces the incomes of those very citizens whose income it is intended to raise.[3]

TABLE 1.1   **Alternative Definitions for Social Problems**

Social Problem Name	Alternative Definitions
Poverty	1. USDA Child Nutrition Program: free school lunches for families with gross income less than $1,739/month 2. Federal SSI cash benefits for a couple having one member disabled or aged and having less than $709/month income 3. Texas Breast/Cervical Cancer Screening: free pap tests/mammograms for incomes under $2,740/month and age over 50
Physical Disablement	1. Unable to work at any occupation for which the person is qualified by experience or education (commonly used by health insurance companies for determining disability) 2. Unable to earn more than $9,720 per year because of physical impairment (definition used by the Social Security Division) 3. Restricted choice among options open to the nondisabled because of impairment (used by Independence, Inc., 1983)

Minimum Wage—Maximum Folly[4]

Federal minimum wage laws represent a tragic irony. In the name of "preventing worker exploitation," "providing a living wage," and "reducing poverty," these measures in fact impede the upward mobility and increase the dependence of the most disadvantaged among us. National leaders, including black leaders, fail to recognize that many economic problems faced by a large segment of the black population are the result of *government-imposed restrictions on voluntary exchange.*

The Strange History of Unemployment for Black Youth

Today's youth joblessness is unprecedented: nearly 40 percent among blacks and 16 percent among whites, nationally. Black youth unemployment in some major cities is estimated to be 70 percent. In dramatic contrast, black youth unemployment in 1948 was 9.4 percent and white youth unemployment was 10.2 percent. In further contrast to today, until 1954 blacks in every age group were *at least* as active in the labor market as whites were.

These facts demand that we challenge the official and popular explanations of current black youth joblessness. Employers have not become more discriminatory. Black youth of earlier times were not better skilled or educated than their white counterparts. Neither can we attribute the problem to slow economic growth. Even during the relative prosperity of the sixties and seventies, black youth unemployment rose—both absolutely and in relation to white youth unemployment. The real explanation lies in the limitations of law itself. By increasing the minimum wage, Congress has caused a significant loss of job opportunities for young blacks. When employers are required to pay a minimum labor *price* of $5.35 an hour, they have no economic incentive to hire workers whose labor *value*, in the production of goods or delivery of services, may be only $4.00 an hour. Congress can legislate a higher wage, but it cannot legislate that workers be more productive. Because Congress has not yet seized complete control of personnel operations in private firms, the minimum wage law thus discriminates against the low-skilled.

Basic Economics and Practical Politics
A law that reduces opportunity for some almost always increases it for others. To see how the minimum wage law accomplishes this, recognize, as economists do, that low-skilled labor and high-skilled labor can often be substituted for each other.

Imagine an employer can build a particular fence by using three low-skilled workers each earning $42 a day ($126 total labor cost per day), or by using one high-skilled worker who earns $110 a day. To minimize labor costs, the employer hires the high-skilled worker.

But suppose the high-skilled worker suddenly demands $155 a day. The fence firm then hires the three low-skilled workers, and the high-skilled worker loses his job.

On the other hand, the high-skilled worker may understand politics and economics. He may now join with others like himself and lobby for a minimum wage law of $50 a day (claiming noble motivations like "prevention of worker exploitation" and "provision of a living wage"?).

Once the $50 minimum wage is law, the high-skilled worker can demand and get his $110 a day—because it now costs $150 to build the fence using low-skilled labor. By law, the high-skilled worker's competition is priced out of the market.

An Incentive to Discriminate
Aside from causing unemployment for some, the minimum wage law encourages racial discrimination. If an employer must pay a minimum of $5.35 an hour no matter whom he hires, he may as well hire someone whose color he likes. Economists would explain this by saying that the minimum wage law prevents the worker from offering a "compensating difference" for less-preferred characteristics.

The same principle applies to groceries. Less-preferred chuck steak can compete with more-preferred filet mignon only by offering a compensating differences—a lower price. If we had a minimum price law for steak of, say, $10 a pound, sales of chuck would fall relative to sales of filet. Because it is *perceived* as less valuable, chuck steak would be "unemployed."

The minimum wage law's powerful incentive for racial discrimination is clearly illustrated in South Africa. There, the white unions are the strongest supporters of minimum wage laws and their counterpart, "equal-pay-for-equal-work" *for blacks!* There, unions advocate these laws with the *stated* purpose of protecting white jobs against black competition.

The Burden on the Young
Young people suffer most from any law that discourages employment of low-skilled workers, simply because the young normally have the lowest skills.

If joblessness merely deprived young people of pocket money, we might shrug it off as another minor consequence of foolish government intervention. But early work experience produces more than money. It teaches job-search skills, effective work habits, and respect for supervisors. It produces pride and self-respect. It lets a worker make mistakes when they are not terribly costly—when there are probably no dependents counting on the worker for continuous income. These labor market lessons are critical, particularly for minority youths who attend grossly inferior schools, where these lessons are not learned.

Moreover, an absence of job opportunity may account for much of the crime and other antisocial behavior among many of today's youth.

Note in this example how the focus is on *unemployment*. What is central for Williams in the material quoted here is that the minimum wage law by creating unemployment "impedes upward mobility and increases the dependency of the most disadvantaged. . . ." Employment is important for Williams because it is the key element in upward mobility and economic independence. Thus, the central social problem defined here is unemployment, the immediate cause of which are certain features of the minimum wage law; the central values that are thought to be threatened here are upward mobility and economic independence. Note that Williams does not tell us exactly what he means by unemployment. It is clear that he is not as concerned about the level of pay as the *number of available low-paying* jobs. He believes that this is the major problem among black youth.[5] Others might disagree.

Social problem analysis should state the concrete measures and indicators of the social problem of concern more clearly than Williams does. Definitions that are specific, concrete, and measurable are useful in these respects:

1. Everyone then knows precisely to what they refer.
2. It is possible to construct comparable estimates of incidence and prevalence so that quantification, importance, and change over time can be judged.
3. It makes it possible to discuss causation. Unless the problem is clearly defined, it is fruitless to discuss causes: What is it that is being caused? It is also fruitless to speculate about "solutions" under these conditions.

Note that here a definition is not "good" or "bad" because you either agree or disagree with it. It is common to have serious disagreement about how a given social problem should be defined. For example, many people have disagreed violently with a definition of institutional racism (a serious social problem, surely) that refers to differential access to institutional resources on the basis of color. That definition implies that if dark-skinned people have lower-quality education (for whatever stated reason), it is first-order evidence of white racism. Such definition is one of the central issues around which the whole school-busing-to-achieve-integration argument has revolved. Are blacks and Latinos the victims of white racism because, for example, their school districts have less taxable property yielding less tax revenue, which results in fewer resources for education in that district? Based on the preceding definition of racism, the example unequivocally constitutes racism. Following some other definitions of racism, particularly those that define racism as overt and intentional discrimination based on color, this would not be an example of racism because no "intentional" discrimination can be distinguished.

The point is that both definitions are "good" insofar as definitions go, irrespective of which you think is the better. The criteria for definitions revolve around clarity, not "truth"; therefore, both definitions are satisfactorily clear. On ideological or value grounds, I would argue that the first definition is preferable to the second, but that is a different issue than whether it is a clear definition.

Earlier, the statement was made that the importance of social problems—in fact their rise to public consciousness—depends not only on the social status of those who speak publicly about them, but on the sheer number of those who are affected as well. Because of the latter factor, you should expect the problem-definition section of careful social problem analysis to give attention to a presentation of the quantitative dimensions—the sheer size—of the problem: estimates of the number of persons (or families), estimates of the percentage or proportion of the total population affected; estimates of the demographics of the problem (e.g., the numbers and percentages of the different ages, sexes, and geographic localities affected). In looking again at the Williams presentation of the social problem of minimum wage, you will see how carefully he has quantified the problem for us. He notes that in 1979, youth joblessness was nearly 40 percent for blacks and 16 percent among whites nationally. He adds demographic data showing that unemployment for black youths in particular cities is as high as 70 percent. He could have carried this kind of analysis even further (and did in other places where his work is published), as you might imagine. Quantifications such as these are often very important in judging the adequacy of social programs and policies to solve the social problem. Without such data, it is impossible to determine whether, for example, the eligibility rules or other features of the program are directing program benefits and services to the people who have the problem or are directing the most benefit or service to those who are affected the most. Furthermore, adequacy of funding for the program cannot be assessed without some idea of how many people are affected. Do not be misled by thinking that quantification is important only in regard to this example concerning minimum wage and youth unemployment; quantification is crucial in the analysis of any social problem. Child abuse, for example, cannot be properly understood without some idea of how widespread it is or the types of people and families in which it appears the most frequently.

Another way in which to deepen the understanding of social problems is to present common variations within the problem category itself. The author of a social problem presentation is very likely to refer to several subtypes of these and expend some effort at distinguishing among them. For example, in discussions about the social problem of crime, distinction is made among the legal subtypes of crime: premeditated homicide, felony murder, manslaughter, and assault. These are legal categories, but they also may serve the social problem presenter well in giving the opportunity to speak of different causes for different subcategories, to speak of different ideological issues, to speak of different prevalence data for each, and so on. In fact, it is not uncommon for the discussion to direct itself mainly to a single subtype, particularly where the broader problem is not well understood or is particularly complex. For example, you are most likely to read about sexual abuse apart from a discussion of child abuse in general. The task of social problem analysis is to track the subclassifications being used, that is, how much and in what regard a narrowing of focus has occurred. One reason for this careful tracking is to avoid being misled by later data that are presented about the problem. Sometimes, for example, social problem presentations will focus only on a subtopic but will present data on the *whole* social problem. Sometimes this is intentional mischief; other times presenters themselves are unaware of the error.

Causes and Consequences

Another factor to consider in doing a social problem analysis is what causal explanations are offered as to why a social problem has come to exist. But sometimes the focus is not on explanation at all, rather on predicting *consequences* that will follow from the social problem. Sorting out this pattern of attributed causes and consequences is at the core of analyzing a social problem viewpoint for causation. A primary goal of the analysis is to discover whether it is the causes (antecedents), the consequences (effects), or both that are of utmost importance to the particular social problem presentation being analyzed. One way to separate antecedents from consequences is to try to diagram, to capture what is being said by setting down on paper what appears to be the causal pattern the author is asserting.

Causal patterns can be described in many ways; one simple method is to describe what will be called causal chains. A *causal chain* consists of a set of events (or variables or factors) arranged in a time sequence that shows the social problem event that is to be explained—what comes before the event and therefore is said to "cause" it and what comes after the event and is said to be a consequence. Causal chains are to be read from left to right so that the "event-to-be-explained" is always some variable to the right of the center of the chain. If only antecedents are of concern, the social problem event-to-be-explained will always appear on the *far* right of the causal chain. Let us now focus only on such causal chains as these, for simplicity. Figure 1.1 presents a simple causal chain "explaining" high unemployment rates (follow the arrows).

It should be clear that this is neither the only, nor even a complete, explanation for unemployment, only one plausible explanation. Remember, the object here is to find

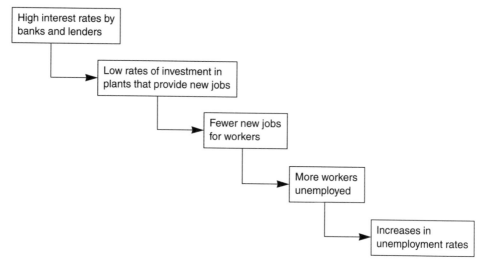

FIGURE 1.1   A simple causal chain "explaining" high unemployment.

Source: Based on Walter E. Williams, "Minimum Wage—Maximum Folly," *The SmithKline Forum for a Healthier America,* 1(6) (September 1979): 1–6.

the expressed *belief* about the causes of the social problem. This causal chain could also be used to explain poverty and economic deprivation because poverty can be a result of the fact that people are just not working and earning wages. However, another author concerned with poverty and economic deprivation might explain it on the basis of high prices rather than low wages. That causal chain might look something like the one in Figure 1.2.

Some causal chains or "explanations" can be very complicated. We can put both these diagrammed causal chains together and add some other features to generate a broader and more complex explanation of poverty. Thus, Figure 1.3 shows how *both* high prices and low earnings produce poverty; it also shows some of the reasons for high prices and low earnings.

Let us now return to Williams's analysis of the minimum wage law and its relation to unemployment. Could we express Williams's argument in the form of a causal chain? I would suggest the example in Figure 1.4 as appropriate to Williams's line of reasoning.

Note that although Williams has not spoken explicitly of an employer's profit motive, it is crucial to understanding his argument. Discussions of social problems do not always make explicit all the assumptions they make in presenting their explanations for the cause of a social problem. One of the reasons for making a special effort to understand an author's explanation for a social problem is to uncover "hidden" assumptions.

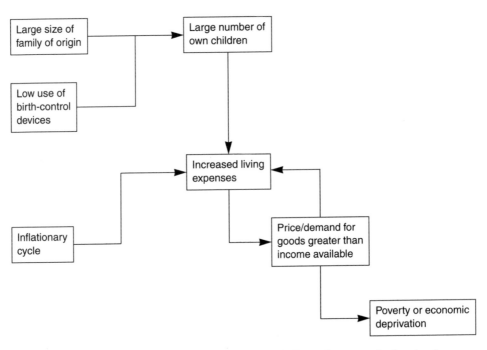

FIGURE 1.2   A simple causal chain explaining poverty and economic deprivation.

Source: Based on Walter E. Williams, "Minimum Wage—Maximum Folly," *The SmithKline Forum for a Healthier America,* 1(6) (September 1979): 1–6.

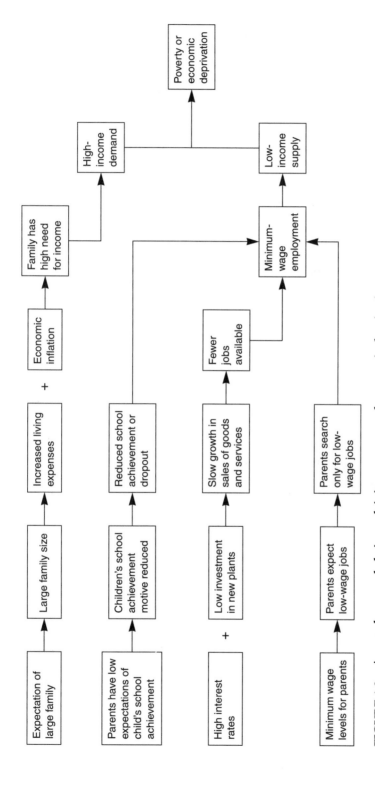

FIGURE 1.3   A complex causal chain explaining poverty and economic deprivation.

Source: Based on Walter E. Williams, "Minimum Wage—Maximum Folly," *The SmithKline Forum for a Healthier America,* 1(6) (September 1979): 1–6.

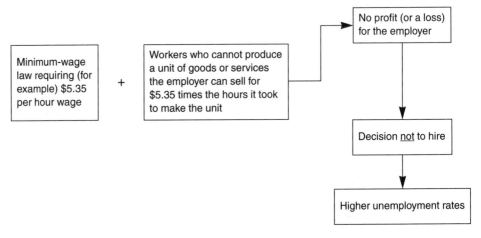

FIGURE 1.4   An analysis of the minimum wage law in a causal chain.

Source: Based on Walter E. Williams, "Minimum Wage—Maximum Folly," *The SmithKline Forum for a Healthier America*, 1(6) (September 1979): 1–6.

Ideology and Values

Another crucial aspect of a social problem analysis is the identification of major ideological positions and value biases embedded in a description of a social problem. For our purposes here, by a *value*, we mean simply a conception of what is preferred. Values express a vision of how things "ought" to be. Note that value statements can be simple or complex, but in the end, they need no justification because they are personal or cultural preferences. For example, if poverty as a social problem is identified by a lack of minimum nutritional standards, a value stance is implied that prefers that no one be hungry. However, if poverty as a social problem is identified by some large difference between annual incomes of certain types of citizens, a value stance is implied that prefers that income be more *equally distributed*, without respect to the differing needs of individuals or any concept of how social merit should be rewarded.

Value statements are usually expressed in phrases using the words *should, ought,* or *must*. For example, the statements, "No one should be hungry" or "Employers should not refuse a job because of an applicant's racial background" are value statements using *should* terms. Value statements are usually more numerous and more complex than can be stated in single sentences. On that account, and for our particular purposes, let us use the term *ideology* to refer to sets of value statements.

Sometimes it is difficult to disentangle value and knowledge statements. Ideology is built from value statements, and explanations and causal chains are built from sentences that describe what *is* the case about one thing or another. These latter sentences are "factual" statements, statements asserting what exists. Recall that value statements are sentences about what is to be preferred. So, it is one thing to say, "No human being *should* be hungry" (a value statement, a statement of preference), but it is another thing to say,

"From 12 to 15 percent of the U.S. population lives in conditions of poverty in which they *are* hungry some part of each week" (a statement of fact). The operating terms are italicized. Again, value and ideological statements feature verbs such as *should, ought,* or *must;* knowledge and factual statements feature verbs such as *are* and *is.* The reason it is sometimes difficult to disentangle value and knowledge statements is that they concern the same event; it is important to distinguish between the two statements because they are intended to deliver two very different messages. The correct reading of the message of the value statement gives the reader of a social problem description advance information about *outcomes* that the author will advocate. The correct reading of the message in the factual statements of the causation analysis will give the reader advance information about the kind of program interventions or policy or legislative changes the author will seek.

Let us now return to the Williams material on minimum wage just to search for examples of the difference between value and knowledge statements. Our conclusion was that Williams's causal argument necessarily entailed a statement about employers' profits. That is a factual statement as it stands—that is, we are saying that Williams implies that employers *do* consider the effect on their profit in making hiring decisions. Note that it would be a value statement if it involved some term such as *should* or *ought:* "Employers *should* consider profit . . . , etc., in their hiring decisions." The point is that his argument does not say that; all it says is that employers *do* consider that issue.

Unfortunately for us, the value statements in the Williams excerpt are not distinguished by the presence of the revealing verbs *should* and *ought.* Therefore, to identify his ideology, we must search for statements whose meaning is not substantially altered by transforming them into statements containing *should* and *ought* terms. For example, we *cannot* take such a statement as "Black youth unemployment in some major cities is estimated to be 70 percent" and transform it into the statement, "Black youth unemployment in some major cities should be 70 percent" and contend that we have not changed the meaning radically. However, we can take a sentence from the first paragraph of the excerpt and transform it into a value statement without altering its meaning. Thus: "Federal minimum wage laws represent a tragic irony. . . . [T]hese measures in fact impede the upward mobility and increase the dependence of the most disadvantaged among us." We can restate this sentence as a value statement as follows: "Impeding upward mobility and increasing the dependence of the most disadvantaged among us are effects of the minimum wage law that we should not allow." What we have done is to take a cue from the phrase "tragic irony" and interpret it to be equivalent to saying that there are effects of the minimum wage law that *should* not occur.

Gainers and Losers

The focus of this aspect of social problem analysis is on three things: (1) *who* loses and gains, (2) *what kind* of gains and losses are involved, and (3) *how much* value is entailed. The reason to examine this angle is that it is not always obvious what losses and costs are of concern; different groups value different kinds of losses and costs. We do not trouble to take a stand about a social problem unless we are concerned about a loss of some kind, so in almost any social problem description, some attention is paid to the issue of losses and costs.

The first principle here is that social problem costs (losses) are seldom, if ever, shared equally among citizens. The first question is, "Who loses most?" In some ultimate sense, there is probably no citizen who is not affected in an indirect way by all social problems. The issue here is to identify those who pay the biggest costs. For example, it is quite clear that the group that pays the biggest cost of the very high rates of crime in inner cities is made up of the local inner-city residents themselves. It is they who are robbed, raped, mugged, and murdered. There are also *indirect* costs shared by all taxpayers, for example, emergency room costs of violent crime. On the other hand, by any measure, the most prominent victims of the "white-collar crime" of tax evasion are the middle-income classes, who pay the biggest share of the taxes collected by the U.S. Treasury. They bear most of the cost of the social problem because they must pay most of the extra tax needed to make up for the evaded taxes.

One of the important costs of the social problem of maintaining the health of the population is the dollar costs of medical care for the aged. Those costs are paid largely through Medicare, a Social Security subprogram financed by the Social Security withholding tax paid by those now in the workforce. The amount withheld from the preretirement wages of those now receiving medical care was always far less than present average costs, so current recipients cannot be said to have paid for the Medicare benefits they now receive. That is not necessarily because of their unwillingness to do so, but simply because (1) many people retired before Medicare was enacted, (2) the costs of medical care have risen enormously in recent years, (3) wages were less inflated in earlier years and, therefore, (4) contributions for Medicare were less. In addition, no one foresaw the incredible advances in medical care now available—for example, the expensive medical technology developed mainly for the older population: bone and joint transplants and heart bypass procedures. The unpredicted costs here are paid from the contributions to Social Security by those who now work and pay withholding taxes. Note carefully that what has been said has not *yet* judged the way these charges are distributed; such judgment will evolve from the *shoulds* and *oughts* of the value and ideology analysis.

Sometimes, very small details designed into public programs make an important difference in who ends up paying the biggest share of the costs. Consider again the example of wage losses for workers permanently and totally work-injured who receive Workers Compensation benefits. Lost wages are the amount a person could be expected to earn (at present wage levels) from the date of injury to the date of retirement. It is a cost to the *worker* when not all of the loss is repaid by the Workers Compensation program. It is a cost to *taxpayers* when the Workers Compensation benefit is not paid at all or is so insufficient that some other public welfare benefits must be paid to keep the disabled worker and his or her family afloat. However, it is a different case when a company buys Workers Compensation insurance coverage that is sufficient to pay the worker's full lost wages but *increases the price of its product or service to pay for the insurance.* Thus, it turns out that the *consumer* is actually paying for the worker's injury. These examples show why it is important to take careful notice of who pays social problem costs; existing social program details can and often do make substantial alterations in what would appear to be the obvious pattern of cost bearing for social problems.

After considering who loses from a social problem, the next issue to consider is the type of loss involved. In the preceding examples, money (or income) was the prominent kind of loss of immediate concern. Other concerns—pain, discomfort, inconvenience, time, and geographic dislocation—are examples of other types of losses that sometimes are discussed in presenting social problems. One obvious example is found in discussions of the social problem of abortion. For some, the concern is the loss and costs of the extinction of human life; for others, the concern is each woman's loss of autonomy over her body and its products. Much of the argument here turns on precisely what type of loss is viewed as important. Similarly, the social cost of a brutal beating might be said to be pain, disablement, discomfort, injustice, shame, and terror—which could be said of most violent crimes, including rape. Although some of these social costs can be said to be subjective in some sense, none would argue that they are unimportant, incalculable, or uncompensable.[6]

Sometimes, social problems incur costs that revolve around the loss of *potential gains* rather than immediate losses, monetary or otherwise. For example, one of the costs for the parents of a severely retarded child may be in what those parents are prevented from doing by way of their own future employment, further education, or professional advancement. They may have to choose among spending their future caring for such a child at home, working, or obtaining further business or professional credentials that would advance their incomes. To the extent that increased income and enhanced employment can increase social standing, the consequence of the social problem of child retardation can certainly incur cost in status. Other social problems also can incur heavy status costs; for example, cost of crime or mental illness to the families of those involved can be negative social labeling that results in losses in both social status and personal esteem.

Finally, consideration must be made of the magnitude of costs—*how much* (whether money or some other measurement). It is convenient to express social costs in dollar terms because that measurement is easily interpreted by a wide audience. There are widely accepted ways of translating almost any kind of loss into dollar terms. The value of life is translated daily into dollar terms when civil courts hand down judicial decisions—for example, whether a physician was guilty of malpractice in a patient's disablement or death or whether a certain dollar value relieved "pain and suffering." We will not discuss further exactly how these more subjective losses are translated into money losses, except to say that economists do it by imagining (or gathering data on) how much most people would be willing to pay either to get rid of the effects of particular pain or suffering or status loss, or how much someone else would demand to take on the problem intentionally. One simple test is to ask yourself, for instance, how many dollars it would take to get *you* to take on the care of a severely intellectually disabled child in your own home or to have it generally known that a close family member is mentally ill or imprisoned for a serious crime. Estimating the *magnitude of social costs of a social problem* is an important process in understanding a social problem because doing so provides at least one standard by which a problem's "importance" can be measured both absolutely and relatively to other social problems.

If the first principle is that social problem costs are seldom shared equally among citizens, then the second principle is that *some people and some social groups actually benefit from others' social problems.* It is quite possible that some social problems are not solvable in any important and immediate sense simply because they create benefits that others are reluctant to give up. The general—albeit unsavory—idea here is that indeed some people do profit from others' misery. The extent to which this idea is true is debatable, but it does not seem wise to assume that such is never (or only seldom) the case. The most obvious evidence of this truth is the documented fact that a small number of people profit handsomely from others' addictions (liquor, tobacco, pharmaceuticals, illegal narcotics, and such). Less obvious is how this principle operates in relation to other more controversial social problems like unemployment, physical disablement, and aging. For example, it is not merely cynical to observe that the lower the general level of employment, the more welfare recipients will be forced into the workforce and, therefore, the larger is the pool from which employers can draw low-wage employees. Employers of unskilled labor would certainly seem to profit from reduced welfare benefit levels and high unemployment. (It is Williams's point that if minimum wages drop, unskilled teenagers will profit as well.)

It would be unfortunate to conclude that only employers benefit from the existence of social problems. One rather well-known line of social analysis views racial and ethnic prejudice and discrimination as one means of establishing an "underclass," a scapegoated "bottom-of-the-social-ladder" group, against whom all other classes and types can be measured and positively valued. Theoretically then, wherever racial discrimination reduces competition from persons of color, whites must gain in terms of money and status. Some believe that the big gainers form the social unrest and racial tensions of the sixties and seventies were not working-class blacks but the black middle class, who achieved gains in income and increased their entrance at educational institutions and their starts up career ladders. Another commonly discussed example is the ability of the health corporations to profit from disease. And, in fact, all professional practitioners profit from social problems; if there were no social problems, there would be no need for social workers or human service personnel at all. But, be careful with that claim. Showing that a professional makes a profit isn't enough to establish that professionals themselves contribute to continuing the existence of a social problem. Professional profit is not a serious issue unless it can also be shown that personal profit rather than benefits to clients/patients or consumers have first priority.

Understanding who profits from the existence of a social problem can reveal the forces that act against its elimination. It is very likely that where a shortage of good housing exists and profits are being made from existing stock, associations of rental property owners, in serving their own interests, will oppose the building of public housing. Similarly, it is unlikely that the American Medical Association will support the creation of a large number of medical schools—despite evidence that all citizens would get better medical care at reduced cost if the patient–physician ratio were decreased. It is equally unlikely that traditional craft unions (plumbing, carpentry, toolmakers) will admit minorities for fear they will become job and career competitors—especially in a stagnant economy in which the threat of competition willing to work for less wages is keenly felt. The point is that the social problems of unemployment, housing, health, and racism all have some built-in resistance to solution simply because they generate strong economic and status rewards for other citizen groups.

The next section shows how conclusions from a social problem analysis are used to shape the basic features of a social policy or program.

Using the Conclusions of Social Problem Analysis to Design Social Policies and Programs and to Judge their "Fit" to the Social Problem

When political scientists, students of government, or sociologists study a social policy or program, their interest is centered on explaining it as a fact of social life; that is, how the policy or program came to be, what broad social function it serves, why it appeared in one form and not another. The social practitioners for whom this book is intended have different questions in mind because their interest lies in how social policies and programs can be instrumental in solving, or helping to solve, social problems for their clients. How much difference does this program or policy make to those who suffer from the effects of the social problem?[8] *Qualitative judgments about the merit of a social program or policy cannot be made without reference to the original understanding of the social problem.* The idea here is that social policies and programs should be judged against the needs and causal analysis implied in the conclusions of the study of the social problem. Social policies should not be designed in the abstract or in relation to more or less random ideas about the nature of the social problem toward which they are directed as a solution.

Table 1.2 contrasts the components of social problem analysis with the basic elements of social policies and programs. What is the relationship between the two?

Consider eligibility rules, in their most elementary sense, as policies that tell who should and should not get benefits or services. Then ask the question, "Does a problem definition influence how such a rule could be constructed?" The most straightforward answer is that ideally an eligibility rule should make services and benefits of the program available *only* to those who have the problem, a determination based on who meets the terms of the problem definition. Conversely, the rule should make it *impossible* for those who do not meet the terms of that definition to receive benefits and services. For example, if the social problem of concern is long-term hospitalization of the chronic psychotic, then an appropriate eligibility rule might be found in the current *American Psychiatric Association Diagnostic and Statistical Manual (DSM-III)*. Thus, the eligibility rule should restrict benefits and services to individuals with "Delusions, hallucinations, or . . . disturbances in the form of thought."[9]

The "fit" with which we are so concerned here is not just a matter of its being logically "neat," because the lack of fit has serious consequences. For example, a program can either overlook needful citizens (underinclusion) or is more expensive than it should be (produces overwhelming cost) because program benefits or services are wasted on those who do not have the problem and do not need the benefits. Furthermore, without a clear eligibility rule in place, it is impossible to determine whether a program or policy had an impact on the problem and thus whether the causal explanations in the analysis were right. Data on the results of the program are useless if contaminated by (1) inclusion of those whose problems the program was never intended to solve or (2) data from

TABLE 1.2   Each Social Problem Analysis Component Specifies an Aspect of a Social Policy and Program Element

Problem Analysis Component	Policy and Program Basic Element
1. Problem definition (terms)	Specifies the terms that must be used in the *eligibility rules* determining who is/is not entitled to benefits or services and specifies the general *goals* to be achieved.
Subtypes	Specifies the specific *target populations*.
Quantifications	Can specify the priorities on the basis of which one *goal* rather than another is chosen when size of the problem is believed to be the determining issue.
	Helps estimate financing needed.
2. Causal analysis	Specifies the particular *types of benefits and/or services* that must be delivered to address the problem.
	Specifies the *type of personnel* required to deliver the services or benefits when causation implicates cultural factors or implies a particular expertise and/or training or experience of the helper.
3. Ideology and values	Can determine choice of type of *eligibility rule* (e.g., means test rather than insurance principle).
	Can determine *goals* by establishing priorities to serve preferred subcategories of the problem.
	Determines *amount of financing* made available.
4. Gainer and loser analysis	Can specify method of *financing* in which dollar loss is clear, ability to pay is obvious, and responsibility for loss can be assigned (e.g., Worker's Compensation).

an ill-formed eligibility rule that excludes either too many or the wrong people. In the example of long-term hospitalization of psychotics, no one would be able to tell whether people with a chronic psychosis and a history of long hospitalization could be helped by a programmed intervention that involved their living outside an institution independently if, for example, nonpsychotic chronically delinquent youngsters and the senile elderly were accepted into the program by an ill-fitting or misapplied eligibility rule. Not only might important resources be misdirected and therefore unavailable to those for whom they were originally intended, but the chance to learn something about the validity of the ideas in the social problem analysis would be lost.

But a few eligibility rules are not constructed out of their relationship to the social problem. Consider that any honorably discharged veteran is entitled to free hospitalization in any Veterans Administration hospital is clearly a welfare benefit according to the generally accepted definition (a material gain resulting from the direct or indirect redistribution of someone else's income).[10] This is not to say that the benefit is undeserved, but only to make the point that the eligibility rule is *not* based on the conclusions from a social problem analysis. Rather, the basis for this eligibility rule is society's desire to *reward* those who in serving their country risked their own lives.

The problem-definition aspect of social problem analysis also prescribes the terms in which the program goals and objectives must be stated. For example, a city's summer recreation program that was originally intended simply to provide adult supervision for out-of-school children transforms its goal into a grand statement about "providing for the child's total well-being during the summer period." There is nothing wrong with concern about children's "total well-being" (although strange that it is only "during the summer period"), but in this instance, the goal is misguided because it is unfaithful to the original conception of the problem.

Before leaving our consideration of how qualitative standards for policy and program design can be derived from problem definitions, recall that there is a subsection of the problem-identification aspect called *subtypes*, which allows for variability within the social problem to be noted and reviewed; for example, there are key differences between sexual abuse, neglect, and physical abuse within the larger social problem category of child abuse. Once a subclass is "declared," there should also be some awareness of its numerical—that is, its *quantitative*—importance. These issues from social problem analysis should guide judgments about whether the goals of the policy or program are directed toward the *whole* social problem or only one of its parts; if the concern is with a subtype, analysis should help determine whether its size warrants priority relative to other subtypes. Size is not the only determiner of priorities, but it is important to understand that magnitude provides the basis for a claim on public resources.

Now let us pay some attention to the relationship between causal explanation and the "types of services or benefits delivered." Earlier, we showed how the most powerful kind of causal analysis proceeds by identifying the factors (variables) believed to be the crucial determiners of the problem. Where that is the case, it should be obvious that the types of benefits or services should be those that are powerful in reducing the influence of those determiners. For example, if the social problem of concern is the physical abuse of children and the causal analysis identifies severe economic stress as the major determinant of abuse, then among the benefits provided by the policy and program must be money, goods, or their equivalent to relieve economic stress. If the causal analysis identifies as the key cause of maternal child abuse, the presence of a nonnurturing, abusive mother who never shows her daughters how to rear children without physical abuse, then the program or policy design simply must provide the substitute parent model that abusing mothers did not get in their own homes.

Even though it would seem that no rational policy or program designer would violate this simple, straightforward, and obvious idea, that is just not the case. Some programs, despite their objective to alleviate child abuse based on an understanding of the problem as described in the preceding theory, in fact only teach about child-development stages. As uplifting (even useful) as that might be, such a program must be judged to be a bad "fit" and an irrational policy. Even the casual observer of social policy and programs does not have to look hard to find bad examples along this line: One program design is based on a causal analysis that identifies (reasonably enough) the major factor in poor social adjustment of some developmentally disabled children as their isolation from ordinary children in ordinary classrooms. However, this same program develops a policy to scatter special-education classrooms for these children throughout ordinary neighborhood schools—but it staggers and limits the daily schedule of the special-education classrooms so that disabled pupils have no chance to associate with mainstream schoolchildren either in the classroom or elsewhere. The fit between the causal analysis and the policy solution is lost because the type of benefit intended as a solution consistent with the causal analysis turns out not to be the one implemented.

Another possibility is that the causal analysis may direct the program or policy to employ only certain types of personnel to deliver benefits or services; that is, the causal analysis creates certain standards for the administrative service-delivery system. As will be discussed in Chapter 6, personnel specifications are an important feature in benefits and services. A common example is a causal analysis that explains that some subgroups of certain ethnic or racial minorities do not apply for important health or school-based services because of the cultural and language barriers created by nonethnic or nonminority personnel. When that causal view is taken, a heavy obligation is laid on the personnel policies of the delivery system: sufficient ethnic or minority personnel must be on-line if the services are to be delivered effectively. Here the issue is not an affirmative-action agenda or a concern with elimination of racially or ethnically biased hiring practices. After all, causal analysis can dictate personnel criteria other than cultural or ethnic features; for example, special expertise, education, or experience.

The analysis of major gainers and losers as a result of social problems is also a source of rational expectations for social policies and programs. These conclusions are particularly relevant for specifying methods of financing. When the loss involved is a tangible material or financial loss, one obvious method of financing is implied: The gainers should repay the losers. In fact, that is exactly what is behind the "victim restitution" programs operated in relation to the social problem of crimes against property (e.g., theft, larceny, and misdemeanors). The causal explanation usually invoked by these programs is that offenders repeat such crimes because (1) doing so costs the offenders nothing out of their own pockets and (2) offenders never have to encounter their victims face to face in terms of being held accountable for their criminal acts. Victim restitution programs, both the direct program cost and the cost arising from the adverse effect(s) of the crime, ideally should be paid for by the offenders themselves. This financing feature is entirely consistent with the causal analysis. Another example is the Workers Compensation program, the goal of which is to compensate workers injured on their jobs so that their income will not suffer irremediable damage. Workers Compensation legislation characteristically assumes that the cause of the income loss is the workplace incident (even though the personal blame for that accident is not assigned and its determination is not made a part of the program or policy—a "no-fault" system). Because the workplace "caused" an income loss, the policy pursued in legislation is to place responsibility on the employer to provide insurance payments to pay the cost of replacing the injured employee's lost income. Table 1.2 shows examples of these expectations.

Summary

Chapter 1 discussed the central importance of social policy in the professional practice of social work and other human services. Social policies both create and constrain the possibilities of any social practice. Central to that understanding is an ability to ferret out the view of the social problem taken by legislative bodies, policy and program designers, political critics, and program and policy administrators. An analytic framework—that is, a set of concepts by which the fundamental dimensions of *any* view of a social problem can be understood—was presented. This framework takes into consideration four activities:

1. Identify the way the problem is defined.
2. Identify the cause(s) to which the problem is attributed and its most serious consequences.
3. Identify the ideology and the values that make the events of concern come to be defined as a problem.
4. Identify major gainers and losers with respect to the problem.

These activities were discussed and examples were given so that readers can learn to analyze social problems. The chapter closed with a discussion of how to use the results of the problem analysis to make judgments of the merit of the program and to design programs anew.

EXERCISES

1. Reread Williams on the minimum wage, page 000, and the causal chain drawn for it on Figure 1.3, page 000. Add "maximizing employers profit" as an explanatory factor (antecedent) to the diagram. Then think how it would affect the total diagram and Williams's causal argument overall.

2. There are both direct and indirect costs paid by those who "lose" and "gain" from the existence of a social problem. Pick a social problem and show both its direct and "indirect costs."

3. Social problem costs, when they seem to involve things that cannot be priced in a handy marketplace (physical pain, for example, or fear of street violence or a neighboring district full of prostitutes and drug dealers, perhaps), can be estimated by imagining that there is such a market where you can pay (expressed in dollar terms) how much as you would be willing to pay to have it disappear (and assuming you had the money). Identify a social problem that annoys you and your friends and estimate what you personally would be willing to pay to be rid of it. Then present the scenario to friends, collect their "price."

4. Do an analysis of the social problem viewpoint expressed in the following historical document. Use the four social problem analysis categories discussed in this chapter.

   Dangers in Half-Dime Novels and Story Papers, 1883[11]
   Satan stirred up certain of his willing tools on earth by the promise of a few paltry dollars to improve greatly on the death-dealing quality of the weekly death traps, and forthwith came a series of new snares of fascinating construction, small and tempting in price, and baited with high-sounding names. These sure-ruin traps comprise a large variety of half-dime novels, five- and ten-cent story papers, and low-priced pamphlets for boys and girls.

   Again, these stories breed vulgarity, profanity, loose ideas of life, impurity of thought and deed. They render the imagination unclean, destroy domestic peace, desolate homes,

cheapen woman's virtue, and make foul-mouthed bullies, cheats, vagabonds, thieves, desperadoes, and libertines. They disparage honest toll and make real life a drudge and burden. What young man will serve an apprenticeship, working early and late, if his mind is filled with the idea that sudden wealth may be acquired by following the hero of the story? In real life, to begin at the foot of the ladder and work up, step by step, is the rule; but in these stories, inexperienced youth, with no moral character, take the foremost positions, and by trick and device, knife and revolver, bribery and corruption, carry everything before them, lifting themselves in a few short weeks to positions of ease and affluence. Moral courage with such is a thing to be sneered at and despised in many of these stories. If one is asked to drink and refuses, he is set up and twitted till he yields or is compelled to by force. The idea of doing anything from principle is ridiculous in the extreme. As well fill a kerosene-oil lamp with water and expect a brilliant light. And so, in addition to all else, there is early inculcated a distaste for the good, and the piercing blast of ridicule is turned upon the reader to destroy effectually all moral character.

Satan is more interested in the child than many parents are. Parents do not stop to think or look for their children in these matters, while the archenemy is thinking, watching, and plotting continually to effect their ruin.

Thoughtless parents, heedless guardians, negligent teachers, you are each of you just the kind that old Satan delights to see placed over each child. He sets his base traps right in your very presence, captures and ruins your children, and you are each of you criminally responsible.

Take further instances of the effect of this class of publications, and then say if my language is too strong. Does it startle and offend? To startle, to awaken, to put you on your guard, to arouse you to your duty over your own children, is my purpose. *Your child is in danger of having its pure mind cursed for life.*

From infancy to maturity the pathway of the child is beset with peculiar temptations to do evil. Youth has to contend against great odds. Inherited tendencies to wrong-doing render the young oftentimes open to ever-present seductions. Inherited appetites and passions are secretly fed by artificial means, until they exert a well-nigh irresistible mastery over their victim. The weeds of sin, thus planted in weak human nature, are forced to a rapid growth, choking virtue and truth, and stunting all the higher and holier instincts. Thus, many a child of dissolute parents is born with natural desires for strong drink, and early becomes intemperate. In his thoughtful moments he loathes drink, and yet there comes upon him a force he is powerless to resist. So, too, the incontinence of parents brings into the world children inheriting morbidly susceptible natures—natures set like the hair trigger to a rifle—ready to fall into shame at the slightest temptation.

We speak of youth as the plastic state—the period of all others when the human soul is most easily molded and character formed. Youth is the seed-time. Maturity gathers in the crop. Youth is the fountain from which the waters of life flow. *If parents do not train and instruct their children, the devil will.* Whether parents deem it important to watch the child or no, there is one who deems it so important that he keeps a constant watch. *The devil stations a sentry to observe and take advantage of every point open to an evil influence.* He attacks the sensitive parts of our nature. He would destroy the finest and most magnificent portion of our being. The thoughts, imagination, and affections he is most anxious to corrupt, pervert, and destroy.

I unhesitatingly declare, there is at present no more active agent employed by Satan in civilized communities to ruin the human family and subject the nations to himself than evil reading.

If gambling saloons, concert dives, lottery and policy shops, poolrooms, low theaters, and rumholes are allowed to be kept open; if obscene books and pictures, foul papers, and criminal stories for the young are allowed to go broadcast, then must state prisons, penitentiaries, workhouses, jails, reformatories, etc., be erected and supported. Expensive courts and high-salaried officials must be employed at the taxpayer's expense, to care for those youths who are ruined, or to protect society against them.

Parents do not permit their children to make a playhouse of a sewer, nor to breathe its poisoned gasses. It is not popular to set diseased meat before the public in any of our numerous hotels or restaurants. Infected clothing may not be offered for sale, much less hawked about the streets. Yet worse evils than these are tolerated and encouraged, even while they are scattering moral death and physical suffering among those whom it is the especial duty of every civilized government to shield and protect—the young.

NOTES

1. P. Pinstrup-Anderson, *World Food Trends and Future Food Security*, Food Policy Statement Number 18 (Washington, DC: International Food Policy Research Institute, 1994).

2. These broad analytic categories were put together by David Hardcastle, a professor at the School of Social Work, University of Maryland-Baltimore, from the work of a variety of sociologists and other students of social problems. I have expanded them and added the details in the material that follows, creating substantial alterations to 1 and 4.

3. Other examples abound. Long stays in mental hospitals are said by some to not only worsen the condition of a number of the mentally disabled, but also to create "insanity" in some patients who were never "insane" in the first place. Some welfare programs, such as AFDC (now TANF), are said to create generational dependency—that is, to produce succeeding generations of children who will themselves be AFDC families.

4. From Walter E. Williams, *The SmithKline Forum for a Healthier America*, 1(6) (September 1979): 1–6. Dollar amounts have been adjusted to reflect inflation. Reprinted by permission of the author and VanSant Dugdale Advertising, Baltimore, MD.

5. Of course, we must understand that Williams was writing for ordinary readers here and in the space allowed could not develop the complete analysis he would have done in an academic journal.

6. The reader may notice that these examples all concern individuals and, thus, may be concerned that this contradicts earlier statements that social problems concern *groups* and not individuals. That problem can be resolved by remembering that all the individuals here are assumed to be members of a larger group in which all suffer from the same problem.

7. U.S. Bureau of the Census, *Statistical Abstracts of the U.S.: 1991*, 111th ed. (Washington, DC: Author, 1991), p. 116.

8. Notice that this criterion for judging a policy or program is not entirely practical from the viewpoint of the government or society because the standard concerns what the policy or program does for *those in need*. Unfortunately, in any view, the interests of the state do not always coincide with the interests of those in need, with those who suffer from a social problem. For instance, it may be easiest, and certainly the least costly, for society at large and a government to ignore the sick, the disabled, and the poverty stricken. The focus on the interests of those in need is a bias here and is consistent with the value positions of the social work profession. The profession takes as one of its goals the elimination of "barriers to human realization." Social problems of concern to the profession are those believed to

be major barriers to many people. See "The Working Definition of Social Work Practice," *Social Work*, 3(2) (April 1958): 5–9.

9. *Diagnostic and Statistical Manual of Mental Disorders*, 3rd ed. (Washington, DC: American Psychiatric Association, 1980). See also P. G. Janicak and S. N. Andrukaitis, "DSM-III," *Psychiatric Annals*, 10 (August 1980): 43–56.

10. Richard A. Musgrave, *The Theory of Public Finance* (New York: McGraw-Hill, 1961), pp. 111–112.

11. From Anthony Comstock, "Dangers in Half-Dime Novels and Story Papers," in Robert H. Bremner (ed.), *Traps for the Young* (Cambridge, MA: Belknap Press of Harvard University Press, 1967), pp. 21–28, 238–242, first published in 1883.

2

Creating the Context for the Analysis of Social Policies

Understanding the Historical Context

BY RICHARD SPANO

Chapter 2 is used with permission of the author, Richard Spano. Professor Spano was asked to write this chapter because of the unique approach he offers to help understand the relationship between history and social problems and social policy. Not only is this approach unique, it translates easily into a method that yields practical results for those to whom it is important to understand why policy and programs are what they have become today.

Introduction

This chapter is concerned with the contribution history makes to our understanding of how social problems are defined and social policies developed. It presents history, and more specifically historical context, as a critical factor in shaping specific thinking and attitudes in all elements of society. The intent here is not to educate historians, but rather to sensitize social workers to a view of social policy as shaped by prior as well as current efforts to resolve social issues.

The Idea of Historical Context

To begin with, it is important to be clear about what is meant by *historical context* as it relates to social policy analysis. In most social work programs, undergraduate students take introductory courses in "Social Welfare as an Institution" and "Social Work as a Profession," each of which has some small portion of its emphasis on history. Sometimes these courses consist of a recitation of dates, people, movements, and structures that represent benchmarks in the development of social welfare and social work: the Elizabethan poor laws, the Social Security Act, the Civil Rights Act, Jane Addams, Mary Richmond, Florence Kelley, the Charity Organization Society, and the settlement house movement, for example. Assuming retention of only these facts, do they help a social worker understand social policy? Probably not.

Although this focus on facts and dates represents the dominant view of history in most social work curricula, at the other end of the continuum are those historians who suggest that the only way to understand history is to know everything about a society during a given era: its music, art, economics, politics, religion, and intellectual climate. Although this is important for historians, the assumption underlying this book is that readers want to prepare for a career in *social work*. Thus, there is the need for something less than comprehensive preparation in history. The way to do that is to learn to be sensitive to some of the more important historical aspects of social policy development without having to relinquish the viewpoint of a practicing social worker. Toward that goal, some ways will be suggested here for you to enrich your understanding of the complex issues associated with social policy analysis.

For our purposes, we are not so much concerned with history as history but with the historical context of social policies and programs; historical context is the soil in which social policy grows and takes root. If social policy is viewed as a plant, historical context consists of the air, water, and ground in the immediate area that will shape the growth of the plant. So it is that the particular interaction of political, economic, religious, and social welfare systems becomes the ground that shapes our analysis of social policy. For example, two conflicting struggles in the 1960s—the domestic War on Poverty and the Vietnam War—illustrate the struggle that can occur when the political and social welfare systems make conflicting demands on the economic system.

One major dimension of historical context refers to the *people and/or organizations that hold a stake in developing social policy in a particular direction.* An example of how potent this aspect can be in shaping social policy is illustrated in the field of mental retardation. Rose Kennedy, President John F. Kennedy's mother, and Hubert Humphrey, a leader in the U.S. Senate, both had a personal stake in seeing to it that developmentally disabled (DD) children received social services. In both instances, their concern came as a result of both having DD members in their immediate families: Mrs. Kennedy had such a daughter and Senator Humphrey such a grandchild. Both Mrs. Kennedy and Senator Humphrey worked tirelessly to improve the treatment and promote their cause.

Sometimes small groups of experts band together and organize to effect a social policy. An example of this is the work of Isaac Rubinow, a statistician and one of the founders, in 1906, of the American Association for Labor Legislation. Rubinow worked as a member of this group for nearly three decades to promote a conception of social insurance that was incorporated in the Social Security Act in 1935. Other examples of these constituent groups include such diverse organizations as the American Medical Association, the American Bar Association, the National Association of Social Workers, the Children's Defense Fund, the American Association of Manufacturers, and the AFL-CIO.

What they share in common is that they seek to shape the process by which policy is developed to fit their own view of the most desired outcome.

From the foregoing, it should be clear how important it is to establish a historical context as a precondition to understanding social policy development. To do that, the practical policy analyst needs to know how current conceptions of a social problem and current actors connect with prior conceptions and actors in a policy area. Having set out what we mean by the idea of historical context, let us now consider some more detailed examples. First, let's think about how historical context affects viewpoints on social problems. Then, let's think about how historical context affects social policy development.

Using Historical Context to Understand Social Problem Viewpoints

In sixteenth- and seventeenth-century England, the social problem of concern was pauperism. Most learned people then writing social commentary about poor people were either churchmen or were educated within theologically dominated institutions. They saw pauperism as an individual moral deficit related to some lack of "moral fiber": pauperism was the product of individual failure or laziness. In general, people were viewed as evil by nature and headed for serious trouble if not kept busy ("the idle mind is the devil's playground"). These attitudes toward the poor reflected the prevailing theology of that era and led to efforts to control paupers rather than poverty. George Herbert's *The Country Parson* illustrates this view. In his chapter "The Parson Surveys," he suggests that it is necessary for the parson to survey his parish to determine the "faults" therein, and that included the sin of "idlenesse."

> The great and nationall sin of this Land [the Parson . . . should] . . . esteem to be Idlenesse. . . . For men [who] have nothing to do . . . fall to drink, to steal, to whore, to scoffe, to revile to all sorts of gamings. . . . Idlenesse is twofold, the one of having no calling, the other in walking carelessly in our calling. . . .[1]

Given this social problem viewpoint, ensuring that everyone had some form of employment should serve to alleviate the problem. Furthermore, once the parson had surveyed his parish and determined the needs, he was to extract funds from the rich members of the parish and carry out his charitable works with the following admonition:

> But he gives no set pension to any . . . for then they will reckon upon it, as a debt; and if it be taken away, though justly, they will murmur. . . . But the Parson, having a double aime, and making a hook of his Charity, he wins them to praise God more, to live more religiously, and take more paines in their vocation. . . . [because they cannot foresee] . . . when they shall be relieved.[2]

Much if not most of this view can be found in the English poor laws of this era: the notion of the need to exert influence and/or control over the poor so that they would mend their ways and thereby take their rightful place in the kingdom of God, and the theological assumptions about the nature of man as essentially lazy and prone toward evil. These concepts legitimated the notion of *social control as a function of charity*.

In the Ypres Plan developed by Juan Vives for the Consuls and Senate of Bruges (Belgium) in the sixteenth century, the blending of church and secular views with an eye toward social control is clearly illustrated.

> We have decreed by an open commandment that none of our citizens presume to let any house to a stranger without our knowledge and consent for else by the daily increase of poor folks greater charge might grow unto us than we were able to bear. . . . Now for all this no man is [hindered from doing] good deeds but every man if he will may give alms privately to who he listeth. . . . Let them not send only broken meats but let them rather send a mess or two of meat even purposely appointed for them so that citizen's children may learn to visit and love the poor men's little cottages. . . .[3]

This view takes note of the economic problems associated with caring for poor people, but draws heavily on the prevailing theology as the basis for explaining the nature of poverty and the relationship of paupers to the rest of society. In fact, this view of poverty was very nearly the only available explanation of the conditions of the poor. Even those few who advocated relief for poor people focused, for example, on the lame, blind, and sick (the individual characteristics of the poor), rather than on social or economic structures, as nineteenth- or twentieth-century commentators might.

Were the seventeenth-century inhabitants of England unconcerned about their fellow citizens? Were they significantly less intelligent than we are? Were they malevolent? The answer to each of these questions is "Probably not." They were probably not significantly different from their twentieth-century descendants on any of these dimensions. However, they were different in that they were products of their history and current social context, just as we are products of ours. Remember, in that period, there was no social science, which meant that there were few explanations to rival individualistic and theological perspectives.

Approximately three hundred years later, in the early 1900s, the American Progressives John Spargo and Robert Hunter studied the problem of poverty in America. They used newly developed techniques such as social survey research methods, statistical and economic analysis, and political ideology to frame the issues surrounding the causes, consequences, and cures for poverty.

Spargo was a radical among the progressives. When he wrote *The Bitter Cry of the Children*, he was active in the Socialist party, although he was identified with that party's moderate wing. In the preface to *Bitter Cry*, Spargo clearly expressed his intent:

> The purpose of this volume is to state the problem of poverty and its effects on childhood. Years of careful study and investigation have convinced me that the evils inflicted upon children by poverty are responsible for many of the worst futures of that hideous phantasmagoria of hunger, disease, vice, crime, and despair which we call the Social Problem.[4]

To achieve his purpose, Spargo compiled an impressive array of statistical information about family income, occupation, number of children, and education and their impact on child nutrition. He took a view of "charity" and the poor that was quite different from George Herbert's (see p. 33). Spargo emphasized the inadequacy of charity as a tool to sustain poor people.

> But it is only too true that charity—that damnably cold thing called charity—fails utterly to meet the problem of poverty in general and childhood's poverty in particular. Nothing could be more pathetic than the method employed by so many charitable persons and societies of attempting to solve the latter problem by finding employment for the mother, as if that were the worst phase of all from any sane view of the child's interest. Charity degrades and demoralizes and there is little or no compensating effecting help. In the vast majority of cases [this kind of charity] falls to reach the suffering in time to save them from becoming chronic dependents.[5]

Robert Hunter was a contemporary of Spargo's, but he was more closely identified with social work. Hunter analyzed poverty, paying special attention to quantifying it and then identifying the factors that contribute to it. Hunter's analysis vacillates between careful study—reflecting the social science perspective—and polemic sermonizing—emphasizing a socialist perspective on the causes for poverty. One of the most interesting aspects of Hunter's analysis is that he takes great pains to separate poor people into different categories: paupers, vagrants, the sick, poor children, and newly arrived immigrants.

These distinctions play an important part in his analysis because they suggest different approaches to the problems of different groups. Hunter's view of the pauper is different in substance from that of George Herbert three hundred years earlier, even though it has a familiar ring. According to Hunter:

> In nearly all cases, he who continuously asks aid becomes a craven, abject creature with a lust for gratuitous maintenance. And he who becomes an habitual pauper undergoes a kind of degeneration. . . . In some cases he becomes almost incapable of self support; he loses all capacity for sustained effort. . . . Avoiding any useful effort, he becomes skilled in those activities which enable him to more perfectly retain his state of dependence.[6]

The significant shift in his view is that he uses a medical rather than a theological metaphor to view the pauper. He "diagnoses" the problem as a "disease of character" and suggests that it affects the actual physical condition of the pauper, using the Jukes studies to support his assertion.[7] The focus of concern is the body, not the soul, and it is to be understood "scientifically," not theologically.

Hunter expresses a good deal more sympathy for the working poor, who he believed made up about 20 percent of the total number of poor. In his conclusion, he admonishes the reader not to believe that all those in poverty are "effortless beings" who make no fight and wait in misery for someone to help them. He concludes the analysis

with a plea for social justice for the working poor that he translates into recommenda-
tions for our basic economic system.

If we placed these perspectives on poverty side by side, it would be difficult to find
many similarities. Were these progressives antireligious? Were they unaware of the
spiritual aspects of their fellowman, aspects so prized by George Herbert? Were they
amoral? Probably not. Possibly they were quite similar to their English forebears on
these dimensions. They were, however, part of the first generation of social scientists
who were developing a rival set of ideas to explain poverty. They chose a "scientific"
rather than a theological framework, which led them to very different conclusions about
poverty, its causes, and its consequences. Note that this does not suggest that social science is a better or a more valid explanation, but simply that it leads to different formu-
lations in a social problem analysis.

Hunter's and Spargo's social science perspectives were early examples in a long line
of scientific explanations of poverty. Hunter and Spargo used economic and political science concepts as useful tools, whereas others used newly emerging concepts from public
health and "industrial sociology" to explain poverty. In the 1960s, there was another
popular conception of poverty, "the culture of poverty," as advocated by Oscar Lewis, a
widely read anthropologist who studied intergenerational poverty cross-culturally. In
part, Lewis's anthropological notion of the culture of poverty was intended to bridge
the gap between large-scale economic and political explanations and the individually
oriented explanations of theology and psychology. For Lewis, the poor family and its
adaptations to the dominant culture were used to explain how this subculture of the
poor developed as a response to poverty. Some of the traits embodied in the culture of
poverty included a lack of effective participation and integration of the poor into major social institutions, a lack of productivity and marginal consumption, an espousal of
middle-class values without the commitment to live by them, and a minimum amount
of organization beyond the level of the nuclear family. At the family level, the traits included the absence of a prolonged childhood, early initiation into sex, free unions, a relatively high incidence of abandoned wives, a trend toward mother-centered families, a
strong disposition toward authoritarianism, and a lack of privacy. On the individual level,
the culture of poverty included a strong feeling of marginality, of helplessness, of dependence, and of inferiority.[8]

The War-on-Poverty programs were consistent with notions embedded in the
culture-of-poverty idea. At an institutional level, Legal Aid and storefront lawyers attempted to make structural policy changes through case law that would help the poor
access goods and services and expand civil rights.[9] At the neighborhood level, the Mobilization for Youth program was designed to intensify participation and a sense of control
over one's environment. At the individual and family level, community mental health services were provided to retard the "disorganization" within the family and the individual.[10] Clearly, the War-on-Poverty programs represented a multifaceted approach that
Lewis's conception suggested as the appropriate means to alleviate the problems resulting from poverty. (Note that Lewis himself would *not* always have agreed with this interpretation of his work.)

Questions to Guide the Search for the Historical Context of a Social Problem Viewpoint

These brief descriptions of social problem analyses of poverty illustrate the interplay of historical context with social problem analysis. Here are some questions that might guide your search to establish the historical context surrounding a modern social problem analysis.

1. Why is this concern being raised as a problem at this moment in history? For instance, in the prior examples, it is appropriate to ask: "Were there no poor people prior to 1601?" The answer is that there were, but poverty was seen as a condition, a simple fact of existence rather than a social problem. A condition does not call for a resolution unless the condition is connected to a value commitment to which existence of the condition is a contradiction. Examples of the forces that shape the problem are complex and often related to events in specific time periods. The 1930s was a period during which economic depression was sufficiently widespread to capture the attention of nearly all groups in America, when urgent economic problems were of such magnitude that they had to be addressed in order for American society to continue. At another time, in the affluent 1960s, concern about the oppression of blacks captured the public's attention. In that instance, blacks raised discrimination as a moral issue and gathered sufficient support from other minority groups and from segments of white society so that long-term changes in our social system resulted. Why were the 1960s ripe for such a change? Why not the 1950s or 1970s?

2. Is this a "new" problem? As we saw earlier in this chapter, our society has wrestled with the problem of poverty for centuries, employed numerous explanations, and developed a multitude of policies and programs. Each time a new formulation of the problem is put forward, we alter the service-delivery structure to account for the change, and sometimes we create a whole new structure. However, in every era, new "problems" are put forward that may have little precedent; for example, the policies and programs regarding nursing-home care are a post–World War II problem that called for novel solutions. Never before had so many people lived so long or families been so loosely knit—both attitudinally and geographically. Those facts provided the historical context for the definition of totally new social problems.

3. What are the precedents for the ideas and values (ideology) being used to define the problem? Sometimes, the current conception of a situation is just a narrow revision of an earlier conception. Note, for example, that there is a contemporary view that poverty is a condition perpetuated by mental mechanisms that develop to adjust to deprivation and are passed down through families. In some ways, this is a view of poverty as a moral degeneration to which the poor become acclimated and that is perpetuated in new generations and by the charity of others. For example, the basic principles enunciated in the Elizabethan poor laws rather dramatically parallel the "individualistic" principles used in the development of President Richard M. Nixon's 1970 Family Assistance

Plan. Rightly or wrongly, validly or invalidly, this is an individually oriented view of poverty that has persisted intact for the last four centuries.

Sometimes, the ideology used to define a problem is almost unprecedented. For example, although the social problem of poverty is defined as having its historical roots in the poverty of women—caused by their occupational segregation, job discrimination, and unequal access to public benefits and services—it comes very close to presenting a new social problem view. Although feminist viewpoints are surely not unique to the twentieth century, their ideological extension to advocating for a position of equality with men in employment and in child rearing probably is unique to this era.

4. Who are the actors now defining this issue as a social problem and how are they different from past actors? Identifying the relevant stakeholders in the problem usually leads to identifying important constituent groups that seek to influence future policy and program development. For example, the battles waged around Medicare and Medicaid in the 1960s included many of the same groups that in the 1930s had argued issues pertaining to the provision of medical care. The beginning of these debates prominently featured points that eventually led to the Social Security Act. Many social service people, politicians, and interested private citizens saw this concern as an essential element in any social insurance package. However, the medical community lobbied hard against this aspect of the bill, and it was removed early in the political process. (The political process will be discussed later in this chapter.) Today, however, the American Medical Association (AMA) and a whole new health care industry are among the important problem definers and supporters of the public provision of medical care.

5. If the issue currently being raised has some historical precedent, what conditions now exist that suggest different outcomes or make society more receptive to change? The suggestion that "history repeats itself" is somewhat misleading. Although certain basic social issues or problems such as poverty persist over time, the policy responses to those problems are never exactly the same. Social insurance provides a good example of a means to combat poverty that was actually not new in the 1930s when Congress passed the Social Security Act. Social reformers like Isaac Rubinow had already proposed various schemes for social insurance in the early 1900s. Those ideas made little impact on society then, in part because they were proposed in a period of relative economic prosperity when society was not threatened economically. Social insurance became a reality in America in the 1930s during the Great Depression, when the resolution of economic problems was central to society's survival.

Along the same line, blacks had been discriminated against in this country for nearly two hundred years before civil rights legislation was passed. Why, in 1964, did we get the Civil Rights Act? In part, the answer lies in casting the treatment of blacks as a matter of social conscience rather than an economic issue. In other words, the civil rights movement, the War on Poverty, and the Vietnam War interacted in a way that made this society sensitive to the redress of grievances that had a longstanding precedent.

Although the answers to these five questions will not provide all the information necessary to develop a comprehensive understanding of the historical context of a social problem viewpoint, the questions do suggest some important areas that should yield valuable information with which to assess a social problem viewpoint. In summary, social problem viewpoints can best be understood as both a product of prior experience on the part of a society and as the unfolding of the current interrelationships existing in that society. The practical policy analyst's task is to identify some of the key factors that lead to the development of a particular problem formulation, rather than to a comprehensive understanding of history for history's sake.

Using Historical Context to Understand Social Policy and Program Designs

Thus far, we have looked at a framework useful in developing an *analysis* of a social problem viewpoint and at how to ground such a framework in a useful historical context for thinking about social problem analysis. In this section, we will use the concept of historical context to see how it affects the implementation of social policies and programs. We will look at policy and program implementations as products of the interaction of political processes and formal organizational structures.

Political Process

Earlier, we described social policy as an expression of society's concern about the need to resolve a specific social problem or issue. For example, so long as there is sufficient clean air to breathe and clean water to drink, these critical aspects of our existence remain outside the purview of social policy. If clean air and water become scarce (whether because of pollution or increased population), their management, distribution, and protection will become subjects for social policy. The underlying idea is that social policy usually reflects society's attempts to manage a scarce resource. Accordingly, there are nearly always competing and conflicting demands made by various groups that shape public policy. These conflicts are expressed through our political system, which generates much of our social policy. The process by which claims are advanced for resources within the political system is called the *political process.*

Our political process has formal and informal dimensions. Its formal aspects are expressed through congressional hearings, public statements put forward by concerned individuals or groups, political platforms, and legislative bills—all of which culminate in social policy being enacted into laws.

Compromises may occur at any point in these formal activities. This happens when some group, organization, or individual exerts influence that alters the makeup of the policy proposals. For example, as a part of its platform, a party may champion a specific proposal such as the Equal Rights Amendment. At any point from the time a bill is introduced, people will try to shape its policy in ways they believe are in their best interest. This effort can occur in congressional hearings, floor debates, public hearings, or joint conferences—all of which are part of the formal political process.

As you examine the political process and how it developed around a specific social policy or program design, two key notions can help guide you in establishing an appropriate historical context in which to understand social policy and program development: (1) the constituent groups—large and small—involved in the process and (2) the nature of the compromise reached. First, identify the various groups that had some stake in the policy. Some of the groups will be private and others public; some will be highly visible and some may keep a low profile; some will have a long history of involvement in the issue and some may be new to the battle; and some will represent special-interest groups whereas others may advocate based on their expertise. The important thing to remember is that each constituent group will have a stake in the process and will try to shape policy and program development to fit its own view of the best solutions to the problem.

The nature of the compromise reached is most often determined in the informal political process. The informal political process is somewhat more difficult to track because it refers to compromises arranged outside formal channels, such as conversations, confidential communications between people or organizations, or decisions made in closed meetings. This information is much more difficult to locate and often requires access to committee minutes, organizational memos, confidential reports and unpublished studies, private notes or diaries, and correspondence between crucial actors in the drama.

Formal Structure

Formal structure refers to the organizational mechanisms established and charged with responsibility for translating social policy and programs from theory to implementation. In some situations, new agencies, bureaus, or divisions are created; in others, social policy is delegated to existing agencies or bureaus that may have similar goals or that in the past have served the population groups toward whom the policy is directed. Oftentimes, the success of social policy depends on the two things: (1) choosing an appropriate organizational structure for policy delivery and (2) designating the appropriate level of government at which the structure is lodged. An example of an agency that played a crucial role—and an unprecedented one—in American history is the Freedman's Bureau. This structure was created at the end of the Civil War to meet the many needs of blacks during their transition from slavery to freedom. The Freedman's Bureau provided settlement, employment, and legal assistance. Furthermore, it was lodged in the federal government, the first time the federal government stepped in to provide directly for the welfare of a group of its citizens. The comprehensive structure of the bureau, coupled with its federal sponsorship, made it possible to achieve some of its objectives. Had the same agency been lodged in state government, its effectiveness most likely would have been severely hampered.

To understand the current role formal structure plays in policy and program development, it is necessary to look at the history of the organization or bureaucratic structure administering the policy or program design and to examine its relationship to various constituent groups. For example, Gilbert Steiner identifies nearly a dozen major organizations interested in the welfare of children. Each has a specific stake in the "children's cause" and defines its objectives in ways that often overlap. These organizations may share related objectives, but they often compete for the scarce resources available to meet them. Organizational survival can become as important as the objectives they seek to reach. Steiner does an excellent job of tracing the effect of these turf battles and personality conflicts in shaping various elements of policies and programs in the field of child welfare.

In *The Children's Cause*, Steiner focuses specifically on tracing the role played by the Children's Bureau in the field of child welfare. The following brief overview of this organization illustrates some of the important aspects of formal structure in policy and program development. The Children's Bureau was created as a result of the first White House Conference on Children in 1909. Answerable directly to the White House, it had remarkably able leadership as well as stability and clarity of purpose. From 1912 until the 1950s, it had only five directors, including such notable social workers as Julia Lathrop and Grace Abbot. The bureau consistently focused its efforts on research—on preparing solid evidence for the development of a policy in the public sector to benefit children. However, from the 1930s on, it was exposed to increasing competition from the newly developing public relief agencies that took over more and more of its turf. By the 1960s, the bureau had become part of the Department of Welfare Administration of the U.S. Department of Health, Education, and Welfare (HEW) and subservient to HEW civil servants. HEW itself was absorbed into the U.S. Department of Health and Human Services.[11] As a result, the Children's Bureau was lost from the sight of its powerful constituent groups and deprived of its autonomous destiny. Formal structure can determine the destiny and influence of a program, and the Children's Bureau could no longer determine autonomously how it should serve children because it had to answer to other civil servants. In its early days, it had answered directly to the White House.

According to Steiner, this loss was the result of the informal influence of Jules Sugarman, an aggressive associate director of the Head Start program, who opposed the assignment of Head Start (then in its early years) to the Children's Bureau. In a confidential memo to Mary Switzer, then administrator of the U.S. Division of Social and Rehabilitation Services, Sugarman was critical of the Children's Bureau and recommended that the solution to its problem was to reduce its role by incorporating it into a new organization or substantially modifying its leadership at all levels.[12] Sugarman's informal organizational activity doomed any chance for the Children's Bureau to assume a new leadership role by taking on responsibility for the Head Start program.

Subsequently, HEW Secretary Robert Finch received a memo from Switzer that further damaged the bureau's reputation and led to its incorporation in a new structure, the Office of Child Development (OCD). Eventually, the Children's Bureau, once the most influential child welfare agency, became an obscure small department in OCD.

It is in this manner that social policy and social problem viewpoints reflect public debates about issues. The informal maneuvering that occurs within and between organizations uses the need to implement policy as an opportunity to provide their own interpretation of the social problem. It is no wonder that ordinary agency practitioners, the street-level bureaucrats, become confused and frustrated when asked to implement policy that reflects compromises at so many levels. Those compromises represent conflicting interests and different purposes all the way back to the time of the first legislative debates on the problem.

The Food Stamp Program: An Example

Before concluding this chapter, it will be useful to see the interplay of historical context, social problem views, and social policy and program design by looking at the food stamp program. The origins of the U.S. food stamp program can be traced to Section 32 of Public Law 72-320 (known as the Potato Control Act of 1935). The last section of this act authorized the purchase of surplus commodities for distribution to needy church groups and families.

The surplus commodities distribution programs were controlled by the U.S. Department of Agriculture (USDA) and administered by the Federal Surplus Commodities Corporation (FSCC). FSCC's purpose was to support farm prices, not to feed the poor. The creation of the program caused concern among the various constituent groups that were claiming an interest in it, including recipients who disliked the distribution system, and the food retailers who did not want normal trade mechanisms disrupted. In this instance, there were two problems existing side by side: widespread starvation and malnutrition caused by the Great Depression and disposal of surplus created by new agricultural technologies. On the surface, the two problems appear to be compatible, but the policy goals of feeding the poor and reducing food surpluses proved to be embarrassingly awkward to achieve.

The organizational mechanism created to meet the two goals was a two-stamp system. In this system, welfare recipients were issued stamps that could be used to buy food at authorized retailers: orange ones, which were purchased at face value by recipients, and blue ones, which were provided for free on a 2:1 orange-to-blue ratio. The blue stamps could be used only to purchase surplus commodities designated by the secretary of agriculture. In theory, the program would reduce food surpluses by making them more available to recipients and reduce malnutrition by increasing the amount of food available for recipients. However, in practice, the program had mixed results. It did not appear to stimulate expenditures on food any more than would have been expected from a cash subsidy. On the other hand, it did expand the choice of foods beyond the prior commodity programs and was advantageous to food retailers as well as producers.[13]

The problem—and thus the policy—regarding these issues again came to public attention in the early 1960s, when surplus food and a concern for nutrition among the poor reemerged as social issues. This time new protagonists were brought into the fray. The goals remained utilization of the nation's food surplus and promotion of the nutritional well-being of low-income persons; however, the political process and formal structures were subject to new stress from politicians who were concerned about the relationship of states' rights to the federal government. A critical factor shaping the eventual food stamp program centered on compromises that needed to be made to ensure support from conservative members of Congress who were concerned about the expanding role of the federal government in the lives of their constituents. The eventual compromise that allowed conservatives to support the food stamp program was that the federal government would determine payment levels (how much benefit was to be given), but the states would determine eligibility standards (who was to receive benefits).[14]

Two social problems—the enormous farm surplus stockpile and feeding of the poor—and their solutions were clearly articulated in the food stamp program from the very beginning, and one structure, lodged in the USDA, was established to resolve both. This suggests some answers to three questions commonly raised about the food stamp program, for example:

1. Why did poor people get so much peanut butter and lard from the food stamp program in the early years? (Answer: Lard and peanuts were glutting the market.)

2. Why is there a stamp program instead of simply giving poor people the cash to buy their own food—especially now that it is clear that the costs of the two alternatives do not differ significantly? (Answer: Continuation of the program requires support of the congressmen from the farm states who have a loyalty and an ideological bent toward a program that was once a useful mechanism for reducing farm surpluses.)

3. Why does the state control the administration of the food stamp program when the federal government pays all its bills? (Answer: The program was caught up in an ideological battle in the 1960s, at a moment in history when increased federal operation of programs was viewed as an encroachment on states' rights.)

To understand policy formulation and program development is to understand clearly the surrounding conditions: poverty in the midst of plenty; the various constituent groups with some stake in the process (poor people, farmers, food retailers, activist groups of the 1960s, and politicians); and the history of compromises meant to implement a specific program. These individual aspects came together in what we call the historical context of social policy and program analysis.[15]

Summary

The study of history for the purpose of creating the historical context for the study of social problems and policy is different from the study of history qua history. For the purpose of the student of social problems, at least five questions are useful in establishing the historical context surrounding a modern social problem:

1. Why is this particular social problem being raised as a matter of concern at this particular moment in history?
2. Is this a new issue?
3. What are the historical precedents for the ideas and values being used to define the issue?
4. Who are the actors now defining this issue as a social problem, and how are they different from past actors?
5. If the current issue has some historical precedent, what conditions now exist that suggest different outcomes or make society more open to change?

In analyzing social policies and programs, there are two important issues to establish in creating the historical context:

1. The Political Process. How causes are advanced within the political system and how this leads to creation of a policy or program; what constituent groups were involved in the process; and the nature of the political compromises necessary to legislate or gather support for the policy or program.

2. The Formal Structure. The nature of bureaucratic and organizational competition that may have been instrumental in deciding where to lodge administrative responsibility for a new policy or program or in shifting such responsibility from one organization or department to another.

These elements of the historical context of policies and programs have important bearing on both the form that the program eventually takes and the extent to which it can be successfully implemented.

EXERCISES

The following exercise is intended to help you gain skill using the framework presented in this chapter. Pick an area of social policy that is currently being debated in your community or state.

1. Identify the relevant actors in the debate. Who are the people and organizations that stand to gain or lose in developing this particular social policy? What appear to be the major areas of contention among these groups? How do they define the problem?

2. Examine public documents, newspaper reports, committee reports, public speeches, and so on, and try to infer from them why this problem is being debated at this juncture in history. Is this a new problem? What, if any, specific events fueled the debate?

3. After examining the definitions of the problem, look behind the words to the ideology being used to shape the definition. What can you tell about the actors' views of the relationship between the problem and social and personal responsibility? Are these new or old arguments?

4. As you look at the surrounding social context, can you identify similarities or differences between these conditions and those affecting prior attempts to deal with this problem? Are there new technologies available? Is a new value commitment evident? Are the relationships among the contending parties different?

NOTES

1. F. E. Hutchinson, *The Works of George Herbert* (London: Oxford University Press, 1941), p. 274.
2. Ibid., pp. 244–245.
3. Karl de Schweinitz, *England's Road to Social Security* (New York: A. S. Barnes, 1939), p. 35.

4. John Spargo, *The Bitter Cry of the Children* (New York: Quadrangle Books, 1968), p. xlii.

5. Ibid., p. 54.

6. Robert Hunter, *Poverty* (New York: Harper & Row, 1965), p. 69.

7. Ibid., p. 318.

8. Oscar Lewis, *La Vida* (New York: Random House, 1965), pp. xlii–xliii.

9. Joel Handler, *Protecting the Social Service Client* (New York: Academic Press, 1979).

10. Leopold Bellak and Harvey Barton, *Progress in Community Mental Health* (New York: Brunner/ Mazel, 1975).

11. Gilbert Steiner, *The Children's Cause* (Washington, DC: The Brookings Institution, 1976), p. 39.

12. Ibid.

13. Maurice MacDonald, *Food Stamps and Income Maintenance* (New York: Academic Press, 1977), p. 2.

14. Ibid., pp. 3–4.

15. The following books represent various ways in which historical context is written; the best single example is Robert Bremner's *From the Depths* (New York: New York University Press, 1956). Other examples are Fred Best, *Work-Sharing, Issues, Options and Prospects* (Grand Rapids, MI: W. E. Upjohn Institute on Employment Research, 1981), pp. 1–9; Judith Cassetty, *Child Support and Public Policy* (Toronto: Lexington Books, 1978), pp. 5–14; Sar Levitan and Richard S. Belous, *More Than Subsistence* (Baltimore: Johns Hopkins University Press, 1979), pp. 29–52; Theodore Marmor, *The Politics of Medicare* (Chicago: Aldine, 1970), pp. vii–ix, 1–82; and Steiner, *The Children's Cause*, chaps. 3, 4, 5.

3

The Judiciary as a Shaper of Social Policy, Program, and Practice

Introduction

To understand the main business in this chapter, how the U.S. Judiciary and its courts of law establish social policy and shape program operations, the reader has to be clear on some fundamentals about how the U.S. government works. The question is: Since the task of the Courts isn't to administer social policies and programs, how can the courts affect them within other branches of government? In this introduction, we will answer that question. We'll begin with a description of the relationship of the Judiciary (the courts) to other branches of government.

Recall that there are three branches of government established by the U.S. Constitution: the legislative, the executive, and the judicial. At the heart of our constitution is the idea that each of these have very different responsibilities and are to be independent of the other as they go about their business. The constitution establishes "checks and balances" between them so that no one branch of government has complete power over the affairs of the nation. So (oversimplifying here), it is the business of the legislative branch, the Congress and Senate, to legislate—that is, to propose and enact laws. It is the business of the executive branch to see that these laws are put into effect through various governmental departments (the President is "in charge" of all government departments and offices). Health and Human Services (HHS) is the relevant example for us here. And it is the business of the Judiciary (the courts) to "adjudicate"—that is, to make judgments about who is right or wrong according to the law: as in (a) disagreements between citizens (civil law), (b) deciding the guilt or innocence of citizens who disobey laws (criminal law), and (c) disagreements between citizens and government agencies (often administrative law). A court order reinstating an ("unfairly") terminated government disability benefit or a court order that revokes the commitment of a person to a mental institution are examples of "checks and balances" in action. The judicial branch of government (the court) is "checking" (or "balancing") the action of the executive branch. Other examples of the same are when a President vetoes legislation that the Congress has passed, when a federal or Supreme Court voids an act of Congress (or regulations imposed by the President) as unconstitutional, when Congress passes certain kinds of laws that clarifies its legislative intentions and thus makes inoperative a Supreme Court decision, or when

Congress denies approval of a Presidential nominee for Secretary of State, for example, or passes by a two-thirds majority a national budget over a Presidential veto. These are all examples of the constitutional idea that a democracy has to have a way to constrain government abuse of power. That idea is worth celebrating since, despite all the "warts" on our form of government, it's kept us free from the worst of tyranny for over 200 years. Before a social policy or program can come before the Judiciary, someone must think a law has been broken. So, let us now look briefly at how laws establishing and funding public social policies and programs come into being.

How Are Public Programs Established and Funded? The Political and Legislative Processes

Public social programs can be established at any governmental level (city, county, state, or federal). Since technical legislative details will vary state by state, city by city, and so on, what follows are not those but the (far more interesting and useful) political processes. Ordinarily, legislation begins with a group of citizens who are concerned about a difficulty they have in common—it is not always so, but we might call it a "social problem." Of course, self-interests can be corporate and financial; no reader should be surprised to learn of the corporate self-interest of Columbia Health Care Corporation in getting Congress to increase Medicare/Medicaid hospital payment coverage or midwestern farm state Senators in seeking congressional exemptions from the Presidential order suspending wheat export trade with India (punishing India for testing a nuclear bomb). Interest groups can also be convened on moral grounds: for or against civil rights of minorities, discrimination on the basis of gender or sexual orientation, and so on.

The *first task* for an interest group is to define its issue clearly and achieve unanimity on what the problem is and what it wants by way of legislation, not always an easy task, by the way. It is crucial since the general public and individual legislators need to know exactly what the interest group wants if they are to give legislative and public support.

The *second task* is to frame a "position paper" that organizes the arguments (pro and con) and summarizes what is known (or unknown) about the issue or problem, perhaps seeking "experts" for advice. Although data and argument may not persuade every opponent, they often can be used to get the support of those who are "on the fence," neutral, or unmoved. The social problem analysis, familiar to readers from the first chapter of this book, is the kind of background necessary for preparing these preadvocacy position papers. It must be done carefully, with one eye on the truth and the other for the center around which political consensus can congeal. Bringing together coalitions of supporters requires compromise.

The *third task* in the legislative process is to create solutions for the social problem of concern, that is, a public policy, program design, or provision (benefit) that will plausibly correct the problem. That is not a simple task to do well; actual legislative proposals vary from excellent to simplistic and all the way to unbelievably simple-minded. "Theories" that suggest interventions or resources or planning have to be converted to practical, financially feasible, concrete program processes and outcomes in order for legislatures to have a basis on which they can rationally decide whether the whole project has merit. Notice that legislators have to have answers to questions from their voter-constituents about the reasonableness of legislation they are being asked to sponsor, promote, or vote for. It is the responsibility of interest groups to provide their legislative supporters with such answers.

The *fourth task* is to organize public support for their issue. In order to motivate legislators to identify themselves with an issue and recruit other legislators as well, large-scale public support is essential. Everything else pales into insignificance without it.

The *fifth task* in the legislative process is to convince a legislator to "sign on" to the bill in the sense of turning the social problem analysis, prospective social program design features, and position papers into a legislative proposal and officially introducing (sponsoring) it as a legislative bill. At that point, it will then be referred to an appropriate committee of the legislature for study and recommendation. Part of the "study" is a legislative hearing on the bill.

The *sixth task* in the legislative process is to organize appearances at the aforementioned Committee hearings with regard to the bill. The purpose of the committee hearings is for committee members to ask questions, receive answers, and debate its merits. Naturally, one function of the hearings is for the committee to gauge the amount of public support for or against the bill. It is to the interest of the supporters of a bill to turn out their fellow supporters either en masse or carefully selected depending on political strategy. Most effective lobbying groups take great care in choosing who expresses to legislators their point of view for or against the proposed legislation. And, take care with exactly what is said. At some point, the committee will vote on whether the bill will go forward to the whole legislature for a final vote. Or, it can vote to "table" the bill for action at a later date. That can be next week, next month, or never.

The *seventh task* in the legislative process is to lobby legislators, other than the one who introduced the bill, for their support when it is finally voted on by the whole (federal, state, or city) legislative body. Supporters need to turn out in strength. Lobbying is most effective when it is coordinated, timed, and clear in what it wants legislators to vote for. Once again, the agenda is to show legislators why it is in their political interest to vote in a particular way on legislation.

Assuming that the bill passed into law, the *last task* in the legislative process is lobbying for money (appropriations) to run the program that is contained in the legislation. It is discouraging in the extreme to work so hard for passage of legislation only to see it gathering dust when no funds are appropriated to get it "up and running." So, it is necessary to repeat lobbying efforts in the hearings of whatever legislative committee (finance or perhaps appropriations committee) controls appropriations. No doubt, "it's a long and a dusty road."

The Regulatory Process Following Enactment

Once legislation is passed (at whatever level of government) and appropriations made, it is sent to the executive branch for the chief executive officer (President, Governor, Mayor, and so on) to sign and implement a program—put into action the provisions of legislation. It is of utmost importance that the practical public policy analyst understand that *the actual form and substance of social programs and policies as they effect ordinary citizens are substantially created, not by legislators but civil servants at departmental and subdepartmental levels.* Legislation usually speaks of social policies and programs in only the most general, yes, even vague, language. Thus, official, regulations coming after the fact of legislation is, very often, the most important time for detailed social program and social policy design. It may come as some surprise to learn that legislators don't design most programs. The reason has partly to do with the amount of time and expertise legislators have, but in an important way, it concerns the politics of legislation. The political reality is that the more detailed a legislative bill, the more likely that someone will find something objectionable in it. Recent federal legislation providing for states to take on new responsibilities for moving recipients of Aid to Families with Dependent Children to incomes from work and wages is a good example. So, legislators will pass the issues of "details" on to civil servants to work out. It is slightly irrational, but there is in it a political wisdom that is charming.

Many public regulations framed by civil servants from legislation are preceded by what are called "Opportunities for Public Comments." They might be administrative department public hearings or simple notices in newspapers and community bulletins soliciting written citizen or other public opinion on the regulations. The executive branch of government is not often *required* to incorporate public comments into changes in regulations but where administrative officers are aware of widespread public opinion on a regulation they might be persuaded to do so. That can mean an opportunity to influence social program design for those prepared to take advantage of it.

The judicial branch of government can wield great power because it can tell social programs the clients that must be served, can totally eliminate programs under certain conditions, and can entitle or disentitle citizens from benefits, among other things. The judicial branch restricts or expands the power of government administrators and officials so that they are consistent with past court decisions, with governmental principles, and (sometimes) with the fundamental constitutional rights of citizens. Virtually all fields of practice are affected by social and organizational policy made by judicial decisions. This includes social workers doing "clinical practice," serving individuals afflicted by various kinds of emotional conditions. Certain policy created by judicial decisions prevents social work and human service administrators from doing certain things: for example, the ruling in *Goldberg v. Kelley* prevents practitioners from terminating public cash benefits without explanation to the beneficiary—an application of the citizen's right under the U.S. Constitution to due process, of which more later.[1] On the other hand, a series of state court decisions has created policy that holds practitioners responsible for taking "due care" to notify people directly who have been specifically and personally threatened with violence or physical harm by the client/consumers of the social worker or human services worker (*Tarasoff v. The Regents of the University of California*, 1976).[2]

Some court decisions make public policy in the sense of holding social workers and human service workers responsible for their professional actions, the explicit policy being that they are accountable to their own professional standards for competent practice. Consequently, they can be sued for their actions (or lack thereof) to the fullest extent allowed by law. Besharov lists a whole catalog of legal horrors that can beset the unwary practitioner:[3]

- *Treatment without consent:* a social worker and her employer were sued by a service recipient who claimed that her [the recipient's] consent to treatment was given only because she was threatened with loss of her job if she did not complete residential treatment for substance abuse.

- *Inappropriate treatment:* ". . . half the claims for erroneous diagnosis made under the NASW insurance malpractice program were based on a charge that the client's problem was actually medical. . . ."

- *Inappropriate release* of a client from hospitalization, confinement, or supervision.

- *False imprisonment:* a client is wrongly detained or committed on the basis of false or inadequate information given to a physician who recommended commitment.

- *Failure to be available when needed.*

Social workers must be aware of these and other decisions not just to keep their practice within the law but to take advantage of social policies that are to the best interest of their client/consumers. In addition to exercising due care with regard to confidentiality, they must be prepared to take strong positions in clinical staff discussions about whether to recommend commitment of a client. Not only must they be wary of participating in agency decisions that may violate a client's civil rights, they must be wary of participating in those organizational decisions that violate social policy in their state. For example, public agencies cannot act arbitrarily and capriciously and must follow their own rules, as long as those rules are legal.[4] It is particularly problematic when public agencies deliberately change administrative rules and regulations, thereby changing laws that Congress has enacted to affirm specific social policies. That was certainly the case when hundreds of thousands of Social Security Disability Insurance (SSDI) beneficiaries were terminated "arbitrarily and capriciously" (illegally, the courts finally ruled) in the mid-1980s.[5]

Social workers and human service practitioners need to be aware of the judiciary as an instrument of social policy as they assist in the preparation of court cases that have the potential to serve and better the interest of their client/consumers. Practitioners can be called to testify in all manner of court proceedings—termination of parental rights, commitment and guardianship hearings, malpractice suits, disputes over public agency benefits, and so forth. It is always possible that their testimony may be crucial in court decisions that break new ground in social policy. In all these ways, social workers must understand that as they interact with the courts they are molding their profession's destiny.[6]

Ordinarily, public policy is initially framed via the political process. But the judiciary can modify or completely negate legislation, so the courts hold trump cards. This fact is simple evidence of the operation of constitutional checks and balances between the legislative, judicial, and executive branches of government. It is a mistake to be misled by the prevalent view that somehow state and federal statutes (enacted legislation) are self-revealing. Certainly, court rulings produce effects beyond those that legislators had in mind. As Ehrmann says:

> The authority of a court to declare laws and official acts unconstitutional is a practice that . . . gives to judges so obvious a share in policymaking that . . . there is little room left for the pretense that judges only apply the law.[7]

The judiciary both creates anew and reshapes old social policy. One example is the *Roe v. Wade* decision, which in effect made abortion a public policy by making it legal for the public sector to provide for the cost of abortions. Another example is the final *Cruzan v. Danforth* decision, which as public policy denied to parents the right to remove life support from their comatose daughter who over an eight-year period had been in a persistent vegetative state. Clearly, those were not public policies made by an elected legislature, and yet they nonetheless were social policy, which has literally meant life and death to other persons. Or consider all judicial decisions on the nature and distribution of education rights and resources: *Brown v. Board of Education* (1954)[8] and the hundreds of education desegregation court orders that followed. Of more direct relevance for human service and social work practitioners are decisions that (1) appointed Court masters to oversee the development of treatment programs for the institutionalized mentally retarded in Alabama (*Wyatt v. Stickney*),[9] (2) stopped the massive terminations of Social Security benefits (cash and medical care) for the disabled during the Reagan Administration of the 1980s,[10] and (3) established welfare benefits as a new form of property to which certain property rights are attached (under specific conditions—*Goldberg v. Kelley*).[11] As stated by Notes:

> The courts in their relationship with public policy are also involved in an evaluative process . . . (which is) interpretive and not . . . political. It is impervious to electoral judgment, unrestricted by the constraints of partisan ideologies and relatively immune to the requirement of (political) compromise. The public policy values the court is free to evaluate are related to but independent from the political values which motivated the existence or absence of a statute. Parliament passes laws, courts decide what the laws mean and in so doing courts react to what they feel are the public policy values that underlie the statute.[12]

Some, who take the view that such decisions deform the original, pristine intent of the framers of the U.S. Constitution, are likely to call such acts "judicial activism." To them the power to make public policy belongs solely with the legislative branch, using the constitution as a stringent framework. This view is popular in conservative circles and for elaborate discussions the reader might refer to journalistic accounts and editorials on the congressional hearings on the nomination of Robert Bork or Clarence Thomas to the U.S. Supreme Court in the *New York Times*. This chapter will assume that, whatever its merits or demerits or whatever is its historical status relative to the founding fathers' intentions, judicial activism is a reality that shapes social policy in this country and any analysis that fails to attend to it is incomplete at best.

Here are a few things to think about in understanding the judiciary as a shaper of social policy. First, in the United States, at least, courts must perform their interpretative magic on a concrete case, a dispute in which at least two parties have an interest at stake and go to court to establish which interest shall prevail under the law. In short, the courts cannot act on abstract issues. In many European countries, the situation is quite the opposite: Judicial decisions *can* be made in the abstract, absent any legislation, pending or otherwise, or absent any concrete controversy between interested parties. Second, courts can shape and frame social policy in regard to administrative rulings as well as legislation—administrative rules are interpretations made by *public officials* about how and when legislation is to be applied in concrete cases.

Finally, practitioners must understand the attitude taken by the courts toward social science, an attitude social workers may find surprising; in fact the courts only reluctantly accept such findings.[13] Webster says that the courts are on unfamiliar ground in dealing with testimony of this kind, and that its plausibility is ". . . never taken for granted as is medicine or law itself. . . .[14] Some might not agree, but Webster is probably correct that there are very few unequivocal social science findings and that because those few quickly find their way into common knowledge, they lose any potential status as scientific conclusions. Not only that, but the typical social science finding is usually stated as a probability, so that individual variability is always an alternative explanation. That is a big problem because always and everywhere the court is concerned with unique, individual cases, not averages; the opposing legal counsel can always argue away the data of social science on the basis that her or his client is simply the plausible exception to the average case.

In court, human service personnel often make ambiguous responses, giving "it depends" answers because they are trained to think conditionally. However, courts want "the truth," definite answers, a categorical yes or no.[15]

The power of the judiciary to shape social policy is embedded in its present power to review legislation and the decisions of public officials. That power was established in the 1800s by Chief Justice John Marshall, in his opinion justifying the majority ruling of the U.S. Supreme Court in *Marbury v. Madison*,[16] the cornerstone of U.S. administrative law. Marshall's fundamental guiding principle was that the direct and current will of the people regarding laws and government must always be served. In part, he feared that legislative alliances did not always represent the will of the people. On the other hand, judicial review was one possible way to remedy the problem when legislatures went so far that they intervened in private affairs in ways that were contrary to the constitutionally established rights of citizens.[17] Hence, the Marshall court also ruled that in principle, the court *could* intervene in private affairs, and so it became possible for the U.S. Supreme Court to concern itself with abortion—with what goes on even *inside* a citizen's body.

A Simple Framework for Examining Judicial Decisions

B. C. Canon's four basic questions will be of use to social workers and administrators in understanding how judicial decisions bear on public social policy and social programs:

1. Whether and in what way new judicial decisions negate earlier legislative acts
2. The degree to which earlier judicial precedents are altered
3. Determining what specific policy consequences follow from a judicial decision
4. How new judicial decisions affect future administrative discretion

Negation of the Legislative Process.   Canon suggests that if we want to think about how a new judicial decision affects public social policy, the first thing we ought to consider is *whether and the extent to which it is a change away from whatever was directly legislated by a sitting or elected assembly* (e.g., the Congress, state legislatures, city councils).[18]

One good example is the U.S. Supreme Court decision in *O'Connor v. Donaldson*,[19] a case that marked the first time a Supreme Court decision recognized the legitimacy of the courts' involvement in activities that earlier legislation clearly had defined to be the exclusive domain of psychiatrists (*O'Connor v. Donaldson*, 1975). What is relevant here is that up to the moment of the Supreme Court's decision, state statutes had clearly assigned to clinicians—psychiatrists in particular—the professional discretion to continue to confine citizens and determine when, where, how much, and what kind of psychiatric treatment was needed. A 48-year-old Florida man, Kenneth Donaldson, was committed to the Chattahoochee State Hospital at the request of his parents. Some fifteen years later, Donaldson and his friends were still trying to obtain his freedom. They did so over the objections of his psychiatrist, who found Donaldson dangerous to himself and others; nor was Donaldson receiving treatment that he could not have received as an outpatient. Donaldson was deprived of his liberty as a free citizen (a basic due process, constitutional, Bill of Rights issue), and the concern of the court was whether he was dangerous. Was he competent enough to avoid "the hazards of freedom," and could he receive the same treatment outside the hospital—conditions that might mitigate the citizen's right to liberty. The court decided that indeed he could, and in doing so, the *O'Connor v. Donaldson* court decision has fundamentally changed that public social policy so that

> . . . no longer can the professional base his decisions as to the most appropriate treatment modality solely on clinical grounds. He must become cognizant of such issues as whether the patient will be viewed as dangerous by a judge or jury, whether the recommended program will be considered adequate treatment or even treatment at all, and whether he will be considered liable for denying the patient his constitutional rights if he continues to hold him in the hospital because he considers him dangerous if a future court hearing finds the patient not dangerous.[20]

Notice how this court decision changed the usual relationships between the legislative and executive branches of government, which implement legislation. The court ruled that prior legislation was unconstitutional and required the administrative branch (in this case, public officials and professionals—probably psychiatrists employed by the state hospital system, usually a state mental health or institutional service—in the employ of government) to follow the court order rather than the legislation.

Judicial Precedents.   Remember that in contrast to European judicial systems, the U.S. legal system is ordinarily guided by earlier court decisions (precedents). So, in principle, the greater the departure from prior court decisions, the more we ought to consider a judicial decision to be important, all other things being equal. Let us take as an example the 1969 decision of the U.S. Supreme Court (reaffirmative in 1997), which found that state laws were *unconstitutional* in using a period of state residence as an entitlement rule for welfare benefits. For two hundred years all states had very stringent residence requirements (usually a year) for a person to be entitled to a state welfare benefit.

Residence requirements created all sorts of problems for poor and low-income citizens, many of whom were necessarily mobile and who qualified for welfare benefits but were not state residents. Consider what a hardship that might be if, for example, unemployed auto workers left Michigan with their families to go to Nebraska to look for work—perhaps an economically rational and otherwise virtuous idea. If they needed welfare benefits until the first check from the new job arrived, they would be out of luck—not because they didn't need it, but because they hadn't lived in Nebraska for a year. In short, the Supreme Court ruled that such state laws are unconstitutional because they hinder the free movement of persons, a constitutionally protected right. Furthermore, labor must have the ability to move freely in order for the economic wheels of the country to grind efficiently. From the day of the Court's decision, states cannot lawfully deny access to welfare benefits simply on grounds of the applicant's residency.[21] In this decision, the Supreme Court overturned 150 years of its own precedent (and perhaps 600 years of British Poor Law).

It is an important example because it reveals that not only are abstract issues of freedom and legal rights at stake, but current and *concrete* agency operations are also at issue. Since the decision, state welfare administrators not only must take the necessary administrative means to stop implementation, but also must prepare budget estimates of what costs the Court's decision will impose on the state's welfare programs. For example, eliminating the residency requirement may add more beneficiaries to welfare rolls where there are high worker in-migration rates. The other side of the in-migration coin, of course, is that it reduces the welfare budget of other states. An influx of workers may benefit a state's economy, but a side effect is increased demand on general assistance and indigent medical care funds.

Type and Effect of Policy Concerned. Canon advises us to think about the type of social policy a judicial decision concerns and its practical effects on operating procedure and policy. These criteria will give direction to our inquiry about the practical effects of the judicial decision. The courts can and do make social policy of two types: (1) procedural policy and (2) substantive policy. *Procedural policy* has to do with rights ultimately derived—indirectly or directly—from the Bill of Rights of the U.S. Constitution: for example, all citizens have a right to a fair trial, an opportunity to confront witnesses, be informed of charges against them, and so on.

Goldberg v. Kelley referred to earlier in this chapter, is a leading example here of how the judiciary creates social policy: in *Goldberg*, the U.S. Supreme Court held that once a benefit is legislated for citizens and administratively granted to them, that interest constitutes a type of property to which due process rights apply. Thus, in this decision, the Court created for Mrs. Goldberg (and others who follow her) a *substantive right* to this welfare benefit. When welfare benefits are interpreted in this light, it is clear that not all of them can be withdrawn by the simple act of administrative discretion. In fact, this judicial decision establishes that once welfare benefits are granted, to withdraw them after the fact, the government must provide *procedural rights:* that is, the client/beneficiary must get advance notice of a hearing in which the action will be reviewed; furthermore, the client/beneficiary has a right to appear and argue his or her point of view, have benefit of counsel, the opportunity to confront witnesses, and so on.

The Supreme Court decided that Mrs. Goldberg had not been given such a hearing and ordered the (Texas) Department of Welfare to do so. Note that in addition to other constraints on their application, these procedural rights do not apply to all beneficiaries or to all benefit programs. *Goldberg* is an important type of judicially created social policy if only because it obliges public organizations that administer benefits to establish fair hearing systems with due process features.[22] Those features are neither trivial from the client's point of view—because they can restore benefits that were illegally or unjustly terminated—nor trivial from the organizations point of view—because they are expensive and complicated to administer.

In summary then, analysis of a judicial decision as a social policy document should always include clarification about whether the issue at hand is one that concerns substantive policy or due process (procedural) issues. It should also include an examination of the practical effects on organizational operating policy and procedures (such as the need to add to or modify fair hearing features as discussed before).

Parameters for Agency Discretion.   Canon advises a fourth consideration in analyzing judicial decisions that influence public social policy: *the degree to which a judicial decision establishes policy itself rather than leaving its details to the discretion of other agencies or individuals.* It is clear that with reference to the residence requirements, the Supreme Court left *no* discretion to state administrators—the court order simply forbade use of this disentitlement rule. An example of how agencies are endowed with discretion is found in the Federal Appeals Court decision of the 1980s that forbade the Social Security Administration (SSA) to use its psychiatric classification as a basis for awarding or denying mental disability benefits.[23] It also ordered SSA to develop a new one based on more contemporary thinking. That instance is a clear example of the Court's leaving the discretion about the specific policy rule to the administrative agency and acknowledging the agency's competence and resources to do so.

Other examples abound, but one of the most extreme is *Wyatt v. Stickney,* a 1972 federal court order that established detailed standards of care that actually redefined public policy regarding institutionalized mental patients in the state of Alabama.[24] In deciding what has come to be called "the right-to-treatment rule," the Court determined that Mr. Wyatt did indeed have such a right, and did *not* place discretion with Alabama's mental health program administrators to decide of what the treatment had to consist. The Wyatt standards have never been overturned. Not only did the Court mandate standards of care, but it appointed a Court administrator for the state mental hospital in question, a magistrate or master responsible only to the Court, to enforce those standards. Part of the lesson of the *Wyatt* decision is about the limits of judicial activism, the big problem courts have in actually enforcing such detailed policy and program provisions.

Using the Canon Framework to Analyze Judicial Decisions That Create or Alter Social Policy

This section looks at some other examples that reveal how Canon's framework can help analyze particular court decisions. The issue of termination of parental rights is a good example for this purpose. Almost all states have statutes about terminating parental rights in cases of child abandonment. Widely varied, they are useful because they demonstrate how different state courts develop both very different and very similar kinds of social policies on this inherently private family matter. Here the long arm of the state intrudes into the very heart of the family, determining in the last analysis such a basic issue as who shall and who shall not remain a member of a family group. Traditionally, courts have relied on common-law criteria to make this determination—whether the parent provided materially for the child or whether the parent was abusive, for example. These criteria proceed from what is taken to be "ordinary common sense," that is, socially inarguable standards for parental conduct. Of course, the social world is a very different place these days, far removed from the simplicity of a tightly knit and traditional agrarian society on whose long-established traditions common law is built. Small nuclear families, geographic mobility, and personal catastrophes such as marital breakup or drug addiction were not a part of the reality of those times; hence, common law did not speak to these contemporary realities. Therefore, the judiciary must consider criteria from other sources in applying its broad discretion in determining whether parental behavior is an indicator of intent to abandon or an indicator that parental responsibility should be terminated.

In terminating parental rights based on concepts that are beyond common-law traditions, courts must of necessity *create new public social policy* (negate earlier legislation). In terms of parental rights, what is at stake is not only the private rights and interests of the child and the parents (and the family kin group), but the public interest in terms of guarding the integrity of a future citizen's (the child's) developmental life, avoiding public expenditures for foster care, ensuring that the child has not only a family identity to carry into adult life, but a family or kin group that will socialize the child to dominant values.[25]

For example, a Connecticut court terminated the rights of the parents of three minor children because the parents failed to ". . . maintain a reasonable degree of interest, concern or responsibility as to the welfare of (their) child. . . ."[26] The Connecticut statute gave only the most general definition of abandonment: ". . . the parents' failure to maintain a reasonable degree of interest, concern or responsibility as to the welfare of their child. . . ." This court was forced to define it more concretely. Note the many very different, perhaps even opposing, interpretations that could be given this abstract definition. For example, some might define church attendance or corporal punishment as a necessary ingredient of "assuming parental responsibility" whereas others might not. Ultimately, the Chignon court decided that ". . . maintaining a reasonable degree of interest . . ." means that a parent had to have continuous, face-to-face contacts with the child over time and thus this mother's average three visits per year to the child, infrequent phone calls and letters, and moving to a neighboring state (Maryland) did not meet that standard. In applying Canon's concepts for the analysis of judicial decisions, we first must think about the degree to which this decision departs from a directly legislated social policy. It is clear that the legislation (state statute) concerned with this matter leaves the crucial operating term "maintaining a reasonable degree of interest [in the child]" entirely undefined. The court then sets about defining the term and giving it concrete meaning, in effect acting to create law independent of the elected legislature. On that account and following Canon's advice, we would take note in our analysis that *In re Chignon* is surely an important court decision with direct impact on citizens in that it sets the basic policy by which state and other social agencies deal with citizens.

In analyzing this judicial decision the second thing to consider is whether the legal issue at hand is one that concerns substantive policy or due process or procedural issues (social policy type and effect). It would be a due process or procedural issue if, for example, the case concerned *the way* in which the hearing to terminate parental rights was conducted, whether the parent had competent legal counsel, received timely notification of the hearing, had a chance to confront witnesses, and so on. As the reader can see, none of those were points at issue; rather, the issue was a *substantive* one: how should child abandonment be defined? This tells us that it isn't the judicial or agency procedures that will have to be reshaped but the way in which the agency defines "abandonment."

In analyzing this judicial decision, the third thing Canon would have us consider is the degree to which earlier court decisions are altered. Unfortunately, the material in which this decision was reported does not give us that information.[27] To complete our analysis of this judicial decision, we will have to locate the decision of this Connecticut court (with the help of our nearest and friendliest law school librarian) and review it for what it has to say about other earlier court decisions on related matters.

The fourth consideration, according to Canon, is the degree to which a judicial decision establishes policy itself rather than leaving discretion to other agencies or individuals. In regard to this decision, we can answer in the affirmative. Indeed *the court went to great pains to establish policy itself and did not leave the matter of defining abandonment to other agencies nor to the discretion of individual state officials.* Note that this is more than just an abstract point: In making a judgment about this analytic criterion, officials are alerted to the fact that the law will not sustain case decisions they make based simply on their own ad hoc criteria. An effective and efficient bureaucracy will take steps to know the law and incorporate it into its operating policy.

Another case (this one in Kansas) created a new social policy when the court upheld termination of paternal rights of a father for the purpose of placing the child for adoption on the basis of his negligence as a parent in attending to the child.[28] Again, the court had to make a decision as in regard to what counted as negligence. The decision was based on a Kansas statute, which specified that the court could grant adoptions without the consent of the natural parents where the parent failed or refused to ". . . assume parental duties for two consecutive years prior to the filing of the adoption petition. . . ."[29] The court decided that the parental effort met this criteria and therefore constituted parental abandonment. In this case, efforts had been limited to Christmas and birthday gifts and a few telephone calls but no financial support, written communication, or other form of emotional support. The court created new social policy in the sense of deciding that absence of financial support, coupled with lack of emotionally significant contact, constituted parental abandonment for any practical purpose and so termination of parental rights was in order. The court was obliged to make such a determination because legislation did not define fulfillment of parental duty so that the Kansas supreme court had no alternative but to exercise its own judicial discretion. Because U.S. courts sometimes take notice of decisions of courts in other jurisdictions as well as by earlier and higher court decisions, that Kansas decision could influence courts in other states.

Finally, the West Virginia Supreme Court of Appeals created new social policy in that state when it upheld the parental rights of a father.[30] Whereas West Virginia Code §548-4-3 provides for termination of parental rights in the instance of abandonment, it does not contain a definition of same. The West Virginia court held that the prospective adoptive parents had *not* shown that the father had abandoned the child because failure to pay child support was not by itself sufficient to constitute child abandonment. The father had sent gifts, cards, money, telephoned repeatedly, paid for health insurance, and written the mother seeking visitation (subsequent to her refusal to allow visitation as a means of prompting him to pay child support).[31] In analyzing this decision following Canon's advice, we would conclude that the West Virginia court had indeed ventured beyond what the elected legislature had decided in such matters.

Canon's next concepts oblige us to consider whether what is at issue here is a substantive matter or a due process right. Clearly it is the former, because, once again, the concern of the court is with what substantively constitutes child abandonment. Note that the father did not contest the procedures by which a lower court had arrived at its decision; rather, the entire focus is on what should be considered as child abandonment and whether the father's behavior conformed to that definition.

Using Canon's third analytic concept, we are led to conclude that in fact the West Virginia Supreme Court did not venture far from earlier court precedents, but based its decision on them, citing an earlier Court decision that provided precisely the definition of abandonment upon which it could base its work. This earlier case in a *local* (lower) court in effect defined abandonment as failure to provide support and maintenance, visit the child or exercise parental rights, responsibilities, and authority.[32] Notice that the West Virginia legislature could have (but did not) incorporate the standards for termination of parental rights from this case into legislation on the matter. Canon's analytic concept yields practical information because (1) once it is known, as in this case, that these criteria for abandonment are part of a whole set of precedents, they become even more important as public agency operating policy in the sense that policy implementers have some certainty that the criteria will have continuity over time; and (2) the decision came (partly) from a state supreme court, which ultimately binds the lower courts with which agencies and officials have to deal.

Using Canon's fourth analytic concept, we can conclude that, as in the earlier case law cited, the West Virginia Supreme Court did not delegate to other agencies or officials the responsibility to make general policy or case decisions but took responsibility to create their own.

Summary

This chapter has shown how the power of the Judiciary to shape social policy is embedded in its present power to review legislation and the decisions of public officials. Judicial capacity can influence social policy of two types: (1) policy about due process and fundamental citizen rights and (2) policy about substantive matters—who gets what, when, in what form and under what conditions, and how benefits are financed. Some basic considerations about the judiciary were presented. For example, the judiciary must consider a concrete case that represents an issue between the vital interests of at least two citizens; courts can shape and frame social policy concerning administrative rulings as well as legislation; and the courts view with reluctance the findings of social science and experimental psychology with suspicion.

Based on the work of B. C. Canon, a conceptual framework for the analysis of judicial decisions with social policy relevance was given. This framework is founded on advising practitioners to be alert to four basic considerations:

1. The extent to which the judicial decision is a departure from legislation passed by a freely elected assembly
2. The extent to which the decision concerns a due process or procedural issue, or a substantive policy issue
3. The extent to which the decision represents a departure from prior judicial precedent
4. The extent to which the court delegated the responsibility to other agencies or officials or took responsibility to make general policy to create their own.

NOTES

1. J. Handler, *Protecting the Social Services Client* (New York: Academic Press, 1979), p. 31.
2. *Tarasoff v. The Regents of the University of California*, Sup. Ct. of California (July 1, 1976).
3. D. Besharov, *The Vulnerable Social Worker* (Silver Spring, MD: National Association of Social Workers, 1985), pp. 2–9.
4. E. Gellhorn, *Administrative Law and Process* (St. Paul, MN: West, 1974).
5. D. E. Chambers, "Policy Weaknesses and Political Interventions," *Social Service Review*, 42 (1987): 87–99.
6. I am indebted to David Brown, J.D., of the legal staff of the Kansas Appeals Court, who kindly read this material and supplied this inviting comment.
7. H. W. Ehrmann, *Comparative Legal Cultures* (Englewood Cliffs, NJ: Prentice Hall, 1976), p. 138.
8. *Brown v. Board of Education*, 347 U.S. 483 (1954).
9. M. Levine. "The Role of Special Master in Institutional Reform Litigation," *Law and Policy*, 8 (1986): 275–321.
10. D. E. Chambers, "The Reagan Administration Welfare Retrenchment Policy: Terminating Social Security Benefits for the Disabled," *Policy Studies Review*, 2 (1985): 207–215, 234–235.
11. Handler, *Protecting the Social Services Client*, p. 31.
12. J. Notes, "The Least Dangerous Branch, *Revue de Droit de McGill*, 34 (1989): 1025–1028.

13. C. D. Webster, "On Gaining Acceptance: Why the Courts Accept Only Reluctantly Findings from Experimental and Social Psychology," *International Journal of Law and Psychiatry*, 7 (1984): 407–414.

14. Ibid., p. 410.

15. Ibid., p. 412.

16. *Marbury v. Madison*, 1 Cranch 137 (1803).

17. D. W. Jackson, "A Conceptual Framework for the Comparative Analysis of Judicial Review," *Policy Studies Review*, 19 (1991): 161–171.

18. B. C. Canon, "A Framework for the Analysis of Judicial Activism," in S. C. Halpern and C. M. Lamb (eds.), *Supreme Court Activism and Restraint* (Lexington, MA: Lexington Books, 1982). I have chosen to use only some of Canon's analytical dimensions, omitting others when they seemed less relevant to the common practice of human service and social workers.

19. *O'Connor v. Donaldson*, 422 U.S. 563 (1975).

20. L. E. Kopolow, "A Review of Major Implications of the *O'Connor v. Donaldson* Decision," *American Journal of Psychiatry*, 133(4) (1976): 379–383.

21. Although the Social Security Act required fair hearings for all programs funded with federal money, it did not specify their mandatory features.

22. D. E. Chambers, "Residence Requirements for Welfare Benefits," *Social Work*, 14(4) (1969): 29–37.

23. *Mental Health Association of Minnesota v. Schweiker*, 554 Fed. Supp., 157 (D.C. Minn., 1983).

24. Levine, "The Role of Special Master" p. 285.

25. What will be lacking in using this issue as an example is the history of its legislative politics in the initial framing of state statutes on termination of parental rights. This issue is seldom an occasion for high-profile political compromise, nor are the constituent (interest) groups either obvious or very visible. Naturally, parents themselves have a stake here, but the activist sentiments of most parents would not be engaged by a legislative proposal on an issue that for them is bound to be only potential, not actual. On that account, the political issues tend to be much more ideological, dividing legislators along lines of commitment to either the rights of parents or the rights of children.

26. In *Re Chignon*.

27. Legal Analysis: "Infrequent Contacts with the Child, Grounds to Terminate Parental Rights in Abandonment Cases," *8 ABA Juvenile and Child Welfare Reporter* (December 1989): 157–158.

28. Matter of Adoption of B.C.S., 777 P.2d 776 (Kan. 1989).

29. Kansas Statutes Ann. §59–2101(a)(1).

30. *In the Matter of Adoption of Schoffstall*, 368 S.E.2nd 720 (W. Va. 1988).

31. Ibid., p. 164.

32. Ibid., p. 158.

PART TWO

A Style of Policy Analysis for the Practical Public Policy Analyst

. . . providence never intended to make the management of public affairs a mystery, to be comprehended only by a few persons of sublime genius, of which there seldom are three born in an age

—Jonathan Swift, *Gulliver's Travels*

Introduction

The first part of this book closed by showing how conclusions from the social problem analysis and the analysis of historical and judicial context might indicate for the practitioner/analyst how particular features of a policy or program were (or should have been) shaped. The next step is to look closely at an actual operating policy or program design to identify its major features. Thus, the first section of Chapter 4 will present a way of "looking closely at" (of describing analytically) social policies and programs. It proceeds by first searching for the six fundamental elements in social policy and program designs. These are fundamental in the sense that they can be found explicitly or implicitly, in one form or another, in every social policy or program. Each element will be discussed, examples will be given, and concepts and classifications will be presented so as to sensitize the observer to their various forms. Once these elements are identified, a judgment is made so as to answer the most basic question: Are these program or policy features "good"?

CHAPTER

4

An Overview of a Style of Policy Analysis

A Value-Critical Approach

This chapter is intended to sort out several important issues that lay the groundwork for understanding the perspective taken in this book and the basic tasks the practitioner as policy analyst will confront. Furthermore, this chapter will prepare the reader for a detailed description of those tasks by discussing the distinction between the value-analytic and the value-critical methods of policy analysis. Arguments will be presented for the value-critical style for the use of social work and human service practitioners, the audience for which this book is intended.

The evaluation criteria essential for that style will be presented and argued in this chapter. Some are argued as essential and others as optional but illustrative of how personal value preferences of the analyst can (and must) be taken into account. These evaluation criteria are so important because they will be used throughout the succeeding chapters of Part II.

The reader should be alert to the fact that much of what will be said about policy elements is simply to show a way to generate an adequate description of a social policy or program. Martin Rein calls this endeavor the *analytic-descriptive* method of policy analysis,[1] that is, an analysis that proceeds (as advocated here) by dividing the whole of a social policy or program into parts

> . . . takes as its task dividing an accepted whole into logically consistent categories; the intellectual challenge is to identify common features that are (or aren't) congruent or consistent with each other. . . .

But for the practical public policy analyst, description is never more than a means to an end because the most important step in analyzing program and policy features is to arrive at a judgment about them, that is, whether they are, in a particular sense, "good," "right," or "appropriate." Policy analysis that remains at a descriptive level, leaving this question unanswered, cannot be a complete, much less a "good," analysis. Coming to judgment is always a value-laden enterprise and a practitioner as analyst should not apologize for that fact; a judgment that would try to be otherwise—somehow value-neutral, in the popular idiom—is hollow in that human judgment must always use value criteria as a foundation. Martin Rein calls this *value-critical policy analysis* and uses that phrase to distinguish it from the analytic-descriptive approach described before. The value-critical approach stands this latter approach on its head, begins with parts and tries to understand the whole that they constitute, the whole that does (or should) integrate them.

The method of analysis presented in this book advocates using *both* approaches serially. It is analytic-descriptive in proceeding first to instruct the reader how to do close description by *disaggregating* the social policy or program into parts (policy elements and the three contexts) and examining them one by one. It follows Rein in advocating the crucial second step, which consists in critically evaluating all of the parts, and how they fit together as a whole using certain strong, value-based criteria by which to make judgments of their goodness, fitness, and appropriateness. In some ways, the analytic-descriptive approach is a way to see clearly how things *should* work. Because in the real world things almost never work out as planned, this second-step, value-critical approach then throws the conventional view (how a program should work) into question and adopts a critical and skeptical view of how programs *actually* work—or don't work.[2] It seeks to uncover shortcomings, inconsistencies in logic, and ambiguities in the everyday program operations. Much of the policy analysis done by political scientists and public administrators does not—in fact cannot—do that, because their method of analysis is so focused on explaining how things *are*, rather than how things *could be* from some value-committed point of view.

Michael Howlett's review of several policy analyses is a good example of policy analysis that stops short of the value-critical appraisal.[3] At issue there is poor people's need for low-cost housing. Howlett's review shows that these theories leave no room for consideration of what they are or are not likely to do for beneficiaries and stops short of considering how cash, as opposed to in-kind housing benefits, extends different kinds of advantages and disadvantages to beneficiaries. In contrast, Howlett's analysis considers things like "complexity of operations," "level of public visibility," and "chances of failure." The point here is that this sort of policy analysis cannot uncover policy shortcomings or throw the conventional view into question, simply because they are not asking the kind of question that would move discussion in that direction. The reader should think of how the questions generated by concern with "complexity of operations" or "level of public visibility" *cannot* encompass how the form of benefit is positive or negative for the beneficiary. (Such factors as "level of intrusiveness" and "adaptability across users" are listed, but the interest in them is relevant only to what problems those factors pose for administration, not for clients.) Of course, program administrators need to be concerned with these issues, but the point is that if the concern goes no further than that, it can be said to favor organizational over consumer/beneficiary issues.[4]

Value-critical analysis seeks to ferret out policy problems using an explicit set of value-based evaluation criteria the function of which is to alert the analyst to specific and problematic policy and program features. In just that sense, value-critical policy analysis seeks to make explicit the "frames of reference" used by implementers of policy—middle managers and street-level bureaucrats among them.[5] The analyst should expect to encounter conflict and divergence between frames of reference of two opposing groups: (1) originating legislators or high-level administrators and (2) middle managers and practitioners. This kind of policy analysis is similar to what Habermas calls "cross-frame discourse."[6] Out of this, dialectic implications for action arise and it is precisely the intention and purpose of this method of policy analysis to generate action from its results. Policy analysis for our practitioner purposes cannot be content with creating abstract academic exercises. The hope is to present a method that will result in reader discontent with the old and a strong motive to create something new and better. The discontent should arise from the analyst's encounter with the operating frameworks of those who actually implement a policy or program. To the reader/analyst who is prepared for it, that encounter reveals the marvelous dialectic between what the legislature, history, and Judiciary fondly hope for and the actual.[7] And, of course, the practical policy analyst should anticipate conflict between these and his or her own frame of reference. The point of this analytic method is not simply to criticize, but to develop a better (more useful-for-clients) way of doing things.

Actually, Rein points out yet another approach to analyzing social policies and programs (one this book will not emphasize) called the *value-committed* approach. This approach

> . . . starts with a strongly held position about how things *ought* to be . . . [and why they aren't] and then works out the implications of this commitment for action. . . . Some Marxists and many social activists, but definitely not all, fall into this category . . . [8]

On several counts, value commitment is an important dimension for social work and human service practitioners. There are moments when they can be plausibly called by their professional commitments to all *three* of these approaches. A calling to "activism" is recognizable in the roots of the social work profession—a calling to actively pursue particular strongly held positions based on fundamental professional values about how things ought to be as against a very different real world. Note that in following that course, the policy discourse will then *not* be about operating details of policies and programs, but about more fundamental social and structural problems—perhaps, for example, about how the whole broad social issue should be conceived from the outset. Such arguments turn out to focus ultimately on fundamental values.

Under certain circumstances, a value-committed approach is irresistible. An example from Central America serves to clarify: From some particular value-committed points of view, there is an inherent injustice in a society in which 95 percent of a nation's assets and income are received by 1 percent of its people, particularly in the face of unemployment rates of over 40 percent, a poverty rate that by local standards approaches 50 percent, and a level of armed violence that makes death and civilian casualties a daily occurrence. For the social work practitioner as value-committed analyst, then, the argument should *not* be whether a policy of in-kind benefits like governmental commodity distributions (e.g., beans, cheese, flour, or meal) is the best way to keep people from starving (not that hunger isn't an important policy issue). Rather, for the value-committed practitioner, the argument *should* be whether this kind of income maldistribution is *just;* the policy argument should be over what is the best means of radically altering it. An appropriate comparison that expresses the futility of small-scale adjustments against a catastrophic environment is that the prevailing state of affairs is "like rearranging chairs on the deck of the sinking *Titanic.*" Examples closer to home might be high-risk industries—coal mining, hard-rock mining, metal refining, lumber milling—or certain kinds of employees—migrant workers in fields sprayed with pesticides or workers involved in the production of nuclear power. For purposes of the value-committed approach, the argument *should not be* whether Workers Compensation benefits should be administered by a public or a private profit-making insurance system (as it is in most states), but about (1) whether some operations of high-injury industries should be permitted at all or (2) whether some industries produce injuries at such a high rate or level of seriousness that any Workers Compensation system design will be deficient. Or take another example: From a value-committed point of view and in the face of (roughly) 15 percent poverty rates in the United States, one of wealthiest countries in the world, the social policy argument should not be about *which* measure of the poverty line is preferred, but about what is the maximum acceptable rate of poverty (*however measured*) in this country.

The value-committed approach will not take the world at face value but seek to impose its vision onto the world and change conditions so that they are more in keeping with the ideal world envisioned. Social workers and other human service practitioners need Rein's distinction among the three types of policy analysis in order to think clearly about which type they will opt for in any given situation. The decision is difficult because a number of questions must be weighed: "What is the 'real' state of the world with respect to the presenting social problem?" "What fundamental values are at stake?" "Is there plausible reason to believe that any audience exists to respond to the policy implications of a given activist approach to the social problem (i.e., will the approach have any chance of success)?"

The merits and difficulties of the value-committed approach will not be discussed in detail here because it seems a better fit with pure political activism, which is beyond the scope of this book—although the professional practice of social work does include that aspect. The world needs all kinds of political activists, including those in the professions. The point here is that professional practice goes beyond exercise of strongly held ideological conviction. Certainly, social work practice includes political activism, but the social worker who wears the policy analyst's hat cannot *simultaneously* wear the political activist's hat. In this style of policy analysis, the two hats are mutually exclusive. Professional practitioners are called to commitment to a rationality that prizes alternative viewpoints and advocates taking them into account. They also are called to commitment to an objectivity that features multiple perspectives. However, *multiple perspectives are not a major feature of the value-committed approach because it assumes that the "truth" is already known and value choices are already made.* The profession is currently much enamored of practice using multiple perspectives about the human condition, so the value-critical approach has a nice fit with the current professional preoccupation in its emphasis on multiple perspectives on the human condition.[9]

The value-critical approach also fits the current professional preoccupation in its assumption that no facts are independent of theories and value biases. Whereas certain kinds of facts are very unlikely to change, the value-critical approach takes the view that the *selection* of facts taken under consideration does vary with the theory used; the approach further posits that it is the very purpose of theory to highlight some facts and ignore (or suppress) others. Note that for the purpose of analysis, the value-critical approach is, like all professions as a matter of fact, both conservative (in its view that the status quo might be worth saving) and radical (in calling the status quo into question).

The value-critical approach also has appeal because it can (and should be) grounded in practice experience. The questions practitioners raise are not just theoretical or just value-driven. In conducting the analysis of a social policy or program, social work and human service practitioners must bring to bear their own practice experience and the experience and perspective of others, not least their clients.

One element of the value-critical approach is that it requires "teasing out" the value biases and frames of reference that lie behind social problem analyses and their associated policy and program designs (ideology, causation, recall). It develops a useful skill in elucidating competing values and frames of reference, a skill practitioners might use when confronted with conflict at any level—personal, familial, organizational, communal, or political. Practitioners need to develop this skill to be able to sort out their own organizational world. After all, each practitioner conducts her or his practice surrounded by competing values and frames of reference. For example, as indicated earlier in this chapter, organizational administrators may have a frame of reference about implementing legislation or court mandates that differs completely from that of the practitioner (the *frontline* practitioner) whose frame of reference about the social program design and the social problem come from an entirely different world: street corners, interacting families, or the corridors of public schools and hospitals. Part of the business of practice is to find some rationalization for practice behaviors or program designs to bridge these competing interests and frames of reference. Social work and human service practitioners at either administrative or direct service levels don't anymore "directly" implement legislation than do physicians "directly" implement medical care out of textbook solutions or Medicare, hospital, legal, even ecclesiastical regulations. Thus, one of the important and persuasive attributes of value-critical policy analysis is that it forces practitioners to analyze for multiple and competing values and frames of reference, to make hard choices among them and to take even their own frames and values into question as they confront the reality of both the social world in general, the world their clients live in, and the daily operating world of organizations, laws, and public expectations.

Still, there is a utility to all this ambiguity in public policy. Social workers and human service professionals need to realize that it is precisely the *lack of specificity* of legislation, court decisions, historical tradition, and organizational regulation that is, in some important sense, the source of their freedom to practice while remaining faithful to their own personal values and frames of reference. Where legislation and regulation is precise and specific, practitioners have little discretion and their tasks lie in, more or less automated decision making. Although practitioners' freedom will be seriously restricted whenever it conflicts with or bursts the bonds of plausible relation to legislation or regulation, nonetheless, it is commonly the judgment of experienced practitioners that *there is almost always more freedom to practice at the limits of organizational rules and regulations than is ever used by most social work and human service practitioners*. The point is, practitioners can protect themselves as well as maximize their freedom to practice simply by having a keen awareness of the relationship between their own values and frame of reference about a social problem and the programmatic features designed to cope with it. A key part of the practitioner's task is to bridge the two, and it is both an offensive and defensive practice strategy to be prepared to do so. The general principle is that a practitioner who can give a rational account of the relationships between what she or he is doing and the various frameworks that administrative or political superiors are using is less likely to experience a serious attack on their competence and autonomy. Martin Rein is very clear on this point:

> We more typically start with practice (action) and then design policies to justify what we do. The sequence is then from practice (action) to design to purpose. *Thus, policy rationalizes and legitimizes actions that arise from quite different processes. . . .*[10] (emphasis added)

The advice here is not to suggest that a seat-of-the-pants behavioral style is really the way social work or human service is best practiced but only to underscore that practitioners and organizations (and street-level bureaucrats) muddle through, work things out, and try to do everything they can to be successful—then repeat what experience shows to be successful. Most likely they *did* begin with a guiding idea for practice, but that idea was shaped by the lived realities of both clients and helpers. The notion is that policy formed out of practice experience serves a useful function in helping to shape the resulting program and practice design. It creates a freer stance from which to conduct a professional practice; here practitioners create programs and are not simply the routinizing, bureaucratic implementer, the tool of higher organizational powers.

The major problem for this approach lies in locating and working with a set of criteria by which to make the value-critical judgment. Particular sets of criteria for each policy element will now be advocated, criteria that seem to be absolutely necessary (though probably not sufficient, of course). Other, perhaps better, criteria could be proposed, certainly, but those proposed herein will force the analyst to give attention to certain features of social policies and programs that are absolutely essential if the analyst is to understand the whole. It is left to the reader to ferret out the peculiar set of underlying, fundamental value biases in the criteria presented here. One such bias is the assumption of rationality, that is, that the best social program and policy is the one that is most rational in the sense of being logically and internally consistent—to wit, consistent with its history, with the judicial decisions that by law it is obliged to follow, with whatever social problem analysis that has been set forth (not, of course, necessarily that of others, the legislature or the organization hosting the program) but with *its own* carefully articulated, rationalized social problem analysis, faithfully executed and taken seriously by practitioners and clients.

So, our list of evaluation criteria will begin with *whether the basic elements of the program and policy are consistent with its social problem analysis.* It can be said that the solution to inconsistency with the social problem analysis is not always to change program features, but one can change the social problem analysis! This is in line with two ideas: (1) Policy as well as social problem analysis can emerge from practice, not always the other way around, and (2) theories are not ultimate truth and should be shaped by practice and empirical experience as well as abstractions.

Other evaluation criteria used here will include traditional ones: equity, adequacy, and efficiency (originally developed for use in economics). Also included are criteria that may be less familiar: trade-offs and access/coverage effects (as I have labeled them). Note that whereas these criteria are intended to be used for critical evaluation of more than one policy element, there are other, criteria that are unique to *a single* policy element.

The next section will give a brief overview of how to do an analytic description of policy and program using the six policy elements. It will then discuss how to do the value-critical aspect of the analysis, using suggested evaluation criteria to judge the ultimate merit of the operating characteristics.

The Policy and Program Analysis Process: An Overview of the Six Fundamental Policy Elements

Six policy elements form the cornerstone of every policy and program presented daily to citizens, program clients, and beneficiaries. It is these policy elements on which the practical social policy analyst ultimately will base judgments about a policy or program. Ordinary sources for information about them cannot always be relied on; and, given the size and complexity of modern social welfare programs, agency staff members, administrators, and policy manuals are not always accurate or completely informed. The six policy elements to be discussed are as follows:

1. Goals and objectives
2. Forms of benefits or services delivered
3. Entitlement (eligibility) rules
4. Administrative or organizational structure for service delivery
5. Financing method
6. Interactions among the foregoing elements[11]

Why study these six rather than others? Because these are the six without which a social policy or program cannot be operated; that is, they are necessary to implement a program or policy system. It is simple enough to do a mental experiment to test out this idea: Suppose you have something very valuable to convey and you neither wish to bury it nor give it to kin or friends. How will you dispose of it? If you want to do it rationally, you will have to ask six questions so as to reach a decision.

1. What purpose or *goal* do you wish to achieve in giving this gift?
2. Given those goals, who is entitled to the gift?
3. In what *form* would the gift be given, assuming you could easily transform it into cash or some other gift?
4. Whom will you select to *deliver* it?

5. Do you want to give the whole gift at once or just the interest earned from principal, or do you wish others to help with *financing* by putting up some of their own money?
6. If the gift is given in cash will recipient(s) spend it for the *purpose* intended? (i.e., interactions in this case between goals and form of benefit)

These same choices have to be made whenever policies or programs for the general good are to be put into effect. In an ideal world, of course, no such choices are necessary because there is an unlimited supply of what everybody needs. Unfortunately, however, in our faulty paradise, a world in which it is *not* the case that everybody has enough, social welfare policy and programs are necessary.

Social policy is concerned with the six elements enumerated because, in the final analysis, they are the basis on which social policies and programs ration and distribute benefits, select beneficiaries and attempt to ensure that money, goods, and services are used efficiently, effectively, and without waste. Some public commentators remark sarcastically that social welfare policy and programs are futile because they attempt to bring paradise to an inherently imperfect world; the reality is quite the opposite—the benefits of paradise are self-selected, self-rationed, and occasioned by justice. *Social welfare policy is about selection and rationing, in an attempt to correct injustice.* Social welfare policy is about a concrete empirical world and the attempt to moderate its sometimes cruel and inhumane effects. We will talk more later about how the challenge to social policies and programs is to be successful in moderating one cruel effect without creating another, more cruel effect.

Table 4.1 lists two additional types of information for each operating characteristic: subtypes and evaluation criteria. When the practical policy analyst studies the policy elements of particular social welfare program or benefit systems, it becomes clear that there are only a limited number of ways in which those criteria are expressed; for example, only about a half-dozen (more or less) subtypes of entitlement or eligibility rules are apparent. That is not to say that an inventive mind couldn't think of others or that certain programs (domestic or foreign) might not have others. Column 2 of Table 4.1 summarizes the main subtypes of policy elements—for example, the main subtypes of forms of benefits are cash, commodities, personal social services, and so on. This summary provides a quick and handy reference for describing the main features of any social welfare service or benefit program. The subtypes listed in Table 4.1 are intended for use by the practical policy analyst who daily encounters a world full of new and old social programs and policies that he or she must evaluate in order to know whether they are useful to clients.

These subtypes are not mutually exclusive; that is, a particular social welfare program or policy may use more than one kind of entitlement rule or financing method. For example, most state Title XX programs that offer social services to various categories of citizens not only have a means test (in most states, only those with incomes less than 125 percent of the state's average income are eligible for free services) but require (in most cases) the exercise of professional discretion—the potential consumer must have been referred for services by a professionally qualified person.

How each operating characteristic is evaluated is discussed in the following section.

TABLE 4.1   Policy Element Subtypes and Evaluation Criteria for a Value-Critical Appraisal of Social Policies and Programs

Basic Policy Element	Types	Evaluation Criteria

Goals and Objectives	1. long term/short term
	2. manifest/latent
		1. criteria specific to Goals and Objectives
		  (a) not just service delivery but end-product
		  (b) clarity, measurability, manipulability
		  (c) inclusion of performance standards and target specifications
		2. implications of Goals and Objectives for adequacy, equity, and efficiency
		3. "fit" of Goals and Objectives with the social problem analysis: problem definition and variables (consequences) in causal analysis

Forms of Benefits and Services	1. personal social services
	  (a) "expert services"
	2. "hard benefits": cash, goods, commodities
	3. positive discrimination
	4. credits/vouchers
	5. subsidies
	6. government loan guarantees
	7. protective regulations
	8. supervision of deviance
	9. power over decisions
		1. criteria specific to Benefits and Services
		  (a) stigmatization
		  (b) target efficiency
		  (c) cost-effectiveness
		  (d) substitutability
		  (e) consumer sovereignty
		  (f) trade-offs
		  (g) coerciveness/intrusiveness
		  (h) complexity and cost of administration
		  (i) adaptability across users
		  (j) political risk
		2. implications of benefit/service for adequacy, equity, and efficiency
		3. "fit" of Benefit/Service form with the social problem analysis

Eligibility Rules	1. means/asset tests
	2. administrative rule
	3. private contract provision
	4. prior contributions
	5. profession discretion
	6. judicial decision
	7. attachment to workforce
		1. criteria specific to eligibility rules
		  (a) over-/underutilization
		  (b) overwhelming costs
		  (c) stigma/alienation
		  (d) disincentive for work
		  (e) incentives for procreational and marital breakup and/or generational dependence
		2. "fit" with social problem analysis: problem definition/target group specifications
		3. implications of eligibility rules for adequacy, equity, and efficiency

(continued)

TABLE 4.1   Continued

Basic Policy Element	Types	Evaluation Criteria

Administration and Service Delivery	1. centralization
	2. federation
	3. case management
	4. referral agency
	5. indigenous worker staffing
	6. racially oriented agencies
	7. administrative "fair hearing"
	8. due process protections for clients' procedural rights
	9. citizen participation
		1. evaluation criteria specific to administration/service delivery
		  (a) has an articulate program/policy design
		  (b) integration/continuity
		  (c) accessibility
		  (d) accountability
		  (e) client/consumer empowerment
		  (f) consumer participation in decision making
		  (g) coping with racial, gender, and ethnic diversity
		2. "fit" with social problem analysis
		3. implications for adequacy, equity, and efficiency

Financing	1. prepayments and the insurance principle
	2. publicly regulated private contracts
	3. voluntary contributions
	4. tax revenue appropriation
	5. fees for service
	6. private endowment
		1. evaluation criteria specific to financing
		  (a) continuity in funding
		  (b) stability in broad economic change: inflation/depression and demographic change
		2. "fit" with social problem analysis
		3. implications of this administrative type for adequacy, equity, and efficiency

Interactions		(No unique evaluative criteria)

Criteria for a Value-Critical Appraisal of Social Policy and Programs

Column 3 of Table 4.1 lists evaluation criteria by which the policy analyst can judge how a particular program has implemented each policy element and, ultimately, the worth of the program and policy system. For example, goals and objectives should be evaluated according to whether they are concerned with outcomes; whether they are clear, measurable and manipulable; and other such criteria. A means test (entitlement rules) should be evaluated on the basis of whether it creates stigmatization or alienation, or off-targets benefits, for example. The method of policy analysis contained in this book actually suggests three general but very different types of criteria for evaluating the features of social program and policy systems.

The first type *uses the social problem analysis as a referent,* the evaluation issue being whether the program or policy has any potential for making an impact on the social problem it was intended to solve. In this mode, the practitioner asks certain questions:

- Do the entitlement rules direct benefits at the entire population defined to have the social problem, or do they only reach a subgroup?
- Do the goals and objectives of the program or policy system "fit" a social problem as defined?
- Can this form of benefit produce a sufficient impact on the causal factors believed to produce the social problem?

The second type is made up of *those traditional value perspectives—adequacy, equity, and efficiency.* For example, one might ask: "Is delivery of commodities rather than cash as a form of benefit a more *efficient* (cost-effective) way to solve the problem of nutrition?" An example of the *adequacy* criterion lies in the question: "Is the counseling adequate to the task of creating change of sufficient magnitude." Similarly, a practical policy analyst might be evaluating a particular service delivery type against both an equity criterion and an adequacy criterion when she or he asks: "To what extent does the case-management style of service delivery increase the ability of the policy and program system to relate to the ethnic and racial diversity of its target population?" It is more than a little useful for the practitioner to be aware of what root questions are being asked (whether adequacy, equity, or efficiency questions) when a program and policy system are being judged for merit.

The reader should be alert to the possibility that many of the questions about adequacy are answered in the context of evaluating the "fit" of a policy element with the social problem analysis. *In fact, one of the most important functions of a social problem analysis is to provide an internally consistent, solid basis for judging whether the policy/program design/ policy system is a "good" one.* For example, a good social problem analysis will describe who is affected and (obviously) the policy/program solution must address those very people in order to be judged "adequate." And, recall, a good social problem analysis will describe the "consequences" at the heart of why the problem is considered to be a social problem—obviously, in order for the policy/program design to be judged "adequate," it has to (plausibly) make an impact on just that problematic condition. The basic question is whether it is believable (or whether there is any evidence) that the program design can do that. Judgments of "adequacy" are not abstract, but refer to the specifics of the social problem analysis.

The "adequacy/equity/efficiency" criteria were developed by economists. When they use them, it is out of a concern for large-scale economic matters: changes in the characteristics of the national workforce, profitability of big industrial employers, gross domestic product, the national wage scales, and the like. Those are surely important matters, but not very useful to social program implementers and designers since they are not factors within their reach. No one likely to read this book would design or implement a program intended to raise the national worker wage scale—though that might, indeed, go a long way toward the solution of some social problems. Economists, bless their souls, do have a good deal to say about how that might be accomplished, though they aren't often right on target. The economists' perspective is to judge the "adequacy" of public policy by how it contributes to an economy that rewards and encourages capital investment and the creation of national wealth. It is nearly inescapable that economists believe that what benefits wealth holders, almost always and necessarily benefits workers and the general population. Although that might be true over some long time spans, it is often not the case for the near term of a few years, the time scale social practitioners and their needful clients work with. They are concerned with immediately presenting problems. Sadly and as anyone knows from having read reliable accounts of large-scale unemployment resulting from large corporations profiting from shifting production overseas, corporate downsizing and mergers, most of the profits in the booming U.S. economy goes into the pockets of those already wealthy, whereas the national income share of the middle and working class remains stable or goes lower. *Thus, judgments of policy/program "adequacy" for the practical policy analyst/practitioner uses the social problem analysis perspective, and its ideological/causal perspective focuses on the consequences for persons and citizens, not on the effects on the "economy."*

The reader can find the economists' focus on equity useful, that is, on whether a policy or program design does treat similarly situated program participants in the same way. Inequities are sometimes (legitimately) designed into policies and programs, of course, but the point here is that inequities need to be searched out, identified, and examined for their consequences, intended or not. And the same can be said of efficiencies. Even though there are prominent exceptions, for the most part, the program or policy that is most efficient or cost-effective is the best choice—if for no other reason, the least cost alternative allows the always scarce social welfare dollar to go to more people in need.

The third type of criteria with which to evaluate policy elements for their worthiness are those used *only* for a particular policy element. Good examples are "includes target specifications" or "performance standards," which can be used *only* for evaluating goals and objectives. Notice that it would make no sense to ask whether some benefit form like a "voucher" has "target specifications." "Target Specifications" are peculiar to goals and objectives.

In summary then, the evaluation criteria the practical policy analyst should use for deciding the merit of the policy elements in a program, service, or policy system will always include

1. the "fit" of the policy element to the social problem of concern
2. the consequences of the policy element with regard to adequacy, equity, and efficiency for clients and program participants.
3. criteria that are uniquely useful for a single policy element but not others

We will save a more detailed look at evaluation criteria for the specific chapters on each policy element that follow this overview.

Summary

Chapter 4 contrasted three styles of policy analysis: the analytic-descriptive, the value-committed, and the value-critical. While recognizing that political occasions will arise during which it is essential, the value-committed approach is rejected because it is not open to new data or conclusions. This fact argues for the value-critical style, which forces into the open whatever ideology is inherent in the analytic method used and the fundamental value commitments of the analyst in whose hands the method rests. Taken into the open, the effects of ideology can be observed and accounted for. Although useful, the sole use of the analytic-descriptive method fails in policy analysis because it commits the analyst to untenable assumptions: for example, that judgments about the "goodness" or "merit" of a social policy or program can be made in a value-free way. Such assumptions are unrealistic because any judgment of social program merit requires judgment of social worthiness—which simply cannot be made absent a strong value commitment. The virtue of the value-critical method is that it forces value commitments into the open and therefore gives both the analyst and his or her audience great freedom in using (or not using) the data produced from the analysis. This approach also enables practitioners to decide whether they are in agreement with the conclusions, to sort them selectively, or to freely substitute their own value biases and draw different conclusions. That sort of freedom can be used at different levels—either with regard to particular social program or policy operating characteristics or with regard to summary judgments.

Value commitments inherent in this preferred method of policy analysis were presented: rationality, logical consistency, and new conclusions reached by a dialectic contrast between various value perspectives on the social problem and the means used to resolve it. Other basic value commitments advocated throughout the presentation of the analytic method in succeeding chapters were also presented; that is, adequacy, equity, and efficiency. This chapter also noted how evaluation criteria vary in their relevance depending on which operating feature of the social policies and programs is under discussion.

EXERCISE

1. *Complete the following mental experiment:* Your physician has just told you that you have a fatal and incurable illness. You have just eight weeks to live. On returning home from the physician's office, you decide not to go berserk today (perhaps tomorrow), at least not until you open your mail. There is an envelope with a strange return address on it, foreign stamps in fact. Opening it first, you learn that you have inherited several million dollars, being the last living heir to a European fortune. A quick calculation shows that you cannot possibly spend it all in eight weeks. Then you decide you do not want to give it either to friends or relatives—your closest friend recently offended you and your closest relative died three years ago. Use the six basic policy elements to decide how you want to dispose of the money.

N O T E S

1. M. Rein, *From Policy to Practice* (Armonk, NY: M. E. Sharpe, 1983), p. ix.

2. Ibid., p. x.

3. M. Howlett, "Policy Instruments, Policy Styles, and Policy Implementation: National Approaches to Theories of Instrument Choice," *Policy Studies Journal*, 19 (1991): 1–21.

4. Ibid., pp. 6–9.

5. M. Rein, Value-critical Policy Analysis, In Daniel Callahan and Bruce Jennings (eds.), *Ethics, the Social Sciences and Policy Analysis* (New York: Farrar and Rinehart, 1983), pp. 83–111. See also A. Weick and L. Pope, *Knowing What's Best: A New Look at Self-Determination* (Lawrence: University of Kansas, 1975), mimeographed.

6. J. Habermas, *Theory and Practice* (Boston: Beacon Press, 1976).

7. M. Piore, "Qualitative Research Techniques in Economics," *Administrative Science Quarterly*, 24 (December 1979): 62.

8. Rein, *From Policy to Practice*, p. x.

9. A. Weick, "Reconceptualizing the Philosophical Base of Social Work," *Social Service Review*, 42 (1975): 218–230.

10. Rein, *Value-Critical Policy Analysis*, p. 87.

11. Elements 2, 3, 4, and 6 were used by Evelyn Burns in a book titled *The American Social Security System* (New York: Houghton Mifflin, 1949) and I assume that (collectively) they are original with her. Her ultimate sources may lie somewhere in the British tradition of social policy studies, of course. Many contemporary authors use N. Gilbert and H. Specht, *Dimensions of Social Welfare Policy* (Englewood Cliffs, NJ: Prentice Hall, 1974). 1 have added new operating characteristics in the belief that they are important to a thorough analysis: Goals and Objectives and Interactions among Elements.

5 The Analysis of Policy Goals and Objectives in Social Programs and Policies

Introduction

The method presented in this book proceeds by first obtaining a close description of social policy or program implementation and then evaluating its merit according to specified criteria. Six fundamental policy elements are essential to implementation of all social policies. Chapter 5 will consider the first—*goals and objectives*—along with the various forms in which they are expressed. The chapter also will describe the difference between goals and objectives, identify sources and problems in locating statements of program and policy goals and objectives, and review their components and functions. In addition, the way in which goals and objectives differ in the personal social services and the problems of setting them in that context will be considered. The chapter will close with an extensive discussion of the task of evaluating the merit of social policy program and policy goals and objectives through the use of suggested criteria. The discussion in this chapter is intended to set a model for later chapter discussions on other operating characteristics.

Definitions and Basic Concepts for Analysis of Goals and Objectives

A goal is a statement, in general and abstract terms, of desired qualities in human and social conditions.[1] It is important to grasp the goals and objectives of a program so as to answer the question: "What is the purpose of this program or policy?" In fact, all elements of the program or policy must be judged on the basis of their contribution to program goals and objectives; the extent to which program or policy elements make such contributions is a measure of the wisdom of choosing them as an instrument of policy operations. Therefore, the program or policy goals and objectives are the programmatic "measure of all things." Program goals and objectives are highly variable, as the following examples are intended to show. The goal of the Social Security program known as Old Age and Survivors Insurance (OASI) is to ensure that citizens will have income after they no longer can work. The goal of the Low Income Energy Assistance Program (LIEAP) is to reduce the impact of increased energy costs on low-income households. The goal of most child abuse programs is to protect or prevent the abuse of children who are too young to protect themselves. It is important to understand that when we describe the goal or objective of a policy or program, we are describing a desired end, *not* a provided service. It is easy to confuse the two when speaking of social policies and programs because programs often are described according to the methods they use to achieve their goals and objectives. Thus, when asked to define the purpose of their program, staff members and executives often say, for example, that they provide counseling or money or nursing care to people who need it. That, however, is not a legitimate goal; by definition, services are not ends in themselves. Thus, the provision of *services or benefits is never, by itself, a legitimate goal or objective of a social program.* To describe services and benefits is to describe program processes (inputs) or perhaps program designs, but certainly not goals or objectives. One of many reasons for *not* including service provision as a legitimate goal is that doing so makes it possible to consider perpetual service provision as a legitimate outcome by which to measure program performance. Think for a moment about how, under these circumstances, a social program can simply continue to give services forever and never have to look at whether it produces an important result. In effect, to express goals and objectives as services rather than outcomes makes it impossible to evaluate a program against its outcomes, rendering such a program essentially nonaccountable. If a social program cannot produce results that meet human needs, the welfare system must direct funding elsewhere.

Here is an example of how this distinction works in practice. Consider this common problem faced by those with responsibility for allocating funds for the delivery of social services. Assume you chair the board of directors of the Barrett Foundation, whose purpose is to fund social programs for general philanthropic deeds, and you exercise broad discretion in doing so. Assume further that while speaking with the director of a local program, the Grant County Counseling Service, the director argues that the organization is a viable, successful operation due to the following reasons:

- Grant has a full staff, each of whom is an expert in three types of therapy (behavior modification, psychoanalytic therapy, and Bowenian marriage counseling).
- The number of clients served has increased by 20 percent this year.
- The number of treatment hours has increased by 35 percent this year.
- New satellite clinic offices were established in six counties over the past year.
- New consulting services were contracted for in two new school districts and in three high schools.

You must decide whether your organization should fund this operation for another five years at an annual budget of around $900,000. Based on the viewpoint about goals and objectives expressed before, the answer is no, because the operations data that are given tell you absolutely nothing about program effectiveness, only about program inputs and processes (mostly counseling), not program outcomes. The data speak only about means to ends, not ends themselves. Goals are not about delivering services (treatment hours, treatment access, consultation, and the like), but about achieving a desirable outcome in regard to the targeted social problem(s). If this board of directors doesn't insist on this, they have no rational means by which to make a decision about funding this program. In an important sense, program outcomes are a public social program's "profit," without which program operations inevitably are taking resources away from opportunities to meet human need elsewhere. One key to the distinction lies in judging whether the program or policy goal or objective could be accepted as an end in itself. For example, could personal counseling be accepted as an end in itself? Not likely, for the mere fact of counseling does not by itself suggest any particular social problem that is being solved. The goal will be revealed by the answer to the question "Counseling for what, to achieve what purpose?"

Different Types of Goals and Objectives

The practical public policy analyst should be alert to the fact that goals and objectives come in a variety of forms. For example, sometimes social programs specify objectives as "long-term" or "short-term." This specification is useful because it can relate to funding—there may be enough money only for outcomes having short horizons and the program may not last long enough to be concerned about a long horizon. Consider a highly politicized social problem like substance abuse. For a time, a drug education program for grade school children was highly publicized and appealed to the general populace. When these programs were first funded, they were fielded with very short-term goals—to increase children's knowledge about the effects of drugs. Once programs were implemented, change was expected to occur over a matter of weeks. In fact, the program was designed to be delivered and the information learned in a very short period of time because funding not only was limited but restricted to a few months' duration. When an intermediate step is crucial to a long-term goal, it is only logical to test for whether the intermediate step is attainable; further dollars await the outcome. The long-term goal here was the reduction in adult, long-term substance abuse, but in that funding environment, the long-term goal was irrelevant from a practical point of view.

Manifest and Latent Goals

A statement about a social policy or program goal is different from sociological statements about the social function served by a particular social program or policy. For example, Piven and Cloward conclude that the primary social function of the U.S. welfare system is to regulate the poor in two ways:[2]

1. To ensure a supply of cheap labor to the economic system
2. To ensure that discontent among the poor does not rise to levels where it becomes a major threat to social order.

These are theoretical conclusions about a social welfare system from the point of view of sociological analysis. Policy or program goal statements are much less global, less inferential, and they are traceable to sources that can be observed "directly"; they are based on evidence from statements in such visible sources as legislative bills, administrative documents, and/or judicial decisions. If sociological and social policy analyses are confused, the policy analysis will suffer because manifest and latent functions are being confused.[3]

A *manifest* function is an explicit, stated purpose. With respect to social programs or policy, manifest functions are discovered through examination of statements in primary documents of concern (legal or administrative) about goals and purposes. As sociologists and anthropologists have long been at pains to point out, social programs, policies, and institutions have purposes or functions (goals) other than those stated publicly, labeled *latent* functions. One widely discussed latent function is served by mental hospitals, which, it is contended, serve the manifest (stated, legislated) function of treatment of mental disorders for the benefit of individual patients; they are also said to serve the latent function of the social control of deviance (control of the incidence of unusual, norm-defying behavior). Another common example is the federal government's Section 8 housing program, which offers substantial rent subsidies to low-income families. The manifest goal or objective of this program is to make safe, adequate, and affordable housing available to the poor. Section 8 housing, located in scattered sites outside the inner-city urban ring, is reasonably expected to be an environmental improvement for low-income families and to reduce urban minority populations. As laudable as these goals and objectives are, some policy analysts argue that their *latent* goal is to gradually depopulate housing projects in inner cities so that they can be torn down and redeveloped as luxury apartments and condominiums. This charge is plausible in that one can easily point to housing projects in metropolitan areas that would be prime real estate development sites. Chicago's inner urban ring is one example in which housing projects are being vacated and discussions are being held as to their future. Whereas, ultimately, manifest and latent goals and objectives are very important (latent rather than manifest goals often drive program features and implementation), the first-order focus in policy and program analysis is on a description of the stated (manifest) goals. Observations about latent goals and objectives, even though speculative, are almost always useful but shouldn't displace focus on what is manifest.

Distinguishing between Goals and Objectives

A *goal* is an abstract and general statement of desired outcomes, and an *objective* is a concrete, operational statement about a desired observable outcome. For any given goal, many different (sometimes divergent) objectives can be written. For example, the goal of Literacy, Inc., a social program, can be stated as follows:

- To increase the ability of native and nonnative speakers of English so that they can accelerate their acculturation

That goal seems specific and in some ways it is. It certainly conveys a clear idea of what the program wishes to ultimately accomplish. Note how this goal *could* admit of several very different objectives:

- To increase reading competence to the sixth-grade level and to the point where employment advertisements can be read with comprehension
- To increase the ability to understand spoken English at a level where conversation with the average U.S. high school graduate can be conducted to the linguistic satisfaction of both parties
- To increase the ability to read and speak standard English so as to eliminate any linguistic barrier to passing the GED high school certificate examination

The idea here is that any one of these statements of objectives would be sufficient to satisfy the goal statement of Literacy, Inc., in any one given program. (It is unlikely though not impossible that such a program would adopt all three as objectives.) Taken together, multiple objectives cannot constitute the total meaning of goals, a direct consequence of the fact that a good, well-defined abstraction admits of an infinite number of concrete empirical instances. Put another way, a good way to think of an abstraction is something whose meaning *cannot* be exhausted by a list of instances, no matter how long.

The nature of goals is that they are quite general and abstract; therefore, they are not ordinarily intended to be directly measurable. Objectives, on the other hand, are intended to be measured. It is not too far out of line to say that the importance of goals is to mark out the general scope (conceptual coverage, one might say) or the theoretical territory of a policy or a social program. The implication is that, for goals, their clear definition is their most important attribute. The importance of objectives, on the other hand, is their concreteness, their observability. Note carefully: When a social program or policy is evaluated by a well-designed empirical study, it is to objectives, not goals, that the evaluative measures are related.

Objectives (Not Goals) Must Contain Target Group Specifications and Performance Standards

If objectives are to be of maximal use, they must clearly specify *who* is to be affected, changed, or whose circumstances or surroundings are the target of change efforts. In specifying a *target group*, the phrase "serving the homeless of the city of Pocatello, Idaho" is not an acceptable target group specification. All terms of an objective need to be concrete: for example, "serving the homeless, those without permanent, warm, secure, sanitary shelter with running water and a stool and those older than 60 years of age. . . ." It is a mistake to write objectives without that kind of specification. Although goals and objectives may seem remote and abstract at program initiation, they take on a serious import when it comes time to evaluate the program for effectiveness because program merit will be judged against the standards implied in objectives.

Objectives (but not goals) must also contain *performance standards*, that is, statements about the extent of the changes or effects the program is expected to have. A performance standard for a housing program might be something like:

> . . . within five years to secure safe, up-to-standard permanent shelter for one-third of the low-income population of Compton, Mississippi, such shelter is to be inhabited by no more than two persons per room, and has running water, sanitary toilets, and electric outlets in each room.

Certainly, the details can be argued, but the phrases "two persons per room" and "running water" are examples of performance standards. Any housing falling short of those descriptions does not meet this standard of performance and thus cannot count as a positive outcome of the program. Another example from the personal social services might be a program for integrating the severely emotionally disturbed into a pattern of community living where the objective is to have each

> . . . person in the program living in a private household shared with at least four other persons, and who takes full responsibility for his/her nutrition, medication, plus has interaction with a nonhouseholder for at least ten hours a week.

In this case, the quoted phrases refer to explicit performance standards for the program. For program consumers for which those standards are not met, that instance does not count as a success for the program.

Most of us would not expect a program with limited resources to serve a total population, but program auditors and evaluators will not make that assumption. Thus, a program objective whose performance standards say it will serve the population of a city means exactly that. If target groups and performance standards aren't specified, goals and objectives will almost always be read to indicate that the program will serve a larger population than is really intended or, for that matter, has adequate resources for. Absent target group specification and a performance standards program, evaluators and those who provide program funds would conclude that the Pocatello, Idaho, homeless shelter mentioned earlier would serve *all* the homeless in Pocatello. If a shelter has accommodations for only ten and there is a demonstrable demand for fifteen, it will almost inevitably be given bad marks because it didn't do what it said it would, never mind after-the-fact arguments that the program didn't really mean what it said.

It is common for legislatures or United Way to cut social service budgets by some arbitrary percentage, often as a simple way to deal with funding shortfalls. When this happens and involves some services that are mandated by law, for example, child protection, it is the legislatively mandated service that will be the program priority. In some cases, that can be a disaster. Since investigation of child abuse reports is mandated by law, that will surely be done, but other nonmandated services will be reduced—follow-up services and treatment most likely. Although it is important to bring child abuse to the attention of judicial authorities, investigations can be an exercise in futility absent the ability of either the court or the social service agency to do anything beyond a radical separation of children from their biological parents.

Not only that. Mindless percentagewise budget cuts can reduce staff so radically that abuse investigations either overlook serious child abuse or result in false reports that can create terrible damage to innocent parents (and in both cases can create substantial legal liabilities for agencies as well). *When such budget cuts occur, social program managers and practitioners are ethically obligated to make clear (and public) how such reductions affect the ability of the program to serve its target group.* Those who make those kind of budget cuts will not be at all pleased to have this news made public. But, there are funding levels below which objectives and performance standards simply cannot be achieved. One way to fight that is to make the consequences plain to the public. One reason to construct target group specifications (and include them in statements of goals and objectives) is to have an established baseline by which the impact of fiscal reductions can be demonstrated.

All of this is to say that is desirable to constrain objectives and performance standards so that the program is never obligated to provide more service than allowed by the budget resources available. One way (not always ideal) to approach this is to set a percentage of a particular target group: "...will serve 30 percent of the homeless" or "...will serve an average of eighty teenage homeless persons over a one-year period." Without hard information, performance standards based on local practice wisdom estimates are better than none at all. Needs surveys can provide reasonably reliable guidance for anticipating service demand; any sensible planning would require them. Sadly, funding is seldom available to conduct them.

Too often, social programs are discontinued not because their program ideas and implementation were lacking or ineffective, but because they failed to reach a target group or performance standard that, with proper foresight, would have been known to be unreachable, given the resources at hand. This happens when administrators and social program innovators become so enthusiastic about their ideas and operations that without realizing it, they overcommit their organization. This is unfortunate because good ideas are scarce. Finally, competition for social program funding is fierce, and interested parties will seize on the others' shortcomings like sharks in a feeding frenzy—all the more reason to avoid being careless about setting target specifications in building objectives.

Purpose of Goals and Objectives

Why have both goals and objectives when, in one sense, they refer to the same thing? Because they serve different purposes. Statements about objectives are absolutely essential for two reasons.

1. They give the operational outcome toward which program operations are directed, and no administrator can make decisions about daily issues like constructing

budgets, distributing money among various program operations, and hiring and firing without a concrete objective in mind.

2. Programs cannot be evaluated for effectiveness unless there is an objective to serve as a measurable standard against which data from actual achievements can be cast.

Program goals are also necessary in that they provide a crucial link between the more concrete and specific objectives, and the public documentary sources (laws, judicial decisions, administrative mandates) that establish the program or policy. Statements in such documents can never be sufficiently specific so that a program or policy can be constructed from them directly. Whatever their source, statements are quintessentially political, the product of political compromise; and political documents can never be truly explicit lest some party takes issue with them. If that happens, it may destroy delicate political, Judicial, administrative, or organizational compromises that were necessary to promulgate the policy or program in the first place. Part of the art of politics is to avoid saying what will offend, and in that way both sides believe the issue is settled. As S. M. Miller states, "... behind every political agreement there lies a misunderstanding...."[4] Program designers must translate these documents into operating programs, and to do that they need to translate the goal in the public document into a statement at a concrete level, that is, a measurable objective. Such a statement at a general and abstract level will encapsulate the basic desired outcomes. Then they need to make a statement at a more specific and concrete level that will direct a choice of specific program operations and program provisions that will move events toward the stated general goal as well as allow observations to be made by which program success or failure can be judged.

The following is one example of how goals and objectives function to provide a link between legislative intent and program operations and to assist operations accountability. A large, private, statewide child welfare program is a major subcontractor receiving state and federal funds for in-home services provided to welfare mothers whose children are at risk for abuse or neglect. The source for these federal dollars is Title XX of the Social Security Act, Goal III/IV which speak of preventing or remediation neglect, abuse or exploitation of children. Notice that the Social Security legislation itself doesn't speak of anything more specific than this general purpose: no definitions, no mention of how it should be pursued. Typically, that is the case for enabling legislation. But the private agency program that will administer these funds, likely the departments of child welfare of the several states, will supply program goals. In this state, these goals were

(a) to preserve, rehabilitate and/or reunite families.
(b) to do this by (note these intermediate goals):
   1. mobilizing the families own resources
   2. increasing family strengths
   3. increasing individual behaviors which support family integrity.

But it is at the level of program implementation, at which people in need (program participants/consumers) come face to face with staff members, that detailed outcome objectives are set forth: that is, those encounters are expected to have the following results:

1. prevention of the child from being placed outside the household (for 70 percent of the families)
2. individual program consumers achieve their individual objectives (75 percent of, in aggregate)
3. and 80 percent of program consumers will be satisfied with services

To see how the concrete outcome objectives are related—as links in a chain—to the intermediate goals, the general goal, and the legislative purpose, look for a moment at Figure 5.1.

This sets out the rough theory that underlies the program: for example, IF we can mobilize resources, increase family strengths, help program participants achieve personal objectives, and so on, THEN we will prevent outside-the-home placement (which is taken to be the rough equivalent of rehabilitating families, which is itself the equivalent

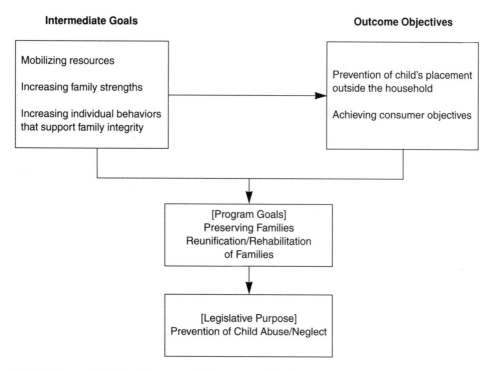

FIGURE 5.1   Linking Concrete Objectives with Abstract Goals and Legislative Purposes.

of preventing further abuse). It is the IF-THEN sequence that defines the rational process here. The reader may disagree that the statement is rational, of course; and data from program outcome measures may show that the statement is false, but that is part of the point—rational process makes clear what is expected and why, data make clear whether those expectations have come true. Program theory and design are discussed in greater detail in Chapter 8.

Setting Goals and Objectives in the Personal Social Services

It is easier to set goals and objectives for a "hard" benefit program (one that delivers goods like housing or food stamps) than it is to set them for personal social services— "soft benefits." The food stamp goal is rather straightforward: to increase nutrition. Notice that the food stamp objective is phrased in ways that shape the buying habits of beneficiaries—thus, junk foods, alcoholic beverages, and tobacco cannot be bought with food stamps. There are other ways to shape buying habits toward improved nutrition. For example, some European Union countries provide a heavy subsidy paid to the retail grocery merchant so that prices for milk and cheese are significantly reduced to the consumer. This strategy hopes to shape buying habits and improve nutrition by making nutritious foods cheaper and more attractive to everyone.

The reader should be clear that it is not only the administrative or program staff or legislation that can set goals and objectives legitimately. In fact, in the personal social services, there is, or should be, considerable latitude for clients and/or program participants to shape and/or set their own objectives. Dedication to practice values like self-determination, maximizing personal choice, and empowerment would lead in that direction.

Personal social services require much more individualized objectives since they deal with individuals who are so different from one another. There is an unavoidable tension between program/policy goals and objectives and personal social service objectives. While practitioners would like to think that they are free to help their clients toward just about any personal objective, it turns out that there are limits on that freedom—in real life, whomever pays the bills (program founders) have a good deal to say about how the money (and time and effort) is spent. The reader might want to consider that this feature (among others) is important in distinguishing private practice from paid employment as a civil servant. It is not a problem peculiar to social service workers. Consider the situation of an attorney for a school district called on to defend a teacher in court. The attorney wants to honor the client's objective, which is to have a judge dismiss the suit as without merit since only that will settle the question in the public's mind: Did she or did she not abuse a pupil? However, if the lawyer's employer, the school district, wants to settle the suit without a public court hearing, the lawyer has no choice but to settle the suit. The deciding issue is who pays the lawyer's salary.

But that problem may never be an issue for most practitioners, since client objectives and the program or policy objectives are often easily tied together at an abstract level. For example, in a residential care home for the mentally retarded, one would expect to see very individualized objectives since functional capacities of residents are likely to be quite variable. Objectives like cleanliness, self-control, increased verbal expression and the like are not difficult to gather under a general objective of increased socialization. But there are clearly specific, quite legitimate practice objectives that an employer of a social practitioner might insist not be included. Readers might want to think of some as an interesting exercise.

Whether a program's goals and objectives are general, that is, the same for all program participants, or are very specific to each person, the program served can have very important consequences. Here is an interesting example showing how highly individualized objectives create an incentive for good personal social services whereas generalized objectives shared by all clients do not. The example is all the more important since privatization of personal social services involving reimbursements from public founders is a highly favored feature of the contemporary social programming scene.

Consider residential care centers in which given sets of specific behavioral objectives for each resident, payment for client care can be based on achievement of objectives, called *targeted reimbursement*. *Nontargeted reimbursement* in personal social service programs has dubious trade-offs. For example, if care providers are paid the same for all clients without respect to their disability or level of care required, there is every motivation for the facility to admit those clients who are *least* disabled. Another example is reimbursement of facilities based on levels of care provided. The trade-off here is that residents are often segregated by whether their care needs are "high," "medium," or "low"—a situation that tends toward the creation of old-fashioned "back wards," where "difficult," "challenging," and "hard-to-manage" clients are "warehoused." The solution that seems to avoid most of these problems is to make reimbursement variable and dependent on client characteristics and level of challenges (code words for special and often difficult behaviors in residential settings). Although creation of a policy and program system that will identify client characteristics and behavioral challenges is itself no small challenge, it may carry a handsome payoff, as suggested by recent research.[6] The point here is that to construct a policy and program system that can accomplish targeted reimbursement and clear and unambiguous goals and objectives are an absolute essential.

Goals and Objectives Vary According to the Developmental Stage of the Program

In program or policy analysis, it is important to understand the developmental stage of the program at that moment. Early on, a preimplementation demonstration stage is now good practice, though it is not routine. Doubtless, social policies and program efforts would be much improved when finally implemented if they were routinely pretested in one of two forms: pilots or models. Models (sometimes called prototypes) are program designs implemented under the ideal conditions for success. The idea is that if they cannot succeed under these conditions, they can never succeed in "real life." Models are very tightly constructed and are not subject to midcourse changes. *Pilot projects* are likely to be the loosest type of demonstration program and the ones whose objectives are most subject to change. A pilot project searches for unexpected outcomes and the program design is changed on a simple trial-and-error basis "to see what happens" as a result. It is the strategy of choice when not much is known about the social problem of concern. Although this approach is social "tinkering" in its most blatant form, there is a clear place for it in the absence of good guesses about the nature of a social problem. The actual objective of such a program is to gather more knowledge or information about the problem and the program, even though the tentative objective may be stated. If that is the case, it is important for the analysis to take that into account and feature it in drawing conclusions about the overall program.[7]

Methods of Identifying Goals and Objectives

Identifying program goals and objectives is not always a simple matter. There is no one source for the documents that are necessary to draw firm conclusions, even in the case of public social policies or programs. What follows, however, is a routine procedure that ordinarily will result in reasonably firm conclusions about the goal(s) and objective(s) of public policies or programs. Note that the procedure does not necessarily need to follow the sequence presented. In fact, the sequence is more or less trivial since conflicting information might be obtained at each "step" described. Such divergence should be considered important benefits of a policy analysis since it sometimes explains why organizations work at cross purposes!

Step 1: Locate the Enabling Legislation

All public social programs are "public" because in one way or another they are funded from the government treasury. Any treasury expenditure must be authorized by the elected officials constitutionally empowered to do so. Authorizations for expenditures are almost always made in terms of "programs" under the administrative control of various governmental departments. Programs are set up by what is called *enabling legislation*, acts that contain some statement about the purpose or goal of the act and for the program.

Step 2: Locate Legislative History

It is important to gain a deeper perspective on policy goals, purposes, and legislative intent, and the best source for doing so is ordinarily called the "legislative history." *Legislative history* refers to a set of official documents or transcripts of legislative hearings and documents accepted as part of the background material studied by members of the legislative committees that considered the matter at hand and framed the legislation that subsequently was passed into law. Legislative history is more readily available for acts passed by Congress, but it is also available at the state level. Legislative histories can be found in any law school library, statehouse library, or university library public documents department. The privately published *Congressional Quarterly* and the publication of Congress called *The Green Book* also contain legislative histories. See Note 8.

Step 3: Locate Staff and Committee Studies and Reports

Other sources of program goals (besides the preamble to the enabling legislation itself) includes *staff studies* prepared for use by congressional committees to study issues that may result in new programs or policies and amendments to existing legislation. Staff studies are usually considered reasonably authoritative sources for statements concerning the goal and purposes of public social policy and programs.

Step 4: Check Other "Official" Sources

There are two main authoritative sources for statements about the goals and objectives of social programs that entail federal funds or administration. One is the official biannual *Social Security Handbook*, published by the Social Security Administration and housed in all federal document repositories. (Nearly all university libraries are repositories or, if not, have this volume in their government documents collection.) Another main authoritative source is *The Green Book: Social Security and Income Maintenance Programs in the U.S.*, which gives exhaustive detail on these programs as well as legislative history.[8] Another source is the guide to means-tested income maintenance programs, published by the Food Research and Action and Council (FRAC) of New York City. The American Public Welfare Association also publishes a means-tested income guide. Other sources, more minimal in character, include brochures and factsheets available at local Social Security offices (e.g., "Understanding Social Security"); local Social Security employees are generally helpful sources for detailed information on programs if questions are specific (although they will not offer evaluative opinions on programs). Finally, the following Commercial Clearing House (Washington, DC) paperbacks are almost always part of the document collections of university libraries: *1996 Social Security Explained; 1996 Medicare Explained; 1997 Social Security Benefits* (including Medicare). The National Underwriters Association also publishes authoritative handbooks on Social Security and Medicare: for example, *Social Security Manual*, 31st ed.

In the search to document public social program goals and objectives, do not overlook the rich resource of official administrative rules and regulations. Although social program administrators commonly prepare public relations material intended to describe programs and program operations, these releases usually are of little help, and often are deliberately vague. Public program operations manuals, on the other hand, are very much public property, although they are not always easy to get (or to use, I might add). For example, the policy manuals for the public agency that operates state foster care and adoption programs routinely list thousands of rules and regulations. The *Federal Register* publishes into the public domain the multitude of rules and regulations and much else that pertains to federal agencies. Buried in these documents are explicit statements about goals and objectives, which, precisely because they are official, can be excellent sources of information on this point.

Locating Sources for Goals in Private and State-Administered Programs

Social programs that are entirely state-administered have documentary sources that are somewhat similar to those for federal programs, although exact titles and sources will vary by state. All state legislatures maintain current legislative history sources, and they can be obtained by a simple inquiry directed to the state legislature's library, usually located in the statehouse. In regard to state-administered programs, look for official committee hearings, staff studies, and reports to committees. A simple inquiry to your local state legislator will usually net a short and helpful discussion with an aide about how to locate the documents desired. Checking amendments to bills as originally written will net information on what was *not* intended. A letter to the legislator who introduced the bill may also provide helpful data about intentions and will usually be answered quickly. Social programs in the private sector and those run by local governments, despite their importance to the total social welfare effort of this country, may not have easy-access official public documentary sources if such programs are not enabled or mainly financed by the state. Therefore, such goals are often fugitive and can be very difficult to identify. Usually, some kind of organizational document is available that supports or mandates the program and therefore can serve as "legislative history." Talk to program and administrators and staff members since verbal reports from them are quite legitimate sources for goals and objectives. In fact, the objectives inferred from direct reports of the "organization-at-work" may be better than formal documents. In researching private sources, you may find organizations that have no overall goal-guiding operations; rather, each staff member has personal and professional goals for her or his practice. You may also find organizations that lack overarching goals, whose only goals and objectives are chosen by clients based on their own preferred outcomes. Based on certain assumptions, both cases are legitimate; note, however, that in neither case is a single social program or policy system in place. In effect, there are as many programs or policy systems as there are staff practitioners or clients. From another point of view, *no* public social policy or program is at work here, and therefore nothing can be analyzed.

Evaluating Program or Policy System Goals and Objectives: A Value-Critical Approach

Introduction

Having discovered the goals and objectives of a social program or policy system, how do we take the important next step, judging whether they are "good" goals and objectives?

Everything hinges on what standards we'll use to define "good." What makes for a good goal or objective depends on what we most "value" in the human condition, so it is on the basis of those values that we want to analyze and criticize goals and objectives. Doing that is what is called a *value-critical analysis.*

The first step is to declare some fundamental value positions. Note that these value positions are not only a matter of an individual analyst's personal perspective for I would like to convince the reader that some value perspectives are implicit in all analytic methods, including this one, and will set them forth here as affirmatively and persuasively as possible.

As the reader might expect, *value neutrality (the attempt to be quite objective) is specifically rejected* in a value-critical analysis because when it comes to statements about the human condition at least, the viewpoint here is that very little can be said in an objective way—such that it is not rooted in a strong set of value commitments and thus inherently subjective. Value neutrality is a seductive ideal, fundamentally negative in its effects because it obscures the inherently value-laden nature of almost all ideas about human affairs. More than a hundred years ago, Max Weber set us straight on this idea, making clear that all social science must be ultimately value-oriented and, further, that we can only save ourselves from utter subjectivity by making explicit (and in advance) the value positions that underlie our conclusions. The views of Weber and others like him are widely accepted but not universally and so readers may disagree here and find themselves in a smaller but still respectable company.

Let us begin by noting that in conducting anything called an "analysis," there must be an a priori commitment to the virtue of logic and rationality as a method of truth seeking. It's not trivial since there is a currently fashionable view that logic and rational analysis is mostly a tool for the oppression of the powerless. For example: "Logic, rationalism and hypothetic-deductive method are being seen not as ultimate strategies for mediating truth claims but oppressive standards that primarily serve to maintain the power status of the truthsayers."[9] Well, surely logic, rationalism and the hypothetic-deductive method are very powerful tools and, like all powerful tools, they ". . . saw finely for either good or ill" (as the saying goes). No doubt these tools have been used as "oppressive standards," but it is equally true that they have made a major contribution to literacy, free speech, participatory democracy, and the birth of the very ideas of minimum nutrition, safe workplaces and public health. It is hard to imagine any of those absent logic, rationalism, the hypothetic-deductive method—themselves the necessary equipage of the enlightenment/rationalist/scientific era of Western civilization. To reject a powerful tool because it can be used for bad purposes is extreme.

The preference here for rationality and logical consistency yields important things. How else might one have a basis for a belief that any program might actually solve a problem, any problem at all? Generalizing from prior practice experience is exactly one sort of act of rationality in the sense that any logical conclusion involves a thought process of the following kind: ". . . this (new) situation is like a former experience in important ways and since this strategy was successful before, *therefore* there is a good probability it will work again." Rationality and logic also give us the freedom from the bondage of using *only* prior experience in developing social interventions. Good thing, for as practitioners and social program designers, we are often faced with human conditions that no one has experienced! It is our good fortune that from within the heart of another sort of rationality (hypothetico-deductive reasoning) can come wholly new ideas for better social program designs, designs whose logical chain lets us "see around corners," that is, to have logical expectations for what we have never experienced. And, in that way, rationality provides grounds for believing that a program design might be successful even in advance of the actual trial run. As commonly said—"yes, that makes common sense," that is, it seems to meet logical expectations.

In the final analysis, I will argue, it is our North American cultural preference for control and prediction and thus the implicit commitment of our political process that demands a rational basis for public expenditures. Legislative, judicial, and administrative accountability demands it. At the level of ideals, public appropriations, in our North American way of doing things, are not distributed simply by virtue of having faith in the person who will spend them. So, it turns out that the political ideology of our society demands rationality as an instrumental means to just and fair dealings with citizens' money. It creates the necessity to have *advance* grounds for judging that a program will be adequate to answer the social problem of concern, equitable for prospective clients or user/consumers, and efficient in obtaining the most value for money expended. It has other virtues: It can provide a consistent standard for performance and a way of specifying how public social programs or policy systems should operate in order to usefully serve program participants as well as the public and collective good.

The reader might already have noticed two other examples of value positions inherent in this policy analysis method: *accountability* and the notion that *product counts.* That means that all social programs, public and private, must be accountable to their relevant funding publics. In the public sector, that means accountability to taxpayers, their elected representatives, and social service consumers. In the private sector, that means accountability to private donors and social service consumers. In its most general sense, accountability simply means that social programs must do what its funding sponsors expect while attending to the satisfaction of program participants. With regard to the former, goals and objectives of a public sector program must reflect their legislative mandates—and so reflect the will of the citizenry whose taxes pay for it. No mystery here: If the legislation and official regulations specify program funding for the purpose of jobs for poor people, then the goals and the objectives of the program system must specify exactly that. *Accountability means that the program must be willing to be evaluated on achieving outcome objectives for specified program participants, whatever else it may or may not do.* Is this the occasion for social control in social programs? Yes and often the case. Although surely it is not always a negative feature, practitioners should always be attentive to that issue and how it might negatively affect the people they serve.

The value position that *product counts* orients the major effort of the program to producing particular results, that is, verifiable outcomes or best results at least cost, whatever else it might do. The perspective here is that social policies and programs are implemented precisely to solve social problems, and their performance in that role is the ultimate measure of their worth. But although these outcomes have the highest priority, note that product is not *all* that matters since there are other matters of priority: A main example is the satisfaction of program participants and another is unanticipated negative side effects of programs and policies.

When we come to personal social services, there are some disconcerting problems with regard to this commitment to "product," this commitment to outcomes that are specified before a single consumer has walked through the front door. Think for a moment about how personal social services are so strongly characterized by "individualization" and how many involve an "empowerment" or "treatment" process. When they are directed at mental, social, and/or emotional disorders, those processes often belie specific outcomes or end products on the view that a treatment or empowerment process worth its salt concerns outcomes that go well beyond the scope of the defined social problem. Many human service practitioners prefer outcomes in personal social services, whatever the "problem" for which the person came for help, to be the prerogative of the consumer/ program participant. Personal social services conceived this way do not always appear to serve as a solution to the presenting social problem; for example, they might make it possible for a person to choose a different "path" for life, where that "path" might be concerned with some immediate and highly individual personal goal: a good friend, an intimate relationship, better housing, a reduced anxiety state are all examples. But, it may be quite plausible that attaining one of those more immediate objectives will create the conditions for *not* living a life driven by or at the mercy of a social problem such as, say, substance abuse, addiction, or spousal abuse. Experienced practitioners know that for many personal social services, the control of consumers over service outcomes constitutes a highly desirable general and radical freedom on the part of the person. And, further, to the extent that consumers *don't* control outcomes, social services can be characterized as authoritarian and strictly in the service of social control. Although those have their uses, they are a last, not a first resort.

But, when *services involve public funds, at some level they must concern the public, not solely a private interest.* So, does that mean that public social services must always deny consumer control over the direction (outcome) of the helping process? No, not quite, but it can unless program designers, managers, and practitioners take it as their task to make clear, to rationalize a connection between consumer control of outcomes, and making an impact on a social problem. No mystery here: At a practice level, think of how often it "makes sense" to engage a service consumer's interest by "working on" particular issues that are of immediate and pressing relevance, sometimes not those that seem directly related to the defined social problem and the goals and objectives of the program. That is, of course, a characteristic of the "strengths approach," now a common intervention strategy for social worker practitioners and social programs. At a policy level, those maneuvers must be related to service outcomes so they create a public understanding of their relationship to the public interest. It is an important policy-level responsibility common to all practitioners.

Recall that in the introduction to this method of social policy and program analysis, four general types of evaluation criteria were cited as necessary for each policy characteristic. In the remainder of this chapter, we will discuss each in order: (1) the fit of goals and objectives with the social problem analysis; (2) certain evaluation criteria specific to goals and objectives; (3) applying to goals and objectives the traditional economic evaluative criteria of adequacy, equity, and efficiency; and (4) those from the analysts' own perspective.

Evaluating the "Fit" between Goals and Objectives and the Social Problem Analysis

Because providing a solution to a social problem is, in our definitions, the manifest purpose of a social policy or program, the merit of any of its features must be judged by how it fits that purpose. Social policies and programs should *not* be designed in the abstract, no matter how strongly they stand as innovative or "good" ideas. This conviction also applies to features, such as policy system or social program goals and objectives, whose purpose is to keep the policy or program going in the desired direction, that is, toward solution (or mitigation) of the social problem. Thus, the fit, goal relevance, and objectives are of premier importance. Unfortunately, a number of social policies and programs are misdirected in this way.

Consider for a moment a program of public child care for working parents. Note at the outset how varied the objectives for such child care can be because definitions of the problem to be solved by such programs can vary so widely. Common objectives for preschoolers (for example) include: providing educational enrichment (develop preschool skills); providing safe and dependable substitute parent care during work hours; developing early cognitive and emotional creativity; providing nutritionally sound, emotionally stimulating, and health-attentive care. Program features of a multitude of day care settings are recognizable in that list. A neighbor who tends to fewer than three children in her own home but provides no explicit educational or creative stimulation exemplifies day care with a minimum of objectives—safe and dependable care. Alternatively, a local franchise of a national day care chain may focus on educational enrichment and development of cognitive and emotional roots of creativity, as well as program components having to do with nutrition, child health, safe care, and the like.

Imagine how different will be the objectives and organizational policies within these different programs. Behind all that is an implicit social problem analysis. In what follows, you will recognize the four elements of a complete social problem analysis (as described in Chapter 1): (1) problem definition, (2) causation, (3) ideology, and (4) gainers and losers. Thus, the favored definition of the social problem to be dealt with for the neighborhood scenario might be the parent's need to have a dependable person to be in charge of an infant during work hours and to feel at ease about the child's nutrition, physical safety, and health. Although this objective may preoccupy many (if not most) day care parents, that is not to say that other objectives are superfluous. The Montessori school scenario has a much more complex, theoretical, even elegant social problem definition in mind. Perhaps their basic concern might be expressed as the absence of age-appropriate stimulation to the child's cognitive and emotional capacities. Whereas preoccupation with a child's safety and nutrition, and the dependability of care may be present, the school or parents may demand more.

The point here is that goals and objectives must fit the social problem viewpoint to which the program is intended to be a solution, and so, for each different social problem/policy/program package, goals and objectives are likely to differ conspicuously. Demonstrating this "fit" is twofold.

First, it is shown by *the equivalence between the terms in the social problem definition and the terms in which the goals and objectives are defined.* Unless this fit can be demonstrated, it is possible that the programmatic solution is irrelevant to the social problem declared to be of interest. Of course, that is a major flaw to the extent that public expenditures are purchasing essentially irrelevant goods or services.

Second, the "fit" between objectives and the social problem analysis is shown by *equivalence between the outcome objectives and the independent variables in the causal sequence of the social problem analysis.* Thus, if the social problem analysis contains a causal chain in which the outcome (independent) variable is child abuse, the objectives of the program must relate to child abuse in some way (of course, there can be other objectives as well), but it is important that the same definitions be used. If, as actually occurs sometimes, program designers have developed a set or programmatic interventions targeted not on child neglect but on physical child abuse, then a serious flaw is involved. It is not difficult to make this kind of mistake in a field in which ambiguous definition is commonplace. It might be made because many continue to think of child neglect as simply a lesser version of physical child abuse—despite substantial research evidence to the contrary (concluding that child abusers inflicting serious physical damage are probably a breed apart). It makes no sense at all to contrive and implement an elaborate intervention directed toward a phenomenon that is entirely different from the one intended. The following sections address the second set of evaluation criteria—adequacy, equity, and efficiency.

Evaluating Goals and Objectives against Traditional Economic Criteria: Adequacy, Equity, and Efficiency

Adequacy

This criteria is applied by assuming that the goals and objectives are *actually achieved* and then asking to what extent will the social problem be reduced? In other words, are the goals and objectives "adequate" to their task? It is a useful question since it might avoid spending scarce money and effort to implement a program when an observant person can tell in advance it won't do the job. Be warned, however, that despite the utter rationality of the question, raising it may not win popularity contests: (1) if a program proposal is the cherished idea of some staff members, raising the question of whether it will do its job may well be taken as a personal insult and bring a hostile response; (2) no one may expect the program to be effective since the intention is only to satisfy a legislative constituency—and the organization will be embarrassed if that becomes public; (3) if the intention behind discussing a program proposal is only a media event to show some "effort" in response to current negative publicity for the organization, the question might embarrass those in command. Readers need to be alert to bringing unwelcome news. "Killing the messenger who brings bad news" is a saying as old as ancient Rome, but experienced practitioners have seen it happen (metaphorically) in modern bureaucratic organizations. The point is not at all to advise against raising issues, only to think before speaking and be willing to brave the consequences.

Traditional economists might want the question of adequacy of goals and objectives answered in terms of how much *reduction in dollar costs of the social problem* is expected. Assuming that the social problem analysis has set forth the relevant dollar costs, then the next question is what savings on those costs should be expected given maximum program success. If the social problem is medical care for the homeless, then some direct dollar costs are such things as emergency medical care for the homeless who are susceptible to physical violence, communicable diseases, and infections of various sorts associated with lack of ordinary medical care and timely treatment. The appropriate question is whether and to what extent the best possible program outcomes will reduce those (or other) costs. For example, one likely consequence of illiteracy is earning less than minimum wages and probable entitlement to such benefits as food stamps and housing subsidies. *Direct costs* are government expenditures like these, expenditures that would not be spent were the problem eliminated. There are also *indirect costs*, and those can be as great as direct costs, though they are more difficult to estimate with precision.

There are ways other than dollar cost reduction by which to make judgments of the adequacy of goals and objectives, however. Although "monetizing," that is, rendering outcomes in terms of dollars saved or earned, is probably the easiest way to do this task, the reader should notice that some goals or objectives don't lend themselves very well to dollar signs. That is often true for personal social service programs; think only of programs directed toward child neglect, for example. It is quite true that it is possible to monetize the negative effects of child neglect, as for the medical costs of malnutrition and the extra educational costs of special education for the learning problems of such children when neglect creates developmental lags. But although that is important, it may be more to the point to evaluate the goals and objectives of a program by asking about its impact on the number of reported incidents of child neglect in a community. Thus, one might evaluate the adequacy of the objectives of a screening program for mothers of newborns by asking how many or what percent of decrease occurs in the incidents of adjudicated child neglect.

Equity

Equity is complicated, but the basic standard is that citizens must be treated similarly by a social policy or a social program as a matter of fairness or justice. The complication is that there are two kinds of equity: (1) *proportional equity*, in which citizens receive benefits or services that are "in proportion" to their relative need for them, and (2) *absolute equity*, in which citizens receive benefits or services in absolutely equal amounts irrespective of their need. Thus, whether the program goal or objective treats one beneficiary the same as others turns on how equity is defined. Two families whose children receive the same standard course of vaccinations (rubella, DPT, etc.) irrespective of income or their ability to pay are an example of absolute equity. In contrast, here is an example of proportional equity. Suppose nutritionists say that it takes a minimum of $220 a month to feed a family of three at barely adequate nutritional standards. Those administering the food stamp program know that if such a family is to pay all its other bills (housing, utilities, etc.), it will only spend $100 a month for food, less than half what they ought. It is well known that at low levels of income, families will pay standard costs like rent and utilities, spending whatever remains on food since, unlike the preceding costs, they can buy more or less of it without immediately disastrous consequences. The food stamp program administrators reason somewhat like this: If a family of three with an income only half the poverty line is provided foods stamps worth $120 a month, it will create enough buying power for food so it matches the $220 per month standard. The heart of proportional equity here is that although benefits are not equal in dollars for everyone, the benefit given *creates* equal purchasing power for food. Notice that program participants can, in justice, be treated both differently and equitably. But if so, it must be justified by an argument that makes use of the proportional equity concept.

Statements of goals and objectives need to be clear as to whether absolute or proportional equity is intended. An example of a statement of objective that embeds proportional equity is: "The objective of the program is to provide transportation to the aged at a cost that, taking into account their earnings, assets, and/or other cash benefits, will not decrease their total spendable income for food and housing." If this program objective is implemented, program participants will get transportation at various costs, depending on what their other money resources are; those with high earnings or assets will have to pay and those with very low earnings might get a free ride. An example of a statement of objectives that embeds absolute equity is: "The objective of the program is to make elderly transportation available at actual cost." If this program objective is implemented, all program participants can use the transportation service at a set fee—the per-user actual cost of providing it—with the consequence being that the fee will be a greater burden on those with low earnings or assets compared to those with high wage earnings or assets.

Equity cuts other ways as an evaluation criterion for goals and objectives. In specifying particular target subgroups in the statements of objectives, some groups will inevitably get more benefits or services or resources than others. Some statements of objectives might express an affirmative action sentiment: "Transportation services will be provided, first priority, for those sections of the community in which ethnic minorities reside." The equity question here has several dimensions. If the ideological position is that ethnic minorities have been historically and systematically deprived of transportation, then proportional equity would justify the priority service given them in the preceding statement of objectives. On the other hand, if the statement of objectives specifies transportation services operated at the county level of government and specifies that they are to be focused on geographic areas closest to the county seat so they can link up with existing city transportation, the system will expand transportation opportunities for those who live on the city fringe but systematically deprive rural residents. The basic question is not answered solely by judging whether equity exists, but, if inequity exists, whether it is rationally justified as a good fit with the overall social problem analysis.

Efficiency

The efficiency criterion cannot be applied logically to the goals and objectives, basically because the concern of goals and objectives is restricted to *outcome*, whereas the concern of efficiency always lies with *means* to an outcome. The center of the efficiency question is always whether there is a better (least costly, more cost-effective) means to achieve a given outcome. Because goals and objectives must refer to ends and not means, the efficiency criterion hardly applies.

Evaluation Criteria Specific to Goals and Objectives

Statements of goals and objectives can be evaluated against the following criteria: clarity; measurability (which only concerns objectives not goals, of course); manipulability; concern with outcomes, *not* delivering services; standards for expected program performance; and specification of the target group at which intervention is aimed. These criteria apply primarily to goals and objectives, not to other operating characteristics.

Clarity

Goals and objectives can only be clear if terms are well-defined; a well-defined term easily distinguishes examples of things to which the term refers from those to which the term is closely related. In other words, meaning of the terms is not left to the imagination. Statements of objectives must be accompanied by definitions for terms whose meanings are uncommon or terms not in general use among the intended public. The following goal statement is unclear because its terms are not subsequently defined and probably are not familiar to most: "The goal of this policy is to raise the level of consciousness about work sharing and its benefits for the unit work group." Note that if the terms *work sharing* and *work group* were defined, the statement might be clear. For example:

> *Work sharing* means splitting one standard 40-hour week of a paid, skilled job into several parts of a workday, each part held by a different employee who works only part-time.

Work group refers to a group of people who are employed by and earn wages from the same employer, working in close proximity to each other at the same workplace.

What we have done here is simply to change the goal statement into what we could now call a statement of objective simply by making it concrete and observable.

The second definition holds a number of definitional options: One could loosen the definition (and include more people) by removing the qualifier "working in close proximity to each other." That would increase the number in the work group but, more important, it would scoop up a very different set of people than is referred to in the first definition. The first would likely include people in relationships usually defined as primary; the second would include those usually defined as primary *and* secondary social relationships. It is easy to see how fundamentally arbitrary definitions are. Choices here depend on the purpose for the definition: Is the interest actually in primary or secondary relationships? Of course, the phrase "raise the level of consciousness" is more abstruse, but it is still capable of definition. The difficulty is that it could mean so many different things that any one definition probably will seem arbitrary and strange to the ear. That may be true, but that is not a fatal flaw here. A handy idea to remember about definitions is the ancient distinction between genera and specie: One acceptable way of constructing definitions is to have the definitional statement tell the general class (genera) to which the thing defined belongs and then tell the things that make it different from all other members of that class (specie). For example, "raise the level of consciousness" means acquiring the cognitive grasp (genera, the general class of things to which this thing belongs) of the contemporary social realities that make work sharing a desirable work option (specie, the feature that makes this different from all other kinds of cognitive grasps).

Measurability

Unless statements of objectives are *capable of being measured,* they are of little use in administering or evaluating a program or policy. Remember, it is only objectives, not goals, to which the criterion of measurability applies. We will not talk about goals here because it is in their nature to be so general as to be immeasurable in principle (as discussed earlier in this chapter). To be measurable means to be quantified, even if only in crude fashion ("none, some, much"). In practice, it seems likely that any term can be measured; all that is required is to give it definitional substance. When definitions are neither given nor carefully constructed, they cannot lead to measurability and that is a serious shortcoming.

Manipulability

Some objectives concern factors that are just not open to change by any conceivable means—literally nonmanipulable. Just to make the point, here are some silly examples: "the goal is to develop in military service personnel the capacity to criticize their superiors in the civilian press." Or "the goal is to enable preschoolers to objectively evaluate their parents restrictions on their behavior." The terms in which goals are expressed refer to factors for which there is no rational basis for expecting change. What would it take to induce a military person to do the one thing that would be most likely to destroy a military career, as the preceding suggests? Probably not anything with which a social program would be capable. And, in the second example, isn't it true that the empirical data on the judgment processes of young children don't support their plausibility?

Sometimes arguments about what is plausibly manipulable appeal to the illogic of the ideas as against everyday experience. The more common use of this criterion calls for some kind of evidence from empirical research—historical, experimental— that would give a rational basis for believing that the variables in which objectives are stated are not open to influence. Consider an objective common among child abuse programs—preventing child abuse incidents. One common kind of prevention program looks to "remodel" potential abusing parents via certain kinds of program interventions, but note it must successfully predict precisely *which* children will be at potential risk. To date, no empirical study has been successful in doing so.[10] So, at present, goals and objectives derived from this kind of child abuse prevention program design would have to be judged negatively because it fails the "manipulability" test: successful intervention cannot occur when the intended consumers cannot be precisely identified. On the other hand, it has been clearly shown that a second abuse incident *can* be successfully predicted and objectives thus focused would pass the test presented by this evaluation criterion.[11]

The demand for evidence of manipulability is not overly constraining since it is entirely acceptable to declare a program to be an experiment. The consequence is to loosen the expectation of achievement and to adopt program objectives as *tentative hypotheses* rather than firm outcome expectations. Later in this book an argument will be made that social policies and programs ought to do more of just that kind of thing, given the limited state of our knowledge. Doubtless, the nature of our enterprise is experimental and exploratory.

Good things flow from this attitude. We are more free and thus more likely to notice unusual things happening when a program is fielded, things no one expected in advance. And because we are speaking about programs and policies that affect human beings, clarity that a program effort is experimental or exploratory is a necessary condition for alerting program participants to that fact; often, it is a legal obligation. Finally, it is only ethical to be straightforward about such matters in dealing with those who make program and policy funding decisions. Too often, and ultimately to our misfortune, policy and program advocates promise more than they can deliver.

Concern with Outcomes Not Services Provided

Concern with ends that are outcomes, not "inputs" or services provided, is another standard that statements of goals and objectives should meet. If you want to make coffee from coffee beans, you put coffee beans *into* the grinder (inputs), then you place the ground beans into the coffee maker and *out* comes brewed coffee (outcomes). No one would confuse the solid beans with the liquid coffee. The standard that must be met by statements of objectives or goals is that they must concern *outcomes, not inputs*. An example common in social work practice in the personal social services is making home studies, that is, those evaluations of the "goodness" or "fitness" of a home for a child in adoptive or foster family care or decisions having to do with which of a child's divorced parents the child should live. It is *not* acceptable to say that the objective of this social program is to "make home studies." Home studies are a means to an end, not an end in itself. A home study is surely not an activity that could stand on its own and be justified. There is simply no use for home studies unless they are necessary for a decision about a child. It is in this sense that we can say, in a commonsense way, that objectives and goals should be able to "stand on their own" as justified.

The Analyst's Own Value Perspectives in Evaluating the Merit of Goals and Objectives

At some point, practical public policy analysts will find that their own personal value positions will intrude on their enterprise. Recall a point made earlier that such value intrusions are important sources of bias and can only be made public to others and the audience for the analysis if analysts themselves are aware of their existence. So let us use some of the author's value commitments as examples of how these are likely to show up in judging the merit of social program or policy system operating characteristics. The concept of client empowerment refers to the idea that the fullest development of human potential takes place in an environment in which it is possible to bring one's choices (empowers those choices) into reality; taking charge of one's life is a common description. It is, at root, the simple idea that one's life can be filled with circumstances that grind into dust the ability to act on the choices one makes: too little money, time, opportunity, training, the moral support of others, skill, vision, energy, health. Valuing client empowerment implies strong medicine, strong constraints on social work and human service policy and practice goals and objectives. For example, in one instance, it might mean that in preference for doing things for people, a practitioner will work toward helping a client take charge, but it also may mean in another instance that the practitioner will take charge of organizing resources for people who (at that moment) cannot do that by themselves. Making available those resources is a means by which it becomes practically possible for the person helped to take charge. Without direct assistance from a practitioner (or others) in providing resources or access to them, taking charge of one's life in regard to housing and education is unlikely. Without training or skills or job opportunities, taking charge of one's work life is impossible.

Goals and objectives of social programs and policies will be preferred by the author-as-analyst when they reflect that idea—when they reflect the value commitments preferred. Now think of a shelter program for the homeless, the goal of which is to help its consumers avoid exposure to the elements; contrast it to one that *also* has goals and objectives reflecting empowerment goals, for example, service consumers learning how to do the following:

- Access medical care (empowering service consumers to maximum physical capacity)
- Access housing market facts and resources (empowering service consumers to search out their own housing)
- Access welfare income maintenance benefits plus skills in applying for a job (empowering service consumers to an independent income and all that implies for their ability to make other life choices)
- Support others who have social problems that are similar to their own (empowering them to help others)
- Form political constituencies for the homeless (empowering service consumers to exert political control over their own problems and work for political solutions of housing shortages, for example)

The last program or policy system will be preferred over the others simply because it has empowerment goals and objectives whereas the others do not. Do not be misled—the intent is not to imply that helping homeless people to survive is somehow trivial. The issue here is to stress how much better is the solution for the social problem whose goal also seeks to empower the homeless in a way that goes a distance toward assisting people to the point where they can work changes in their own lives and live in circumstances that allow them to pursue the choices they make freely. The fact that it might be preventive is important to me only because it reduces preventable basic human pain (always a value preference for almost anyone involved in delivering human services and because less recurrence is an efficient use of resources—it makes available those resources for better work with fewer people or for work on other important social problems).

Such value choices can be complicated because they are not benign in every respect or they sometimes impinge on the delivery of "best" or "better" services to everyone. That happens because a broad objective (like empowerment) requires so much in the way of additional program services. In a world where finite resources and demand for services exceed availability, doing more for some client/consumers often means doing less for others. When some get so much that others may get nothing, those with nothing are unlikely to agree that my value choice is a better one. Although I don't believe the preceding choice is always the best, in some instances, I am persuaded it is and here is the best case I can make for it. When a social program does only a little for everyone in need, it may be that a little can be worse (or at least not better) than nothing—that is, its contribution to the solution of the problem is either minuscule or may create even worse problems. Under many conditions, homeless shelter programs can be examples of the potential for that result. It is one thing for a shelter program to provide benefits in the aftermath of community disaster—tornadoes, hurricanes, earthquakes; it is another when the disasters are personal (or perhaps singularly economic). If a homeless shelter cannot provide enough services or benefits to make it possible to escape from the shelter, it can create a permanent resident population of those who cannot deal with the circumstances that brought them there in the first place; being "institutionalized" is not far around the corner. Before the advent of psychotropic medication for psychosis, mental institutions were very much in that position. Income maintenance programs like SSI, which currently has a maximum grant of $575 per month for a single person, will help people survive but not move beyond that level of existence. The viewpoint in this book is that one aspect of the empowerment idea is that it assumes that people are continuously changing organisms, so that new paths (sometimes, but not always positive and growthful) are necessary as environmental conditions, experience, and social circumstances change around us all. The idea is that social programs, policies, and practitioners *ought* to keep that in mind and see their work, their goal, as a continuous effort to enable human potential to come out from under the grind of circumstance—and perhaps even from the outcomes of what we tentatively call not very wise or good choices.

Some Special Problems in Evaluating Goals and Objectives in Personal Social Services

There are some special problems in applying criteria such as these in the personal social services as opposed to applying them to the delivery of public service utilities or hard benefits like cash and commodities. In hard benefit programs (food stamps or housing), the steps in delivering benefits are reasonably direct with few if any intermediate steps. Many personal social service programs or policy objectives can have many *intermediate steps* in a whole social treatment process. For a personal social service agency that deals with the social problem of unemployment, its plausible objective might be retraining of unemployed workers in certain high-demand skills for a particular local job market. Thus, learning to operate a word processor might be one of several objectives; others might include learning how to read city maps to find addresses of employers or learning interviewing skills and how to fill out job applications. If obtaining employment is the ultimate objective, then the preceding examples are clearly intermediate to the ultimate objective.

Many personal social service programs or policy objectives contain *intermediate steps* in a whole social treatment process. Processes cannot be legitimately included as terms in a statement of objectives—not because they are unimportant, but rather because they cannot "stand by themselves" as serious outcomes *if no other outcome happens* as a result. As soon as a tangible outcome can be concretely specified, for example the outcome of a psychosocial treatment—higher morale or less anxiety—it is exactly the tangible, and measurable outcome that can then legitimately be thought of as an objective. Indeed there might be several such intermediate objectives. They could clearly stand on their own as outcomes—almost no one would argue these days that it isn't ultimately a contribution to a worker's skill to be able to use a word processor. They "stand justified on their own" in a sense for which foster home studies could never qualify. There is no use for home studies except for decision making. There *is* a use for word processing skills almost anywhere in today's employment market. When intermediate objectives are present, they must be accompanied by other objectives to which they contribute with the full expectation that the program or policy will achieve both the intermediate *and* the ultimate objective.

Another problem in constructing program and policy goals and objectives in the personal social services is that objectives will, of necessity, be highly individualized because, after all, that is precisely one of the defining features of personal social services. Recall how "hard-benefit" programs such as OASI (Social Security retirement) are governed by strict entitlement rules and that entitlement is a matter of demonstrating one's membership in large groups (over age 65, Social Security contribution history)—no individualization there! Those rules govern everyone who applies and the objectives of the program are the same for all beneficiaries. Contrast that with personal social service programs like day care for the aged, in which the main feature is to set client/user goals that are unique to the elderly individual—increase social interaction, increase attention span, reduce anxiety and disorientation. Whereas many user/consumers might share some of these goals, not everyone would. So, it turns out that for each client there may well be an individual program; the individual learning plan for the education of the developmentally disabled is just another example. What is important is that in the abstract, the program has some goal that is applicable to all user/consumers. Increasing the socialization skills and personal comfort of the aged person might be one example; increasing learning levels for the developmentally disabled might be another. This interesting twist that characterizes personal social service programs adds an additional complexity to evaluating their goals and objectives, that is, the practical policy analyst must judge whether there is a fit between these highly individual objectives for user/consumers and the general goals to which the program is committed. And, of course, that is exactly the kind of value-critical judgment that the practical public policy analyst should be prepared to make.

Finally, the practical public policy analyst should keep in mind that the personal social services often have obvious *social control* objectives. On that account, personal social service goals and objectives should express them explicitly. For example, some organizations (courts and other legal and quasilegal agencies) that probation counselors work for have explicit social control objectives: mental institutions, youth detention centers, and camps are not very different. In fact, mental health clinics often have explicit social control tasks when they work with clients whose attendance at the clinic is court-mandated, whether for preliminary diagnostic evaluations or for treatment. When that is the case, organizational goals and client objectives should clearly express that. When a client is legally committed to residence at a state mental institution and the problem for which he or she was committed is, say, exhibitionism, then that behavior should be included among others in any statements of treatment objectives. Although it seems obvious, in practice, the principle often is violated in favor of others that ignore the very problem that created the basis for legal commitment. For example, a treatment program that increased self-concept, as desirable as that might be, will not be acceptable if it cannot show findings that such decreases, say, hostile behavior.

Human service and social work practitioners frequently are uncomfortable with social control purposes and they are easy to ignore. To conduct a value-critical analysis of personal social service programs, the analyst should look to see whether the program expresses those explicitly lest this feature be lost from sight. There is nothing intrinsically negative about the idea of social control or using public funds on its behalf. It is, after all, likely to be the reason the program is funded! To be clear on that matter with clients and organizational personnel is taken as a value position here in the belief that to obfuscate it only leads to serious problems with user/consumers who eventually will encounter it anyhow. Few of them are confused on this matter. Few adoptive parent/clients are confused about the fact that their friendly social worker who is supervising the last few months of their adoption actually can take their child away under certain conditions. Few children who are clients of social workers and human service workers in mental and penal institutions are confused about the fact that those workers exercise considerable control over whether and when and under what conditions they will be allowed to leave the institution. The value bias at work here opts for honesty and openness with clients; believes that "putting everything on the table," so to speak, is one of the conditions required for being helpful to people. Sometimes that may rule out the possibility of helping people achieve objectives that require close personal, trusting, nonauthoritative relationships. Nothing is gained and perhaps everything can be lost by avoiding the issue of the existence of the authority factor in relationships when in fact that is the case. Social program goals and objectives should reflect that.

Summary

A goal is a statement, in general and abstract terms, of desired qualities in human and social conditions. Goals are an answer to the question "What is the purpose of this program or policy?" All elements of a program or policy must be judged on the basis of their contribution to the program goals and objectives. The program or policy goals and objectives are the programmatic "measure of all things." When the goals or objectives of a policy or program are described they point to desired ends, not providing services. That is essential because a program or policy system with commitment only to providing service can never be held accountable but could continue service provision indefinitely despite no tangible results. Goals can be manifest (public and explicit) or latent (unstated). Whereas a goal is an abstract and general statement of desired outcomes, an objective is a specific, empirical, operational statement about a desired, observable outcome. For any given goal, many different (apparently divergent) objectives can be written. Goals can also be long-term and short-term.

There are several general types of evaluation criteria the practical public policy analyst should use in judging the merit of goals and objectives: (1) those that concern their fit with the relevant social problem analysis; (2) from which the meaning of the traditional criteria of equity, adequacy, and efficiency are drawn; (3) those that are specifically relevant to particular policy elements; and (4) the personal value commitments of analysts themselves.

A good fit between the social problem analysis and the goals and objectives of a program or policy system is a matter of demonstrating the similarity between how their terms are defined. A statement of a goal or an objective is clear if its terms are well-defined; a well-defined term is one that easily distinguishes actual examples of things to which it refers from those to which it is closely related. Unless statements of objectives are capable of being measured, they are of little use in administering or evaluating a program or policy. The criterion of measurability applies only to objectives, not goals. Many personal social service programs or policy objectives contain intermediate steps (not necessarily ultimate outcomes) in a whole social treatment process. Goals and objectives in the personal social services create special problems because they must be highly individualized. After all, that is precisely one of their defining features. The fact is that personal social services can be and often are mandatory and operate with quite obvious social control objectives. Personal social service goals and objectives should express those explicitly where that applies.

EXERCISES

1. Two of your friends are arguing: One says that the reason for high schools in the United States is to keep teenagers out of the labor market for as long as possible so there will be less competition, better pay, and more jobs for adults; the other says that the school district charter says that the goal of high schools is to teach teenagers the skills they need to get a good job. What does the material in Chapter 5 teach you about goals that would help you sort out that argument? Is one or the other or both right, and why?

2. The Indian Child Welfare Act (P.L.95-608, 95 Stat. 3069) (Sec. 3) says that "it is the policy of this Nation to protect the best interests of Indian children and to promote the stability and security of Indian tribes and families by establishment of minimum Federal standards for the removal of Indian children from families and placement of children in foster or adoptive homes which will reflect the unique values of Indian culture. . . ." It also says (Sec. 101[a]) that "in any State court proceeding for foster care placement of or termination of parental rights to an Indian child . . . the court . . . shall transfer such proceeding to the jurisdiction of the tribe (Tribal court) . . . absent objection by either parent or the Indian child's tribe. . . ."

Write a one-sentence goal statement and a one-sentence statement of objective from the preceding quotations, using your own words. Write a short paragraph justifying the difference between the two statements, telling why one is a goal and the other an objective.

NOTES

1. P. Rossi, *Evaluation: A Systematic Approach* (Beverly Hills, CA: Sage Publications, 1979), p. 58.
2. F. F. Piven and R. Cloward, *Regulating the Poor* (New York: Pantheon Books, 1971).
3. R. Merton, *Social Theory and Social Structure* (Glencoe, IL: The Free Press of Glencoe, 1957), pp. 51–53.
4. M. Rein, *From Policy to Practice* (Armonk, NY: M. E. Sharpe, 1985), p. xii.
5. Although there is a tendency in the literature to conclude that Congress in the 1930s never intended OASI to provide a living wage but to be a supplement to workers' savings, that is plainly not the case, as a reading of the legislative history of the Social Security Act will show. It defies common sense as well because Congress was well aware that almost no worker in the depression of the 1930s would have savings in this amount, either then or in the expectable future.

6. S. Geron, "Regulating the Behavior of Nursing Homes through Positive Incentives: An Analysis of the Illinois Quality Incentive Program (QUIP)," *The Gerontologist*, 31 (1991): 291–301.

7. J. A. Pechman and P. M. Timpane (eds.), *Work Incentives and Income Guarantees* (Washington, DC: The Brookings Institution, 1975).

8. U.S. Congress, Joint Commission on Labor, 1991, 2nd Session (Washington, DC: U.S. Government Printing Office, April 21, 1991). See also, Ways and Means Committee, House of Representatives, *The Green Book*.

9. D. Saleeby, "Building a Strengths Perspective for Social Work," in D. Saleeby (ed.), *The Strengths Perspective in Social Work Practice* (New York: Longman, 1997), p. 23.

10. D. E. Chambers and M. K. Rodwell, "Promises, Promises: Predicting Child Abuse," *Policy Studies Review*, 8(4) (Summer 1989): 749–793. The comments here concern "secondary prevention." Another kind is called "primary prevention" and doesn't require identification of individuals who are "at risk" of abuse (here children), rather it applies an intervention to a *whole* population to achieve its objectives (e.g., an educational program in child development undertaken in all high schools that is to raise the understanding of age-appropriate infant/child behavior in the general population of those who will soon be of child bearing age.)

11. Ibid.

6 Analysis of Types of Benefits and Services

Introduction

Because there are so many types of benefits and services, sorting them out is, unfortunately, a complicated matter. Here's one approach to it. First, consider social welfare benefits to be any income transfer in a *nonmarket* exchange. That means you count as welfare benefits any money you receive for which you haven't either labored or traded for goods of some kind. It is a common way to define welfare, and done that way, it includes anything from a free school lunch to a government guarantee of a corporate loan. Benefits thus defined can also include nonmaterial things like increased "power" over organizational decisions, positive discrimination like giving preference to the hiring of minority group members, as well as "expert services" like we all get from physicians and lawyers. That's because, ultimately, all of the preceding examples translate into cash. In this chapter, we'll be discussing common types everybody refers to as "welfare" benefits and services, but we'll talk about uncommon types as well. Criteria that can be used to judge the merit of benefits and services will be discussed. Finally, examples will be given of benefit packages to illustrate how benefit and services are commonly received in sets as well as singly.

A Classification Scheme for Benefit and Service Types

Practitioners need a clear grasp of the most common social policy benefit and service alternatives. This classification scheme will assume that any of these benefit forms are interchangeable—which may mean positive or negative consequences.[1] A benefit form can only be judged *relative* to the available alternatives, so it might help to see how, in very different ways, each benefit form could be used to solve the same social problem.

Assume that a low-income, working-class family has exhausted its insurance coverage for mental illness. Derek and Drusilla Orkney, both in their mid-thirties, have four children and live in a moderate-size urban area on the eastern seaboard. Derek is a welder in a manufacturing plant, and Drusilla is a waitress at a neighborhood tavern. The Orkneys' children range from age seven years to eight months. Drusilla is suffering from a recurring psychosis, an illness first diagnosed when she was fifteen. This is her fourth episode. She has delusions of being pregnant with the second Savior, fights with those who frustrate her low tolerance for contradiction, and hallucinates about visitations by the Holy Spirit. When agitated, she paces the floor and pays no attention to her appearance or to others around her. She cannot care for her children now; nor can she work. It is difficult to predict how long she will be unable to function. Derek also fears she will injure the children.

What different types of benefits could remedy or reduce the harm of this situation to the family. Consider Drusilla. Derek wanted a psychiatrist and inpatient psychiatric hospital treatment for Drusilla, what we will call *expert services*. These days, if Drusilla gets those at all, it will most likely be in a community hospital unit, perhaps operated as a part of her local community mental health center. Her hospital care has to be subsidized by public funds since she has exhausted her insurance coverage, and the reason tax money provides the subsidy is likely to be because the community considers illness a danger to her children—anywhere considered a social problem of importance. But the city or state that provided the funds could have chosen many other types of solutions (or partial solutions). Not likely in reality, but they could have chosen a policy that would simply issue a check to the Orkneys in the amount of the charges on presentation of the hospital bill. That is called a *cash benefit*. Even though the benefit is in the form of a check, the issue defining a cash benefit is how negotiable is the face amount. If it is exchanged for the face amount, it is a cash benefit. In the Orkneys' case, the benefit is both a cash benefit and for expert services.

In a later chapter, readers will be asked to think broadly about who gains and who loses from all forms of benefits and services, but let us here note a feature of cash benefits that is commonly overlooked: Cash welfare benefits also benefit merchants that welfare beneficiaries patronize. *A welfare dollar paid to a merchant (grocery store, clothing store, whatever) by a welfare recipient is the economic equivalent of a dollar the merchant receives from anyone else.* What is meant by that is simply that welfare dollars, like other government dollars, contribute to the economy by providing employment in retail establishments as well as in the wholesale suppliers who manufacture the goods sold by the merchant. It is not true that welfare dollars somehow vanish into the marketplace with no positive economic impact.

The policy options can become much more complex. Suppose that the public policy was to pay private hospitals to provide care for citizens afflicted with illnesses like Drusilla's, but rather than giving the citizens cash, the public treasury gave money directly to the hospital. If this amount of money in this case was directly related to the costs incurred by Drusilla, then this type of benefit is a *credit*. The public treasury *credits* the Orkneys' account at the hospital with a certain amount. Derek will pay the rest of their bill (if the government doesn't pay it all). As in the preceding example, there are two benefit forms here—expert services and a credit. If the public treasury pays the hospital for anticipated costs of the "average patient,"[2] a cost related to a group and not to any one citizen, the benefit looks more like a subsidy (more on this later). *Credits* and *vouchers* are prepayments or postpayments to a purveyor of benefits and services. The difference between a credit and a voucher is that a voucher is a written authorization to receive a benefit or service; the choice of purveyor is left with the consumer or beneficiary. The distinction is important because vouchers retain a good bit of consumer sovereignty. A credit is prearranged in such a way that the benefit or service can be received only by the purveyor chosen by the organization that provided the credit. An example here is the "grocery order" given to an applicant from local county or private funds, an "order" that can be redeemed only at particular grocery stores.

There are still other benefit forms that could be used as instruments of public policy. For example, a public policy could adopt a *subsidy* approach to help its citizens gain access to expert services for the treatment of mental illness. In return for a guarantee that the particular facility would serve all or a stated portion of low-income clients, the state could give hospitals 50 percent of their start-up costs and 70 percent of their net operating costs (or some fixed percentage of each). Even though the state is not directly paying the Orkneys' hospital bills, it is paying them *indirectly* through this institutional subsidy. The hospital may agree to accept the government subsidy as settlement for the account of any low-income patient. Once again, two benefit forms are at work here—expert services and a subsidy. There are a number of public subsidies at work in the United States. Government payments to purchase computers for educational centers; passenger railroad service operations; national, state, and local highway construction; the operation of community mental health centers; many day care centers; and the education of developmentally disabled children are all examples of public subsidies.

Note especially that what makes the subsidy a distinct benefit form for our purposes here is that the intended beneficiary may be several steps removed from receipt of the actual cash transaction. Also note that, as is the case with most other benefit forms, many citizens—other than those for whom the subsidy is directly intended—indirectly and substantially benefit from public subsidies. With respect to government subsidies to purchase computers for universities, students obtain a substantial benefit—they gain marketable computer skills they might not otherwise have. The computer industry is a gainer because it sells more machines, given the government subsidy. The Medicaid program, which subsidizes medical expenses for low-income patients, also benefits the hospital industry by picking up costs for services that hospitals cannot deny, services for which they cannot expect to obtain payment from patients. Hospital employees—including social workers—also benefit.

There is a small but useful distinction between market and wholesale subsidies. Those we've discussed so far are *consumer subsidies*, those in which the public treasury supplies monies to provide an indirect benefit to a particular population sector or group so as to serve the national self-interest. The focus of consumer subsidies, their intended purpose, is to benefit consumers, not producers. Consumer food subsidy is a common form of social welfare benefit worldwide. In Britain in past years, the price of bread, cheese, and milk has been subsidized at rates that reduce the price to the consumer some 21 to 40 percent. The government picks up the difference between the price grocers pay to the producers and the price received from consumers. *All consumers*, regardless of income, receive the benefit of this subsidy.

Market subsidies, on the other hand, focus on benefits for producers, not consumers. In a market subsidy, there may be no one who receives goods or cash supplied by the government treasury; nor is there always an identifiable product involved. Some agricultural market subsidies are a good example because the subsidy here is not cash or the availability of a product, but a guarantee of a particular price to farmers for specific crops they raise. Under certain conditions, market forces do not generate a price that covers the cost of production for farmers. So, wheat, corn, and soybeans, for example, have a "support price," and when market price goes below that, wheat growers will get the difference between the support price set by the government and the market price.[3] Note now that the intention of farm support prices is not only to benefit individual producer/farmers (though there is much disagreement over the issue), but in part (as declared) to ensure that the "family farm" remains as a viable unit in the U.S. economy and that those producer/industries that depend heavily on farmers as consumers are assured a strong market for their products (farm machinery, steel, rubber, fertilizer, and such). There are market subsidies in industries other than agriculture, of course. Scarce defense materials (such as uranium and tungsten and even tanker ships) are often in line for government subsidies because of their wide use in the economy and the government's wish to have them available should need arise.

None of the preceding exhausts the benefit forms by which the government could pursue its general policies. It could choose to provide expert services only to those who, because they were unjustly denied in the past, are in very special need. *Positive discrimination* is a benefit form that attempts to restore equity where inequity has prevailed in the past. Applicants for the benefit are not treated identically or equally. They get special treatment now as a way of remedying unequal treatment in the past. Affirmative action laws and certain administrative procedures are examples of positive discrimination, a special benefit made available to three groups—racial and ethnic minorities, disabled persons, and women—membership in which is, by public policy, deemed prima facie evidence of past discrimination with regard to employment. These groups are commonly given hiring priority for university faculty and many civil service positions. Clearly, there is little debate about the intent, although widespread public debate in the United States continues on whether the benefit of positive discrimination is a useful and/or effective means by which to right a wrong. Judicial decisions and state legislatures have recently prohibited many kinds of positive discrimination.

Three other types of benefits common in the United States are loan guarantees, material goods and commodities, and protective regulation. *Loan guarantees* have been a public policy favorite when the population sector of concern was the middle class or the business community. A common example is the FHA Program, which provided federal government guarantees of mortgage loans for private dwellings. If the home owner defaults, the U.S. government will pay off the loan. If no money changes hands, how can the loan guarantee be a benefit? It turns out to be a significant benefit because it will often result in a substantial loan from a bank when, without the guarantee, no money would be forthcoming and sometimes at lower interest rates. As with all other benefit forms, of course, others will benefit nearly as much as the home owner (the primary intended beneficiary): the home builder, the banker, the materials supplier for the home builder, to mention only a few. Loan guarantees are not made to individuals only. The U.S. government has made massive loan guarantees to businesses and whole sectors of industry. The 1990 bailout of the U.S. savings and loan (S&L) industry is perhaps the most extravagant example. It is clearly the most expensive federal intervention ever, with cost estimates currently running around $230 billion. It makes prior ventures along this line (including investment subsidies to the poor and middle class) pale by comparison. Note especially that these financial guarantees to S&Ls do not necessarily produce a single job or build a single unit of private family housing (arguably a predictable result of other government loan guarantees mentioned in what follows). Nor are main beneficiaries either the poor or the middle class, few of whom are large savings and loan investors. Indeed, S&Ls may once again be a financing resource for middle-class housing, but at the present moment, no one is making the case that there is shortage of such housing or no other financing resource available. Of recent memory are also the federal guarantees of loan monies to the Chrysler Corporation, without which the automaker would probably have gone bankrupt. Even New York City was bailed out of financial difficulties by a government guarantee of its debt. Slightly more removed in time is the loan guarantee to the Lockheed Corporation, without which the aircraft industry would have been minus one of its oldest and largest members. In the case of Lockheed, once again the primary economy is not the only beneficiary; aircraft suppliers and related materials industries also benefited.

An example of *material goods and commodities* (in-kind benefits) is the distribution of surplus farm products like cheese, flour, and bacon by the federal government. Although little remains of the formerly large Federal Commodities Distribution program, it still operates on Indian reservations. Goods and commodities are as tangible and valuable a benefit as a direct cash grant. *Protective regulation* is a form of protected access to a market. The most familiar examples are public utilities (an electric or natural gas company), but regulation is also applied to telephone companies and airlines. Protective regulation is a welfare benefit because some regulations virtually guarantee the utility an annual profit; an exclusive franchise to sell a product people believe they cannot live without implies that the company cannot help making money if only it prices its product at more than its anticipated costs, year by year. There are benefits to the public-at-large that result from protective regulation. When utility companies were first formed in the United States, many went bankrupt in the process of trying to meet the intense competition that emerged, and in some cases, the public had no service at all. One of the major justifications for protective regulation rests on preventing a repetition of that history. Airline deregulation, which allows virtually free competition among airlines, has resulted in a mixed bag of disadvantages and advantages: sometimes ultracheap fares but a worrisome reduction in service.

Finally, there is another benefit form that entails no transfer of money: *the delegation of power over decisions.* A typical example is the allocation of board of director positions to persons who are consumers of services or in some way are particularly well suited to represent consumers. This benefit encompasses the right to make decisions that serve the self-interests of the group with which the decision maker is affiliated. Of course, such a benefit is intended to benefit a group, not a particular individual. The issue of how much power is given in such instances and how much is necessary to make the benefit effective (what constitutes token representation and how much representation is required to constitute an effective bloc of power) will be discussed in Chapter 8 on service delivery systems. Notice here that these last benefit forms are not likely to be useful as a solution to Drusilla Orkney's problem; it would be an unusual social problem analysis that would suggest protective regulation, loan guarantees, or power over decision making as solutions for the Orkneys' problems. So, protective regulation is probably the limiting case with respect to benefit and service forms regarding the social problem of mental illness.

After considering all these various types and forms that government benefits and services can take as ways of responding to social problems, the reader should be mindful that governments don't necessarily *have to* respond with a program to deal with a social problem. In fact, they often don't respond at all! Politicians can make all sorts of responses to public concern about social problems. Sometimes they are simply the substitution of shadow with substance—window dressing hoping to pass for serious effort. A legislator or a public bureaucrat can express lots of indignation about the existence of a social problem, propose or actually investigate same at almost no political cost whatsoever![4] It is not the point that legislative investigations or departmental research aren't important, rather that in either case, it can represent *a lack of will* with respect to promoting actual solutions to problems if indignation, exhortation, and research aren't followed by serious proposals.

Summary of Types[5] of Benefits and Services

At least nine major forms of benefits and services are common in the U.S. social welfare system. They may be used singly or in combination; very often a single benefit may represent more than one benefit form. Whereas one form of benefit may appear to be obviously superior, the merit of any particular benefit form ultimately depends on the logic of its connection with details of the social problem analysis and the program or policy goal. The forms of benefit are summarized in Table 6.1.

TABLE 6.1   Major Forms of Benefits and Services

Benefit/Service	Definition
Material goods/commodities	Tangible benefits (e.g., food, shelter, clothing)
Cash	Negotiable currency, exchangeable without loss in value
Expert services	Skilled, knowledgeable performances by credentialed professionals
Positive discrimination	Benefits directed to protected groups to redress past inequities
Credits/vouchers	Prepayments or postpayments to purveyors of benefits and/or services. A *credit* can be used by a beneficiary only at purveyor(s) chosen by the organization providing the credit. A *voucher* can be used at purveyor(s) chosen by beneficiary.
Subsidies	Payments made to a third party (e.g., federal funds to private hospitals)
Government guarantees	Government promise to repay loan in event signatory defaults
Protective regulation	Grants of exclusive or near-exclusive right to a certain market as a result of lack of competition
Power over decisions	Right to make decisions that serve self-interests of a particular group with which decision maker is affiliated

Multiple and Interrelated Benefits

It would be a mistake to leave the reader with the conclusion that most social policies and social programs pursue their objectives through single benefit or service strategies. Although there are instances of that, it is not the general case, especially in relation to programs that intend to deal with the social problem of poverty. It is common for citizens to think of programs like Social Security or even unemployment security as providing only a single benefit, but in fact eligibility for one benefit form very often automatically qualifies a person for multiple benefits. The fact of interrelated benefit packages certainly makes the analysis of social policy with respect to benefit forms, in particular, a lively and complex venture. It is not surprising that programs and policies should have more than a single kind of benefit; after all, we have already seen that multiple goals or objectives are commonplace. Where that is the case and where such goals are diverse it would be expected that different benefit types and thus multiple benefits would occur. Lewis and Morrison found that multiple benefits can occur in two major forms: (1) benefits from one program can alter benefits in other programs and (2) program benefits can change personal tax liability.[6]

The U.S. Unemployment Insurance (UI) program is an example of a benefit that generates multiple benefits: eligible, involuntarily unemployed workers might receive both a cash payment, services from the state vocational and rehabilitation service, and referral to employers searching for workers. The purpose of rehabilitation services is to retrain the employee and to provide trained and ready-to-work employees for employers. Maintaining the stability of a large workforce for the economic enterprise of the country as well as for relief of unemployment is a goal of the UI program. The TANF program (Temporary Assistance to Needy Families) is another example of a highly complex package of benefits and services. It is difficult to elaborate because of interstate variation, but the list that follows characterizes the most general case: a cash benefit, a medical card, special food allowance for infants and pregnant mothers, vocational training, family planning services, and so forth. Notice that elements in this benefit package are mostly compulsory: vocational training programs and job searches are compulsory for mothers once their children are three years old. Sometimes "benefits" can be used punitively against clients: sterilization, family planning, and abortion. Further, some program policies automatically disqualify a recipient from benefits from another program. We will discuss those complex examples in Chapter 10, which deals with program and policy interrelationships.

Criteria for Evaluating the Merit of Benefit and Service Types

Stigmatization, Cost-Effectiveness, Substitutability, Target Efficiency, and "Trade-Offs"

Whenever there is a benefit to be given in remedy of specific tangible need, it can be given in the form of cash or it can be given it in the form of directly consumable articles (e.g., food or clothing). The question is: "Which form is best, why, and from what point of view?" Almost all U.S. public benefits available in maintenance programs could be given in-kind. The issue touches on more than income-related benefits. Think for a moment about the delivery of medical care benefits and services. A cash approach would give dollars directly to families in need, that amount equivalent to whatever was the price of the necessary medical care. This benefit is most commonly given not in the form of cash, but in the form of a credit or voucher—a strategy that is more related to an in-kind benefit than a cash strategy.

Such examples serve to illustrate how the evaluation criteria apply to this general question. From the consumer's point of view, the major difference is the degree to which a choice can be exercised with regard to the goods or services delivered—the evaluation criterion we earlier called *consumer sovereignty*. From the benefit giver's point of view, the major difference is the ability to exercise control over the nature of the article and the way it is consumed—the evaluation criterion we earlier called *target efficiency*. If a family needs cheese and you give them $5 to buy it, the family can decide whom to buy it from, when to make the purchase, under what conditions, and at what price—an example of maximum consumer sovereignty. If you give the family a letter telling the cheese store to give the family $5 worth of cheddar and to add it to your bill, the choices that can be made by the family are thereby limited. But notice that from the point of view of the benefit giver (the person who is paying for the cheese), it may be important to restrict the choices. For example, the benefit giver may get a special price from the cheese dealer if a great deal of cheese is purchased this way and our cheese dealer can purchase more economically if he can count on volume sales. Not only that, the merchant knows that no advertising expense is incurred. Thus, the benefit giver is able to help more hungry people because cheese can be purchased for less in an in-kind, rather than a cash, benefit form. Under this condition (but *only* this condition), giving the benefit in an in-kind form satisfies the evaluation criterion of cost-effectiveness—the benefit is delivered at a cost that is effectively the lowest relative to the other available and practical forms and means of delivery.

Note that it is also true that the benefit goes directly for the specific social problem of concern—hunger. This is an example of the evaluation criterion called target efficiency, a virtue here because the efficiency involved makes it possible to benefit more hungry people. There is not much else to do with cheese except eat it, though a genuinely imaginative person might use it to catch mice, sell it to a neighbor at a cut-rate price, or trade it for another commodity. And, of course, there is a well-known street trade in food stamps. Best estimates are that they sell for around 50 cents on the dollar of face value in most urban centers.

Here are the arguments against the preceding conclusions. With regard to the lower expense of in-kind benefits, they say, it is not entirely clear whether economies of scale work in a way that inevitably yields a lower unit cost than cash (and thus generate a cost-effective benefit form). A person can take the view that the only way to establish a true cost is through an exchange in a free market, even a cheese market. How can the benefit giver really know that the price charged by the cheese merchant was the best price on that day for that amount of cheese of that particular kind? Whereas the price quoted the in-kind benefit giver may have been the best price the benefit giver could have obtained that day, suppose there was a cheese crisis the day following; if the family had cash with which to deal, they might have obtained twice as much cheese for half the price. On the other hand, the cheese merchant may have had bad luck selling his Swiss that week and would've sold twice as much to the family for half the price. (Of course, it might also have worked in exactly the opposite direction.) The same argument raises an objection to an extension of social control via the purchase of cheese. The cost to the family is a lack of consumer autonomy, and that makes them even more dependent and less able to cope with the stresses of life. After all, this argument goes, independence and self-reliance are built on experience in such small matters as deciding whether to buy cheddar, swiss, or mozzarella. Notice how important are the details, for it is on them that the ultimate conclusion depends.

Notice the *trade-offs* operating here between the various evaluation criteria. A trade-off occurs when the policy system has to suffer some disadvantage in order to get another advantage. In general, benefits delivered in the form of cash increase consumer sovereignty and reduce target efficiency. Another example of trade-offs is with regard to programs to reduce poverty. When such programs create low unemployment (a virtue), economists believe that they will invariably increase inflation (a vice) as more employed workers become consumers with money to spend. Although considered by economists to be a "side-effect"—and certainly it is in the sense that it was not intended—it is undeniably an important effect on the lives of most people. But then it pays to notice that economists aren't always right: In the 1994–1998 period of historically low unemployment rates, inflation did not, has not, appeared as economists predicted.

Somewhat more serious is the argument that the price of in-kind benefits is *stigmatization*. When the consumption or acquisition of benefits is public, certain kinds of items become associated with "being on welfare," and negative attributions are made to those so identified. Although someone seen eating a slice of cheddar cheese attracts little attention, it certainly is the case that disparaging comments are made to people who spend food stamps in grocery stores (a mild form of in-kind benefit). And it certainly is the case that children are cruelly insulted when "welfare tickets" are required to be presented in school lunch lines. According to Terkel, local welfare agencies bought certain kinds of shoes and dresses during the depression, and those who wore them were sure to inspire negative comments from others.[7]

Some of these objections to in-kind benefit forms do not apply in all instances; it is surely not the case that all noncash forms stigmatize recipients—not all consumption or delivery of the article or good is public. For example, one way to avoid public consumption or delivery of foodstuffs in a noncash form is to use a subsidy method that was common in England. If the U.S. government wished to increase the nutritional level of its low-income citizens, it could subsidize the price of a popular food to the point where it could become the least expensive, most nutritious food available (e.g., bread or milk products). The public treasury could subsidize the bakers or grocers, perhaps 40 cents a loaf; every month, those vendors would tote up how many loaves they sold and submit a bill to the public treasury. In return, they would agree to sell bread for half the former price, maybe 35 cents a loaf. Thus, the consumer gets bread at a reduction and the baker or grocer still makes a profit. Would the consumption of bread increase? Very likely. Would consumers be stigmatized for buying bread? Not very likely, because everyone pays the same price. Would the benefit go only to those who "really" need it? No, because there would be considerable "seepage" to those not in low-income brackets (again, a question about the target efficiency criterion). Would this form of the benefit be more cost-effective than cash? That question can be answered only through the empirical study of increased nutrition as a result of the increased use of the subsidized foodstuffs. The increase in nutrition resulting from the cash-benefit strategy would also have to be studied and the net results of the two compared.

Note that the cost of achieving the nutritional goal is the cost of the subsidy for the foodstuffs actually bought by the poor; the cost of the destigmatization of the in-kind strategy is exactly the cost of subsidizing the foodstuffs bought by the nonpoor. Thus, in this case, the exact cost of the "trade-off" can be specified. Those who strongly support cash benefits argue that such a benefit form clearly has an advantage along the lines of ensuring consumer sovereignty by means of which receivers maintain control over when, what, and how things are bought. From the consumer's point of view, that autonomy is a major issue.

The Political and Public Administration Viewpoint

But, how does all this look from the benefit giver's view, the perspective of the legislature, and the public program manager? Politicians and bureaucrats have their own preferences for benefit forms, as well as evaluation criteria of their own. Linder and Peters think that one such is *administrative complexity*, for example.[8]

It's only natural to expect that public administrators will value a benefit form that is simple rather than complicated to administer. It would seem preferable to administer a fairly simple program delivering a partial cash subsidy to the elderly to pay part of their winter heating bill rather than administer an in-kind commodity program for the same purpose—one in which the benefit would be gas or oil or electricity (or cow chips for that matter), which the government owned and would deliver directly to consumers. Think of the problems of storage, delivery, services, and all the rest. A cash benefit places the responsibility on the beneficiary for obtaining the product needed and thus avoids the administrative complexities. Or, consider a program that delivers services for severely mentally ill children. Such a program may involve such complexities as administering income or asset tests to a wide variety of income levels (e.g., to determine whether to charge for hospitalization); coordinating the program activities of a wide variety of professionals; facing high costs per case and "treatment" strategies of uncertain and sometimes controversial validity to consumers potentially capable of deviant and antisocial behavior. On the other hand, the public policy may choose to deliver this benefit in a form that simply subsidizes the costs of such services in the private sector by the consumer. In this case, the public administrator looks to the cost issues and struggles with determining whether charges are fair and whether services were actually delivered, but certainly that is less complex than taking responsibility for their actual delivery. The form taken by the benefit is determining here. Material, hard benefits are obviously simpler to administer than personal social services, which are often intangible and often controversial as to their effectiveness. It is quite likely that less complex practices also entail *low administrative cost*, another evaluation criterion of preference to public administrators and political figures who must account to the public in such matters.

Another evaluation criterion common to public administration and the political context is the extent to which the benefit form is *adaptable across different kinds of users*.

A subsidy (equivalent to cash) is obviously quite adaptable to different kinds of users: those who heat with gas versus electricity; those who live in apartments versus their own homes; those who live in rural areas versus central cities. An in-kind benefit may not be so adaptable across the diverse users in those examples. *Political risk* is also an evaluation criterion in this context; for example, the level of public visibility of the benefit form may be an issue here. The cash-equivalent subsidy for the winter heating program for the low-income elderly is quite invisible in that such programs can be handled via the U.S. mail. Note, however, that even if benefit receipt were visible, in this case it might be a political advantage rather than a liability; the viewpoint in our society is that the low-income elderly are surely "deserving poor," and that a politician who helps them projects the image of a social and moral conscience—good political images, no doubt. Contrast the level of political risk via the high public visibility of a program that generates benefits in the form of psychiatric services for severely mentally ill children. Because such children are capable of social deviance, they can be highly visible to a sensitive public and if the benefits (no matter how great or obvious the need for them) are delivered to a population group that is considered deviant, the political risk is high. It is widely believed among social historians that the popularity of mental institutions as a benefit form for the severely mentally ill or shelters for the homeless are, in the first instance, appealing to politicians and public administrators simply because such institutions effectively reduce their visibility to the public (hence the political risk) of the targeting social problem and the people who are subject to it.[9]

Finally, another evaluation criterion, *potential for failure to reduce or soften the impact of the social problem*, should attract the attention of the reader. There are few social programs that have an unmitigated record of success. New programs should actually be thought of as experimental ventures and should be proposed to decision makers as exactly that. Too many unkept promises, too many disappointments on the part of those who fund programs create an enduring pessimism that will come to haunt social program providers in the future. This evaluation criterion points to that issue; surely, before politically astute legislators make a public commitment in support of a social program, they make calculations of their potential for failure. Those who seek funding should be prepared to make statements about the probability for success of their program design. Further, they should also be prepared to make proposals as clear experiments on ideas that have no history. Experimental failures are not a moral mistake; program failures, for which success has been widely advertised, are immense political mistakes.

Criteria for Evaluating the Merit of Benefit Types: Consumer Sovereignty, Coercion, and Intrusiveness

This section considers an evaluation criterion that is preferred by this author/analyst: *consumer sovereignty*. One argument for its generally positive effects is that it allows for making choices. The cash benefit expended contributes to the support of the general public economy in ways that in-kind benefits cannot. Cash benefits support ordinary businesses and ordinary employers and employees. In-kind benefits, if they are to achieve their major advantages of economy of scale and expense reduction, must enter a special market at the producer and wholesaler levels—certainly not the same retail market corridor used by the ordinary citizen/consumer. Support of that market "bypasses" many "free markets," and in a way, that costs jobs because employers will not need the employees that are created by the additional cash demand for goods and products. In the long run, this argument speaks to the appealing idea of creating more employment and more taxes paid by a mechanism that remains faithful to a cash market system; cash benefits ensure that "the consumer is king." The point is that, in contrast to in-kind benefits, cash benefits have some (albeit limited) capacity for welfare-expenditure reductions just because cash benefits create some free-market employment and in-kind benefits don't (in general). One wouldn't expect that free-market advocates would prefer a welfare benefit form that takes welfare beneficiaries *out of the free market* in the ways outlined before. Radical free-marketeers often find in-kind benefits attractive on the view that in-kind benefits are socially stigmatizing and thus makes "welfare" unattractive.

Still there are those who seriously advocate for in-kind benefits. Alva Myrdal, the 1983 Nobel Prize winner in economics, is an example. Most of the arguments discussed before can be read in greater detail in her work.[10] However, Myrdal makes two other points we have not covered in the above and that are worth noting because they concern cogent arguments from an advocate for in-kind benefits but about their limitations. The first is that the issue of consumer choice is not very relevant when it comes to benefits targeted primarily toward children; children seldom exercise much consumer choice in poor families. The second is that in-kind benefits cannot be seriously preferred where family income is not adequate in the first place. In the last analysis, Myrdal comes out for restricting in-kind benefits to secondary needs, nonbasic food, shelter, and clothing. With that view, then, it would seem that the kinds of benefits Myrdal really advocates as appropriate for in-kind forms are items such as medical care, education, perhaps clothing, but surely expert services.

The issue of *substitutability* of goods, also important to Myrdal, refers to the possibility that a public policy or program the intent of which is to increase food purchases, for example, may not do so because more food is *not* purchased because the family uses food stamps to purchase the same amount of food they would have bought ordinarily; the money released by the availability of food stamps can then be used to buy other commodities of choice; the net gain, then, is not necessarily in food items. For example, the socially conforming family may use the extra purchasing power to buy books or more vegetables for the children. The less socially conforming may use it to buy illegal drugs, clothes, or a good time. Substitutability is an important idea because it shows how the in-kind benefit, when it concerns items that are vitally necessary for survival, may not always be an effective way of controlling the consumption pattern, amount, or kind of benefit received. The same argument might be made with respect to the provision of vouchers for medical care, physician prescriptions, and credit for child care or work clothing, for example. Substitutability is probably a criterion that has wide relevance to the evaluation of the merit of benefit forms, whatever those benefit forms might be.

Consumer sovereignty is a virtue because it works against coerciveness and intrusiveness of government in the lives and private affairs of citizen-recipients of public benefits. *Coerciveness and intrusiveness into private lives* should be conceded as an important criteria for evaluating benefit and service types. It is important for readers to remember that intrusiveness into private affairs can violate a citizens right to privacy—which itself derives from constitutional provisions. Being a recipient of public benefits doesn't change that. Obviously, some types of benefit and services are worse offenders than others in this respect. The greatest potential for this offense is when beneficiaries are dependent on public benefits for their very physical survival. That would direct us to means-tested programs like TANF, Food Stamps, or SSI for the disabled or aged. Their means tests must be repeated at intervals in order for the program administrators to carry out their responsibility to see that beneficiaries are still actually eligible: for example, beneficiaries may be living a shared life with a household member who is working and earning but not be reporting it as household income. Notice that reporting it requires revelation of the beneficiaries personal relationships, where that would ordinarily be considered "private affairs" were the person not a welfare beneficiary. One of the reasons means tests are objectionable is that they cannot easily avoid this kind of intrusiveness. But notice in contrast programs like Social Security Retirement and Disability, which are usually means tested but only at the level of individuals not households. No need there to be concerned about who else is sharing a household, a bed, or an income as in TANF or Food Stamps.

AFDC, in particular, had a history of notorious intrusiveness. The best example is the public welfare staff/County Prosecutor "night-riders" in Newburgh, New York, who routinely stationed themselves outside recipients' dwellings after dark to see who came and went. It was a county-administered program at that time and the local policy concerned what was called the "man-in-the-house" rule: Any recipient who had a "man-in-the-house" (anytime after dark presumably) lost their benefits (illegally as it turned out). The point is that the eligibility rule has to do with who shares a household income, *not* with who sleeps together. Besides being a violation of citizens' privacy rights, knowing that there was a "man in the house" doesn't necessarily tell you anything about household income sharing, though recipients were disentitled just on that basis. The reader shouldn't conclude that this is an argument against administrative rules, rather it is an argument about how such rules should be applied with due respect for their legality. And it is advice to practitioners to be alert to abuses of that kind.

Of course, the reader must realize that there are social programs whose very nature it is to intrude into private affairs, the obvious example being families whose children are being severely physically abused. Notice that the issue there is social control but of a kind that *is legally sanctioned.* Although that cannot justify just any kind of intrusion or coercion, it is an important distinction because when the intrusion has occurred by court order, it also means there is a way of remedying abuses through the court system and the legally required defense attorney. In contrast, administrative, extra-judicial coercion and privacy intrusions occur buried in organizational privacy, without clear and ready remedies.

Criteria for Evaluating the Fit of the Benefit/Service Type to the Social Problem Analysis

Whatever the type of benefit, the basic question is whether it "fits" the social problem analysis, that is, "fits" compatibly with the definition of the problem. One way to approach this question of "fit" is to look at what the problem definition implies as the most promi-nent "needs" of the people who have the problem and ask whether the benefit the pro-gram delivers is relevant to any of them. If it is not, then the benefits are clearly off target and irrelevant to the social problem. They may even be desirable yet not a relevant ben-efit. Think of an after-school recreational program for children who are disruptive in classrooms. As desirable as this recreational program might be (perhaps it provides after-school hours supervision for working parents when no adult is at home), if the program cannot make a case for some linkage with classroom behavior, then the program fails the "fitness" test. Notice that you might create a "fit" by a design for the recreational pro-gram that tailors itself to outcomes that are relevant to decreasing disruptive classroom behavior in some way. That is, of course, exactly the point: If the tailoring is a strong, the program activities would likely be much more specific than just simply "recreational"—recall that the definition of recreation is "doing what you want, when you want."

The policy and program analyst should also look at the social problem theory and, in particular, its derivative—the social *program* theory. Note that program theory will specify some set of factors as preferred outcomes and describe how to set in motion a chain of events (or processes) to obtain just that outcome. The benefit/service type must be one of those events, causal antecedents likely to set this chain of events in motion. And, there must be a plausible and logical argument as to why this benefit would be ex-pected to have that result. That is what "fit of the benefit/service type" is all about. If that argument is not there, then there is no "fit."

There are some historical examples of bad consequences as a result of this lack of "fit" with the social problem analysis. In the 1970s, federal payments to states for foster home care were raised to 100 percent of state costs. There was an entirely innocent mo-tive on the part of the U.S. Congress: States complained that they didn't have funds to provide all the foster home care they needed to protect children from abuse and neglect. The legislation and the federal dollars appropriated made cost-free foster home care avail-able to states. The benefit/service was a bad "fit" to the social problem of concern. The so-cial problem wasn't just the lack of foster home care—couldn't be, since foster home care is never more than a means to some other end. In this case the "bad thing" that identifies the social problem was the neglect and abuse of children. Clearly, foster care protects chil-dren from immediate harm, but it doesn't by itself change anything for next year or the year after that. As it happened, within the year, there were massive increases in the num-bers of children removed from their homes and placed in public foster home care facili-ties. It would appear that cost-free foster care created large-scale overuse of this service.[11] Not only that, many believe that cost-free foster home care funding was a major factor in children continuing in long-term foster care, "stuck" there for interminable periods. That phenomenon came to be called *"foster care drift,"* a phrase referring to children who nei-ther return to their own homes nor are placed in permanent adoption. Foster care drift has bad consequences: Many children in foster care for long periods literally lose their place in families since families are living, organic things, changing with age/stage development of their members and adapting to the surrounding social and economic circumstances. *The program of cost-free foster home care actually created a whole new social problem*—foster care drift—an outcome that should be kept in mind when initiating new social programs.

It is a great temptation for legislators, policy makers, and social practitioners alike to believe that a personal social service can (somehow) substitute for a necessary material need. It is almost always a mistake to believe that job training can provide a livelihood when the economy itself is not at that moment providing jobs for that particular person, that various "counselings" can help a mother find a way to deal with an aggressive child acting out when she has to work two jobs and twelve hours a day in order to feed and provide shelter for her family. That is not to say that personal social services are never effective, only to say that they can only be effective for people who are at least minimally fed, housed, and clothed. It would seem to be obvious, but the history of the provision of social welfare benefits in the United States shows that important and very costly mistakes can be made in that regard. In legislating the 1962 amendments to the Social Security Act, social workers and other human service proponents convinced Congress that personal social services should be institutionalized as a major strategy against the problem of poverty. It wasn't exactly a new idea—the emergency relief legislation of the depression era in the early 1930s had provided for special units of social workers to be available for difficult cases on an individualistic basis to those who were poor and/or had personal problems.[12] Prior to that time, private charitable agencies as far back as the Charity Organization Societies of the mid-1800s included social workers as part of a system to tailor cash assistance to individual characteristics and to plan and implement service and benefit delivery. In its 1962 amendments, the Social Security Act provided the first federal statutory instance in the United States for the general provision of personal social services to families on relief. According to Morris, at the same time Congress increased the federal dollar match (to state funds) to 75 percent for this purpose as if to underscore their commitment to the "rehabilitation" of the poor via personal social services.[12] This effectively put into practice the idea that services were an inextricable part, if not the major strategy, for a solution to the problem of poverty. The social problem viewpoint was that the cause of poverty was an interaction between lack of material resources and some personal attribute (attitude, cultural approach to work) and was amenable to change by a service strategy: family, group, and individual counseling; job and parent training; referral agencies; and service coordination, which avoided duplication of services. Indeed, the very name of the federal agency responsible for basic income maintenance programs (e.g., AFDC) was changed to the Family Service Administration.[13]

Congress was convinced to increase appropriations by hundreds of millions of dollars for services and the training of personal social service workers on behalf of those ideas. Federal expenditures for personal social services increased from $194 million in 1963 to a billion and a half dollars by 1972.[14] Unsurprisingly, services weren't successful in reducing poverty. The money was directed at what was perceived to be the shortcomings of individuals rather than the shortcomings of the economic system. The mistake was to think that these services could somehow substitute for the problems of an economy that created most of the poverty in the first place.

Here is an instance of a social problem analysis shown by subsequent events to be dead wrong and it reveals, on the one hand, the limitations of the criterion of fit with the social problem analysis. On the other hand, it shows how important it is to remake the social problem analysis when that is the case. An obvious alternative hypothesis is that the social problem is caused by external and environmental, not personal, attributes. Such errors are common mistakes, evident in much of social welfare history of the Western world. Modern instances of comprehensive job training programs and quintessentially personal social services that offer training in job skills, job search, and job application are relevant examples. The best training, education, and job referral systems cannot make up for a bad job market or low earnings combined with (for example) high child care and transportation costs. The English historian Barbara Wootten puts it this way: "It is always easier to put up a clinic than tear down a slum . . . we prefer today to analyze the infected individual rather than . . . the infection from the environment."[15]

But it isn't that difficult to take all this history into account and then recreate a social problem analysis based on a broader economic and social system viewpoint. If one did, the implication would be reasonably clear that the most obvious cause of poverty is lack of money and the most obvious remedy is via material benefits: cash and/or adequately paid, full-time jobs. History shows that such jobs can be increased by a wide range of governmental public policies including (but not limited to) the following:

- "Trickle-down" policies that give tax cuts to employers and investors to invest in new industrial plants and equipment to create new jobs (very slow in producing effects and with sizable benefits to the wealthy)
- Governmental policies to place new orders to private business for military equipment, roads, bridges and hydroelectric power dams in employment-distressed regions (quicker effects for the middle class but expensive and controversially cost-effective for the poor)
- Projects directly administered by the federal and state government to construct public buildings, roads and bridges, and national park facilities (like the Works Progress Administration (WPA) and the Tennessee Valley Authority (TVA) during the 1930s depression) (quickest for the poor but controversially cost-effective for the product produced and politically very controversial in the United States, though not in Europe)

And, of course, there is an incident in world history that, although not so intended, dramatically demonstrates the effectiveness of public policy remedying poverty by hard benefits like money or food or the access to opportunity for the ordinary jobs that produce it. In the 1800s, Great Britain, stubbornly ignoring the relationship among crime, poverty, and general economic distress, decided to solve its problem of an immense overload of civil prisoners by shipping them off to their colonies in Australia and New Zealand—out of sight, out of mind, out of trouble. No one believed that these colonial societies would be successful. As hindsight shows, not only did that happen but successful modern social and economic structures were built on a populace of convicted criminals. The desire to work and the ability to compete and survive are shown by this example not to have been lacking in the convict society. The economic and social development of these countries is the premier example of the importance of having available sufficient economic opportunity created by public social utilities (when the private sector cannot provide it). Given abundant land made available by explicit public policy in the form of subsidies, land grants, transportation, and settlement, a society made up of convicted criminals created a hard-working, ordered, socially conforming and economically productive life.[16] The mistake in the British approach to its social problem of crime was an ideological error in the British understanding of the problem of criminal behavior—the problem was thought to be one of moral lack, not of economic opportunity. However, when given a labor market that provided opportunity, these early Australian and New Zealand settlers took advantage of its benefits and turned them to their own self-interest. Personal social services were not required. At the most concrete level, one might say that the lesson to be learned from this history is that the problem of overcrowded prisons is simply to find new, undiscovered continents or vast ocean islands as resettlement sites for criminals; a wiser conclusion is that it takes very dramatic, hard-benefit-oriented mechanisms (jobs and money) to produce a major impact on serious national poverty and crime and no personal social service strategy—training, rehabilitation, job search sophistication, however well financed or conceived—can substitute for it.

Criteria for Evaluating the Merit of Benefit Forms: Adequacy, Equity, and Efficiency

We have already considered "adequacy" and "efficiency" in the earlier section on the "fit" of the benefit form with the social problem analysis. But there are moments when *equity* has a special relevance to the choice of benefit type. Educational vouchers, it turns out, is a good example here. Here is the argument. Suppose that instead of providing neighborhood schools for children, a school district decides to issue educational vouchers. When presented to a private school, the school district will guarantee payment of a child's tuition costs from tax funds. Commonly, educational vouchers pay tuition costs up to the dollar per pupil costs in the local school district—some places that could amount to, say, $5,000 per year per child, not an insignificant sum of money. Those who object to this form of educational benefit argue that for most private schools, the tuition is more than the voucher will provide, so that only those families with greater-than-average income who can make up the difference can take advantage of them. And, if a significant number of parents choose vouchers and private schools, the number of citizens who support public schools will not only diminish, but actively oppose their improvement since they are paying double educational costs. Indeed, with less pupils, per pupil costs rise, and at some point, these cost increases mean less will be provided for public school students. Some voucher opponents argue that ultimately vouchers mean that public schools are only for those of less-than-average income and will not have enough support from taxpayers to avoid serious deterioration in teaching staff, curriculum offerings, not to mention buildings and facilities.

That is, of course, a consequence that is seriously inequitable because it falls primarily on low-income citizens who are least able to accommodate to it. The issue here is not that vouchers are inevitably inequitable, only that where it creates inequities, the voucher policy design must have features that eliminate it. Vouchers can have some important positive qualities, particularly the increase in what we have earlier called "consumer sovereignty"—parents can exercise free choice over what kind of school their children attend. The *trade-off* here is between that free choice and the inequity in the form of lower-class schooling it visits on children who remain in public schools. There are a number of ways of reducing the inequity. Most of the solutions turn on different ways of equalizing educational costs so that every parent has the opportunity to send their children to private schools: for example, private schools could be prevented from charging more than the local district per pupil costs, the school district could subsidize private schools at a higher rate than their own per pupil cost, and so on. Note that all the previous discussion avoids other important issues in public payments to private schools, notably the issue of church–state separation.

Summary

Nine types of benefits and services were presented for use in the analysis of social programs and policy provisions: cash, material goods and commodities, expert services, positive discrimination, credits/vouchers, market/wholesale subsidies, government loan guarantees, protective regulation, and power over decisions. Criteria for evaluating the merit of benefits and services were presented: fit with the social problem analysis, fit with the program design, potential for stigmatization, target efficiency, cost-effectiveness, consumer sovereignty, substitutability, and "trade-off's," among others. Interrelationships between benefits and benefit packages accruing from more than a single program will be the sole concern in a subsequent chapter of this book.

EXERCISES

1. Review the exercises in Chapter 5. Now think of a way the government could provide emergency substitute care for children without a government agency recruiting and selecting foster homes.

2. Write a paragraph expressing some conclusions you have drawn about whether the alternative benefit forms you have proposed in answering Exercise 1 do better or worse on the four evaluation criteria for forms of benefit discussed in the chapter.

NOTES

1. M. Howlett, "Policy Instruments, Policy Styles and Policy Implementation: National Approaches to Theories of Instrument Choice," *Policy Studies Journal*, 19(2) (1991): 1–21.

2. Of course, the U.S. Medicare system had reached that point by 1990 and now finances hospitalization under a diagnosis-related group (DRG) system in which the same (average cost) payment is made for patients whose diagnosed medical conditions lie in the same DRG.

3. Of course, sometimes the U.S. government has worked out agricultural subsidies in ways that require direct federal ownership and handling of grain: for example, there have been times when the federal government would actively take ownership of wheat, corn, rice, and soybeans and store them for years in their own granaries located across the country. They would do this as a way of "artificially" creating low supply (acting to "corner the market" and thus control prices), so as to increase demand and therefore increase prices paid to farmers for what grain they either retained or grew next year.

That is still a market subsidy because its purpose is directed toward producers, not consumers. This is only a different mechanism for working it out.

4. G. B. Doern and R. W. Phidd, *Canadian Public Policy: Ideas, Structure, Process* (Toronto: Methuen, 1983).

5. The reader might wish to consult Martin Rein, "Poverty, Policy and Purpose: Dilemmas of Choice," in *Social Policy: Issues of Choice and Change* (Armonk, NY: M. E. Sharpe, 1983), for a somewhat different and more abstract classification of benefit forms: social amenities (what here were called public social utilities), investment in human capital, welfare transfers, rehabilitation, participation (of the poor), and aggregative and selective economic measures. Whereas Rein calls these benefit "strategies," ultimately that is what Table 6.1 amounts to. Rein's list is useful but in the list presented here, the benefit forms are more mutually exclusive and concretely descriptive of exactly what the benefit is.

6. G. Lewis and R. J. Morrison, *Interactions among Social Welfare Programs*, Discussion Paper No. 866–88. Madison: Institute for Research on Poverty, University of Wisconsin, 1988.

7. S. Terkel, *Working* (New York: Avon, 1992).

8. S. H. Linder and B. G. Peters, "Instruments of Government: Perceptions and Contexts," *Journal of Public Policy*, 9(1) (1988): 35–38, 56.

9. L. Stone, "Madness," *New York Review of Books*, July 10, 1988, 8–12.

10. A. Myrdal, *Nation and Family* (Cambridge, MA: The MIT Press, 1968). See also Gilbert and Specht, *Dimensions of Social Welfare Policy*, pp. 81–102.

11. A. Kadushin, *Child Welfare* (New York: MacMillan, 1986).

12. Robert Morris, *Social Policy of the American State* (New York: Harper and Row, 1979), p. 120.

13. Ibid., p. 121.

14. P. Mott, *Meeting Human Needs, a Social and Political History of Title XX* (Columbus, OH: National Conference on Social Welfare, 1976).

15. B. Wootten, *Social Science and Social Pathology* (London: Allen and Unwin, 1959), p. 329.

16. M. A. Jones, *The History of the Australian Welfare State* (Sidney: Allen and Unwin, 1988).

7 Analysis of Eligibility Rules (Who Gets What, How Much, and Under What Conditions)

"That's not a regular rule, you invented it just now," said Alice. "Yes, and that is the oldest rule in the book," said the King.

—Lewis Carroll, *Alice in Wonderland*

Introduction

Fifty years ago, textbooks on economics referred to air and water as examples of "free goods." So far have we come from that more plentiful time that it is now difficult to cite any example of a free good: free in the sense that it is neither rationed, regulated, nor priced. Because no social welfare benefit is a free good, rules and regulations allocating such benefits abound. Such rules and regulations are not dispensable. As long as the demand exceeds the supply of benefits and services, some rule or principle must be used as a guide for deciding who gets the benefit or service and who does not.

Social work practitioners need to understand eligibility rules because they work daily within the context of these guidelines and use them at all levels of complexity. For example, the practitioner may need to seek exceptions from those rules to meet a client's special need; or need to understand the eligibility rule to decide whether to advise a rejected client to seek an administrative hearing on the issue. As an agency representative, the practitioner needs to understand the details of the rule so the applicant has the same chance to receive a benefit as every other citizen.

Social work and human service practitioners must also live with the fact that they are in the business of denying as well as qualifying clients for benefits—a hard fact of life that is a consequence of scarce resources. In an earlier chapter, the argument was made that finite resources is one reason social policies had to be invented; in one sense social policies are the vehicle by which social resources, services, and benefits are rationed when there isn't enough for everybody under every condition. So, as long as there are insufficient resources for every conceivable social need, every time a benefit or service is given to one user/client, it takes away the opportunity to give it to another one in need.

Eligibility rules are the vehicle for rationing benefits and services. On the positive side, they seek to target resources on those who need them or those who need them most. If they are off-targeted and go to clients who don't need them then, at some point in time, someone who does need them will go without.

It is a mistake for practitioners to think they can just "work harder" somehow to deliver services to clients so that *no one* will go without. Practitioners' time is also a scarce and expensive resource, every bit as scarce and expensive as cash. It is tempting to think that a way around this problem is to deliver services via a "first-come, first-served" eligibility rule. Although that rule has qualities of "rough justice" that are somehow appealing, the justice involved is probably illusory. Think of how a "first-come, first-served" rule gives a not necessarily merited advantage to those who *by chance* hear of the rule or the service first; there is no particular justice in that. At some point, those who implement that rule will run out of resources, so that denying clients has only been postponed. First-come, first-served is not inherently a bad eligibility rule, but it has no great virtue either— why shouldn't it be preferable to give preference to those who are, on some basis, most needy? Indeed, the practitioner may even be responsible for constructing such rules at some time later in their career and at that moment there is at stake a professional responsibility for good service to clients. Where a policy does not meet the needs of clients adequately, neither the exercise of simplistic eligibility rules nor a large dose of moral indignation will suffice to discharge professional responsibility. Practitioners are responsible for advocating their clients' needs even to their own administrative superiors as well as to their colleagues in other agencies who have resources that clients need. Furthermore, practitioners are responsible for joining with others in pursuing legislative or judicial advocacy as a remedy.

Types of Eligibility Rules

The decentralized disarray of the U.S. welfare system creates literally hundreds of public and private programs that offer welfare services and benefits. Each has a somewhat different set of rules for determining who gets what, how much, and under which conditions. Faced with this bewildering variety, we need to reduce its complexity by some kind of scheme that will render it understandable. The purpose of the following scheme is to group together eligibility rules so that we can talk about "types" of eligibility rules without the trouble of weighty discussions about lightweight differences. Many schemes serve this purpose—none perfect—so we will borrow heavily from one that seems well suited to the purpose. It was devised by Richard Titmuss, a student of social policy in the British tradition of Beatrice Webb, Beveridge, and others.[1] Titmuss was tentative about this analytic scheme: "This represents little more than an elementary and partial structural map which can assist in the understanding of the welfare complex today."[2]

- Prior contributions
- Administrative rule
- Private contracts
- Professional discretion
- Administrative discretion
- Judicial decision
- Means testing (needs minus assets and/or income)
- Attachment to the work force

Eligibility Rules Based on Prior Contributions

Eligibility for many important social welfare benefits is established by rules about how much advance contributions have been made to the system that will pay the benefit later. A prominent example are benefits paid by the U.S. Social Security system: retirement income for workers and survivors (OASI), disability income for workers and dependents (SSDI), and payments for medical care services (Medicare) for both the disabled and the retired.

Exactly how much prior contribution is required varies with the age at which benefit is drawn and the type of benefit in question; but some *prior contribution* is always necessary. In general, 40 quarters of prior contribution is required although for those under 30 years of age, it is less. The prior contribution of which we are speaking comes from the worker and the employer and in matching amounts, calculated by a complicated formula and expressed as a percentage of workers' wages written into legislation. As of 1998, 7.65 percent of wages (up to $68,400) were paid by both employer and worker as a contribution to the Social Security Trust Funds. It is from those Trust Funds that Retirement, Medicare, and Disability benefits will later be paid. Note that some citizens receive benefits not because they made prior contributions but were dependents of those who did: spouses, children, and other legal dependents of contributing wage earners.

The basic ideas behind the prior contribution method of establishing entitlement are the same principles that lie behind all private insurance schemes: (1) payment in advance provides for the future and (2) protection against the economic consequences of personal disasters is best achieved by spreading the risk among a large group of people. When Social Security was first established, it was intended to be based on just such insurance principles and benefits were to bear a strong relationship to contributions. That relationship has eroded over the years so that in 1997 the benefits received by the average Social Security new recipient will equal the Social Security tax (contributions) paid while working (plus expected interest) in 8.3 years. From that perspective and since life expectancies of those retiring in 1997 are 15 years for men and 19 years for women, the new 1997 recipient will get at least twice as many years of benefits as years of contributions.[3]

The insurance principle has come on hard times in the Social Security system lately, largely because Congress has continued to enact larger benefits than were ever anticipated in earlier years when financing was being planned, and the ratio between the number of working contributors and the number of retiree beneficiaries has changed substantially (more on that later). The prior contribution strategy is subject to a number of problems, one is insensitivity to demographic changes. There are also strong inequities for employed women and spouses who both pay Social Security contributions: Upon retirement they will receive no more than 50 percent more benefits than if she had never paid Social Security contributions at all (the maximum family benefit is approximately 150 percent of the benefit of the spouse who has the best earning record). In an insurance scheme that was absolutely faithful to the insurance principle, the married couple's benefit on retirement would be based on the contribution of both husband and wife, plus whatever interest and dividends accrued over the years during which the contributions were made. It must be said, however, that to date there is little actual loss on this account since the average Social Security beneficiary has actually paid for only about half of what is received in benefits. On that account and contrary to a common myth, *no present Social Security beneficiary household would have come out better had they paid the same amount of their total combined Social Security contributions into a private insurance scheme.* That may change for those earning, say, twice average annual incomes (at or above $65,000 per year). Since they pay Social Security tax on a much larger share of their annual incomes than in previous years, by 2025, retirees who have earned twice average incomes will have to receive benefits for more years than they can expect to live in order to recover what they've invested in Social Security payments (and expected interest).

The feature that makes Social Security work to the advantage of those who are retiring now is that (1) there are income transfers at work and (2) profitability is not a factor (not least because there are no sales or marketing costs). The Social Security system is, in fact, transferring income from those who are now working to those who are no longer working—the retired, disabled, or users of Medicare benefits and from high earners to average wage earners.[4]

Eligibility by Administrative Rule and Regulation

Although eligibility rules for public social programs may be laid out in some detail in the law, seldom are they sufficiently detailed so that no administrative interpretations need be made. Thus, *administrative rules* are made to clarify the law. This is an advantage to client/beneficiaries because it gives social workers and other human service staff members a means by which to administer the benefit or service program even-handedly and reliably, so that people similarly situated given similar benefits. On the other hand, administrative rules restrict the freedom of staff members to use their discretion, that is, to judge need for the benefit or service in individual circumstances. So, even though administrative rules may work toward greater equity, they may also be a less effective response to unique individual circumstances. There are some eligibility rules that are almost fully spelled out in the law, and the Food Stamp program is probably the best example. Almost all of the details necessary to determine whether a citizen is entitled to food stamps are built into the law. The exact amount of assets, as well as income, is specified by family size in the text of the act, along with definitions of what constitutes a household. Consequently, no discretion is needed in determining whether (for example) a live-in friend of either sex should be included in determining household size. The administrative rules for the TANF (Temporary Assistance for Needy Families—the replacement for the old AFDC) program, on the other hand—are so numerous and concern so many different topics that they are bound into ponderous "manuals." These administrative tomes not only include the state and federal statutes relevant to the program but (mainly) they address how those laws are to be interpreted. On reason for the complexity of eligibility rules in the TANF program is they are "means-tested," meaning that eligibility is established by a test of whether a person's assets and income are greater than some official standard of need for a given family size. Apart from all the administrative rules that concern how to count assets and income, the TANF program has to be built on numerous administrative rules that tell the staff who sign the eligibility documents how to interpret the law: for example, should a child's paper route income be counted as family income or should Aunt Lily's inherited piano count as an "asset?" It is in the character of administrative rules that they can be modified over time; if they are devised by administrators, they can also be changed by administrators. Therefore, it is important to know whether a certain entitlement rule originates with judicial decision, administrative rule, or individual staff discretion, for on that fact depends the probability for change—staff decisions certainly are changed more easily than are formal ("manualized") rules or statutes. Further, as you might imagine, the method, resources, and time used to effect changes differ for each rule source. Chapter 8 will discuss the details of administrative appeal hearings that are required by law for all social programs established under the Social Security Act and for many programs that receive federal funds.

Eligibility by Private Contract

Strange as it may seem, it is possible to become entitled to a public benefit through the provisions of *private contracts*. The Workers Compensation system is constructed this way.[5] In every state, employers are required to purchase insurance policies from private insurance companies (or a state insurance fund) to pay to workers money for income and medical costs to replace what is lost through work injury. There is nothing optional about the law, and employers are subject to substantial fines for noncompliance. In this case, the benefit form is a cash payment plus a voucher for medical expenses.

Another source of entitlement to public benefits in which private contracts are involved is purchase-of-service contracting (POSC). In the past decade, more and more welfare services—counseling, legal advocacy, special education, day care, and some transportation services (e.g., for the elderly and/or disabled)—are delivered by private contractors. In the case of purchased services of various kinds, the state actually pays the bill (or some of it) directly to the private purveyor of the contracted service. Because the state is the purchaser of services, the state can insert conditions into the contract concerning who can obtain the service, for how long, and under what circumstances.[6] Not only state and federal governments subcontract for services; private charitable organizations do so as well.[7] For example, private hospitals "contract out" to private profit-making corporations the operation of psychiatric units—Horizons Corporation and Humana operate many such units nationwide. Another example is a midwestern private social agency that operates a "high-tech foster care" program for its state. This program serves severely emotionally disturbed children who cannot be cared for in the ordinary family foster home setting. In both these examples, the entitlement rules embedded in the private contract determine who is eligible for services.

Services provided under Title XX of the Social Security Act is another example of the extensive use of POSC. Title XX is intended to provide services ". . . aimed at the goals of: (a) Achieving or maintaining economic self support to prevent, reduce, or eliminate dependency, (b) to prevent or remedy neglect, abuse or exploitation of children and adults unable to protect themselves, (c) to provide services to individuals in institutions."[8] Although Title XX did not require POSC from private contractors, it certainly anticipated it, because specific provisions in the act (subpart G) set out what had to be included in such a contract.[9] In 1996, most of the 2.8 billion dollars of Title XX expenditures were purchased from private purveyors under this act rather than being provided directly by the state welfare agencies. Payment for services under POSC arrangements can be either by fixed-price, reimbursement-at-cost, or performance contracting. In *fixed-price* contracting, the governmental body pays the contractor a price that remains stable over a set period of time; the main reward for the contractors depends on their ability to estimate costs accurately and to administer the program within those constraints. A *reimbursement-at-cost* contract insulates the contractor from unexpected costs and is often used for research or program development for which it is difficult to estimate costs. *Performance* contracting rewards contractors for achieving program objectives at certain levels and penalizes them financially for failing to do so. Incentives for goal attainment are built into the performance contract in various ways. For example, Wedel and Colston cite job training, job placement, maintaining frail elderly in their own homes, and so on, describing in detail a performance-based contract between the state of Oklahoma and local community mental health centers. The contract featured the use of financial awards for those centers delivering services that exceeded the contracted amount of service provided and the assessment of financial penalties for those centers whose performance was not up to par.[10] Performance contracting is not without some problems, one of which is the ruling of Michigan's attorney general that contractors could not be held responsible for failure to meet performance goals specified in the contract. Among other problems is the difficulty in always being able to specify some numerical criterion by which good and bad performance can be distinguished and the potential conflict over how the enduring profit motive in performance contracts creates incentives to shave services in ways that, although not mentioned in the contract, may degrade them.[11] Clearly, successful POSC and performance contracting require participants, both government and contracting service providers, who are sophisticated in pricing, administrative controls, and close monitoring.[12]

Eligibility by Professional Discretion

One of the most widely used sources of entitlement is the *professional discretion* of individual practitioners. A common and concrete example is eligibility for medical benefits, which is always contingent on the discretion of the physician (or physician surrogate). Almost every licensed profession controls part of the entitlement to some kind of social welfare benefit: dental care for TANF children is entitled in part by the judgment of dentists; foot care for veterans is entitled in part by podiatrists; legal advocacy for low-income people is entitled in part by the judgment of lawyers; eyeglasses for low-income mental patients are entitled in part by optometrists; foster care for children is entitled in part by social workers. In each case, the entitling profession whose judgment is necessary is presumed to have some expertise about the matter. More often than not, such a presumption is correct, though there can be exceptions. Social work and human service practitioners must keep in mind that such discretion can be challenged in an administrative or judicial hearing, and where such discretion seems prejudicial to their clients practitioners have a professional obligation to help their client challenge it. Sometimes professional discretion is the leading evidence that severs children from parents, as in child physical abuse, sexual abuse, or neglect cases. The opinions of therapists and diagnosticians (both physicians), clinical psychologists, and social workers are commonly used. No doubt those opinions are important and often accurate, but social workers and human service workers should be wary of a blanket assumption about the validity of those very difficult judgments.

Eligibility by Administrative Discretion

Another kind of discretion that serves as a source of eligibility for social welfare benefits is *administrative discretion*. A common example of this is the policy in some states and counties that allows a county welfare worker to distribute small amounts of cash and credits for food, housing, and utilities to poor people who apply. This kind of policy is characteristic of the General Assistance programs (less than half the states have them). General Assistance is financed by the local government and is usually oriented toward short-term emergency budgets. The staff member must account for the funds only in the fiscal sense; administrative judgment is seldom called to account, and there is little systematic effort to document its accuracy. However, there are more important examples of administrative discretion. It is indeed widespread and the source of such extensive power throughout modern public organizations that, according to Michael Lipsky and Michael Brown, there may be serious question as to whether staff members at the lowest level or the chief executive actually controls the organizational operations.[13,14] All general organizational policies and administrative rules must be interpreted and applied to individual situations, so it is important to understand that such interpretation and application necessarily involve significant personal judgment—a form of administrative discretion—on the part of the staff member. For example, a state patrolman sees a person stopped at the side of a highway and diligently applying a newspaper to the bare rear end of a five-year-old child. In a hairbreadth, the patrolman is dutybound to make a serious decision about whether to stop and make inquiries. His decision is essentially administrative because it comes out of the role he fills as protector of persons. Later, he may have to make an even more serious decision. Was what he saw simply a child who had tried the parent's patience and was being disciplined within acceptable bounds? Or was it a cruel physical attack that will leave black-and-blue bruises or break the skin of a child too young to defend himself? The discretion entailed here concerns interpretation of the state child abuse statute. Does this instance, and the data selected to report it, constitute an example of what the statute delineates? The statute will not reveal to the patrolman what rules he should use for its interpretation; it will not say how inflamed the bruises should be—or even whether black-and-blue rather than red bruises count. Nor will it always protect the officer from consequences if the parent claims illegal detainment or false arrest. The same situation is faced by the social worker or the physician while examining a hospital emergency room patient. Here, however, it is *professional* discretion that is being asked for. Their task is to render a professional opinion about the matter, and they are prepared by training and experience and specifically empowered by law to make that judgment. The difference between professional and administrative discretion is source of authority of each: Professionals exercise discretion because of the authority of their professional preparation and training, whereas administrators exercise discretion because they are appointed by their superiors to do so.

There are important examples of administrative discretion gone amok, so that social work and human service professionals should be aware that administrative discretion—as important and humane as it can be—also can be used in ways that work to the detriment of their client's welfare. Few cases are so flagrant as the massive disentitlement of the chronically mentally ill from Social Security Disability benefits during the early 1980s Reagan administration. Although it is not a common case, it is useful to summarize briefly here to illustrate this point. At that time, the Social Security Administration (SSA), ostensibly concerned about the rising costs of the Social Security Disability system, began a systematic effort to reduce approved benefit claims and to terminate the benefits of the chronically mentally ill whom the SSA believed to be unable to prove their illness. Some 150,000 beneficiaries had their benefits canceled during those few years. Not only the mentally ill were disadvantaged; there are documented cases of rejected applicants with severe cardiac conditions who died in the waiting rooms of Social Security offices.

The mechanisms by which this was accomplished included changes in the standards used for mental disabilities and attempts to impose a "quota" on SSA hearing judges for benefit denials—judges were expected to hand down a constantly increasing number of benefit denials. If the quota was not met, they were subject to considerable harassment: reassignment, or mandatory attendance at lengthy "educational seminars," for example. The Association of Social Security Administrative Law judges appealed these measures on the grounds that they constituted unlawful interference in the fair-hearing appeals system established by the Social Security Act as independent of administrative authority. The Association won on those grounds, after verifying that indeed there were systematic, illegal, plainly political attempts to influence the outcomes of the fair-hearing system. Thousands of appeals of disability denials ensued, sizable proportions of which were successful. It is clear from the data available that disabled beneficiaries who persevered in challenging the administrative decisions of the SSA increased their chances of a favorable decision to nearly 80 percent. The higher the federal appeal court rendering the decision, the more likely was a decision against the Administration.[15] Only through the efforts of both legal advocates and social work and human service advocates were these reversals accomplished. This example should give heart to practitioners that advocacy can succeed and, when conditions warrant, should be a part of their daily work.

Practitioners who advocate in these matters should understand that the most important issue in these cases was whether the SSA had *followed its own rules* in denying disability claims. That is the standard required by administrative law, and it is the most common ground for appeals. The law does not often call into question the substance of an administrative criterion for eligibility for benefits or services, but it does require that when specific criteria are established for public benefits, the agency must adhere to them *and* apply them equitable among applicants. If rules change, the changes must be made public and published in certain ways. In a very concrete way, administrative rules are the "rules of the road," and justice requires that citizens know about them so that they can equitably pursue claims to which they may be entitled. On that account many (though not all) rules of due process apply: due notice, opportunity to know the grounds for denial, opportunity to present testimony in a fair hearing, and the like. (Some of these rules will be discussed in Chapter 8.)

Eligibility by Judicial Decision

Judicial decisions are important sources of eligibility, virtually ruling applicants in or out of program benefits and services. (So important is it that all of Chapter 3 was devoted to the whole issue of the Judiciary as a source of public policy.) After a program has been in operation over a period of time, it is very likely that a contention will arise either about a point in the enabling legislation or whether an administrative rule or discretionary judgment was faithful to the spirit and intention of the law under which the program or policy was established. Appeals to the Judiciary for clarification of the law are routine and in the end they can become as important as the legislation or administrative rules themselves. Sometimes judicial rulings prevent administrative rules from excluding people from benefits. An example is the 1969 ruling of the U.S. Supreme Court on the constitutionality of what were then called "residence requirements." Under residency rules in effect at the time, citizens of a state had to establish permanent residency over a specified number of days, weeks, months, or years (usually one year for the old AFDC program) as a condition of entitlement. (Residency is an ancient eligibility requirement going as far back as the Elizabethan poor laws in England.) In 1969, the U.S. Supreme Court held that such requirements were unconstitutional infringements on citizens' (labor's) right of free movement between states.[16] Presumably, the same applies to TANF, the program replacing AFDC.

Some judicial rulings operate not only to prevent exclusion from a program, but to positively assert eligibility where none existed before. In one of the most familiar, *Brown v. Board of Education* (1954),[17] the U.S. Supreme Court ruled that all children are entitled to an equal opportunity for education, regardless of race. It was truly a landmark decision and marks the beginning of a whole era of efforts to establish civil rights, benefits, and services. Paternity determinations serve as a source of judicial entitlement to the child support payments by nonsupporting fathers, even though such entitlement may be viewed by some as a mixed blessing. There is now available a clinical test, the human leucocyte antigen (HLA) test, which will rule out, with 97 percent accuracy, whether a given individual is the father of a particular child. Nearly two-thirds of all courts accept use of the HLA test in paternity cases, with full confidence in its results.[18] And now even more accurate (99.9 percent) DNA genetic material matching tests are well accepted by the courts. When evidence is accepted and decisions are rendered about paternity, eligibility for child support payments from the adjudged father is established by court decision. Another kind of judicial ruling that represents a source of eligibility is somewhat unusual, but it occurs in the process of the judicial review of all children in "temporary" foster care and is now required by law in most states.[19] Begun in New York State in 1971, that state's court review statute provides that for eighteen months, the Family Court will review cases of all children in involuntary placement and determine whether they shall be discharged to their biological families, continued in foster care, freed for adoptive placement, or placed in an adoptive home. In essence, this is a decision by a judge as to whether a child is entitled to parental care, adoptive placement, or foster home services.

Eligibility by Means Testing

One of the best-known and most widely used of all eligibility rules is a *means test:* Income and assets are totaled to see whether they are less than some standard for what a person is believed to need. If the assets and/or income exceed this standard then no benefit is given; if assets and/or income are less than that standard, the person is given a benefit in such an amount that total assets and income are equal to the standard. The central idea is that where assets and income are up to the standard, the person "ought" to have enough to meet his or her needs.

Despite its apparent simplicity, the whole idea turns out to have enormous complications. For example, there is the issue of what to consider as income. Some means tests concern both assets and wages (SSI and TANF), whereas others concern wages alone (Workers Compensation). Benefit amounts and types of beneficiaries turn out to be very different depending on which version of the means test is used.[20] Note the world of difference in terms of administrative complexity between income only versus income and assets with regard to the test. Income is almost always a matter of record (often public), is often in the form of cash, and, therefore, can be immediately valued. Assets are usually held privately and, because they are seldom a matter of record, determining their valuation is often problematic. Then there is the question of how to establish a standard of "need" against which to cast income and/or assets. Even determining what minimum nutritional need is can be very controversial; the same goes for "minimum" need for housing, clothing, and on it goes. As a result of the difficulty of arriving at a consensus on these issues, a different "standard of minimum need" applies in almost every state. In 1991, the state standards of need for the old AFDC programs—by any standard never a princely sum—varied by as nearly 300 percent! For a family of three in the contiguous 48 states, the standards varied from the lowest, New Mexico ($317 per month), to the highest, Vermont ($1,160 per month).[21] Means-tested eligibility procedures also vary with respect to whose income and assets are being considered when the means test is calculated. For some programs, focus in on individuals (e.g., SSI) or on families (e.g., the old AFDC now TANF); in others, it is on workers (Workers Compensation); in still others, it is on households "who purchase food together irrespective of blood relationship"

(Food Stamps); and in still others, focus is on blood-related families (Title XX, Child-Support-Parent Location services). Table 7.1 summarizes some of the wide variability that can be found in concrete, selected social programs with respect to means-testing policy. Means are tested along three major dimensions: (1) type of resource counted (wages and/or assets), (2) concept underlying needs, and (3) beneficiary unit (child, household, worker, and such). These dimensions are useful in knowing what to look for in analyzing means tests as entitlement rules.

Establishing Attachment to the Workforce

Where social welfare programs are aimed at the primary workforce, that is, the working populace, it is of crucial importance to determine eligibility by a means that will qualify *only* those who are part of the workforce (lest benefits go astray). This is done by setting a minimum to be contributed (via wage deduction at a workplace) that will entitle a person to benefit. Note that in many programs that require prior contribution for eligibility, not just *any* prior contribution will do; it must be a particular minimum amount, over a specific time, that counts for eligibility. The U.S. Unemployment Insurance (UI) program is a major example of this mechanism of entitlement. The goal of the UI program is to benefit those who have some significant work history—the program does not now intend, nor has it ever intended, to benefit those working part-time, only in casual employment, or only for insignificant wages. Although specific rules vary state by state, UI typically requires the worker to have received wages for at least six months and to have received at least $200 in wages during each prior three-month period. The purpose of such eligibility requirements is to establish that the worker has some significant "attachment" to the workforce. The Social Security Retirement and the Disability Insurance (DI) program have a similar policy built into their prior contribution policies,

TABLE 7.1   Variability in Means-Testing Procedures for Selected Social Programs

| Program | Type of $ Counted | | Concept Underlying Idea of "Need" | Beneficiary Unit of Concern |
	Wages	Assets		
TANF[a]	Almost all	Almost all	Absolute minimum subsistence	Child
Food Stamp	Almost all	Almost all	Nutritional adequacy; income less than 125% of poverty line	Household: those who buy food together
OASI	Half of wages earned ages 62–70	None	Low to adequate living standard	Worker
SSI[a]	Almost all	Assets over $2,000 in general	Absolute minimum subsistence	Individual

[a]Varies by state, but these are the best general rules.

but Workers Compensation is not concerned with limiting coverage to those with attachment to the workforce. If a worker is injured on the first day of the first job ever, and the employer carries Workers Compensation insurance, that worker is eligible for benefits appropriate to the injury as provided by law.

Criteria for Evaluating the Merit of Eligibility Rules

Fit with the Social Problem Analysis

Correspondence between Eligibility Rules and the Target Specifications of the Social Problem Analysis.   For a program or policy to be a coherent solution to a social problem, those who receive the program's benefits and/or services must be included within the group whom the social problem analysis identifies as having the problem. Recall from Chapter 1 on social problem analysis the necessity of social problem definition containing "... concrete observable signs by which the existence of the problem can be known." *Those concrete indicators, subtypes and quantifications are main sources from which entitlement and eligibility rules must be drawn.* Eligibility rules that don't correspond to those indicators will off-target the program benefits and services. If poverty is defined as annual cash income less than $15,569 for a family of four, then at least one of the eligibility rules must restrict the benefits of a cash assistance program to those with that level of income. If inability to attain a university-level education is defined as one problem for families with annual incomes less than $20,000, then the same stricture applies. If the social problem of providing income support for the physically and mentally disabled is defined as applying to those with a verified disability and proven inability to work for the next six months, then indeed the eligibility rules are about verifiable standards for determining disability and the inability to work for that period of time. The quantifications embedded in the social problem definition are the basis for the target specifications that must be a part of well-formed goals and objectives and it is to those that eligibility rules must be relevant.

A central question is whether the entitlement rules expand or reduce the agency's ability to bring its program to those who are affected by the social problem. And recall that definitions in the social problem analysis can always be changed to widen target specifications and thus provide an improved answer to that question. Note, however, that doing so may have serious consequences. First, an enlarged target specification of those who have the problem might create large increases in program costs. Second, a narrower target specification might very well change the causal factors on which a program design should focus and thus the whole program design. The reader should not interpret this as advice against changing a social problem viewpoint, rather it is to alert the unwary. With experience viewpoints on social problems become more sophisticated and hopefully better program designs emerge.

Correspondence between the Eligibility Rules and the Ideology of the Social Problem Analysis.   Eligibility rules do more than just reflect target specifications, they also reflect general ideological positions that underlie or are associated with the viewpoints from which a social problem is defined. An example is commitment to the work ethic, an idea that refers to the common belief that work is inherently virtuous and that the virtue of a citizen is related to work effort and work product. English poor laws required work tests as a condition for eligibility; that is, one way a person proved he or she was poor was to be willing to accept placement in a nineteenth-century workhouse. The modern U.S. equivalent is the requirement that unemployed food stamp recipients be registered for work referrals at their local state employment agency. That requirement is itself a condition of eligibility and thus an eligibility rule. It reflects an ideological commitment to the idea that citizens should expect to work for their own bread and that if they don't, they should have to show that no work is available or that they are unable to do the work that is available. The "relatives responsibility" policy is another instance of eligibility ideology. England's Elizabethan poor laws, as well as U.S. social policy, provided relief for the poor but were constrained by the common ideological commitment to the idea that families were always primarily responsible for their members. Thus, the underlying practical understanding of the social problem of poverty was that three descending generations in the family group—grandparents, their adult children, and their children's children—must be poor before any individual member was deemed poor. The eligibility rules for the expenditure of public funds for the poor reflected that ideology: Parents were financially responsible for the relief of the poverty of their children, and children were responsible for the relief of the poverty of their own parents.

Good entitlement rules for personal social services must have an ideological fit with the relevant social problem analysis. For example, in the field of mental health, there is an interesting split between ideological positions: One implies that severe and chronic psychosis is a problem of greatest concern, and the other implies that prevention of mental health problems is the premier priority. Thus, for the eligibility rules to be consistent with ideology here, the former would have entitlement rules for mental health services and would give priority to those with psychotic behaviors, whereas the latter would give priority to those considered to be major "at-risk" groups—those considered to have high potential for the development of mental health problems (however, those problems are defined). Of course, that applies only under conditions where resources are insufficient to provide services for both, but that is almost always the case for social policy and program systems. For a different example, consider child protective services. If the ideological position implies that children should never be considered to be a cause of their sexual abuse by an adult, then the rule that entitles them to protection by state intervention should also entitle them to remain in their own homes while the adult perpetrator is required to leave. That is a modern practice, of course, not universally followed as a matter of public policy on child protection.

Criteria Specific to Eligibility Rules

Stigmatization.   The manifest purpose of eligibility rules is to ensure that only those whom the program intends to provide with benefits are in fact included as beneficiaries. Certainly, there are also latent purposes, and some social scientists believe these have clearly negative effects as well. Side effects of some eligibility rules may have such serious consequences that they outweigh benefits received. Some argue that these side effects are intentional, the sign of true latent (and negative) purposes of a social program. Two of the most widely discussed side effects of eligibility rules are stigmatization and alienation. To be *stigmatized* means to be marked as having lesser value, to bear the burden of public disapproval. There are many meanings of *alienation*, but here the term refers to the subjective sense of being estranged from the mainstream of the society in which one dwells. How is it that an eligibility rule or mechanism can produce such strong negative social effects? Both alienation and stigmatization are serious side effects that are believed to be associated with many consequences (suicide, social deviance, tendency toward serious crime, and chemical addiction).

To understand how eligibility rules can produce these strong side effects, think for a moment of what is entailed in an application for a means-tested public assistance program like SSI or TANF. (Recall that TANF offers both cash benefits for all citizens whose income is less than some "official" needs standard *and* personal social services designed to do such things as increase parenting effectiveness, offer children foster care, and help single parents get jobs.) Basically, the application requires a person to lay bare the details of his or her financial and work history in order to document income and assets. Thus, it requires a person to reveal all details about when jobs were left (for whatever reason), when spouses or children were abandoned—without regard for unflattering details. The application requires a person to say some or all of the following: "I'm broke. I can't keep a job. I left my last job because I had to go to jail (or the mental hospital). I couldn't be enough of a success in school to get the credentials so people would hire me. My parents, relatives, husband have all left me and don't care enough about me to help out." Revealing such details to a stranger cannot help but make the strongest constitution quiver in the telling. The ordeal is self-stigmatizing because the teller can no longer hide what may be humiliating facts—at least one other person knows. The more a person believes he or she is regarded negatively, the more likely will that opinion be believed and the stigma accepted as real. The stigmatization that appears to result from eligibility rules associated with the TANF or the old AFDC program is widely discussed in the literature.[22,23,24] The Pettigrew article contains an excellent survey of the studies of labeling and stigmatization of welfare recipients.

It is important to observe that not all entitlement rules are associated with this kind of stigmatization. Few elderly feel stigmatized by the application process guided by the eligibility rules of the Social Security Retirement or Disability program. Nor do people feel stigmatized by the means tests involved in the application for student loans (BEOG [Basic Economic Opportunity Grant] or NSDL [National Student Direct Loan]) or, for that matter, the means test inherent in payment of income tax (if your earned income is more than $15,000, for example, and you have no more than three dependents you are "eligible" to pay some income tax). Two factors distinguish a means test involving an application for TANF from a means test involving a loan for attending college or university and illustrate how stigmatization occurs. (1) The reason for application for TANF (say) is most likely to be something that must be apologized for or explained. In contrast, the reason for applying for a BEOG or NSDL loan is almost never the occasion for an apology or explanation; to the contrary, it is likely to be occasion for congratulation or recognition that a person is about to embark on a path of high social regard—going to college.

The same applies to the instance of the means test entailed in paying taxes: The very fact that a person struggles over filling out forms and takes a long time at it suggests a person who has considerable assets and income.

The *worst* consequence of the means tests involved in a BEOG loan application is that a person would have to look elsewhere for funds or delay going to school for a year. Contrariwise, the *best* consequence of the means test for TANF or the old AFDC is that a person will receive a poverty level income and medical card.

Some years ago, George Hoshino suggested that, in a phrase of Gilbert and Specht, the means test did not have to be mean-spirited.[25] Hoshino suggests that one of the main reasons for the negative effects of the means test as a way of determining eligibility is that it places great stress on determining unique individual needs when all that is really required is to determine average need for categories of family size, age, and so on. Verification of assets is a process filled with arbitrary and specious judgments of the market value of mundane goods. As any experienced social worker knows, the administrative cost of such determinations far outweighs the relatively small misplaced benefit that might be given were the verification of the value of highly personal assets simply ignored. It was a considerable step forward when the means test for the Food Stamp Program cleverly avoided these pitfalls and determined need on exactly the basis Hoshino suggested in earlier years—that of some concept of average need (for food, in this case) and by "average" deductions for major items like cars, houses, and insurance policies.[26] Although there may be the rare applicant who has a house full of expensive new furniture and who might not declare it when applying for food stamps, this would certainly not characterize the majority of food stamp applicants. The administrative cost of tracking down that odd exception outweighs any saving that might result.

Every eligibility rule needs to be scrutinized for potential stigmatizing potential. One important thing to look for is the extent to which receipt of benefit is a matter of public knowledge. Free school lunches are a good example: If a student is required to show a voucher, a form, or a ticket that can only be obtained upon demonstration of inability to pay, then having to show that voucher in public to receive the meal is stigmatizing in our society where the general social norm disvalues people with low incomes. This eligibility rule would be judged to be deficient on this criterion. There are ways to "destigmatize" the meal benefit: If the ticket for a free lunch is issued for an amount that is larger than a single meal—so that it is a credit that is spendable on diverse goods and services provided by the school (books and athletic fees) and which must be purchased by *all* students—then the fact of who paid for the ticket is withheld from the public and fails to be stigmatizing.

Off-Targeted Benefits.   Another criterion for judging eligibility rules and their associated procedures is the extent to which benefits are directed to population groups who are not the main object of the program. One example from the early 1980s concerned the NSDL funds for college and university students in the United States. NSDL loan funds were very attractive to students in those years because their interest rates were far below the existing market rate of around 7 percent. The difference between the interest rate on the loan (some as low as 3 percent) and prevailing high interest rates in 1981 on such things as long-term savings accounts (12 to 17 percent) was so much that some students who already had sufficient school funds took out an NSDL loan simply to make a little money by banking it at a higher interest rate. Every year the cost of the interest on the loan was $300 (3 percent of $10,000), whereas the long-term savings account yielded perhaps as much as $1,700 (17 percent of $10,000). The net profit on this no-effort enterprise would have been the difference between the dollar yield of the two interest rates, that is, $1,700 - $300, or $1,400 total. It would be hard to think of a way to earn more than $100 a month more easily.

There aren't many examples of porous eligibility rules as outrageous as that and, in fact, that gaping wound in the design of this eligibility rule was closed by raising interest rates on loans to competitive levels. But eligibility rules such as this should be judged negatively since the off-targeting is significant and has no obvious impact on the social problem. In fact, it represents off-targeting of the worst kind in that it takes away money for income transfers from those who are most clearly in need of them and because the government that made the loans possible had to borrow at market rates, the profit for those who took advantage of the opportunity was and probably still is being paid for by taxpayers like you and me. It is important, nevertheless, to notice that some instances of off-targeting are intentional and not always a bad thing.

In fact, some social policies are operationalized in ways that purposely produce "seepage" of benefits to nonmembers of the target group. Perhaps the best example of off-targeting intended to produce positive results is the Social Security Retirement program (OASI). As noted earlier, the program is nonstigmatizing because its designer ensured that nearly *the whole population would receive benefits* (because nearly all were entitled since they contributed as workers). In the usual case, social programs that are universal cannot stigmatize or alienate since it joins a citizens to their peers rather than identifying them as "apart," or "less worthy." In fact, the actual cost of "destigmatizing" this (or any) program is precisely the cost of the off-targeting. Though the total cost is not relatively large, OASI does off-target benefits; those with earned income of as much as $43,500 annually can still receive some retirement benefit.

There are other ways to avoid stigmatization besides universalizing eligibility. Here is an example, one that failed becoming law in the 1970s by only a single vote. Its virtues are that it does avoid stigmatization, has simple eligibility rules, can be administered without constructing yet another bureaucracy, and is probably more fair than other alternatives because most administrative discretion is removed from the eligibility process. This proposal would abolish all existing cash and cash-equivalent programs (TANF, Food Stamp, SSI, and UI programs) and replace them with a cash benefit that will provide a minimum subsistence standard of living for those who, *for whatever reason*, do not have a minimum amount of income and/or assets. The program would use the regular IRS administrative procedure for collecting income tax as a means of distributing benefits to the poor, a system generally called a negative income tax (NIT). Originally called the Family Assistance Program (FAP), the program was first sponsored in Congress in 1974 by the conservative Republican Nixon administration. The basic idea is that every three months, people would file an income tax statement. If their total income and assets were less than some designated poverty line, they would receive a monthly amount over the next three months that, when added to their past three-months' income, would equal the poverty line for their household size. When income exceeded the poverty line, that household would incur a tax liability and be required to pay the government additional tax dollars. This scheme was neither clearly universal nor clearly selective. In fact, the system carefully selects and benefits most those in greatest need, even though all citizens can potentially benefit and the system is nonstigmatizing in that there is almost no public revelation of benefit receipt. The Nixon administration scheme was automatic in that it was operated by the Internal Revenue Service and had a built-in work-incentive feature. Using 1997 figures, if there was no earned income, the family would get a standard "base payment," a fixed-dollar amount. Families could work and still keep part of the "base payment." For example, the first $8,000 of earned income was excluded from consideration and doesn't affect the base payment at all. The next $8,000 of earned income, however, reduces the base payment by $1,000 because for each earned dollar above $8,000, the base payment is reduced by 50 cents. The base payment is reduced even more for earned income above $16,000—for each earned dollar in this range, the base payment is reduced by 75 cents. More and more of the base payment is taken away as earnings climb, but each dollar earned up to $18,000 will still continue to add something to the family coffers and thus continue a work incentive. A point is reached where finally the base payment is totally wiped out by the reductions for earned income.

In contrast to the negative income tax program, which targets benefits heavily on those presumed to be most in need, there is a program called "Children's Allowances." It is semiuniversal since it benefits every household having children irrespective of their level of need. Some form of Children's Allowances operate in nearly every country in the western industrial world except the United States (including countries such as Germany, France, and Ireland). Canada has had a children's allowance since the 1930s and Great Britain since 1945. Although benefits are usually small, they are a significant addition to family finances for poor people. Proponents often argue that it targets benefits directly on children and their needs in ways that other (more or less) universal programs don't in that benefits are paid directly to mothers.[27] The German Children's Allowance type benefits in 1997 were DM 220 per month for the first child (and an exchange rate around U.S. $1.80 per German Deutschmark). With respect to off-targeting of benefits, the Children's Allowance strategy involves considerable seepage, depending on how one perceives the program objective. If the objective is to supplement incomes, the seepage is very large—more nontarget groups than poor will receive the benefit. If the objective is to increase the standard of living of all families with children, whatever their present income level, then there is probably much less off-targeting. However, there can hardly be any sense, from any point of view, of increasing the standard of living of those families already at the top of the income distribution scale. Finally, note that the NIT idea must always involve some kind of means and asset test. It is the presence of this feature in NIT and the lack of it in Children's Allowance that always generates controversy over whether there is strong off-targeting in any Children's Allowance scheme. An additional point of vulnerability for Children's Allowance proposals is that the benefits must be very low per family or else the cost is overwhelming. Simple arithmetic will show that a payment of $100 per week per child in a nation with 50 million children would cost $260 billion per year—more than the cost of the U.S. defense budget. Though child advocates would not find that unseemly, no doubt it would be an unacceptable division of the pie to the advocates for other constituent groups, like the American Association of Retired Persons (AARP) or AIDS advocates. It is important to note that Children's Allowance schemes are not inherently bad proposals, but they are neither cheap nor insignificant in that their redistributive qualities would require a radically different national consensus in the United States about the importance of children and the justice of large-scale income redistribution programs.

Trade-Offs in Evaluating Eligibility Rules

So, if off-targeting has both "good" and "bad" effects, how is the practical public policy analyst to judge between them? It is an important question and doesn't yield to a simple answer. Let us use the concept of "trade-off" to characterize what we will be considering here. It is not an exotic idea, rather one we all use in working out our everyday lives: To get one or another good thing sometimes means having to endure some bad things. Usually, we choose so that the good outweighs the bad—but not always: If I have only enough money to buy badly needed new household appliances—perhaps a refrigerator, a washer-dryer, and a stove, but I also need a better used car, the choice is not so simple. Here is the trade-off: If I buy the appliances, I buy freedom from having to go to the laundromat, enjoyment of a new stove, ability to store food longer and therefore shop less often. In return, I have to endure an unreliable car that spends weeks in the repair shop, which forces me to depend on friends or public transportation. So, how does the ordinary person living an ordinary life make that decision? The answer ultimately depends on the relationship to what one values and disvalues—in a word, preferences. Now let us consider what those value/preferences might be and how a person might go about making decisions based on them.

The most obvious decision rule rests on a preference for getting the "best-value-for-money." Taking into consideration only the most obvious costs and savings, one might add up the costs and savings of choosing (in this example) to buy appliances: Suppose their total cost is about $2,000 and from that I can subtract the savings from avoiding laundromat costs (say, $200 a year). But I must also add in the expected cost for car repairs (about $800 a year) and the extra public transportation costs (about $600). If a better used car will cost about $6,000, then (using out-of-pocket costs as a standard) I would be about $2,400 better off to buy the appliances and forgo the better used car: $2,400 = $6,000 − $2,000 − $200 − $800 − $600. A notable feature of the best-value-for-money standard is that it can depend on whether I want to make it work for the long or short term (these figures only take into account the first year). With every passing year, I lose another $1,400 in transportation costs. Simple arithmetic shows that in three years, I am $1,800 the net loser. Furthermore, when my appliances begin to need repair, I will go deeper into the hole. Thus, in the long run, I would be better off, dollarwise, in choosing the better used car; but in the short run, I am better off choosing the appliances. Still that doesn't take into account those preferences that are more difficult on which to put a dollar value—my preference for saving time and trouble by having a dependable automobile. Best-value-for-money is an obvious standard for choice, but it won't sort out whether I would prefer the convenience of a reliable car compared with the convenience of new appliances. Choosing among trade-offs that involve social programs is no different in principle—whereas costs are important, they are not always (and in all ways) the crucial issue.

When we think about public benefits, trade-offs are ultimately cost *and* value issues—is the public interest better served by exercising a preference for avoiding stigma and increasing costs (as in Children's Allowance or Guaranteed Income Programs) or by exercising a preference for lower costs (e.g., in which case, the monies saved can be spent on reducing other social problems) at the expense of creating stigma for beneficiaries (as in the means-tested TANF program)? There are many other examples of trade-offs; in fact, almost all policy and program choices involve trade-offs of one kind or another and because they ultimately are settled on value/preference grounds, it is one additional reason a value-critical perspective is essential for the practitioner. Two concepts are used to examine some types of trade-offs: vertical equity and horizontal equity. *Vertical equity* refers to the extent to which resources are allocated to those with the most severe need—the kind of close target efficiency spoken of earlier in this and other chapters. *Horizontal equity* refers to the extent to which resources are allocated to *all* those in need.[28] The point here is that, given scarce resources, there is almost always a trade-off between vertical equity and horizontal equity—the difficult (sometimes tragic) choice between meeting a little of the need of *all* those afflicted and adequately meeting the need of those in *most serious* difficulties. There is no consensus on the value/principles on which that decision can or should be made. Other important criteria for evaluating eligibility rules involve trade-offs are discussed in what follows.

Overwhelming Costs, Overutilization, and Underutilization

Bad eligibility rules can create severe overutilization and thus serious cost overruns. Medicare is a leading (and interesting) example in that cost containment is a major problem for Medicare and, in some views, a problem due to an overly generous, eligibility rule. The entitlement rule for Medicare is universal all beneficiaries of OASI are automatically coentitled to Medicare. Medical care for an aging population is an expensive business because they need more care and there is a rising proportion of the elderly in the population. Not only that, but both absolute and relative costs of medical care have risen exorbitantly over the past decade.

But the problem is also due in part to the rising success of medical technology. For example, such procedures as bypass operations for heart disease are now routine. Kidney dialysis is at present included as an acceptable medical procedure for Medicaid beneficiaries. The problem is even more complex because the long-term health benefits for both are debatable—kidney dialysis will extend life about ten years and heart bypass procedures last on average about five years before death or before having to be repeated. The debate is about whether adding zero to ten years onto the life of a post–65-year-old citizen is the best expenditure in view of the pressing health needs of children and working adults in the United States. Recall that all policy systems operate under a condition of finite resources, so that every dollar spent for kidney dialysis and heart bypass procedures is a dollar that cannot be spent on disease prevention for children: The United States still does not make routine immunizations for smallpox, diphtheria, and typhoid available to its children, even though many Third World countries do so. The value-critical policy analyst must search for the value stance from which this policy choice is made. Universal entitlement to medical procedures of debatable benefit are filled with great ethical issues, vexing and ambiguous in the extreme; no surprise they don't get the public discussion they deserve in the halls of Congress. As a nation, we seem unable to face these issues squarely. The consequence is that when it comes to the choice of which medical procedures will be universally provided for the people, it may be determined by which drug or medical supply or hospital corporation lobbies Congress most persuasively. Nothing inherently wrong with profit making but profit making is an imprecise tool, often blunt and cruel, when it comes to cutting out choices of who lives and dies. Note that priorities for scarce research and care money are now embedded in the Medicare/Medicaid policy system. But where should first priority lie: AIDS, Alzheimer's, developmental disabilities, chronic mental illness, or for neonatal care—newborns, born at less than one pound, ten ounces? Here are some quotes about the nature of such neonatal care:

- About half will live but three-quarters of those will have serious neurological damage.
- All stops are pulled out, . . . we are doing virtually everything that can be done to keep these children alive.
- One national study in 1988 revealed that a third of neonatologists said they had changed their medical practice and were treating babies they thought had nothing to gain and a lot to lose from aggressive medical care.
- After three months in the hospital, which cost close to a million dollars, . . . the triplets came home. All had grade 4 brain-bleeds making it virtually certain that their brains were damaged. (*New York Times*, September 30, 1991, p. Al)

These data are an example of an overwhelming and uncontrolled cost burden on the medical system in general. Because recent estimates suggest that such care is extremely expensive and that the babies' chances for surviving into adulthood as fully functional adults are quite slim, on what value/preferences shall such choices be based?

The basic value problem is highlighted because public policy has avoided the basic value issue. It is not a "scientific" decision. Clearly, some public medical benefits can create their own unlimited demand. Where private physicians control treatment and where physicians fear legal suit for not providing maximum care and treatment, neither the patient nor the government is in a position to curb the use of modern technology (although health insurers seem to do so!). One of the reasons that Medicare and Medicaid costs have risen so rapidly is that nearly all the aged can qualify for benefits under one program or another.[29] But it is quite clear that the issue is not simply *who* is entitled, but also for *what benefit. The basic question U.S. social policy has not yet answered is: "On what value premises shall medical care, indeed life and death, be rationed?"*

Some eligibility rules create underutilization; that is, program benefits are not taken up by the people for whom they are intended. There are several important examples of underutilization in the United States, some more serious than others. One that perhaps is less serious is the low "take-up" rate of the Low Income Energy Assistance Program (LIEAP), a federally financed program initiated by the Carter administration with the object of subsidizing increased energy costs among the low-income population. The entitlement program rules rested heavily on a reasonably flexible and nonstigmatizing income test, but there the public was poorly informed about exactly how much benefit was possible. In fact, in many states the LIEAP benefit was certainly more than a trivial amount—sometimes covering an average of 150 percent of the total cold-weather energy costs of the average household.

One more serious example of underutilization of a public benefit program is the SSI program offering cash income maintenance benefits for which a means-tested entitlement rule is in place. The take-up rates for this program run between 55 and 60 percent.[30] Although it is not entirely clear that this underutilization is totally an eligibility rule problem, there are suspicious signs: SSI is a program for which both the aged and the disabled qualify and, for complex reasons, much of the underutilization concerns the disabled. The eligibility rules have a very complicated procedure for entitlement determination, which appears to qualify only those completely and totally disabled for long periods; also, it was originally designed for physical, not mental, disabilities. For example, it ordinarily disqualifies those who can only work some of the time, which, of course, applies especially to those disabled for reasons of mental illnesses like psychosis, manic depression, or schizophrenia. Reestablishing benefits takes as long and is as complex and demanding as the original application—seldom less than several months and often more than a year. Also, it is well known among the disabled population that the outcome of application is unpredictable at best. It is reasonable to expect that rational people will hesitate before committing themselves to pursuing such benefits, especially when they involve heavy expenses in time, long-term doggedness in documenting medical treatment and diagnosis and not trivial monetary sums for a population that has no discretionary income. The mentally ill are not the largest proportion of the homeless, but they are a significant group. Homelessness creates public costs, an illustration of the point that underutilization doesn't automatically create cost savings in tax dollars, for example, jail stays, emergency medical care, and street violence.

Overutilization and underutilization criteria have special applications in the personal social services. A leading example of eligibility rules that create unintentional underutilization are programs for older caucasian and minority children who, otherwise available for permanent adoption, nevertheless remained in foster care for lack of parent/applicants. Until the 1980s, child-placing agencies that had adoptable minority children in their custody in fact contributed to their problems by holding to certain eligibility requirements. For example, requiring separate bedrooms for children, typical middle-class income levels, a nonworking mother for infants, and/or formal in-office interviews held in a distinctively white middle-class office environment. Such eligibility rules actively disentitled working-class and minority and ethnic parent/applicants from consideration in two ways. First, "working-class" and minority status can mean absence of average incomes, and working mothers; therefore, if an eligibility rule is based on average income or the presence of a nonworking mother, it disentitles many minority applicants and single parents except those with incomes above the average compared with their own racial group. Such a rule offends against the *equity* criterion because it systematically disentitles based on social class status that has nothing to do with any feature of the social problem the program is intended to solve.

Second, some people from minority and ethnic groups have limited experience in making "formal applications"—in fact, the whole idea of "applying for" children and having their parental and social competence judged is an experience outside the realm of their cultural expectations. For most such groups, not only is taking responsibility for others' children not unusual—whether children from their own families or otherwise—it is usually negotiated in face-to-face encounters and in familiar surroundings with little or no expectation that motives are under scrutiny. Whereas there is good reason for adoption agencies to be concerned about applicants' motives for parenting, any good eligibility rule will take cultural practices into account and not run hard against them. Agencies have dealt with this by featuring initial contacts in the applicants' home, church (or other religious site), or lodge; sometimes, these contacts have been initiated by friends or acquaintances. In that way, the whole encounter in adopting a child occurs in the context of a familiar social network where the agency staff member, although a stranger, is at least "vouched for" by someone already trusted.

Here is another extreme example, this one from the eligibility rules apparently in use by some public Central American child-placing agencies: Part of the application process involves psychological testing via such measures as the Minnesota Multiphasic Personality Inventory (MMPI). Firsthand interview data suggest that the results of such tests have serious implications for adoption placement decisions.[31] In fact, a requirement for MMPI screening is listed in the administrative documents of one Central American public adoption agency. Screening is an issue because local Central American adoption agencies commonly have in their custody a number of local children of color (e.g., indigenous Indians and Caribbean blacks), including infants and preschoolers, children whose only hope for kinship associations of their own are non-Indian (most frequently Latino) families. Those agencies report that adoption by local non-Indian citizens is uncommon. Psychological screening of this kind as an eligibility rule creates underutilization because it is so alien to the applicants' experience (leaving aside the cogent argument about its cultural transferability to a Hispanic culture or the doubtfulness of its ability to predict good parents or screen out the mentally distressed). That alien nature of psychological testing discourages scarce applicants. And, news about agency experiences spreads widely in minority communities by word of mouth, especially among potential adoptive applicants, and that further discourages applications.

These considerations probably apply equally well to other personal social services such as mental health and counseling services where their delivery takes place in formal clinics and office buildings. That is one reason why, years ago, "street workers" and "outreach" programs were invented—to create access to services when they could be encountered in the everyday and familiar lives of the people for whom they were intended, rather than limiting formal application to unfamiliar, hard-to-get-to office settings. In small communities, it can be stigmatizing to enter a building known to be the community mental health center. Certainly, that applies to more controversial birth control and/or abortion locations.

Clearly, eligibility rules for insurance-covered services can be sources of under- and overutilization. Insurance companies find eligibility rules for mental health services to be problematic, not least because for mental and emotional illnesses or problems, the need for treatment and what constitutes adequate treatment are debatable in the field—debatable in a way that appendicitis or diabetes or athlete's foot for that matter is not. Insurance companies need to ask where is the clear and definable point at which a patient is not helped by further office visits for the purpose of increasing "self-awareness," self-concept, or "personal insight." As might be expected, insurers don't find underutilization a problem, but if eligibility rules for insurance coverage aren't on target, underutilization can lead to a tragic results.

The general solution insurance companies have resorted to is to place arbitrary dollar or time limits on mental health and/or counseling service—$1,000 a year for outpatient services or fifteen days of inpatient services is not an unusual standard. Costs are an issue and insurance companies have a telling point, one that the psychotherapy industry has yet to answer, coincidentally, because the insurance principle requires ability to forecast use (via some actuarial design) in constructing rate schedules for prepaid insurance premiums for health coverage.

Overutilization of mental health and counseling services, where the financial rewards are generous to therapists continuing services to essentially healthy individuals for personal growth and fulfillment, may have contributed to this situation.

On the other hand, the health insurance industry is not noted for its leadership in this regard either; between the two, sizable underutilization and overutilization continue because of the arbitrary nature of the "caps" placed on mental health and counseling services.

Work Disincentives and Eligibility Rules

Almost all agree that eligibility rules should be evaluated against their potential for work disincentives. The argument about whether cash benefits in social welfare income maintenance programs cause people to choose benefits over work for wages is several hundred years old. A major concern during the Speenhamland experiment in England in 1795, it is presently a concern of U.S. economists and politicians as they attempt to reduce welfare costs.[32] Both economic theory and common sense would seem to indicate that cash benefits from the public treasury could strongly reduce work effort on the part of the ordinary citizen—why would anyone work if they didn't have to? Both the question and the answer are complex issues that for years have eluded practical resolution and scientific experiment. Who, after all, would give money to someone just to see whether he or she would continue to work, work less, not work at all?

In fact, that experiment has taken place. The economic theory behind the income guarantee experiments runs a little like this:

> One person can view time as being divided among three activities: working for wages, working at home, and enjoying leisure time, depending on relative opportunities and rewards. The reward for market work is money income, which ultimately is used to buy goods and services. One of the goods that people may "purchase" is leisure, but each person pays a different price, one equal to his or her wage rate. Economists theorize that the amount of nonworking time "bought" by a person depends on two factors: (1) the wages that must be foregone and (2) the amount of nonwage income that is available to the person. As a person's wages rise, leisure (non-work) time becomes more expensive. So, besides the question of whether public benefits cause less work effort, two other questions arise: (1) whether if there *is* less work effort, it is due to the fact that leisure time becomes more expensive as income rises, causing people to regard increasing leisure costs as "expenditures" or (2) whether with more income, people value increased income less and are willing to substitute leisure for work.

These questions have vexed discussions of welfare reform for many years. The U.S. Office of Economic Opportunity (OEO) undertook a series of large-scale experiments beginning in New Jersey in 1968 and extended in the 1970s in Iowa, North Carolina, Colorado, and Washington state. These experiments, all long term (five years for the most part), were carefully designed and instrumented, and strong attempts were made—not always successfully—to insulate them from external contaminating influences. We will focus here on the Seattle-Denver Income Maintenance Experiment (SIMDIME) because it was the last in this series and provides the best data. It had the largest sample among all the experiments, in that it included around 5,000 one- and two-parent families of black, white, and Hispanic ethnic origin. In SIMDIME, the families were assigned either to one of several experimental groups receiving cash assistance payments at various levels or to one of a control group of families who received no experimental payments but continued to receive whatever benefits they were eligible for under current governmental programs. Hours of work of experimental families were compared with hours of work of the control-group families during the course of the experiment. First, the results showed no significant difference between responses by racial or ethnic background, holding all other characteristics constant. Next, some decrease in work effort was shown when people got an income guarantee, but the difference was small and differed significantly for women compared with men. The report has this to say about the results:[33]

> The results for husbands show, for example, that if a family's preprogram annual income was $4,000, a cash benefit that raised income by $1000 would cause the husband to work about an hour less per week . . . the effects on a wife in a family with the same income would cause her to work two hours per week less. . . . However, since wives usually have lower wage rates than their husbands, a given benefit reduction rate usually would have a smaller dollar effect on the wife's net wage than on the husband's.

The experimenters note that these results are as expected since "wives probably feel the greatest necessity to work when other family income is low and have more freedom to respond to changes in income or wage rates when the family income is initially high." Husbands, on the other hand, are more likely to feel that they "should" work, no matter what the circumstance. Table 7.2 presents the results of the effect of the income guarantee on work effort for all four work-incentive experiments. Although some of the wives' reduction in work hours appears large, observe that the authors interpret this as a relatively small-scale response. "Since wives in poor families usually work relatively few hours to begin with, the large percentage change in their labor supply effort amounts to relatively small numbers of hours."[34] The net result, as stated before, is that a $1,000 increase in the family's income "causes" the wife in a poor family to work only two hours less per week. Recall that at the time of this experiment, the minimum wage was around $2.75 per hour and that was the prevailing wage for those women. So what should be our conclusion about the work disincentives of social welfare programs offering cash benefits like this one? A conservative conclusion, faithful to the facts the experiment reveals, would be that the effect is there, but is very slight, probably insignificant to most people. The experimenters believe that the results from all four of the experiments show a "striking similarity," particularly considering that the experiments provided different sets of benefit levels and benefit reduction rates, that they took place in states with widely differing tax and transfer systems, and that different criteria were used to select the four samples.[35]

One result of the Guaranteed Income experiment should not go unnoticed: There was a marked increase in the proportion of marriage dissolution under the impact of an income guarantee. It was about the same for whites as for blacks but noticeably greater

TABLE 7.2 Estimated Percentage Reductions in Work Hours in Four Income Maintenance Experiments

Control/Experimental Group Differences as a percent Control Mean[a]

	New Jersey (White Only)	Rural Wage Earners	Gary, Indiana	Seattle-Denver
Husbands	6%	1%	7%	6%
Wives	31	27	17	17
Total	13	13	8	9
Female heads	[b]	[b]	2	12

[a]These estimates are weighted averages of the response in hours worked by different study groups. Because of the technical problems in estimating the response of black and Spanish-speaking groups in the New Jersey experiment, estimates reported here for New Jersey are for whites only. Recent reanalysis of the New Jersey data provides evidence that the response of these groups is similar to that of whites. Total responses (and base hours) include only husbands and wives in the Gary and Seattle-Denver experiments; in the other experiments they include other family members as well.

[b]None included in the experiment.

Source: The Seattle-Denver Income Maintenance Experiment, Midexperiment Results and a Generalization to the Natural Population (Stanford, CA: Stanford Research Institute and Mathematical Policy Research, 1978), Table 2, p. 64. Reprinted by permission.

for Latinos.[36] One important consequence here is that if a national income guarantee program were put in effect, the proportion of female-headed, single-parent families would increase substantially, particularly for whites and Latinos. Remarriage rates for blacks under conditions of income guarantee is sufficiently high, so it would not affect the proportion of single-parent families among that subpopulation. Taken at pure face value, many would probably agree that this is a negative feature of an NIT or any guaranteed income program. Note, however, that these facts can also be interpreted to mean that greater good prevails when women (and men) have the economic support that allows them to make free choices about ending "bad" marriages.

Procreational Incentives, Marital Instability, and Generational Dependency

Other criteria for evaluating eligibility rules, especially cash-benefit programs, are the extent to which they provide incentives for procreation, marital break-up, and/or the dependency of the children of families who receive public benefits. The possibility that citizens conceive children in order to become eligible for, or to increase, welfare benefits, surfaces regularly as a matter of public and political discussion. For some, the issue is the amount of benefit per additional child, and for others it is simply that where benefit eligibility is tied to the number of children in families it is possible that it serves as a significant childbearing incentive. The latter issue is usually argued from a social problem viewpoint that is ideologically committed to the notion that work is a highly valued instrumental activity and that citizens have a predominant propensity *not* to choose work if there is an available alternative—no matter how grim. It is certainly possible to conceive of a person who would endure the physical discomforts of bearing children as the preferred alternative to working, but even if the standard of living it afforded was considerably less than a poverty line existence and if the attached stigma was extreme, such a choice is neither economically nor socially rational. What are the costs of bearing and rearing a child, when measured against the welfare benefit gain? Where such calculation is made, only the person who could *never* expect to work at all would find it to her advantage to bear children just to obtain an increase in benefits. In states with generous means-tested benefits, the benefit increase per new child amounts to about $80 monthly and the increased cost of rearing another child—even by very modest standards of living—are several times that sum. Surely, there will always be a few people who make irrational choices that work against their own economic self-interest but to rebut such an argument, we only need assume that the ordinary person acts in ways that will be of most economic benefit to herself or himself. Furthermore, there is every reason to believe that the average poor person, well acquainted with the realities of life at the poverty level, does that in serious matters of everyday life. In fact, Goodwin's study suggests exactly this point: His data clearly show that most poor people wish to work, believe that work itself is virtuous, and expect to work profitably most of their lives.[37] But we must be careful of this argument when applied to the case of the teenage mother/welfare beneficiary who still lives with her own parents. To the extent that she doesn't bear the full weight of the extra cost of an additional child, there may be an incentive to have more babies just to obtain the benefit increase.

There is persuasive evidence *against* the notion that financial incentives stimulate childbearing in the results of programs in countries that need to increase population rapidly: Attempts to do so are made through social welfare programs that grant benefits, often sizable, to citizens who bear children. The most massive of such programs was the French attempt to raise their birthrate in a population decimated by World War I after France lost half its male population. Both Sweden and more recently Canada have made similar attempts for similar purposes. All these programs have been *entirely unsuccessful*. It is worthwhile noting that in Third World countries as standards of living and wage rates rise, along with increased literacy and educational attainment of women, birthrates go down rather dramatically.

In summary, does the fact of eligibility for welfare benefits serve as an incentive to procreation? Given the evidence reviewed before, it is very unlikely that there is any such effect in a population or even any of its subgroups, though there may be some marginal and individual instances. There is, of course, no wisdom in forming large-scale public policy around small marginal effects. We are left with the conclusion that increasing benefits with family size does not create an incentive to further childbearing.

Another widely discussed issue is that public benefits like the old AFDC (now TANF) create marital instability: Do families split in order to meet the condition that the major wage earner be absent from the home? Nancy Murdrick studied that issue directly through data on when AFDC applications occurred relative to the marital split and observed differences between high- and low-income families with respect to the same issue. Study results are clear. The data show that most AFDC applications occurred nearly two years after the split. Murdrick concludes that the AFDC application is a response to the consequences of the split, not a premeditated outcome. Nor does it matter whether the applicants had an above-average or below-average income prior to their split.[38] Surely, some couples do split up just in order to qualify for welfare benefits, but the policy-relevant issue is what is the case for *most* people. Once again, the issue of policy trade-offs is relevant: Doing good policy for the general population may create some negatives for a smaller number of others.

Earlier studies support Murdrick's conclusions. It does not appear that AFDC applicants contemplated applying for AFDC before the split, nor that possible eligibility somehow stimulated it.[39] Further, it appears that the expected wage rate, rather than expected AFDC benefits, is the significant factor in predicting marital splits. Given these results, it seems that the contention that AFDC actively creates marital instability is doubtful. However, there is no doubt that for children, it eases the financial crisis caused by the marriage breakup—which, of course, is the main program intention.

Yet another problem said to be a consequence of eligibility for public welfare benefits is that, generally speaking, citizens who now receive public benefits were reared in families who depended on public benefits, and that this current generation will produce children who also will live at the expense of public benefit. In its most rational form, this argument over generational dependency (as it is sometimes called) asserts that social and personal identity are crucial in determining the choices made about work and "getting by." It assumes that a child who grows up in a family in which there are no models of working to make a living will simply follow the pattern set by adults, that he or she will search out the welfare option. In its more unsympathetic form, the argument asserts strong antisocial, deviant motives to both parents and children in poor economic circumstances. In order to make this argument plausible, it would seem necessary to assume that generational dependency must involve primarily those children whose families spent long periods as welfare beneficiaries, short-term since the learning of role models and the socialization process referred to is not a short-term matter. No current explanation or approach to socialization suggests otherwise. If that is the case, the data from the Michigan Panel Study of Income Dynamics bear strongly on the plausibility of the generational dependency argument.[40] This study, which has few challenges to its methodology or conclusions, shows clearly that only 12 percent of all welfare beneficiaries had received benefits for as long as four years, cumulatively. The authors conclude that there is little support for the existence of a sizable welfare class, that the most characteristic welfare recipient receives public benefits for about two years in succession, and then may move on and off benefits for two considerably shorter periods of time later in their lives.[41] If there is no large number of persons who spend long years on welfare benefits, it seems unlikely that the necessary conditions are available in which the mechanisms that are said to create generational dependency can work. Of course, this only shows that if generational dependency exists at all, it is a small-scale problem. Other studies, based on less extensive data than the Rein and Rainwater study, support the preceding general conclusions. Podell's extensive study of a large sample of New York City welfare beneficiaries concludes that about 15 percent of the group in the mid-1960s were reared in families that were publicly assisted at one time or another.[42] Less than 10 percent of the group had both parents and siblings who had been public welfare recipients. It is noteworthy that in both the Rein and Rainwater and the Podell studies, the definitions of *welfare dependency* are very loose ("receiving over half the total income from public funds" in the latter case and simply "to have received any income from public funds" in the former). Finally, a study by Baumheier in the early 1970s draws the conclusion that the magnitude of second-generation public assistance dependency is quite small.[43] Whereas some might consider a 10 to 15 percent rate of intergenerational dependency a significant problem since the welfare dollar costs of this group is high, it would not seem to be a good characterization of the AFDC-TANF recipient group as a whole.

Opportunities for Political Interference via Weak Eligibility Rules

At one level there is every reason to believe that political influence is one route to the entitlement to public benefits for individuals and groups—of course, social programs are a vehicle by which political interests are (and should be) expressed. But once the program or policy is implemented, it becomes bad social policy for citizens, or groups of them, to be either eligible or not simply because of political influence that circumvents the legislative or judicial processes that keep social policy as an expression of the will of the people in a democracy. Equity is the value issue here. Citizens in a democracy should have equal access to public benefits, and that access should not depend on who one knows or doesn't know. Nor should it depend on the desire of the executive branch of government to shape a social program in ways that it couldn't achieve through the regular channels of the legislative or judicial process. There is an unusual modern example of the latter, which we will briefly review for its value in illustrating the great danger posed by eligibility rules that are vague and uncertain in administration. Well-formed eligibility rules are not valuable just for their tidiness, rather that they might avoid political intervention in the operations of social programs, an intervention of a particularly vicious sort for vulnerable people. This example, from the mid-1980s, concerns the Social Security Disability Insurance (DI) program.

Probably the premier policy problem of any social program for the disabled is to construct a useful and stable definition of *disablement*, and the DI program is no exception. Robert Ball, chief actuary for the Social Security Administration for many years, reports that the slippery DI definition of disability allowed opposing biases to be used within one rather short period of time.[44] The reason for its "slipperiness" is that it leaves one part of the eligibility rule to medical and *administrative discretion*—the determination of whether a disability exists in fact. Thus, administrators and physicians were left to liberal interpretation of medical facts. One has only to look at the sizable proportion of initial application decisions that were reversed and "re-reversed" at every stage of reconsideration and appeal to realize that what is technically called "interjudge reliability" was a hallmark lack in this eligibility process.[45] Over a ten- to twelve-year period beginning in the 1970s, reversal rates on disability denial appeals rose to nearly two-thirds of all appeals; in regard to mental disabilities, reversal rates reached as high as 91 percent of all appealed denials of benefit applications.[46]

In explanation, Robert Ball noted that in the early years of the program, ". . . I can assure you gentlemen, that the general attitude . . . [was] wanting to pay claims."[47] To the point, it is notable that in this climate, even though Congress expressly forbade the Social Security Administration (SSA) from reversing the findings of state disability determination units, it did so regularly (to the advantage of applicants).[48] However, under the prodding of a Congress worried about rising program costs and a presidential administration looking with disfavor on most welfare benefits, SSA began by a variety of means to administer a very different definition of the term *disability*. Clearly, SSA was able to turn the DI system around simply by the strength of its own ability to reinterpret the definition of disability and change some of its procedural mechanisms: In five years, DI benefit allowance rates were cut in half, terminations increased, and total costs slowed significantly. ". . . [D]isability examiners have become more conservative in the way in which they interpret and apply standards [for DI awards]."[49]

Despite the significant changes that had already occurred, with the 1981 inauguration of President Reagan, who had made explicit campaign promises to reduce the size of entitlement programs, not only were new applicants under fire, but the disabled who already received benefits were affected as well. Unprecedented terminations of thousands of DI beneficiaries took place between 1980 and 1985: 71,500 in 1980; 98,800 in 1981; and 121,400 in the first five months of 1982—with 360,000 expected to be terminated in

1984.[50] "In the 1960s, the loose and ambiguous definition of disability could not constrain a [Democratic, neo–New Deal] political administration determined to expand the program any more successfully than it could in the 1980s constrain a [Republican, conservative] political administration determined to reduce the size and costs of the DI program."[51] Now another highly placed Social Security administrator could say, mimicking Robert Ball's earlier statement, ". . . I can assure you gentlemen, the general attitude [in the Social Security Administration] is to deny, deny, deny. . . ."[52] Intelligent programs cannot be administered under such conditions of radical changes in programs as exemplified before. Seriously disabled beneficiaries have had reason to expect that they could count on their benefit income in one year, only to learn a few years later that despite no change in their condition, benefits will be withdrawn. Worse, they learned a few more years later that many if not most terminations were illegal in the first place, so that if they reapply there is good chance that their benefits will be reinstated (*Minnesota v. Schweiker*, 1983; Social Security Regulations no. 83-15, 16, 17s, 1986). On such grounds as outlined before, it is clear that this policy system was in ragged disarray.

The definitional ambiguity of disability with which the DI has (and still does) operate has been used by parties of opposing political persuasions to expand and contract the program at will. Note that it is possible to increase substantially the clarity and reliability of medical disability determinations, as Mashaw (and Nagi before him) have clearly shown, by fairly simple attention to definitional clarity, plus well-known modern research and investigative practices on making clinical judgments. It is also clear that there is every reason to expect further political adventures into the Social Security system absent the correction of this policy problem. "If the same policy weaknesses that made possible the political intrusions into this social program are still in place when the next liberal administration comes into office, it will simply use the very same weaknesses to restore the system to its former condition."[53] Such a political scenario would continue into infinity, a prospect that is not in the best interests of the country or its disabled citizens.

This example teaches two key lessons: First, it highlights for us from Mashaw the conclusion that there is nothing inherently wrong with using expert judgments as a basis for eligibility rules. Second, it shows that some conditions are necessary to keep the process on track and functioning. Social researchers have learned of those requirements: define very carefully the thing to be judged, train and orient judges to apply only that definition within a specific procedural context, and indoctrinate new judges into that system, a few at a time. This process is not inexpensive, but almost any trained researcher can achieve a 90 percent agreement with almost any set of judges making even complicated judgments. Costs will surely be less than the direct administrative costs of disentitling and reentitling disabled beneficiaries time and time again.

Summary

This chapter presented concepts to assist the practitioner in understanding the variability among common eligibility rules and procedures. The following types of eligibility rules were discussed:

- Prior contribution
- Administrative rule
- Private contracts
- Professional discretion
- Administrative discretion
- Judicial decision
- Means testing
- Attachment to the workforce

Whereas the ultimate test of the merits of any particular eligibility rule is its "fit" with the social problem conception that underlies the program or policy under consideration, special problems are likely to be created by eligibility rules. The practical analyst should examine the available data and the general workings of the policy or program to search for evidence of the following special problems:

- Stigma and alienation
- Off-targeting of benefits
- Overwhelming costs
- Overutilization and underutilization
- Political interference
- Negative incentives and disincentives (work, procreation, marriage, and so on)

The presence of any of these special problems works against the achievement of a functional policy and programs—against adequacy, equity, and efficiency.

EXERCISES

1. What is the difference between the eligibility rule known as administrative discretion and the one known as administrative rule?

2. What are the consequences of basing eligibility for social welfare benefits solely on the type of entitlement called "attachment to the workforce"?

3. There are three branches of U.S. government: legislative, executive, and judicial. What role does each play in establishing the eligibility rules for TANF benefits? What may each branch do to affect eligibility rule once the TANF program is established? (Remember, no state is required to have a TANF program.)

4. What is the major difference between professional discretion and administrative discretion as methods of determining eligibility for social welfare benefits or services?

NOTES

1. The scheme concerns only "selective" eligibility rules. However, this book will not consider the traditional selective versus universal distinction in regard to (among other things) eligibility rules, siding with Titmuss in his belief that its utility for the practical policy analyst is only marginal.

2. R. Titmuss, "Welfare State and Welfare Society," in *Commitment to Welfare* (London: Allen and Unwin, 1968), pp. 130–134.

3. G. Kollman, "How Long Does It Take New Retirees to Recover the Value of Their Social Security Taxes?" 94-149 EPW. (Washington, DC: Congressional Research Service and *The 1996 Green Book*, 104th Congress, 2nd Session, November 4, 1996, House Ways and Means Committee, Print No. 104-14, p. 112, Table 1-50).

4. H. Aaron, *Economic Effects of Social Security* (Washington, DC: The Brookings Institution, 1982), pp. 12–16, 67–73.

5. Only in the United States is the Workers Compensation system operated as a private enterprise.

6. K. R. Wedel, "Designing and Implementing Performance Contracting," in R. L. Edwards and J. A. Yankee (eds.), *Skills for Effective Service Management* (Silver Spring, MD: NASW Press, 1991), p. 86.

7. K. R. Wedel and S. W. Colston, "Performance Contracting for Human Services: Issues and Suggestions," *Administration in Social Work*, 12(1) (1988): 73–87.

8. "Social Services Programs for Individuals and Families, Title XX of the Social Security Act," *Federal Register*, 40(125) (June 27, 1975): p. 27335, sec. 228.

9. *Annual Report to the Congress on Title XX of the Social Security Act, Fiscal Year 1979* (Washington, DC: U.S. Department of Health, Education and Welfare, Office of the Secretary, 1980), pp. 38, 45.

10. K. R. Wedel and S. W. Colston, "Performing Contracting," p. 75.

11. Ibid., p. 81.

12. Ibid., p. 348.

13. M. Brown, *Working the Street: Police Discretion and Dilemmas of Reform* (New York: Basic Books, 1981).

14. M. Lipsky, *Street Level Bureaucracy: Dilemmas of the Individual in Public Services* (New York: Russell Sage Foundation, 1980).

15. D. E. Chambers, "The Reagan Administration Welfare Retrenchment Policy: Terminating Social Security Benefits for the Disabled," *Policy Study Review*, (1985): 207–215.

16. D. E. Chambers, "Residence Requirements for Welfare Benefits," *Social Work*, 14(4) (1971): 29.

17. *Brown v. Board of Education*, 347 U.S. 483 (1954).

18. H. D. Krause, *Child Support in America* (Charlottesville, VA: The Mitchie Company, 1981), pp. 330–340.

19. T. B. Festinger, "The Impact of the New York Court Review of Children in Foster Care: A Follow-up Report," *Child Welfare*, 55(8) (1976): 515–544.

20. AFDC beneficiaries live below the poverty line and seldom during their whole lives work at jobs that pay more than minimum wage, whereas Workers Compensation beneficiaries almost always earn average incomes and do at least semiskilled work.

21. *Characteristics of State Plans for Aid to Families with Dependent Children* (Washington, DC: U.S. Department of Health and Human Services, Social Security Administration, Office Administration for Children and Families of Family Assistance (Part Two, Table 1, 1991), pp. 409, 455, 488.

22. J. Feagin, *Subordinating the Poor* (Englewood Cliffs, NJ: Prentice Hall, 1974), pp. 103–118.

23. T. F. Pettigrew, "Social Psychology's Contribution to an Understanding of Poverty," in V. T. Covello (ed.), *Poverty and Public Policy* (Cambridge, MA: Shenkman, 1980), pp. 198–224.

24. Susan Sheehan, *A Welfare Mother* (New York: Signet Books, 1976). *Social Security Benefit Rates*, Leaflet NI 196. Department of Health and Social Services (HMSO), 1990.

25. G. Hoshino, "Simplifying the Means Test," *Social Work* (July 1965): 98–103.

26. N. Kotz, *Hunger in America* (New York: The Field Foundation, 1979), pp. 28–29.

27. *Child Benefit*, Leaflet CH1. Department of Health and Social Security (HMSO), 1990.

28. S. Danziger and K. Portnoy, *The Distributional Impacts of Public Policies* (New York: St. Martin's Press, 1988), p. 124.

29. That is because 85 to 95 percent of the U.S. workforce is covered by the Social Security system, so they are automatically eligible for Medicare when they receive retirement and disability benefits.

30. J. Menefee, B. Edwards, and S. Scheiber, "Analysis of Non-participation in the SSI Program," *Social Security Bulletin*, 44 (1981): 3–21.

31. Data were gathered by author in personal interviews with public (and private) child-placing staff and administrators while conducting research on exportation of Central American children to Europe and the United States for adoption in Honduras, El Salvador, Guatemala, and Costa Rica (1991–1992).

32. Speenhamland was an English town whose council solved its poverty problem by providing bread—not cash—to needy persons. There was a public outcry from those who believed it would destroy all incentive to work.

33. *The Seattle-Denver Income Maintenance Experiment, Midexperiment Results and a Generalization to the National Population* (Stanford, CA: Stanford Research Institute and Mathematics Policy Research, 1978), p. vii.

34. Ibid., 11–12.

35. Ibid., 12–14.

36. M. T. Hannan, N. B. Tuma, and L. P. Groeneveld, "Income and Marital Evidence from the Income Maintenance Experiment," *American Journal of Sociology* (May 1977), pp. 1200–1201.

37. L. Goodwin, *Do the Poor Want to Work?* (Washington, DC: The Brookings Institution, 1972).

38. N. Murdrick, "Use of AFDC by Previously High and Low Income Households," *Social Service Review*, 52(1) (1978): 110.

39. B. Bernstein and W. Meezan, *The Impact of Welfare on Family Stability* (New York: Center for New York City Affairs, 1975), p. 99.

40. M. Rein and L. Rainwater, "Patterns of Welfare Use," *Social Service Review*, 52(4) 511–534.

41. J. N. Morgan et al., *Five Thousand American Families: Patterns of Economic Progress*, vol. 1 (Ann Arbor, MI: Institute for Social Research, 1974), pp. 1–9.

42. L. Podell, *Families on Welfare in New York City* (New York: The Center for Study of Urban Problems, 1968), pp. 28–29.

43. E. C. Baumheier, *Intergenerational Dependency, a Study of Public Assistance in Successive Generations*. Ph.D. diss., Brandeis University, Waltham, Massachusetts, 1971.

44. M. Derthick, *Policy Making for Social Security* (Washington, DC: The Brookings Institution, 1979).

45. Chambers, "The Reagan Administration," p. 4.

46. U.S. Congress, Senate Subcommittee on Oversight of Government Management of the Senate Committee on Governmental Affairs, "SSDI Reviews: The Role of the Administrative Law Judge," Hearing Report, 98th Congress, 1st Session (June 8, 1983), Appendix, memo from Carl Fritz to Louis Hays, Chief of the Appeals Division of the Social Security Administration.

47. Derthick, *Policy Making*, p. 310.

48. D. Goldsborough et al., "The Social Security Administration: An Interdisciplinary Study of Disability Evaluation" (Washington, DC: George Washington University Law Center, 1963), mimeographed, pp. 98–100.

49. M. Lando, A. Farley, and M. Brown, "Recent Trends in the SSDI Program," *Social Security Bulletin*, 5(2) (August 1982): 50.

50. J. Mashaw, *Bureaucratic Justice* (New Haven: Yale University Press, 1983).

51. Chambers, "The Reagan Administration," p. 7.

52. Mashaw, *Bureaucratic Justice*, p. 37.

53. Chambers "The Reagan Administration," p. 15.

8 Analysis of Service-Delivery Systems and Social Program and Policy Design

He who would do good to another must do it in minute particulars. General good is the plea of the scoundrel, hypocrite, and flatterer.

—William Blake, 1784

Introduction

This chapter concerns a basic policy element called administering and delivering social services. First, the heart of the matter, the social program or policy design, will be considered since that, precisely, is the most important thing a service-delivery system delivers. Readers need to learn how to develop program designs out of program theory, so that will occupy an important place here. Types of service-delivery organizations will be examined so that readers can readily recognize them in the field. The chapter ends with a discussion of evaluation criteria for judging the merit of service-delivery programs and organizations.

Social Policy and Program Design

In the most fundamental sense, providing a solution to a social problem is the main reason for being that a social program or social policy can claim. And the only manifest reason for being of an administrative or service-delivery system is to provide the means by which that solution can be implemented. To be sure, there are many latent sociological reasons as well (see Chapter 5 on goals and objectives), though we will not focus on those here. Let's call the basic root of that solution *program or policy* design (for the sake of simplicity, hereafter referred to as a *program design*). The program design consists of sets of carefully defined program activities that the staff or the implementing organization intends to deliver or undertake on behalf of its consumer/beneficiaries. These activities are the heart of the social program; however, the program has many other parts because programmed activities must have a context—it is like a theatre production that must have an actual location, a stage or set and a cast, among other things. So it is for a social program: It must have a geographic location (a neighborhood street corner, a center, or office, but it could be a tavern, as well); it must have a cast (practitioners), it must have costumers/makeup/lighting folks (program consultants), and it must have creative and administrative staff like producers/directors (clinical supervisors, program directors, and the like). But, the heart of the "drama" is the practitioner cast and the program design, a "sort of" script to which all the organizational actors play. We'll call that script the *program specification*. Figures 8.1, 8.2, and 8.3 show, respectively, an example of a common (program) theory concerning the physical abuse of a young child, a program design, and a program specification based on the theory.

The word *theory* is being used loosely here to mean only a rough-and-ready sketch of a sequence of activities performed so as to make a difference and achieve the desired outcome(s). The logic of these connections (i.e., how and why certain activities are sequenced) is not given here, but if it were, it would set out basic premises about the events

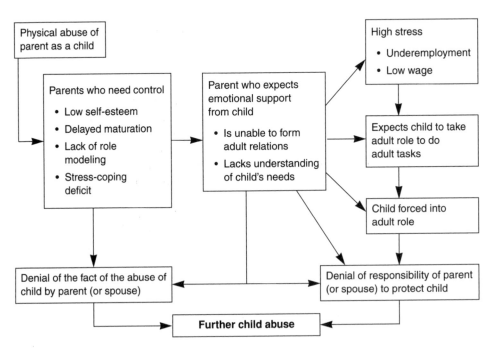

FIGURE 8.1   Program theory.

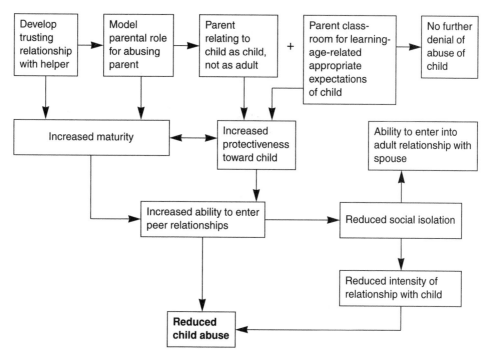

FIGURE 8.2   Program design (essential program elements involving child abuser).

described and the reason they are connected to the desired outcomes. These rough-and-ready sketches are the fundamental ideas that highlight the cause-and-effect relations that are presumed (whether on good evidence or not) to lead to the stated outcome that represents—wholly or in part—a social problem solution.

This section will describe this fundamental aspect of social policy and program service delivery so that a judgment can be made as to whether a clear and credible program/policy theory and design are present and accounted for. *The presence of a clear and credible program theory and program design is an important evaluation criterion, one by which the merit of a program of service delivery should be judged.* Note that we will stress this aspect of service delivery and administrative systems. The direct administration of such systems is beyond the scope of this book since this text is directed to social work and human service practitioners, those whose primary task it is to implement program design features rather than to provide organizational context in which that activity occurs.

Program Theory

Program theory is important for obvious and nonobvious reasons. First, it obviously is the source from which the program activities are drawn; absent a program theory,

I. Program theory

(the selected variable)
Parent expects child to take on adult roles and tasks
    ↳ Parent who expects emotional support from their child and the child to be responsible for adult tasks and roles

II. Program design

(intended to decrease the effect of the preceding "selected variable")
(a) Teaching the parent age-appropriate expectations of children
    1. teaching *not* expecting adult roles/tasks from child
    2. teaching *not* expecting emotional support from child

(b) Practitioners modeling doing of these age-appropriate expectations with the child (in the parents presence)

(c) parent model doing of these age-appropriate expectations with the child in practitioners presence

III. Program specification (example)

(a) Content to be taught and learned by parent
Age-appropriate behaviors: What to expect of a child:
    being held/crying/demand for affection

1. self-feeding	6. staying close to home
2. toilet training	7. getting ready for school
3. bedtimes and naps	8. helping with housework and meal preparation
4. dressing	9. ability of child to "be a best friend"
5. caring for siblings and other children	

(b) Educational processes must include:
    1. Video demonstration of age-appropriate expectations
    2. Discussion of content by peer parents in group
    3. Parents role playing the expectations with peer tutor
    4. One-on-one opportunity for discussion of special problems with practitioner

FIGURE 8.3   Program specification.

program activities would probably amount to random choices at best, assorted and un-coordinated "good ideas" at worst. If we care about the people who suffer from social problems, then it seems only right that we care enough to program a sensible and coordinated set of activities we have reason to believe will make a difference (and for which we would want to be held accountable) and then see to its implementation.

Second, for nonobvious reasons, program design is essential to program management in that it is required as a measure of observing the program in order to assess the quality of its implementation. What would one monitor (observe) without some idea of what program activities are intended to produce the desired outcome? For example, it is possible to observe *whether* the program performs organizational tasks, has credentialed staff, files reports, pays bills, completes other paperwork, and observes staff communication protocols to specification and on time. However, the heart of such observation in terms of quality assessment is whether program activities were in fact implemented *to specification*, that is, in a way that makes it plausible that it will achieve its stated outcome(s) (the partial or whole solution to the social problem). That assessment is of more than passing interest to program managers because overseeing the program essentials is key to their task; it is on such observations that management decisions about personnel, organizational change, allocation of program resources, and the like, are made.[1]

Third, and perhaps even more important, unless one knows whether the program was implemented successfully and with sufficient intensity so that positive outcome could be expected, even outcome data that show success cannot be attributable to the program effort. Put simply, just because the program occurred prior to the positive outcome is not sufficient reason to think that the program caused the outcome. It is possible that any number of other factors about clients and external conditions were responsible. Recall here the standard distinction between correlation and causation: Correlation is not sufficient reason to attribute causation. The scientific standard for attributing causation is "control" over factors that the experimenter hypothesizes will produce change, control in the sense of ability to consciously manipulate them, put them in place in conjunction with things to be changed. That, as well as other things, is what implementing a program design achieves.[2]

Fourth, a good program theory will contain statements that are essential to high-level planners whose role is to decide when and where else such a program might be successful.[3] Good program theory speaks about the *conditions* required in order for it to achieve the desired outcomes. That is important because the kind of theory social programs use is generally very specific, perhaps even local—dealing as it does with the particulars of problems, people, and cultures. The specification of those conditions is an important function of program theory. Notice in Figure 8.1 that one of the factors is "high stress (underemployment/low wages)," which is an example of a factor so important that failure to attend to it in the program design may result in failure to reduce or eliminate child abuse, the desired outcome. On that account, such attention might be a necessary condition (alluded to before). It is difficult to specify all such conditions because very often we simply don't know enough to do so. Our theories soften in the face of hard unyielding realities of the everyday life of program users and program personnel. For example, even the most clever and devoted case manager or social work practitioner working with the chronically mentally ill cannot do his or her main job—acquiring resources for clients—if (as is too often the case) basic housing, public income support, and essential medical care are simply unavailable to this population. This instance is, of course, just another example of how services are no substitute for food, shelter, and medicine. It is critical to understand those as basic conditions for successful outcomes for a case-management program. Good programs have been dismissed as bad theory when they don't show positive outcomes, when in fact the conditions for positive outcomes are absent. Good intervention ideas are too scarce to let that happen.

Chapter 1 referred to causal chains in a social problem analysis. We should take some pains to distinguish causal chains from program theory. Understanding the causes of social problems does not necessarily guarantee knowing enough to do anything about them—the factors that created the problems may be beyond reach of ordinary programmatic interventions. That is particularly true of the "soft" benefits of personal social services (though it also can be true of "hard" benefit programs). For example, no act of intervention will restore the loss one suffers from the death of a family member. Nor can anyone identify the exact factor that creates most chronic mental illnesses. Knowing so little about such imponderables means that the program objective may be simply remedial—taking the hardest edges off the consequences. In that case, that *is* what program theory should be about. Just on this account, theoretical causes of social problems may differ notably from the causal sequences in the social problem analysis. That difference will also be the case when social program or policy objectives are intended to deal only with a partial aspect of the social problem (e.g., the stresses and reactions of family members to an alcoholic parent or spouse).

Finally, the idea of multiple causation is important in understanding why causal sequences at the social problem level may be different from those at the program design/ intervention level. Multiple causation holds that there may be more than a single cause (or a single causal sequence) for any given human problem. Thus, *it is quite possible to assist people with problems other than by working just to reverse the same factors that were causal in the first place.* It is a fortunate idea because—again—the historical roots of certain social and personal problems are beyond our interventions; we can no more restore dead family members to life than we can go back and undo personal tragedies, cataclysmic weather, or catastrophic economic events. Note that the route *into* poverty is not necessarily the way out. Note that the route back to a solid and sustaining marriage is not necessarily to redo the past, but rather to help a relationship reestablish itself on an entirely different basis—changes in role descriptions, occupations, preoccupations, and the ways of the loving heart. The good program designer and the wise and witty interventionist understands that human beings have wings as well as roots, as the saying goes.

Program Specification

Now let's turn to the details of *program specification*. When the practitioner or program designer turns to the problem of playing out the theory in the "real world," he or she quickly discovers that program theory cannot be directly implemented since it is, by nature, entirely an abstraction. The problem is how to make the thing concrete, how to choose concrete instances of those theoretical ideas. Doing that is not so mysterious, an ordinary thing, something most of us do every day. What do we do when we keep locking ourselves out of the house because we left the keys inside? We develop a sort of minitheory about why it happens using some observations, facts, and some logic. For example, we recall that we always leave the key ring in the coat last worn (fact) and forget to take them out the next day (fact). The idea that springs to mind (program theory) is simply to put them away in a place where we'll see them the next time we want to leave the house. Or we remember that there's only one key for three roommates (fact) and the last one to leave has to put the key under the outside doormat; then (we theorize) if everybody had their own key, I could put mine on my own key ring, which I recall as a fact that I've never locked inside the house. Problem solved?

Oops, no, not quite. Notice that the idea "everybody has their own key" doesn't make keys appear like magic, rather they have *to be made*. And that is the idea of program specification—it instructs a person, very concretely, what has to be done to make good outcomes done. So, the program specification here looks like this: (1) take the key to the locksmith, (2) get the keys made, (3) pay for them, (4) test them out to see if this duplicates actually work, (5) distribute them to the roommates. Unless each of those steps are completed, no solution to the problem is obtained! Could there be other program specifications? Sure—throw away all the keys to make sure nobody locks the door . . . ever! But that may involve some not-so-pleasant consequences—some program specifications (and theory) are better than others.

Here is an example of how a program specification is drawn from a real social program theory. First, in Figure 8.1, there is a diagram of a program theory and the reader will notice in the diagram a variable called "Parent who expects emotional support from their child" (in last line of the center box). And notice that there is an arrow indicating a consequence of this, which is that a parent "lacks understanding of a child's needs." The program design in the lower part of the figure selects this last variable with the idea that reversing it will, ultimately, go some way to prevent further abuse of a child. The designer expects to reverse it by including a parenting classroom for "parents to learn age-appropriate expectations of a child," one of which is that a child cannot be expected to be a major source of emotional support for their own parents. The idea here is that this expectation can be reversed by "learning" some basic, straightforward things like this about child development. Ultimately, this program design anticipates that if parents view their child as just a child not an adult, it will engage their "natural" drive to protect them, rather than look to them as an adult capable of giving emotionally support.

If the objective is parental learning, the program specification, the program activities here, must be about teaching abusing parents' age-appropriate expectations: Thus, it must include, at least, (1) content about age-appropriate expectations and (2) specific educational processes dedicated to mastering that content (e.g., group and individual classroom exercises, readings, group discussions providing opportunity for parents to learn the content). Notice that this will require yet another theory—this time explaining how parents learn new things. The specification must be sufficiently detailed so that an observer can tell by looking whether that is what is happening in program activities.

Program design and program specification are essential to practitioners in order to give them concrete ideas of the service they are providing. They are essential to managers for monitoring the quality of program operations. Program design answers the question of *what to observe* (monitor) in order to know whether ". . . things are going right." Thousands of things "happen" in the daily work of a program, and no one could possibly observe them all (nor would anyone want to). A clear program design and specification shows what program activities are important for a manager to keep track of. The heart of what she/he is observing lies in whether those activities were implemented according to specification. In the foregoing example, the issue would be whether the specified content about age-appropriate expectations was *actually* presented to program participants. And, were class exercises and discussions *actually* taking place, whatever else was also happening. The reason the manager needs to be concerned is that if it is not happening, there is no reason to expect positive outcomes. That's bad for program participants and, ultimately, bad for the service-delivery organization. That all is the foreground for the important outcome measure: Did the parents actually learn what was intended? Some bright reader may think: "What if positive outcomes happen even if a program design isn't actually implemented to specification?" Good question. Here are some answers. "Spontaneous remissions"? Not likely. Either something was happening in the lives of these parents that no one is taking account of *or* practitioners were doing something right that needs to be identified and learned from—might be replicated in whole or in part for the benefit of others. Good programs take care to do that.

Some practitioners might be offended by the idea of "program specification," believing it would take the natural flow, the intuitive interchange out of the helping process. But, that's not the idea here. Program specification is not an exact "script" for practitioners, only a minimum description of practice activities that sets out helping processes that *have* to be done. Along the way, practitioners and program participants discover many human needs and problems that must be met and dealt with in order that people can actually benefit from the program. Nothing is automatic here. It isn't that program specifications prescribe boundaries for the helping adventure, as much as they identify places that have to be visited. Exactly the paths followed in wandering through the geography of a helping encounter is a matter of the art of conducting a helping relationship. The stage-play metaphor may still be helpful here: Although no actor invents her own script, she is the *central figure* who delivers the message to the audience. Because she is free to interpret within her performance, she gives the script its meaning—and it is to the actor that any drama, helping or otherwise, owes its life and its vitality.

Some Different Types of Administration and Delivery of Social Service Programs, Benefits, and Services

Neither love, money, nor good intentions alone is sufficient to get benefits and services to masses of people who need them. Some kind of organizational system is necessary to deliver the benefits or services to bridge the gap between problem and solution. In its original sense, to describe something as bureaucratic was to call it thoughtful in pursuing logical, effective, and efficient means to specific ends; of people working together in a set of defined roles when clear divisions of labor and authority enhanced the effectiveness and dispatch with which responsibilities were accomplished. That is still a portion of the ideal of organizations, certainly those we are concerned with here. Let us now consider some different types of organizations.

Centralized Service-Delivery Systems

Authority is always important in "centralized" organizations; there it is *always* clear where authority resides. It is pyramidal, the highest authority at the peak, usually residing in a single chief executive officer (CEO). That office will include *support staff* who have specialized duties: an information systems staff responsible for routine data gathering and care of its computer systems, a legal staff, someone who is responsible for buildings, and, of course, accounting. The *line staff* are administrative officers (e.g., program directors and supervisors) who carry out the CEO's directives having been delegated his or her authority over all other personnel and actions in the lower-level departments and offices of the organization. Hence, it is easy to show the "lines of authority" in an organizational chart, which reveals who is responsible to whom, who carries what responsibilities, and how one office or department is distinguished from another.

In contrast, some organizations are "decentralized," when different departments and offices are under *only* the authority of the CEO and report directly to her or him—*no* supervisors or department heads. In a large organization, that can mean that each department has greater freedom to develop its own ways of operating, ways that may be different from other departments; of course, in a small organization, such "decentralization" might only mean that a CEO has more chance for close supervision of operations. In a large organization, the number of "layers" of authority between any department and the CEO can be (but isn't always) a measure of how much freedom it has in designing its own operations. The number of authority "layers" is equivalent to the number of administrators, including the CEO, who must authorize an action the administrator or staff member wants to take.

But note, at some point, an organization becomes so large that an informal local organizational autonomy sets in. There is some size at which no CEO (or even lower-level administrators) can personally monitor organizational operations; hence, given a sufficiently large size, lower-level departments are shielded from close oversight and thereby gain a measure of informal autonomy. Like little colonial outposts of the 1800s, far removed from the capital of the empire, they begin to set their own style and rules—often (but not always) for the better. And it is not only size but geographic separation that can produce this result; statewide social service programs, for example, as in geographically large U.S. states with large rural areas scattered widely throughout a number of county or city local offices, gradually work out their own styles. On this account, organizational charts should be viewed with some suspicion since they show the "planned" state of affairs, seldom up to date in any case and ordinarily not reflecting how things actually work.

Local administrators and staff can and do exploit the freedom suggested before to the advantage of program consumers. Personal social service practitioners and programs should exploit it since they are likely to require individualized services for consumers. It's not a subversive suggestion, rather a perfectly straightforward matter. If the service given is a test for a drivers license, it is simple enough for a state office to give local offices in a state routine procedures planned in the abstract and geographically removed. But, if services are for abused or neglected children or the homeless, a "one-size-fits-all" set of administrative procedures is unlikely to meet program participants needs. Readers should notice that the perspective here favors decentralized administration for personal social service programs and centralized administration for programs delivering hard benefits like school meals programs, housing subsidies, and food stamps.

Centralization has other common problems. One is the time it takes for a centralized organization to make decisions. Unless authority is clearly delegated and the conditions for making decisions at levels lower than that of the top executive are clear to everyone, decisions, even simple, obvious ones, will often be time-consuming when passed on to a higher executive level.

Most important, since a centralized organization has many executive or supervisory "layers," there is, necessarily, a large distance between clients/program consumers and administrative decision makers. That is a problem because those who plan the organizational future, as well as make day-to-day decisions about services, can be far removed from the way the organization deals with program participants and how those program consumers respond. In this sense, it is fair to say that although centralization increases formal accountability within organizations ("easily identifies who is at fault"), it also decreases accountability to those it serves. Rapp points out that this kind of organizational structure ". . . reinforces the tendency to maximum nonresponsiveness to clients and their welfare. . . ." And he makes clear that the focus in centralized organizations is on control over operations, most usually on the basis of what the organization, rather than what its consumers or program participants need: reporting and data gathering, adherence to policy rules, and so on.[4]

Client-Centered Management and "Inverted Hierarchy" Service-Delivery Systems

Social service–delivery organizations, especially public social services, can be notoriously unsatisfying places in which to work. Staff who work directly with clients are often overburdened beyond counting, pay is low, and organizational support is often absent in the extreme. And, in an important way, centralization is one of the reasons for those problems. But, it is only the most obvious reason. *The main problem in centralized organizations is that the organization is centered on its own structure and survival and has little time or energy to be client centered, much less to care for its practitioner staff.*

Rapp and Poertner have designed an alternative to the traditional, centralized service-delivery agency and called it "inverted hierarchy."[5] They believe it will deliver better social services precisely because the driving metaphor is client-centered. Rapp and Poertner, like all good paradigm breakers, stand the idea of centralized structure/authority on its head: at the top of the organizational hierarchy in place of CEOs and administrators are clients and direct service workers—all other personnel in the organizational are (chartwise) below and in service of them. The task of management is not to control, but to assist those who are most directly in contact with people in need. Rather than focus on control and monitoring direct service workers, managers main function in this type of organization is to provide organizational help in four ways:

1. making clear what is to be done and expectations for those doing it: literal modeling by managers of the idea of client-centeredness, helping workers to reframe clients situations, clarifying service plans, and so on.
2. providing the tools to do the job (resources, adequate time, and equipment)

3. removing obstacles and constraints: large caseloads, less paperwork, meetings, office noise, and so on.
4. creating ". . . a reward-based environment . . ." in which successes of direct service workers are made noticeable and responded to positively by those around them so that the organization becomes a place for work that is satisfying, full of pride, and pleasurable.[6]

This "client-centered management" goes well beyond its historical roots in this field; the principle is "managers venerating people called clients." It refers to specific managerial behaviors:

1. managers must have frequent friendly and respectful contact with clients
2. managers must assume client advocacy as their task[7]

When Rapp and Poertner speak of managers' responsibility to "create" organizational focus, they mean a focus on clients and client outcomes plus ". . . an obsession with achieving (them). . . ."[8]

Federated Service-Delivery Organizations

Federations are two or more organizations that agree to cooperate and coordinate their services in certain, usually limited and precisely specified, activities. For example, several nonprofit day care programs may agree to have one of them take responsibility for advertising services, and receiving and processing applications. In return, other programs may take responsibility for food service and another for building maintenance, and yet another for on-site nursing services, and so on. Recreational programs such as the YWCA, YMCA, and Boys Club may agree to focus services only on specific neighborhoods so that they cover a whole community without duplication. The hoped-for effect of federation is to serve the total need (or at least a greater proportion) and serve it in a way that avoids duplication of effort while making efficient use of available resources. Note that in federations, no program necessarily gives up any authority over its internal program operations *except* about what agreements specify. And, of course, federation is voluntary, so no program makes a commitment it cannot revoke after the terms of the agreement have been completed. Most federation agreements specify time periods. Tucker has described five types of interagency federative and cooperative efforts:[9]

- loaning staff to another organization
- locating staff at same office site
- delivering the same service jointly to agencies
- combining delivery of one service with another
- consulting with other agencies in a formal way

Federation has some well-known difficulties. One such is that it is difficult and often time-consuming to resolve conflict over how the terms of a federation agreement.

Few agreements can be written so clearly that all contingencies are spelled out and, of course, the unanticipated always occurs. Federations exist because of the desire for voluntary cooperation and should the thread of cooperation be broken by conflict, a stalemate can occur and the enterprise is threatened. Voluntary cooperation involves a good deal of negotiation. There is nothing wrong with that, but sometimes there is no time for it and sometimes negotiation isn't successful. One of the strengths of centralized authority is that it only takes a single person who is "in charge" to make a (potentially quick) decision.

Case Management Service-Delivery Systems

One strategy for solving integration and coordination problems in the complex system for service and benefit delivery is case management. *Case management* relies on settling the responsibility for organizing and delivering services and benefit packages on a single person—the case manager. This practitioner must assess client need, plan for the provision of services and benefits to meet those needs, identify and acquire commitments from other organizations and service providers to deliver those services and benefits for a whole range of client needs (housing, medical care, employment, legal services, child day care, nutrition, personal counseling, and so on). Case management can go beyond just assembling "packages"; it can range from constant monitoring for quality to responsibility for seeing that clients get to the right places at the right times. It can also extend to actively advocating for clients' rights on behalf of benefits and services that may be unjustly withheld. Case management is also a product of extensive frustration in the field with the high degree of specialization in the functions performed by different agencies. So specialized have these functions become that differences between services and eligibility rules virtually mystify the uninitiated. One of the case manager's tasks is to clarify for clients the service and benefit choices available and what is necessary to gain access to them.

Although there are many versions of how case management should be pursued, three styles illustrate the variability. The most simple approach proposes that the case manager act as a broker of services, one who has little direct contact with clients but simply identifies needs based on clients' direct requests, locates organizations that offer relevant services and benefits, and refers clients to them. Responsibility for making direct contact rests with the clients' own initiative. A second version of case management views the case manager as a therapist devoted to healing but one who actively pursues, monitors, and evaluates the provision of treatment, services, and benefits other than what the case manager can provide directly. That pursuit, monitoring, and evaluation occur in tandem with the therapist/case manager's treatment/services. A third version, taking exception to the presumption of client "deficit" or "pathology" implied in the second version, seeks to organize and orchestrate resources focused on an assessment of client and client social network strengths and assets. This is done in an effort to support and augment these strengths in service of the client's greater functioning in an ordinary community.[10] Thus, the case manager's assessment of need is focused on strengths assessment rather than on diagnostic implications for "treatment." Resource acquisition is done with a dual focus on person-environment interactions and with a strong commitment to client participation in both decision making, resource acquisition, and quality monitoring. Ditchbank describes these contrasts in the following way:[11]

> The client in the community needs a traveling companion, not a travel agent. The travel agent's only function is to make a client's reservation. The client has to get ready, get to the airport and traverse foreign ground by himself. The traveling companion, on the other hand, celebrates the fact that his friend was able to get seats, talks about his fear of flying and then goes on the trip with him.

As Rapp and Chamberlain note, "The travel companion is an enabler engaged in a human relationship with the client but is not a therapist focused on the internal dynamics and psychiatric symptoms."[12] Indeed, there is some important research support from six studies over ten years for the success of the "strengths-based case management model." In two small experimental studies, one has shown statistically significant reductions in hospitalizations for the strengths-model case management group, though one study did not.[13] A larger but post-hoc correlational study "suggests that clients in the strengths-model case management group had fewer hospitalizations or emergency room visits."[14] In other studies (both experimental and nonexperimental), other outcomes associated with strengths-based case management were community living skills and appropriate community behaviors,[15] greater overall physical and mental health,[16] greater tolerance of stress,[17] and reduced family burden,[18] among others.

As a design for service delivery and administration, the "strengths-based case management" model, Rapp says, requires certain organizational ("structural") features to be in place as *necessary conditions for implementation*.[19] Here are some examples; note their importance and particularity:

1. Team structure for service delivery: case planning, mutual support, passing on knowledge of resources, and so on.
2. BA-level workers can be case managers but ". . . require access to specialists, particularly nurses . . . and experienced mental health professionals as team leaders. . . ."
3. Workloads for case managers shouldn't exceed 20, nor average more than 12 to 15.
4. Case management service should be of indeterminate length while expecting intensity to vary, of course.
5. Twenty-four-hour, seven-day-a-week access to crisis and emergency services, preferably involving the case manager.
6. "Case managers should have ultimate responsibility for client services, excepting medication, and retain authority even in referral situations."

Staffing with Indigenous Workers as a Service-Delivery Strategy

Indigenous Workers.   An *indigenous worker* is a nonprofessional who has had personal experience with the social problem of the clients being served.[20] As used here, the term *indigenous* refers to its common dictionary definition: originating in, growing, or living naturally in a particular region or environment. Thus, with respect to poverty, an indigenous worker is one who "lives naturally" in an environment of poverty. With respect to criminal deviance, an indigenous worker is a person who has been convicted of a crime and spent some time in prison. The classic example of the indigenous worker is the reforming alcoholic who is an active member of Alcoholics Anonymous (AA). The theory behind the indigenous worker strategy assumes that some social problems generate a particular culture or lifestyle or, according to Oscar Lewis, a "design for living" that has the social problem as a central reality to which life adjustments and responses must be made.[21] Those who have lived with a particular social problem have in fact become intimately acquainted not only with its reality, but with the cultural response to it. Such people know its customs, its language, and its common patterns. That knowledge, born out of experience, enables that person to establish communication more quickly and effectively with those who continue to live with a given social problem. Alcoholics readily speak of the unique subculture of the alcoholic experience—how it yields a common pattern of life and a common language for those life experiences and how difficult it is for an alcoholic to believe that anyone who has not experienced alcoholism can understand it.

There are other social problems that develop a strong subculture. The most obvious example is that of substance addiction, the habitual use of chemical substances. Heroin addicts tend to form a discrete social group in their communities (though, as is the case with alcoholics and all other subcultures, loners exist among them); the life of individuals and the cultural group center on the central fact of demand, supply, and use of the chemical. Language, manners, and customs grow up around its use and are shared among group members. Knowledge of those cultural features of the addict's community gives the indigenous helper the critical edge in establishing communication and credibility more rapidly and more effectively. Perhaps less common—but certainly not less serious—is the use of indigenous workers to defuse encounters with staff of service-delivery systems that clients experience as humiliating, abusive, or traumatic. Keep in mind that social class, racial differences, prejudices, and biases can be the sources of experiences that are so humiliating and abusive that clients will do terrible things to themselves to avoid repetition of the experience: They will go hungry, refuse to seek medical care, or refrain from seeking redress when innocent and convicted of crimes that carry serious penalties.

Also understand that in some geographic areas where racial minorities comprise a very large proportion of the population, the actual encounter between such minorities and outsiders may be infrequent; after all, the literal meaning of ghetto is "an isolated section." Children of ghetto minorities may have their first encounter with people different from themselves only on visiting or being visited by a staff member of a social service agency. The encounter may be particularly revealing; having a black or Latino child feel the visitor's skin to see whether the white rubs off is not a scene that whites are particularly prepared to understand, much less handle well. The extensive use of indigenous workers can facilitate services and reduce serious misunderstandings, trauma, and abuse that can result from tense encounters between ethnic groups and naive whites. Use of the indigenous worker seeks to increase the probability that the staff member whom the client first encounters will be able to respond in ways that are culturally and socially sensitive and empathetic with the client's problem. Whereas the primary intent of using indigenous workers is to produce better service for consumers, there is good reason to believe that there also can be specific benefits for the indigenous worker as well. For example, the helper-therapy principle asserts that those vulnerable to a problem who set out to help others with the same problem are very likely to benefit simply by being involved in the helping process.

There is no clear understanding about why this is so; the principle is simply an empirical observation of outcomes. The helper-therapy principle may be just another version of the common wisdom that in helping another to learn, one learns as much in the process. The indigenous worker approach as a service-delivery strategy does have some basic problems and some limitations despite its appeal. Clearly, the indigenous worker idea is effective only with social problems that generate a subculture that is sufficiently unique so that it cannot be easily learned, understood, and incorporated by the ordinary nonindigenous helper. Also, it turns out that the career of a particular individual who performs in an indigenous worker role is fairly short. The tendency of the indigenous worker is gradually to take on the attitudes and values of the professional staff of the nonindigenous organization. That process goes by other names—socialization and cooptation, for example. It is certainly natural enough that a person should assimilate to the norms and outlook of those positioned to befriend, reward, and punish. It is not necessary to refer to a conscious motive on the part of organizations that employ indigenous workers to accomplish this, it is sufficient to cite socialization as a natural process in human groups.[22] Close observers of indigenous workers in Head Start and Community Action Programs (CAPS) report that it takes about eighteen months for the indigenous worker to be acculturated to the organization that pays the worker's wages. In other words, eighteen months may be about as long as one can expect an indigenous worker to retain a view of the social problem of concern that is sufficiently allied with client views so that it gives the indigenous worker a unique value perspective.

Referral Agencies in Delivering Social Service

Any system of agencies and organizations involved in delivering social welfare services and benefits can be a puzzle for clients and helpers attempting to solve problems. In any given metropolitan area, hundreds of agencies, programs, and organizations offer multiple services and benefits under widely varying conditions for diverse target populations. This is one reason why benefits and services are inaccessible to people who need them. Sometimes the organizations are so numerous and the nature of their services and entitlement rules so ill defined and difficult in terms of distinguishing one from the other that it requires direct experience to judge exactly where a certain client with a certain problem should be referred for services or benefits. Where this has been identified as a problem, one solution has been to create a special agency whose sole purpose is to ensure that clients get to the appropriate agency. Such a solution is the embodiment of an attempt to solve a problem of accessibility—a problem created by the fact of agency overlap, duplication of services, and the general disarray of the social welfare service-delivery system in the United States.

Referral agencies often assume a client advocacy role as well, viewing their responsibility as extending further than the simple supply of information to clients about the "best" source of help for their problem. Most referral agencies are also committed to advocating their clients' needs to the agencies to which the clients are referred. The purpose of this advocacy is to ensure that once the application is made, the clients get the services and/or benefits to which they are entitled by right, policy, or law. In this sense, then, the referral agency acts as both a "front door" for all the community's agencies and as a "door widener" for clients to get what they need and what they are entitled to. Advocacy practices vary widely—following up with a phone call on each client to ensure that the client-agency contact was made, helping a client file an application for a "fair hearing," referring a client to legal counsel to get a special judgment as to whether the agency's actions or policy interpretations were correct. Some referral agencies broaden their functions to include what are commonly called "doorstep" functions; that is, the agency's reason for being is to serve all persons who "appear on their doorstep." They are free to serve as just a referral agency and, commonly, that is the most frequent service, but where services are not available or cannot be made available by some combination of expert choice of referral and client advocacy, the agencies' commitment is to serve the clients' needs. It is in fact a radical professional commitment to undertake to serve all clients' needs. One of the stated functions of "doorstep" agencies is that of constant monitoring and assessment of the adequacy and range of social services in the community, and of planning for additions or extensions when indicated by experience. In Great Britain, a whole program has been devoted to the development of referral agencies and is directed toward the development of "Citizens Advice Bureaus" whose purpose is to provide referral services and, where necessary, client advocacy.[23]

Program Consumer/Beneficiary, Client-Controlled Organizations as a Service-Delivery Strategy

Organizations delivering social services or benefits organized and operated by the very people who they serve has developed with some strength over the years. It has strong historical roots among groups driven by the "self-help" idea, for example, in the neighbor housing programs initiated in England in the mid-1800s when the idea seems to have first arisen of helping poor people in neighborhood groups arrange for funds to buy their own derelict houses and rehabilitating them with what we now call "sweat equity." Habitat For Humanity is a contemporary example. But such "mutual aid" societies for all kinds of purposes both economic and sociocultural, have been developed by tribal societies (and later discovered by anthropologists) all over the world. In the contemporary world, they are often different than that; they are rather "advocacy" or "activist" political organizations among the poor or oppressed. Since they have no money or goods to share mutually with each other, their organizational focus is on ensuring that people actually receive what legislation or public policy has already established is due them as help in solving their difficulties. Examples are many: the National Welfare Rights group, Family Focus, and so on.

Racial, Ethnic, and Religious Agencies as a Service-Delivery Strategy

Instead of simply ensuring staff members who either have a special cultural understanding or who speak a special language, a whole organization can be developed that is exclusively devoted to the special social welfare needs of specific groups. Various kinds of such service-delivery organizations currently exist: Some state income maintenance programs have established special units to serve Asian populations; at one point in the early 1970s, the Black Muslims were frequent sponsors of child care and emergency relief agencies for black inner-city populations; many metropolitan inner cities have had medical facilities that traditionally served only blacks. Probably the most common example of ethnic- and race-oriented service-delivery organizations are the black adoption agencies that responded to local black communities whose children were embedded in the public foster care systems. As Fanshel, and others since have shown, the likelihood of these children leaving "temporary" foster care before they are self-supporting is distressingly small.[24]

At one time, it was believed that the black community did not have the foster parents or adoptive parents needed to serve these children. Those who pioneered black adoption agencies believed that the reason black people were not forthcoming to serve these children was the barrier to application posed by confrontation with an all-white staff and the formal nature of foster care or adoption application forms, as well as interviews required in a formal office setting instead of in the home or even in a familiar neighborhood. Also problematic were the extensive discussion of past psychological history and the high fees required. Adoption agencies to serve black consumers were created to construct a program that would give black applicants more reason to believe that their applications and life circumstances would be received with sympathy. Further, it would avoid a confrontation with all-white personnel on unfamiliar grounds in unfamiliar neighborhoods. In fact, some of these agencies have been dramatically successful in increasing both the number of foster and adoption applications from black families and individuals and the number of permanent placements of black children. They demonstrate clearly that prior statements about the barriers presented by an all-white staff and the application process of the traditional child-placing agency were probably correct. It is worth noting that even though this service-delivery innovation seems to be one of the few undeniable successes in the delivery of child welfare services in years, it still lacks widespread support and is still controversial. Nevertheless, in some places where black adoption programs have been operating for a few years, healthy black infants are being placed in adoption where they weren't before.[25] As important as these special ethnic agencies are in the solution of some severe social problems, this service-delivery strategy was not alone a sufficient answer. Availability of "adoption subsidies" was a crucial factor in the recruitment of black homes for black children."[26]

Black adoption agencies are a special contemporary example of the private voluntary program, which has been so prominent a part of the U.S. social welfare scene for so many years. It is easy to forget that before the 1930s, the major burden of the social welfare effort was carried by private voluntary agencies. Many of those voluntary agencies were ethnically and religiously oriented, oriented to alienated and often stigmatized subcultures that were similar in social status to today's U.S. black or emigrant Hispanic, Asian, and Caribbean population. Out of that social position grew ethnically and religiously oriented social welfare agencies intended to serve the needs of their cultural parent group. The black adoption agencies are an independent but parallel development, an interesting commentary on the hardiness of the ethnic self-help, mutual-aid phenomenon. There has also been the contention that special agencies to serve ethnic and racial interests are prohibitively expensive because they duplicate the efforts of the mainline social agencies. Certainly, there is little question that they are duplicative; whether they are "expensive" from a cost-effectiveness viewpoint (from the result obtained) is another question.

Criteria for Evaluating Service Delivery

Introduction

The important question here is what should we want in the way of a "good" service and benefit delivery system? We will offer several criteria specifically for evaluating service-delivery systems—features that characterize organizations good at accomplishing tasks with effectiveness and dispatch.[27] Thus, benefits and services should be, for example, (a) *integrated and continuous,* (b) *accessible to clients and beneficiaries,* and (c) *the organization delivering them should be accountable for its actions and decisions.* The traditional economic criteria used earlier in evaluating other program elements, *adequacy, equity,* and *efficiency,* are not useful here since they concern the actual benefit delivered: for example, the "adequacy" of, say, an educational program for decreasing unprotected sex or whether this program is the most "efficient" relative to other available program designs with respect to delivering that outcome at least cost. Our subject here, the service-delivery system, is a means to that outcome, not an end product itself.

Evaluating Program Administration and Service Delivery: Services and Benefits Should be Integrated and Continuous

Social welfare organizations and systems often deliver more than a single program benefit or service. On that account, problems of integrating different program operations, benefits, and services are always an issue. For example, if system or program parts are not integrated, clients may be continually sent from one office to the next without understanding the reasons for being shuffled around, frustrating to say the least. A benefit-delivery system can be constructed to avoid that situation. For example, since people likely to qualify for the federal Food Stamp program are also likely to apply for benefits/services provided by state public welfare agencies, the Food Stamp program uses state-administered welfare agencies (e.g., the agency administering TANF) to determine eligibility and deliver benefits. This is an example of a service-delivery system integrating services by coadministration and colocation. It avoids determining eligibility twice and avoids the potential beneficiary having to go to more than one office to accomplish that task, saving some administrative costs in the process.

With deinstitutionalization and the closing of many state mental hospitals, patients with serious mental illness are being discharged into communities without medical care, vital medication, food, or housing. It is a serious problem in both integration and continuity of care. When a service-delivery and benefit system continues to have such problems, the system is said to be fragmented. Certainly, that is generally the case in the United States, where the severe and chronically mentally ill among low-income groups without health insurance are now being cared for in local jails and state and federal prisons. Linda Teplin of Northwestern University found that 9 percent of men and nearly 19 percent of women in local jails in her area were severely mentally ill; nationally, ". . . more than 1 in 10 of all those in jails are known to suffer from schizophrenia, manic depression or major depression."[28] With the closing of the state mental hospital system jails have become the first line for the treatment of the mentally ill. And, without state mental hospitals, mental patients easily get into criminal difficulties and thus into state prisons, where they get what is nearly the only psychiatric treatment available for those unable to pay regular hospital and physician costs. That, despite the fact that it is ". . . 2–3 times more costly to provide treatment in prisons than in community clinics. . . ."[29]

Another leading example of service-delivery system discontinuity is the Social Security Disability Insurance (SSDI) program in which entitlement rules legislated by Congress require that a person declared disabled for work and thus entitled to SSDI monthly cash benefits is *not* entitled to Medicaid care until one year later! The disabled might be entitled to Medicaid, but that only applies if they are very poor; if their SSDI benefit is more than (roughly) $550 for a single person, it is enough income to disqualify them for Medicaid. Thus, there is built into SSDI a systematic service and benefit discontinuity so that the assetless, financially distressed disabled, they who are very likely to need medical care, cannot receive it until a year after they are certified to be disabled.

Another important example of service system discontinuities and nonintegration are child welfare services in the United States, probably one of the most fragmented, disintegrated systems in all of the U.S. social services. Local juvenile courts make the decision to place children in state care and custody though they (commonly) don't administer child welfare services, but rely on state or local welfare departments to do so. Thus, the decision to place children in care is divorced from the actual administration of care and both are divorced from the responsibility to provide funding for same. One could hardly devise a more fragmented, disintegrated, discontinuous system.

Evaluating Program Administration and Service Delivery: Services and Benefits Should Be Easily Accessible

Another criterion for "good" service-delivery organizations and systems is that they should be easily accessible to people who need them. Accessibility refers to the extent to which obstacles prevent ready use. Such obstacles might be geographic location, location far away from where potential consumers actually live or work or far removed from public transportation thereto. Another example are complicated application procedures, for example, requiring lots of reading or writing when the likely consumers may not be literate; and having only English speakers for consumer groups when English is not their first language. If personnel cannot speak the language of potential clients, services and benefits are not fully accessible to them. That is an important issue in the United States, where there always and in every generation significant emigrant and refugee subpopulations concentrated in particular areas: these days that would be Mexicans, Asians, Central Americans, Haitians, and, most recently, Russians and Eastern Europeans.

Cultural but not necessarily linguistic differences can also be an obstacle to access of needful clients to important benefits and/or services. Some Latino, Asian, or Native Americans with serious medical or psychiatric conditions have sometimes been unable to take advantage of treatments prescribed by Anglo physicians and programs because Western medicine sometimes has a very different style of healing. Native healers (*curanderos*) are commonplace among Latino cultures of all regions and certainly common to Indigenous North American tribal groups.[30] Some medical programs have employed native healers as part of the treatment staff for relevant consumers.[31] With the blessing of native healers, use of Western procedures are likely to be more acceptable for these consumers.[32] It is a way of making services accessible.[33,34] Generally speaking, two strategies have been used to remove obstacles to use of or entry into programs and service-delivery systems: staffing with "indigenous workers" and constructing special "referral agencies." See the subsections earlier in this chapter in which they are discussed at length.

Evaluating Program Administration and Service Delivery: Organizations Should Be Accountable for Their Actions and Decisions

Accountability is the third ideal characteristic of a service-delivery system. The following example examines a service-delivery system, an agency concerned with child abuse as a social problem. Suppose a report was made to this agency of a case of a suspected child abuse but that the report remained uninvestigated for two months. Meanwhile, the child was beaten to death by one of the parents. The agency's accountability in this turn of events must be questioned. Be clear that the thing for which the agency is directly accountable is the lack of response to the report.

The service-delivery agency can be said to have a system for accountability if the following conditions are met:

1. It is possible to identify which staff member decided not to respond to the abuse report.
2. It is possible for both the staff member and immediate superior to identify the specific organizational policy that justified that decision.
3. It is possible to identify the staff member's immediate superior for a quick supervisory review and opinion of the staff member's decision not to respond to the report (or lack of attention to it at all) with respect to its conformity to agency policy.
4. If there is substantive disagreement with the preceding opinions by outside third parties, there is a regular procedure (e.g., administrative hearing) by which such disagreements can be heard and resolved.

These are the minimum standards if accountability is to be a factors in the operation of a service-delivery system; more and better features might be involved. If organizations and service-delivery systems can respond to criticisms simply by denying that any overall policy is in operation, the organization cannot be held accountable. In other words, if *no* particular staff member can be held responsible, then, of course, no one can be held responsible. When failure to respond to a report of child abuse is associated (causally or not) with the subsequent death of a child, it is a travesty of justice to try to affix responsibility only to find that "no one was responsible." That is why accountability is such an important feature in the character of an organization; with out it, irresponsibility and injustice go unmended.

Although many mechanisms are used to render service-delivery systems accountable as discussed earlier, two of the most prominent will be detailed: (1) administrative ("fair") hearings and procedures by which clients can appeal decisions that affect their benefits or services, (2) constitutionally derived due process protections of clients' procedural rights.

Administrative ("Fair") Hearings and Appeal Procedures. Fair-hearing procedures are a common part of the service-delivery system of many social service programs. In fact, the Social Security Act requires a fair-hearing procedure for all programs established by the act (OASI, AFDC, UI, DI, Medicare, and so on). A fair-hearing procedure is one in which a client or applicant is given the opportunity to appeal to an administrative tribunal or a judge who hears arguments of both sides. This tribunal reviews agency policy, practices, and enabling legislation and then renders a decision for or against the agency or the complainant. The administrative judge is duty-bound to hold the agency to decisions and actions that are consistent with agency policy, tradition, or legislative mandate. The judge can require the agency to reverse it prior actions or decisions and/or change its policies and procedures.

Fair-hearing system most commonly use judges employed by the system that is being question. On that account, the U.S. fair-hearing system is not entirely independent of those who must submit to its scrutiny. On the other hand, the job performance of the administrative judges who operate the Social Security Administration (SSA) fair-hearing procedure are subject to review only by other administrative judges. However, during the early 1980s, judges were subject to unusual scrutiny by a new (Reagan-appointed) chief judge—clearly, the first historical record of blatant presidential political interference with the administrative apparatus of Social Security or the congressional power to set public policy for the agency.[35] The judges association filed suit in federal district court asking for a desist order against such practice. The conclusion about presidential political interference was supported by the entire bipartisan committee, including prominent Republican congressperson. State welfare departments administering income maintenance programs also have fair-hearing procedures, but note that in many state systems, the "judges" often are agency administrators with no supervisory responsibility for the decision being questioned and pressed into auxiliary service as administrative judges. Clearly, such judges cannot be completely free to make decisions that go against the interests of the organization that employs them. Every social practitioner should be able to counsel clients on use of the fair-hearing procedures in force in local social service and health agencies and income maintenance agencies. If they feel that policy decisions affect a client adversely and that a decision is inconsistent with past policy, is arbitrary or capricious, or is blatantly prejudicial or discriminatory, practitioners can and should help clients access fair-hearing/procedures.

Practitioners should be prepared to help clients get fair hearings even if the policy interpretation that works to their disadvantage was made by the very agency for which the practitioner works—which is not uncommon. The first loyalty of a professional is to the client, and when there is a conflict of interest between client and organization, the professional obligation is to ensure that the client's interest is served. That may mean that the client's advocate may have to be someone other than the practitioner, and if that is the case, it is not difficult to secure the services of another professional to advocate for the client on this one issue.

Due Process Protections for Clients' Procedural Rights with Respect to Social Welfare Benefits and Services and Administrative Discretion.
Scholars and practitioners are in virtual agreement that policy rules are never entirely adequate as a guide to action or decision in concrete, practical, day-to-day situations. The human condition is too variable, so that even the best policy statements fall short of accommodating the complex and finely textured relationships between organizations and the people they serve. Absent a rule to guide action, staff members use the only recourse left to them, their own "best judgement," which can be wrong in any given instance. Among writers and researchers on policy and organizational problems, such recourse is called *administrative discretion*. But, like strange and marvelous lights in the night sky, it needs careful watching. Administrative discretion can be a threat to the substantive rights of citizens, whether they are social service beneficiaries or service consumers. Administrative discretion can also be a threat to the procedural rights of citizens in claiming social welfare benefits or social services. *Procedural rights* are those elements in a decision-making process

that are required for decisions to be made with the openness, fairness, and impartiality that natural justice demands. In the United States, federal and state constitutions provide for due process of law where interests in life, liberty, or property are at stake. Prior to the 1970s, social services or social welfare benefits were viewed as gratuities in which citizens had no property interests. These benefits were granted at the discretion—not the obligation—of the government. Reichs's concept of "new property" interest became ascendant, and the crucial case was *Goldberg v. Kelley*, decided in 1970.[36]

The key issue in that case was whether the constitutional due process requirements applied to welfare benefits. The U.S. Supreme Court held that they did indeed. Note that the Court did not find that citizens have a substantive right to welfare benefits, only that once a statute grants an interest or a right in a welfare benefit, then that interest must be protected by the constitutional due process requirements.[37] The Supreme Court recognizes that administrative discretion can indeed threaten the procedural rights that protect the possibility of just and equitable decisions. What does constitutional due process require of administrative decisions about eligibility for, continuance of, or changes in welfare benefits or services? Whereas it is true that the Social Security Act has always required programs to have a fair-hearing procedure as a way of redressing grievances, it was little used and the procedures were variable prior to the 1970s, when they became one of the principal battlegrounds for the welfare rights movement.

The following is Handler's appraisal of what is required of a fair-hearing procedure:[38]

- The right to timely and specific notice of the action taken by the agency and its basis. The norm is that the written notice must be in a form that the person can understand and allows reasonable time to prepare for the hearing.
- The right to appear at the hearing, to give evidence, and to argue a point of view. Sometimes allowing a recipient to present his or her story only in writing and not orally in public will not satisfy the due process standards. The Supreme Court has noted potential lack of writing ability by welfare clients. The right to call witnesses exists generally, but is not unlimited.
- The right to counsel. In recent years, the Supreme Court has retreated on this matter, though some precedent still stands.
- The right to confront and cross-examine witnesses.
- The right to an open or public proceeding. "Due process does not require an open hearing in certain kinds of administrative hearings (prison discipline cases and school cases)," according to Handler.
- The right to an impartial decision maker. The crucial issue is how much prior exposure to the case biases judgement. It appears that in some cases, the Supreme Court has allowed decision makers to have substantial involvement.
- The right to a decision based on the record and to written findings of fact and conclusions of law. It is very important to understand that in granting the application of due process requirements to "government largesse" (like welfare benefits and services), the Supreme Court conditioned the grant in important ways. The general

principle is that due process requirements apply in any given specific instance only to the extent that there is a balance between the following three elements:

- the seriousness of the grievance to the person receiving the welfare benefit
- the need for any particular due process procedure in order to resolve the grievance fairly
- the costs in time, money, and other resources to the administrative agency

This means that the balancing test described previously is the most explicit guide available to the "general rules" in determining what constitutes an acceptable attention to due process requirements.

Evaluating Program Administration and Service Delivery: Citizens and Consumers Should Be Participating in Organizational Decision Making

Citizen participation is the involvement of consumers and citizen representatives in policy decisions of a social service–delivery organization. Citizen participation is intended to increase the accountability of the organization to its consumers and the general public who pay bills. Involvement of laypersons or consumers of agency services in policy decisions is believed to curb the career and professional self-interest of staff members. Such involvement exposes professionals to fresh viewpoints and, in the case of citizen participation by consumers, to a view of service form the receiving end. The point of consumer involvement is to constrain policy decisions toward the needs of clients rather than the needs of the community or the service-delivery staff. The problem with citizen participation as a strategy to increase organizational accountability is twofold. One, it doesn't happen very often; laypersons or service consumers are not given significant power over policy-making decisions. Two, if they are, they may not be very interested in taking that much responsibility. Nearly every author who writes about community participation notes the frequency with which citizen participation actually refers to token representation. Not only have observes of the scene in the United States—like Arnstein, Kramer, and Weissman—included this style of participation in their typologies of community participation, but British policy analysts and observers note it with regularity.[39]

It should be clear that because power is the crucial factor, meaningful citizen participation cannot be said to occur unless it is actually exercised. The conditions for its exercise are as follows:[40]

1. Citizens must constitute a significant (perhaps 1/3) voting block, not just a token portion, of the whole.
2. Citizens must have the right to initiate actions, not just respond to the agendas of executive managers.
3. Organizations must help citizen board members cope with formal procedures (like Roberts's Rules of Order) and technical language they may find unfamiliar.

The War on Poverty of the late 1960s and early 1970s featured citizen participation as a central element in program strategy. The CAP (Community Action Program) agencies were a central administrative device by which program benefits and services were delivered to neighborhood target areas. CAP agency boards of director were elected by the neighborhood areas they served. One of the five major Head Start program areas was parent participation in the policy-making and program evaluation efforts of Head Start, which itself was "governed" by an advisory board made up of the citizen consumers. It seems safe to say that the War on Poverty programs spent remarkable effort and energy orchestrating citizen and consumer participation. The net gain in citizen participation of any kind, let alone effective participation, was disappointing in most instances in both programs. One of the facts about which there is little debate is that volunteer participation in organizational decision making is a strongly class-biased trait. Citizen participation is essentially a middle-class phenomenon; middle-class people take to it naturally, apparently, whereas blue-collar people do not see it as either very important or potentially very productive (though they surely might not express it in exactly those words).[41,42] Neither Head Start nor CAP programs serve middle-class populations, so it should not be surprising that participation efforts were not productive. As Jones, Brown,and Bradshaw point out, it is not so much a matter of "apathy" as an essential pessimism about the likelihood of assuming an influential role.[43] Given documentation of the high probability that citizen participation was nothing more than tokenism in Head Start and CAP, it is a fair conclusion that blue-collar attitudes are in fact a correct assessment of the situation! Blue-collar people seem to have a grasp of this issue that neither professionals nor middle-class "joiners" seem to have. To balance the disappointing performance of the massive efforts by Head Start and CAP agencies to succeed in a full and serious citizen participation program, let us now turn to a description of a successful effort. Many believe that the Family Centre Project (also known as the Laurence Project) was the most significant antipoverty program ever undertaken in Australia. Perhaps it is best that Director David Donison speak for the project.[44]

> Radical, pioneering and iconoclastic in theory, and in practice full of human drama, the Family Centre project appeared to its staff to embody the very heart of the issues facing social work in the Australia of the mid-70s. The following description of the Project used by the Brotherhood of St. Laurance in its publicity material outlines the Project's essential elements. In 1972 the Brotherhood took the major decision to terminate its established Social Work Service and the Youth and Children's Services and to set up an innovative and experimental anti-poverty program designed to test new ways of assisting poor families. The overall objectives of the Family Centre Projects were to demonstrate, with a small group of poor families who had been long-term clients of the Brotherhood, that changes in their economic and social conditions and opportunities were a precondition for change in their family and societal relationships, and that it was toward such changes that social work intervention would be directed. Through the first three years of the Project, the emphasis was on the redistribution of resources and power within the programme, with the implication that such changes are necessary in the wider community if power is to be effectively attacked. Among the features of the Project were:
>
> (a) A universal income supplement scheme in which every family was entitled to a weekly subsidy to maintain its income at a set level;
> (b) An emphasis on "development work" rather than "casework";
> (c) A commitment to the "de-professionalisation" of the relationship between social workers and clients;

(d) The introduction of programme in which the families ultimately took over the control and running of the Project;

(e) A growing emphasis on welfare rights, self-help and social action.

Another interesting and more recent example of citizen participation and empowerment as an accountability mechanism is the rise of citizen review panels for the purpose of monitoring, case by case, foster placement of children in long-term care. The function here is to keep a constant public tab on children in public care to ensure that they do not somehow get lost from sight. These "external" reviews can occur either alongside the more ordinary case review systems that have been put in place in many states or can occur independently (in addition to them). Citizen review systems of this kind were stimulated by provisions of the 1980 Child Welfare Act.[45] Although their net effect on accountability awaits a future study, they have certainly stimulated considerable discussion and been effective in raising public consciousness of the problem of accountability with respect to foster care programs.

Evaluating Program Administration and Service Delivery: Organizations and Their Staff Must Be Able to Relate to Racial, Gender, and Ethnic Diversity

Organizations delivering social services cannot always resort to the creation of subunits serving ethnic or racial groups or, sometimes, even hiring staff who are ethnically or racially similar to groups served by the organization. Absent that, direct service staff and administration have to be able to relate to ethnic diversity; Caucasians must learn to deliver services to whatever ethnic, gender, and racial diversity shows up on their front doorstep (and when it doesn't conform to demographic expectations, seek out the explanation). And vice versa as well. Experience shows that it is wise to assume that professionals and other service-providing staff have been socialized into whatever were the cultural prejudices concerning ethnics and races, minorities of their families, and communities of origin. So, if their consciousness in this regard has not been raised, it is the responsibility of the program and its organizational host to do so. No program design, however well executed, can overcome staff attitudes where racism, sexism, and ethnic prejudice abound. Organizations need to seek consultation with their own staff members who have relevant ethnic and racial backgrounds or seek regular external consultation if no such staff exists. Service-delivery programs and their organizations should be evaluated on their attention to this issue. There is every reason to expect that racism, ethnic bias, and sexism on the part of service-providing staff management is present, that it has entirely insidious effects, and that it will not, somehow, go away by itself.

Summary

This chapter presented some leading and contemporary types of benefit and service-delivery organizations and discussed their strengths and weaknesses. Guidance for deriving program designs from program theory and program specifications from program designs were set forth. A set of evaluation criteria for the practitioner/policy analyst to use in judging the merit of specific "real-life" service-delivery organizations (or proposals for same) were offered, among which were the presence of a clear and credible program design, program specifications, service integration and continuity, program and organizational accountability, and the ability of the program and its host organization to relate to ethnic, gender, and racial diversity within its target populations.

EXERCISES

1. What is the difference between centralization and federation?

2. What practical difference would it make in which organizations you chose to work, and in the day-to-day conditions under which you would work?

3. To what does due process refer? What does it have to do with human service or social welfare clients, programs, and policies?

4. How would you determine whether a fair hearing meets due process requirements of the law?

5. What are the major differences between administrative and professional discretion?

6. What is citizen participation with respect to social welfare service-delivery systems and organizations? What is its main purpose?

7. In applying for a job at a social welfare organization, you are told the agency surely has "a lot of citizen participation." What question(s) would you ask to determine whether that is really the case?

NOTES

1. K. Conrad and T. Miller, "Measuring and Testing Program Philosophy," in L. Bickman (ed.), *Using Program Theory in Evaluation.* New Directions for Program Evaluation Series (San Francisco: Jossey-Bass, 1987) pp. 19–42.

2. Of course, the fact of successful program implementation will not guarantee proof that the program features "caused" the outcome either. The only claim here is that it is a necessary condition for such an attribution, even though insufficient by itself.

3. L. Bickman, "The Functions of Program Theory," in L. Bickman (ed.), *Using Program Theory in Evaluation.* New Directions for Program Evaluation Series (San Francisco: Jossey-Bass, 1987) pp. 5–18.

4. N. Gilbert and H. Specht, *Dimensions of Social Policy* (Englewood Cliffs, NJ: Prentice Hall, 1974).

5. C. A. Rapp, *The Strengths Model* (Oxford: Oxford University Press, 1998), p. 170.

6. Ibid., p. 175.

7. Ibid., p. 167.

8. Ibid.

9. D. J. Tucker, "Coordination and Citizen Participation," *Social Service Review*, 54(1) (1980): 17–18.

10. C. A. Rapp and R. Chamberlain, "Case Management Services to the Chronically Mentally Ill," *Social Work*, 28 (1985): 16–22.

11. W. S. Deitchman, "How Many Case Managers Does It Take to Screw In a Light Bulb?" *Hospital and Community Psychiatry*, 31 (1980): 789.

12. Rapp and Chamberlain, "Case Management Services," p. 5.

13. M. Modrcin, C. Rapp, and J. Poertner, "The Evaluation of Case Management Services with the Chronically Mentally Ill," *Evaluation and Program Planning*, 11 (1988): 307–314; C. Macias, R. Kinney, O. W. Farley, R. Jackson, and B. Vos, "The Role of Case Management within a Community Support System: Partnership with Psychosocial Rehabilitation," *Community Mental Health Journal*, 30(4) (1994): 323–339.

14. C. S. Ryan, P. S. Sherman, and C. M. Judd, "Accounting for Case Management Effects in the Evaluation of Mental Health Services," *Journal of Consulting and Clinical Psychology*, 62(5) (1994): 965–974.

15. Modrcin et al., "The Evaluation of Case Management Services," pp. 307–314.

16. C. A. Rapp and R. Wintersteen, "The Strengths Model of Case Management: Results from Twelve Demonstrations," *Psychosocial Rehabilitation Journal*, 13(1) (1989): 23–32.

17. Modrcin et al., "The Evaluation of Case Management Services," pp. 307–314.

18. Macias et al., "The Role of Case Management," pp. 323–339.

19. Rapp, *The Strengths Model*, pp. 189–190.

20. G. Brager, "The Indigenous Worker: A New Approach to the Social Work Technician," *Social Work*, 10(2) (1965): 33–40.

21. O. Lewis, "Culture of Poverty," *Science*, 188 (1975): 3–54.

22. D. A. Hardcastle, "The Indigenous Nonprofessional in the Social Service Bureaucracy: A Critical Examination," *Social Work*, 16(2) (1971): 56–64.

23. J. Baker, *The Neighborhood Advice Project in Camden* (London: Routledge and Kegan Paul, 1974).

24. D. Fanshel and E. Shinn, *Children in Foster Care: A Longitudinal Investigation* (New York: Columbia University Press, 1978).

25. Kansas City Black Adoption Program, J. Hampton, Director, personal communication, May 22, 1985.

26. L. B. Costin and C. A. Rapp, *Child Welfare Policies and Practice* (New York: McGraw-Hill, 1984), pp. 370–371.

27. N. Gilbert and Paul Terrell, *Dimensions of Social Policy*, 4th Ed. (Boston: Allyn & Bacon, 1998), pp. 150–151.

28. "Prisons Replace Hospitals for the Nation's Mentally Ill," *New York Times*, March 5, 1998, p. A1.

29. Ibid., p. A18.

30. D. Sharon, "Eduardo the Healer," *Natural History*, 52 (1980): 32–49.

31. W. McDermott, K. Deuschle, and C. Barnett, "Health Care Experiment at Many Farms," *Science*, 175 (1972): 23–30.

32. Ibid.

33. E. Ginzberg, "What Next in Health Policy," *Science*, 188 (1975): 1182–1186.

34. J. Goering and R. Coe, "Cultural Versus Situational Explanations for the Medical Behavior of the Poor," *Social Science Quarterly*, 51(2) (1970): 309–319.

35. D. Chambers, "The Reagan Administration's Welfare Retrenchment Policy: Terminating Social Security Benefits for the Disabled," *Policy Studies Review*, 5(2) (1985): 207–215.

36. J. Handler, *Protecting the Social Services Client* (New York: Academic Press, 1979), p. 31.

37. Ibid., p. 32.

38. Ibid., p. 28.

39. S. Damer and C. Hague, "Public Participation in Planning: A Review," *Town Planning Review*, 42(3) (1971): 224; D. Phillips, "Community Health Councils," in K. Jones (ed.), *The Yearbook of Social Policy in Britain, 1974* (London: Routledge and Kegan Paul, 1975), p. 106.

40. K. Jones, J. Brown, and J. Bradshaw, *Issues in Social Policy* (London: Routledge and Kegan Paul, 1979), pp. 106–108.

41. K. Newton, *Second City Politics* (London: Oxford University Press, 1976), p. 84.

42. For a dramatically convincing elaboration of this theme, see George Orwell, *The Road to Wigan Pier* (London: Golancz and Song, 1937), p. 37.

43. Jones et al., *Issues in Social Policy*, p. 106.

44. D. Donison, *Power to the Poor* (London: Blackwell, 1979), pp. 12–13. For a current description, see Tim Gilley, *Empowering Poor People* (Sidney: Brotherhood of St. Laurence, 1990).

45. L. B. Costin and C. A. Rapp, *Child Welfare Policies and Practice* (New York: McGraw-Hill, 1984), pp. 370–371.

9 Concepts for the Analysis of Methods of Financing

BY ROSEMARY CHAPIN

Introduction

The way services are financed has profound impact on service provision. For example, services funded through voluntary contributions may cease to exist if contributions decline. On the other hand, services financed publicly through general revenue appropriations may be subject to legally mandated restrictions on service eligibility and method of service delivery that do not reflect professional standards of "best practice."

Service access and provision are also dramatically shaped by reimbursement, or payment methodology used to reimburse service providers. Public agencies are increasingly moving away from direct service provision; instead, public money is used to contract with, or purchase needed services from, private providers. This shift amplifies the importance of understanding how provider reimbursement or payment methodologies influence service access and provision. For example, if private providers are reimbursed the same amount for serving clients with intense service needs as they are for serving clients with minimal needs, providers could be expected to target service to clients with less intense needs. This often overlooked influence of reimbursement design on services is highlighted in this chapter.

To be effective, social service practitioners need to understand how methods of service financing shape service delivery and, ultimately, clients' lives. Some basic types of financing are common to social welfare benefit and service systems the world over. The following five classifications can be used to analyze financing of social welfare benefits and services in the United States.[1]

1. Prepayments and other variations on the insurance principle
2. Voluntary contributions
3. General revenue appropriations
4. Direct out-of-pocket payment by consumer
5. Corporate/employment-based funding of benefits

To analyze a social policy or program adequately, it is necessary to grasp which of these types of financing (or combination thereof) are used to fund the social program or policy under consideration. However, that analysis alone will not provide enough information for the analyst to draw conclusions about the relative merit of the financing method and what changes might be needed; therefore, certain key questions (outlined in what follows) on eight special aspects of financing will be germane to nearly any type of financing and will provide the additional information needed. These questions also need to be considered so as to judge the implications of a particular type of financing for a specific policy or program.

1. What is the immediate source of funds?
2. Are funds adequate to pay for the cost of providing needed service?
3. How is fund security and year-to-year funding continuity ensured?
4. What mechanisms are used to ensure funding stability in the wake of economic and demographic changes?
5. What is the distributional effect of this method of financing?
6. How are funds transferred from point of collection to point of service or benefit provision, and at what cost?
7. What methodology is used to reimburse the service provider?
8. What is the impact of this method of funding and provider reimbursement on the client?

The relevance of a question will vary based on the form of financing under consideration. In the following examination of each major financing type, these eight questions will provide the basic framework for the analysis.

The Insurance Principle: Prepayments and Other Variations

The insurance principle enjoys wide use in the financing of benefits and services. Any financing method that relies on a "share-the-risk" mechanism and the payment of premiums before benefits can be received is, by definition, making use of an insurance principle. The basic concept of the insurance principle involves a group of people banding together and pooling some portion of their assets so that when an uncommon but disastrous event befalls one of the group, that person can recover the loss from the pool of assets. Life, health, and fire insurance are only a few examples of the insurance principle commonly in operation in our society.

Early insurance pools centered around commercial ventures. The intent was to provide some protection against loss of cargo or other property to a specific disaster such as fire or the sinking of a ship. Gradually, the insurance concept was expanded to protect individuals against a larger variety of losses and eventually to individual personal disasters, such as disability or loss of health. Even predictable, universal, and financially influential events such as old age are now covered by insurance. The insurance principle, originally developed in the private sector, is currently at work in the public sector protecting citizens against illness, unemployment, old age, and work injuries that interrupt the capacity of workers to support themselves and their families.

In the United States, a number of the public social welfare programs established under the Social Security Act employ the prepayment insurance principle. These include the Old Age and Survivors Insurance (OASI) program, the Social Security Disability Insurance (DI) program, and hospital insurance (HI) under the Medicare program. The first question to be examined when attempting to analyze these programs is: "What is the *immediate source of funds for social welfare programs?*" The source is prepaid contributions from both employer and employee of a given percentage of wages collected with the total Social Security payroll deduction.

The question of *adequacy of funding for Social Security* has been hotly debated. In the early 1980s, a great deal of press coverage was devoted to the idea that Social Security was going broke. Although political motives were undoubtedly present, one of the reasons that the balance between Social Security contributions and benefits was getting out of hand was that Congress was trying to protect aged and disabled beneficiaries from inflationary depletion. In a period of rapid inflation, retired and disabled workers living on Social Security benefits experience severe reductions in their living standards if benefits do not increase along with the cost of living. In response to this problem, Congress *indexed* benefits, that is, passed a law that increased benefits in proportion to the increase in the Consumer Price Index (CPI). Although this strategy does help to mitigate the problems faced by the retired and disabled workers and their families, the trust fund from which benefits are to be paid is drawn down when wages do not increase as fast as the cost-of-living index (or even when they decrease). Recognition of this problem resulted in amendment of this method of adjustment. Now, in any year that the combined reserves of the OASDI trust funds fall below 20 percent of expected benefits, the cost-of-living adjustment is limited to the lesser of the increase in the CPI or the increase in national wages.[2] In fact, there was no genuine crisis, even though there were some technical problems that needed to be resolved (as discussed before), and some funding decisions that needed to be made. In one sense, what was presented as a crisis was simply the widespread recognition of what had been the case for years. The system operated on what was essentially a "pay-as-you-go" basis. Since 1960, about 90 percent of yearly contributions to the trust fund were being used to pay current beneficiaries.[3]

The Reagan administration moved to deal with these problems soon after taking office. The original Republican proposals were radical, including elimination of cost-of-living increases, elimination of all minimum benefits, and reductions of benefits across the board. By the fall of 1981 widespread grassroots opposition to those proposals, combined with weak congressional support, was apparent.

There are several lessons to be learned from review of these political maneuvers. First, they illustrate the widespread support for the Social Security system, a major reason for optimism about its continuing soundness. The American people clearly want the problems solved and the system continued. Proposing reduction or elimination of benefits is done only at considerable political peril. Second, it is very difficult to predict consequences of changes in a system as massive as the Social Security system. Additionally, administrative expense of undergoing changes can be prohibitive, and changes can take a very long time to implement. Third, the system has shown resilience in the face of politically motivated attempts to reduce benefits. Because the system is nonstigmatizing and almost universal in its coverage, citizen beneficiaries are willing to defend the program.

Social Security withholding tax is an example of what are called *earmarked revenues.* By earmarking or restricting taxes to certain uses, resources are often protected against the uncertainties of the annual political process of appropriation.

When considering issues of *fund security and year-to-year funding continuity,* it is simply impossible to predict precisely the economic vagaries of the next seventy-five years. Projections of the adequacy of the system are made by Social Security actuaries, based on certain economic and demographic assumptions considered likely to occur. Given these assumptions, it is expected that large reserves will continue to develop in the combined OASDI trust fund during the 1990s and the early part of the twenty-first century. Projections over the next seventy-five years anticipate a small deficit (approximately 5 percent), which may require a modest benefit reduction or payroll tax increase after the year 2020.[4] These mechanisms may ensure *funding stability* in the wake of economic and demographic change.

The Social Security trust fund is the major mechanism used to collect and hold prepayments. The guarantor of the soundness of that fund is the government of the United States. The dollars collected *each day* are invested in U.S. Treasury Bonds, and interest is accrued at regular ongoing long-term rates. Investment policy for Social Security funds is a complicated issue. Some economists have illustrated how investing such enormous funds could result in severe disruption in the financial world if they were invested in ordinary ways and could affect the capacity of the Federal Reserve system to manage the economy.[5] *Year-to-year continuity* of the programs is dependent on the U.S. Congress, which specifies the percentage of wages to be taxed for each program, the relative employer–employee share, and other possible changes.

The method of financing used to provide Social Security benefits is particularly prone to problems because of *changes in national demographics.* When there is low birthrate among the workforce and, simultaneously, large-scale retirement of older workers, it means that there are fewer active young workers to pay for more retirement benefits. This is a problem not usually associated with financing based on the insurance principle because prepayment methods ordinarily deal with this by storing up funds in advance. It is a problem peculiar to this prepayment type of financing because benefits are ultimately tied to workforce wages.

The *distributional effects of Social Security* are often misunderstood and merit careful attention. Substantial *income transfers* are involved in the Social Security programs, and the presence of these income transfers is one reason Social Security can be deemed a social welfare program. It also must be noted that many economists have concluded that ultimately the worker's *and* the employer's share of the Social Security withholding tax is paid by the worker. At a certain level the employer's contribution may be considered additional wages that would have been paid to a worker had the payroll tax not been in effect.[6] Social Security contributions currently collected are used to pay benefits to current retirees, many of whom have not paid in anywhere near the amount of their long-term benefits. Based on this information, it is clear that a major income transfer is taking place. Money is being transferred from those presently working and paying Social Security withholding to those now retired and drawing benefits. Another important welfare transfer occurs because retired married women who have worked outside the home typically draw on their husbands' earning record and seldom on their own. A married woman who meets basic eligibility requirements is entitled to one-half of the amount of her husband's benefit. Because many women earn much less than their husbands, benefits based on their work history are less than the spouse's benefit. In that they cannot receive both benefits, these married women who draw on their husbands' earning record never draw more in benefits than if they had never worked at all. This is a direct violation of the insurance principle. One explanation given in defense of this striking inequity is that it was enacted as an attempt to pay benefits proportional to what a *couple* "needs" and not proportional to what they contributed.

When analyzing the distributional effect, it is important to consider not only the costs but also the indirect monetary benefit that may accrue to those paying the direct costs of Social Security. Most current Social Security beneficiaries have not fully paid for their retirement or medical benefits. However, the children and grandchildren who are now paying into the program do obtain a "benefit" in the sense that Social Security pension and Medicare health benefits help their retired parents maintain their independence without added financial support from their children. This facet of the program can be overlooked by those who currently pay Social Security taxes and who feel burdened by Social Security payroll deductions.

The federal agency that administers the OASDI program is the Social Security Administration (SSA). The Medicare program (HI) is administered by the Health Care Financing Administration (HCFA). There are differences in the way money is *transferred from point of collection to point of service or benefit provision* under the various parts of the OASDHI program. Social Security taxes are forwarded to the federal government by the employer, and benefits in the form of monthly checks are sent directly to eligible recipients by the U.S. Treasury Department. However, hospital benefits provided under the Medicare program, which was added to the Social Security Act in 1965, are paid out in a different manner. Medicare provides prepaid insurance primarily for the elderly, as well as voluntary medical insurance. Health benefits, paid under the Medicare provisions of the Social Security Act, do not go directly to the beneficiary but rather are paid to the health service provider. This makes it necessary for the federal government *to devise and implement payment or reimbursement methods to determine how much to pay providers for what services.* As Medicare costs continued to climb, cost-control strategies received increased attention. There is now little argument that cost control must be central to any publicly funded health care program if it is to survive. However, the way in which reimbursement methodologies are designed has profound impact on the client. For example, elderly patients may find that physicians in their area will not accept Medicare patients because they consider the accompanying paperwork too demanding and the payment level too low. Reimbursement design issues are discussed in more detail in the following section.

Additionally, any treatment of the *impact of the Medicare reimbursement* on recipients must include discussion of the significant reduction in poverty resulting from the elderly no longer being overwhelmed by hospital costs.[7] For millions of elderly Americans, their only defense against the crippling costs of health care is Medicare. Researchers also point out that during the ten years immediately following enactment of Medicare (1968–1977), mortality rates dropped sharply. In fact, the increase in life expectancy during that ten-year period accounted for almost one-third of the increase that the elderly as a group experienced from 1900 to 1975. Although factors in addition to the advent of Medicare influenced this increase, the access to health care that Medicare made possible—especially for the elderly poor—was an important ingredient in this change.[8]

At the same time, many elderly people believe (incorrectly) that major portions of long-term nursing-home care will also be covered by Medicare, whereas in fact, Medicare pays for approximately 2 percent of those costs.[9] In fact, elderly people in need of long-term nursing home custodial care still must be impoverished before they can be eligible for long-term care assistance under the means-tested health care Medicaid program.

How Social Security programs are financed has profound impact on recipients in a number of other ways. First, financing the program with payroll taxes based on the insurance principle has removed the negative stigma from recipients. Second, social insurance programs, especially Social Security, have done much to reduce poverty for the elderly in the United States. A U.S. Bureau of the Census report (1988) indicated that these programs have done more to reduce poverty and income inequality than either the American tax system or public assistance.[10] Although most people who receive monthly Social Security benefits are middle class, millions would drop below the poverty threshold without the health and income security benefits provided through OASDHI. Additionally, lower-income beneficiaries receive a greater portion of their retirement income from Social Security. The program was designed to pay a greater return in relation to amount contributed for the lower-income worker. Thus the program is even more crucial to the survival of the low-income retiree.

On the other hand, it also must be remembered that the Social Security payroll tax is a substantially regressive tax. That is, people with higher income do not pay a higher proportion of that income for Social Security tax purposes. In fact, the Social Security payroll tax may be the largest tax paid by low-income workers. This fact has special significance for minority workers. Because minority workers typically enter the workforce earlier, work at lower-paying jobs, and generally have a shorter life expectancy, the charge has been made that Social Security discriminates against minorities at risk.[11] As Kingson points out, this charge fails to recognize that minority members are more likely to receive survivors and disability benefits under Social Security. They also receive *proportionately* larger benefits because of the special low-income provisos described before. This discussion is not meant to suggest that Social Security could not be improved. However, it is important that attempts to reform Social Security are made with a clear understanding of the enormous benefits as well as shortcomings of the current program.

Besides OASDHI, there are other public social welfare policies that are pursued through programs financed through a prepaid insurance-type scheme. Unemployment insurance (UI) is a good example and is, in fact, also established by the federal Social Security Act. UI financing can be understood using the same general set of ideas as those used to analyze OASDHI. Although space does not allow for that analysis here, it is worthwhile to notice that there are as well several important differences. First, unemployment insurance is a *joint* federal–state program financed primarily by unemployment taxes levied by both the state and federal government. The source of the prepaid contribution is primarily the employer, although in some states the employee contributes. Second, *adequacy of the program varies from state to state*, for it is the state that sets the amount and duration of UI benefits. Although states are not required to have UI,[12] all states do because the federal government simply taxes them for the program anyway, even if the states' workers receive no benefits (a sizable inducement, indeed). Third, each state collects the advance payments made by employers and deposits them in the federal UI trust fund, administered by the Secretary of the Treasury. The U.S. Congress can lend or give money to the state when the state fund is in danger of depletion. Such crises may result from inflation, recession, and economic hard times, or poor advance planning by the state. Fourth, in contrast to OASDHI, employers contributing to the UI program are "experience-rated," that is, if an employer has a history of high unemployment among its workers, the mandatory prepaid payments to the UI will be set at a higher level. OASDHI has no such feature; people paying DI withholding tax are not required to pay more if they work in hazardous occupations and are thus more likely to be disabled or in occupations (like construction) where employment is unsteady or seasonal.

The impact on the beneficiary of UI financing via state and federal taxes is complex. In that states set amount and duration levels, the result is inequitable treatment of workers from state to state. Also, legal requirements are placed on the worker as a condition of receiving these public funds. Although UI is a work-related benefit, recipient behavior is regularly monitored to make sure that the beneficiary is applying for work. The benefit received is proportional to the salary earned before the recipient became unemployed. The benefit typically equals about 50 percent of previous earnings up to a statutory maximum.[13] However, it never is equal to previous earnings and is paid for a limited time period. Thus UI is actually a vehicle only for aiding recently employed persons who have lost jobs through no fault of their own. It can be used to empower workers in the short term in that they can (legitimately) spend some time looking for a job that pays at least what their previous job did without suffering a total loss of support for themselves and their families. It is not a vehicle for dealing with chronic long-term unemployment in a changing job market. In areas experiencing a shrinking job market in their manufacturing sector, people who lose their jobs may find their benefits have run out in six months to a year and before they find a job that pays anything close to previous earnings. Then, when the breadwinner takes one of the more plentiful jobs in a fast-food restaurant or a convenience store, the family's standard of living may drop dramatically; often no health benefits are provided.

Other social welfare programs that the ordinary citizen may fail to recognize as social welfare transfers are financed through the insurance principle and prepayment. These include federal flood insurance and crop insurance for farmers, for which prepayment is required. Such programs are experience-rated and subsidized by the U.S. Treasury general fund.

Voluntary Contributions

Historically, private voluntary financing has been the predominant way of funding social welfare benefits and services. However, public financing now overshadows voluntary financing to such an extent that despite continuing assertions about the potential of the voluntary sector to assume more of the social welfare burden, there is little real expectation that the private voluntary sector will ever again play a dominant role in social welfare. However, voluntary financing continues to be the source of funding for many important new *initiatives* that advance the cause of social justice and are used as prototypes for some of our most successful public programs. For example, voluntary financing was crucial for the civil rights movement. Although help in the form of legal assistance, moral support, and use of the U.S. National Guard was eventually forthcoming from the federal government, money to fund the early civil rights movement came in the form of voluntary contributions. Additionally, some of the early work on which Head Start was based was financed by the Ford Foundation.[14] These are examples of controversial and experimental initiatives that resulted in vital contributions to the social welfare effort in the United States. Voluntary contributions are crucial because it seems unlikely that controversial, experimental, and political initiatives such as those cited will receive significant public funds during their formative stages. Indeed, voluntary contributions may be the *only* way of ensuring financing for such social welfare efforts.

A few examples of publicly financed controversial client advocacy programs come to mind, but they seem to have shared a common fate of lost funding and obliteration. One such example is Mobilization for Youth (MFY) (an early effort that supplied some of the important program models used in the old War on Poverty programs); the Community Action Programs (CAPS) of the War on Poverty, and Model Cities. In retrospect, Model Cities was especially political and controversial in that *it totally bypassed the states* and put money into the hands of powerful political figures in cities. That meant that state-level political figures (i.e., the governors and legislative leaders) could not control and direct funds in ways that could serve as political rewards and punishments. State political administrations soon successfully lobbied Congress to change the process.

Legal aid is a well-known example where this generalization about inability of publicly funded and highly political social programs to survive opposition may not apply. Federally funded legal aid programs have provided legal counsel for the poor since the 1960s and have resulted not only in the relief of personal legal difficulties but also in federal court decisions that have shaped crucial social policy at national and state levels. For example, legal aid attorneys halted the attempt of Reagan administration appointees to systematically disentitle the chronically mentally ill to Social Security disability insurance benefits. Legal aid attorneys also routinely draw political fire because they represent the poor in landlord–tenant disputes. Even so, federal funding, although reduced, still supports legal aid; only congressional action and the energetic efforts of the American Bar Association (ABA) have ensured its continuance.

Legal aid operations have survived despite the need of their staff to take strong and unpopular stands in representing poor people in court, because legal aid also serves an important and current agenda of the ABA. Strict U.S. Supreme Court decisions require that all citizens charged with serious offenses be represented by legal counsel, which would *not* be forthcoming without legal aid services in local communities unless local lawyers gave substantial services free of charge. Even with legal aid in place the need is sufficient (given the yearly reductions in the legal aid budget) such that some state legislatures have imposed a mandatory fee (fine?) on those attorneys who do not volunteer legal representation for indigent clients. The success of legal aid indicates the general principle that public agencies that politicize their mission and operations cannot long survive, *except* where a controversial program can capture the financial self-interest of a powerful political constituency like the ABA—an example of "the exception that proves the rule."

Many current civil rights efforts designed to secure basic rights for women, for the disabled, and for gays and lesbians are financed with voluntary contributions. Some current welfare services that are privately financed are rape counseling centers, black adoption programs, shelters for battered women, and the growing numbers of privately financed emergency food storehouses and soup kitchens.

Voluntary financing has *at least three kinds of sources:* (1) individuals, (2) foundations and trusts, and (3) corporations. Differences in their tax status shape the quantity, locality, target, and duration of their contributions. Individuals target much of their social welfare contribution dollars toward highly visible and locally represented efforts like the American Red Cross, the United Way, and health-related programs like the American Cancer Society or the American Diabetes Association. Although corporate social welfare dollars are vital to these efforts, corporate giving in large volume is also directed toward educational research and medical institutions. When corporations are closely held (a few people own most of the stock), their social welfare contributions may be channeled through their own trusts and foundations (for example, the Ford Foundation).

Any discussion of the source of voluntary giving would be incomplete if the voluntary giving of family members (primarily women) were overlooked. Still the major source of help for people in need, family volunteer efforts have some important implications. On the one hand, these efforts go unrecognized by public policy makers because women do not receive Social Security credits or other benefits in return for providing major portions of the care needed for the nation's young, elderly, and disabled. This oversight can mean that these care givers have no disability or survivors' benefits and will face old age with inadequate retirement benefits. On the other hand, policy makers are often meticulous in their efforts to ensure that public financing not be used in such a way that family care giving would be reduced. Indeed, the increased emphasis on keeping people at home and in the community who were once cared for in public institutions, might be a way of shifting even more of the cost of care giving back on women. Certainly this will be the result if adequate public financing of home-based and community-based services does not accompany the closing of state institutions and the push to keep people in their home community.

Judgment of *adequacy of voluntary funding* depends on what functions our society calls on the voluntary sector to support. Conservative politicians can be counted on to call for a return to the traditions of "volunteerism" and voluntary contributions as a way to fill the gap caused by social welfare retrenchment. The reality these days is that many of the voluntary agencies depend heavily on publicly funded contracts. For example, Lutheran and Catholic social services, as well as many other religious-affiliated service agencies, receive Medicaid funds to provide residential services to mentally retarded people. When public funding is cut back, many voluntary agencies lose funding. Therefore, they are hardly in a position to fill a gap and in fact may have to lay off workers and discontinue services.

If government funding is curtailed, the corporate sector will be asked to provide more needed revenues for services. Indeed, corporate giving currently accounts for about 22 percent of the contributions to United Way nationwide.[15] Also, corporations fund a variety of model programs, efforts designed to help inner-city youth stay in school, provide for children of cocaine-addicted mothers, and reduce teen pregnancy. However, corporations make donations from discretionary funds, and as the economy improves, discretionary funds increase. As Karger has pointed out, when there is a recession, corporate executives are not in a position to commit to social services funds that the corporation may need later to weather the economic downturn.[16] Yet, it is during times of economic downturn that significant increases in need for social services can be expected.

When considering *year-to-year continuity of private voluntary contributions*, the goodwill, altruism, and tax benefits generated are important factors. Dependence on the goodwill and altruism of private financial benefactors has resulted in interesting variability in the kinds of programs that have received continuing support. On the one hand (as mentioned earlier), many privately financed programs are rather conservative—the American Red Cross, the Girl Scouts, and the YWCA are examples that come immediately to mind. In contrast, radical social programs and social policies were pursued by Saul Alinsky's back-of-the-yards community organization, which was privately funded. History also bears out this variation. For example, the Tolstoy-inspired communities and the Robert Owens New Harmony, Indiana, experiments in radical utopias were privately financed in the 1800s. They stand in contrast to more conservative private efforts of the same era that were intended to solve social problems—such as the charity societies that attempted to alleviate unemployment and poverty with a combination of advice and moral exhortation.

Another factor that influences voluntary giving is the tax benefit available to donors—the result being that the benefits and services supported by these private donations are being indirectly funded in part by uncollected tax dollars. Congress regulates who can receive these tax benefits and under what conditions. For example, requirements for tax-exempt status for charitable foundations or trusts were tightened by the Tax Reform Act of 1969, which included the following requirements for charitable trusts and foundations: (1) They must expend at least 5 percent of their total assets each year. (2) Foundations must pay a 4 percent excise tax on their assets. (3) Their activities and assets must be made public. The logic of this law is that the tax exemption of a charitable foundation or trust is based on whether that foundation serves the public interest. Therefore, its operations and assets should be a matter of public record. A number of trusts and foundations have been motivated to expend money when their tax exemption was threatened by noncompliance with this law.

The Tax Reform Act of 1986 required that individuals itemize their income tax return if they wanted to claim contributions to charitable causes as deductions. Because middle-class contributors provide much of the revenue for the voluntary sector and because middle-class workers are less likely than upper-income groups to itemize their returns, this also reduces incentives for voluntary giving. The *distributional effects of private voluntary financing* are insignificant here because the money goes to such a large and diverse number of beneficiaries.

The costs accrued (profit made?) *between the point of collection of contributions and the point of provision of services* merits consideration. There is recurring controversy about the cost of collecting voluntary contributions and returning them to service recipients when the exorbitant administrative costs of fund raising of some voluntary agencies come to light. It is incumbent on human service professionals to look carefully at these costs to judge their appropriateness, and to expose them if they are excessive.

Because many people turn first to the voluntary sector—especially their churches—in time of need, *the impact of voluntary financing* on the person in need may be enormous. Many times the restrictions on receiving help are much less stringent than legally mandated and often free of stigmatizing eligibility rules that may be attached to publicly funded programs. These voluntarily financed services may be accessed at a time when individuals have not already depleted most of their personal resources. Volunteer services like home repair services, shopping, and transportation for the elderly may make it possible for the individual to maintain independence. They are not offered as a last resort but rather form part of the ongoing community support that undergirds us all and helps us to maintain what we mistakenly call "independent" lives.

General Revenue Appropriations

In terms of *funding sources*, many social welfare benefits and services are funded by general welfare appropriations made from the public treasury. That is, money from taxes, property, sales, and income are put in the public treasury, which Congress or state legislatures use for the purpose of administering social welfare programs. Local jurisdictions (counties and cities) may also levy taxes and provide services. General revenue appropriations fund a wide range of social programs at various levels of government: AFDC, Medicaid, Food Stamps, U.S. Public Health Service programs to control disease, home care programs for the elderly, and education and school nutrition programs.

The Supplemental Security Income (SSI) program is an example of a program financed entirely with federal general revenue appropriations. SSI is a means-tested program intended to provide a minimum safety-net cash benefit for aged, blind, and disabled persons and to supplement the benefits of other public programs for low-income persons. Each year Congress must decide how much benefit to pay and what services to give, calculate the cost, and then appropriate sufficient funds from the general treasury.

The Social Security Act was amended in 1972 to include the (SSI). Besides SSI and the social insurance programs previously discussed—UI and OASDHI including Medicare—the Social Security Act as amended now includes federal and state public assistance to poor families with dependent children under AFDC, and federal and state assistance in paying medical costs (Medicaid) for some categories of the poor. Clearly, various methods of financing have been devised for funding different components of the Social Security Act. Both AFDC and Medicaid require "matching funds," which are contributed from federal, state, and in some cases local general revenue.[17]

Matching-fund programs specify the percentage of contribution for the services for each level of government involved as a condition of receiving such financing. The immediate source of funds for these programs comes from both federal and state general revenue appropriations, which in turn come in large part from taxes paid by individuals. Sometimes county and city public funds are also part of the funding mix. AFDC is a good example of a matching-fund program that relies on both federal and state general revenue appropriations for its immediate source of funds. The federal government is obligated to match the dollars each state appropriates for AFDC, subject to certain limitations, with additional federal dollars appropriated from the general treasury. The percentage of the costs covered by the federal match is based on the state's per capita income and varies from state to state.[18] AFDC was established as part of the Social Security Act in 1935. However, in contrast to OASDHI (discussed earlier in the chapter), AFDC is a means-tested program paid for out of general revenue appropriations.

Adequacy of AFDC also varies from state to state. States are allowed to determine their own need level. In 1991 only five states provided AFDC benefits for a one-parent family of three persons equal to even 75 percent of the poverty threshold; thirty-four states provided benefits at less than 50 percent of the poverty threshold. Even when the food stamp benefit and AFDC benefit are combined, less than one-half of the states provide benefits equal to 75 percent of the poverty threshold.[19] AFDC, which primarily benefits poor children, is much less adequately funded than SSI, the means-tested federal program for aged, blind, and disabled recipients. SSI payments for an individual are at 74 percent of the poverty line for an elderly individual. In contrast, the median state AFDC benefit amounts to approximately 42 percent of the poverty level for a family of three. Because cost-of-living increases are not given often—in fact some states have reduced benefit levels—the value of the benefit is actually decreasing in many states.

The federal government took most of the responsibility from the states for financing the major means-tested income maintenance program that serves "worthy" poor people—the aged, blind, and disabled. However, AFDC continues to depend in part on state funds (about 25 percent in general), and this means there will be wide variation from state to state in willingness to care for families and in financial resources available to do so. When considering *issues of continuity and funding stability*, reliance on state funding means that when a state is in the midst of a deep recession and families are even more desperate, AFDC benefit levels may be cut because of declining state revenues. New state and federal appropriations are made annually for AFDC.

The *distributional effect of AFDC* results in increased income for poor families. However, the general public seems to believe that this distributional effect is far greater than it actually is. The bulk of spending on social welfare is often thought to be going to support of AFDC families. This is certainly not the case. In fact, AFDC and child support enforcement efforts together account for only 1 percent of federal spending.[20] The *impact of AFDC funding* on the client has already been discussed in relation to issues of equity and adequacy given the variation in benefit level from state to state and the overall inadequacy of the benefit.

It is also important to know other ways in which the tax system can be used to finance benefits and services. For example, earmarked taxes (mentioned earlier) are a special kind of tax that states and local jurisdictions may use to finance some types of social welfare programs. Local county/city mill levies on either property or sales to support local services for mental health or the developmentally disabled are good examples of earmarked tax. These levies can be locally mandated and controlled. Although typically the levy is small, it can still allocate important portions of the budget for local personal social service programs. Some of the earliest earmarked taxes for social welfare programs were included in public health mill levies that most communities have had for years. Some public health programs, mental health services, and services for the developmentally disabled or the aged may be funded in this way.

Some benefits are financed out of taxes purposely not collected, or taxes refunded. For example, the Earned Income Tax Credit (EITC), enacted in 1975, provides tax credits for low-income families with children.[21] The EITC is remarkable in that this type of financing is typically reserved for benefits for the *non*poor. Use of the tax system to create incentives for businesses and home ownership has long been an accepted means of providing benefits to the middle class and the wealthy. Use of tax expenditures—that is, uncollected taxes, allows provision of benefits without stigma or marked expansion of bureaucracy. Although the maximum amount currently available under the EITC is not substantial, the concept on which it is based holds considerable promise for helping the working poor with children.

Block Grants

The federal government also allocates money to the states for social welfare services by providing *block grants*. These grants come with varying restrictions on how, when, and for what purposes they can be spent. The immediate *source of funds for block grants* are taxes collected at the federal level and transferred from the general treasury to the states and thus to the local taxpayers from which they originally came.

Federal grants to states requiring the expenditure of public monies on particular problems or in regard to particular groups of citizens have a long heritage in this country. The Morrill Act used monies generated by the sale of lands in the West during the westward expansion of the past century to establish all of what are called land-grant colleges and universities, schools generally devoted to agriculture and engineering. Kansas State University, Iowa State University, and Texas A&M University were all established as colleges of agriculture and mechanics.

Of special interest to social workers and others in the human service professions is the social services block grant, the intent of which is to finance personal social services. The enabling legislation for the social services block grant is Title XX of the Social Security Act, as amended in 1981. It is important to understand that Title XX is one of a long series of aid-to-states programs by which the federal government provided incentives to states to expand their personal social service systems. Through the 1930s and for many years afterward, responsibility for the personal social services belonged to states, local government, and private charitable agencies. In 1956 the federal government began providing a 50–50 matching fund to states that wanted more elaborate social services. In 1962, the federal share of the match was increased to 75 percent, and rehabilitation was added as a basic goal for social services.

Rehabilitation was a legitimate social service program objective. However, there was considerable confusion about what was meant by "rehabilitation." Federal expenditures for social services rose in large increments during the next decade. By 1967 it was apparent that "rehabilitation" using case-centered or family-centered approaches to ameliorate poverty was not having the desired effect. Congress was disenchanted with the whole approach and began emphasizing on-the-job training programs for welfare clients, various work-incentive schemes, and work-support programs like day care for working mothers. Results after the change in emphasis were similarly disappointing. In 1975 Congress enacted Title XX of the Social Security Act. Under original Title XX legislation, the general revenue funds of the federal government were provided to the states, on a 75–25 matching basis, for the purpose of providing programs of personal social services. A $2.5 billion cap on federal social service expenditures was already in place, and that ceiling was continued for Title XX.[22]

When Reagan assumed the presidency in 1981, he was determined to reverse the trend toward increased federal responsibility for social welfare by shifting these responsibilities back to state government and the private sector. Increased use of the block grant concept was part of the New Federalism strategy. Block grants now provide federal funds to state or local governments for general functions such as welfare, health, mental health, education, law enforcement, and community development. The money must be spent for the general function specified, but beyond that states and communities decide how to use the funds. The Reagan administration preferred block grants to *categorical grants*, which require federal review and approval of specific applications for defined activities by state and local government.

In 1981, the Reagan administration convinced Congress to radically amend Title XX. State matching requirements were eliminated, but federal contributions to social services decreased. Examination of Title XX funding from 1980 to 1990 provides dramatic evidence of the decline in funding. During that period Title XX funding declined in real terms by 38 percent.[23] Total federal government expenditures are currently capped at $2.8 billion, with states being free to use the money as they wish. The services most frequently provided are day care for children of welfare mothers and in-home services for the frail elderly.[24] Persons mentally ill or mentally retarded, drug and alcohol abusers, and abused children are examples of other groups who, depending on state decisions, may receive services provided in part with funds from the social service block grant. States choose what social services they will offer, to whom they will be offered, and the method of service delivery. Federal Title XX funds are allocated on the basis of state population.[25]

Reagan also collapsed funding for mental health services, drug abuse, and alcohol abuse into the Alcohol, Drug Abuse and Mental Health block grants, details of which will be discussed in Chapter 10. The amount of money available to states to provide these services was also reduced. As a result, *adequacy of funding* for such services became severely diminished, especially in states with few resources with which to augment the federal funds. *Year-to-year continuity for* these block grants depends on annual reappropriations from Congress. Professionals who have strong altruistic and economic interests in more social service programs and employment lobby hard for these appropriations. *Distribu-*

tional effects of these income transfers are not significant because funds are so small relative to the number of persons receiving direct benefits.

When considering the *impact on clients* of this method of financing, an additional factor not previously covered in the discussion of impact of other financing methods merits attention. Citizens who are concerned with the aged, with the developmentally disabled, with the poor, and with particular ethnic groups compete heavily for Title XX funds, as well as for other block grant funds. The principle with which this book began was that *where resources are finite, a dollar spent on one group will be a dollar withheld from other groups.* Of course, it is possible that state public competition may be more "democratic," for at least public opinion will be invoked, and public debate will occur about the relative seriousness of social problems as well as the relative merits of specific programs. It is true that final decisions about *which* social problems are of primary importance must be value oriented, and it may be that such values can best be gauged by local public opinion and debate. However, attempts to depart from traditional program approaches to social problems may receive more opposition on a local level. The social welfare effort could lose some of its (scarce) ability to be creative and innovative, and groups that fail to attract powerful advocates or constituencies, or whose client/consumers are considered "unworthy," may not receive anything approaching a fair share of the available resources.

We do know that policies and programs became more innovative in the years when responsibility for planning and administration was moving away from the local to the federal level than had previously been the case. For years, state-level service advocates had struggled to create "mothers' pensions" (an early AFDC-type program) and unemployment insurance programs. One reason that these social problems were taken up by the federal government is that the states absolutely failed in their efforts. That bit of history seems to be either forgotten or ignored by those currently charmed with the push to return administrative and financial responsibility for human services to the states. Despite many years of effort by hard-headed, reform-minded citizens, only New York State ever developed an unemployment insurance system on its own initiative. The various state income maintenance schemes, such as they were, did not remain solvent for long during the Great Depression of the 1930s. Prior to the 1930s, only five states were operating old age assistance programs, and although half the states had mothers' pensions, the benefits were totally inadequate.[26]

Reimbursement Mechanisms

In addition to assuming increased responsibility for resource allocation, state welfare administrators and workers are now being asked to assume new responsibilities for the purchase of service from private providers. In the past twenty years, there has been a dramatic shift from public provision of needed service to increased reliance on the private sector for service provision. These services are purchased with public monies and states must construct provider reimbursement or payment methodologies to determine the rates to be paid.

Method of reimbursement has profound effect on how services are provided. For example, there was unprecedented growth in child foster care when the federal government began reimbursing states for foster care costs at a rate of 100 percent of total costs.[27] Simultaneously, there was no fiscal incentive to states to keep and support children in their own parental homes. This reimbursement pattern drove services inevitably toward foster care placement.

The importance of careful reimbursement design is magnified by changes taking place in the public sector. Direct service provision in public facilities such as large state institutions is decreasing for a variety of client groups, including those with mental illness and developmental disability. As these large state facilities downsize or close, private for-profit and nonprofit providers have increasingly been called on to provide community services. With the growth of privatization, human service professionals in the public sector who are attempting to design effective community service strategies increasingly find these programs are dependent on contracts with private providers. At the same time, human service professionals in the private sector may find themselves frustrated by reimbursement system restrictions that do not provide payment for those services they feel would be most effective. The challenge is to design reimbursement systems that support the policy and program goals of a service system.

However, professionals often see the results of poorly designed reimbursement systems. For example, case managers working to place a severely disabled and mentally retarded person in the community may find that no provider will accept this client because the provider is not reimbursed more for the additional services required for this client compared to more independent clients. Clients' lives are affected by these reimbursement design decisions.

Although it is tempting for human service professionals—especially those with number phobia—to think that reimbursement issues are beyond their scope, this is simply not the case. First of all, human service professionals are the "listening posts"; they must make sure that information on client impact gets back to those who design the reimbursement systems. Thus, practitioners can help to empower clients and their families to tell their stories firsthand by guiding them to the policy makers. Practitioners can also advocate in behalf of their clients.

Second, human service professionals must understand the incentives erected by reimbursement systems so that they can attempt to reduce client harm when such incentives are destructive and have confidence in them when they are not. For example, when provider reimbursement for treatment of child abuse is contingent on the child remaining in foster care, the human service professional may have to work harder to facilitate timely return of the child to the parental home. On the other hand, if a portion of the reimbursement is linked to return of the child to the parental home, it will be an incentive for timely return. Note that if the incentive is very strong, the practitioner will need to take care that children are not returned prematurely.

Third, human service professionals are often designed into the reimbursement system as gatekeepers. Public policy makers need reimbursement system designs that allow them to predict future costs of service provision and thus exert some control on these costs so that services can be paid for with available tax dollars. In order to do this, service access must be limited, and amounts of reimbursement must be controlled. By exercising professional judgment in individual cases, the case manager is in a key position to make such decisions. Case managers may be called on to determine who is eligible for a given program, what services may be reimbursed for a specific client, and even what amount will be reimbursed. Even though case managers have written rules or criteria to be followed in making their decisions, typically there is room for professional discretion. When human service professionals find themselves in a pivotal role in a reimbursement system they do not understand, it is difficult to make decisions that both safeguard consumers' rights and make most effective use of scarce tax dollars.

Two concepts basic to understanding reimbursement systems are unit of service to be paid for and amount to be paid. *Units of service* to be paid for include per day (or per diem), per treatment episode, per head (capitation), total budget, or per outcome. Table 9.1 illustrates some examples of positive and negative incentives created for providers based on choice of units of service to be reimbursed.

TABLE 9.1 Examples of Reimbursement Incentives

Unit to Be Reimbursed	Valence of the Incentive (from Point of View of the Provider)[a]	Description of the Incentive
1. Reimbursement on a per day basis as long as condition persists	+ Incentive	Provider is not pressured to discharge prematurely
	– Incentive	Late or no discharge is rewarded; client improvement may result in lost revenue for provider
2. Reimbursement for a specific service	+ Incentive	Provider is rewarded for giving most profit-generating services irrespective of effectiveness
	– Incentive	Public funding agency may mandate use of cheaper or less-profitable services irrespective of effectiveness
3. Reimbursement on the basis of outcome	+ Incentive	Promotes achievement of desired outcomes rather than limiting focus to structure and process
	– Incentive	When treatment process is crucial, this type of reimbursement may be negative because it stresses (pays for) outcomes, not process; thus, it may reward provider for shortcutting the care process essential to client well-being
4. Reimbursement on basis of diagnosis	+ Incentive	More reimbursement is provided for conditions requiring costly services
	– Incentive	Providers may overdiagnose in order to maximize reimbursement
5. Reimbursement on a "per capita" basis	+ Incentive	Predictability of reimbursement
	– Incentive	Underutilization of service is rewarded

[a]The valence of an incentive has everything to do with some particular ideological point of view—what is preferred as outcome and process.

If unit of service paid is per diem as long as the condition persists, the provider may be rewarded for the client's lack of improvement. Also, because a variety of services are "bundled" into the per diem payment, clients may be getting services they do not need. For example, a developmentally disabled client who simply needs a place to stay and some minimal supervision may be receiving unwanted additional hours of community skills training in the evening because it is part of the service package bought by the per diem paid to the group home. On the other hand, a per diem is a simple and unambiguous unit of service.

Payment on a per service basis requires first that some method of determining eligibility and price for each and every reimbursable service be determined. Here there is an obvious incentive for the provider to provide the most profitable service as well as a large number of services, even if they are ineffective.

Payment for outcomes can promote achievement of desired outcomes, but to achieve this effect outcomes must be priced and someone must decide how much to pay for what outcome given a specific client's base level. If client's base level of functioning is not considered, there is a strong incentive for the provider to concentrate efforts on clients who show the most potential for achieving the desired outcomes, and to not admit or to abandon those clients who have the least potential for achieving the desired outcome. These examples are intended to help point out how unit-of-service decisions influence clients. Although space does not allow for elaboration of incentives for each possible unit of service, it is important that human service workers consider these issues in relation to the service they provide. Workers need to think through very carefully the incentives being created by unit-of-service options so they can help protect their own practice and, most important, their clients from perverse incentives.

The method used to arrive at service cost also has powerful implications for clients. Methods may include negotiation, bidding, grants, reimbursement based on last year's allowable costs plus inflation (prospective payment system), or payment for costs incurred (retrospective payment system). Negotiation involves the provider and the funding agency mutually agreeing on rates to be paid for service, a system that provides flexibility but also may result in widely differing rates for different providers serving similar clients. Bidding usually involves submission of a proposal that includes specifications of service(s) to be provided and cost of service. Competition between providers may be increased by this method. However, awards may hinge more on the providers' proposal writing skills than on the quality of service provided or the needs of the clients in their catchment (service) area.

After initial certification as an authorized provider, service vendors may also be reimbursed on a retrospective basis. That is, the providers submit allowable costs and are reimbursed by the public agency. If designated providers are assured they will be reimbursed retrospectively based on submission of reasonable costs incurred in providing service, they can provide services they feel the client needs without fear of not being reimbursed for their costs, which may include a certain amount of profit. On the other hand, this method may result in uncontrolled, unpredictable (even spiraling) costs for the public funding agency. Therefore, public agencies may adopt prospective systems whereby providers are reimbursed based on last year's costs plus inflation. This results in more predictable costs, but it also makes it difficult for providers to take clients with more severe needs because reimbursement will be based on what they spent last year on clients with less intense needs.

Human service professionals need to question how their services are reimbursed. They need to understand the incentives and disincentives created by the unit of service and the method of payment used for reimbursing their agency. Additionally, if their agency must submit an annual cost report to a public agency as part of the reimbursement process, this document is usually public information from which a great deal can be learned. Examination of the annual cost report can show what percentage of payment goes to direct care of clients, to administration, to property costs, and, sometimes, the percentage of profit.

Having a basic grasp of the reimbursement system may help practitioners understand the decisions of their supervisors. Additionally, without a rudimentary grasp of the reimbursement system, human service professionals cannot make the necessary decisions required to help their clients most effectively. Finally, the human service professional must consider the overall adequacy of the rate being paid for service. When it is obvious that the amount being reimbursed is inadequate, they must lobby their public officials and the private sector for adequate funds.

Direct Out-of-Pocket Payment by Consumer

Most citizens are familiar with admission or user fees requiring direct, out-of-pocket payment by the consumer. Such fees are charged by public facilities such as state and national parks and municipal swimming pools. Direct out-of-pocket payments are also used to partially finance some social welfare programs. Charges are paid individually by the client and are related to some unit of service delivered. Examples include fees for placing a child in adoption, day care fees, and fees for counseling services offered by public and private social agencies.

State medical hospitals and institutions for the mentally ill or developmentally disabled extract consumer payment for services in ways that other public programs ordinarily cannot. For large bills for clients who may be indigent at the time of service, most states file a lien on the client's estate or property. Payment is then collected upon client's death or upon client's receipt of an inheritance.

State or county welfare departments may offer a variety of services to families who are not poor and charge them based on a sliding scale keyed to family income. For example, disabled elderly people may receive services designed to help them maintain independence even though their incomes exceed poverty thresholds. The use of such a strategy makes it possible for states to offer services to economically vulnerable families and to those who may be endangered by social problems but not yet economically overwhelmed by them.

Obviously, the *source of financing for direct-pay programs* is the consumer. The mechanism that provides *continuity of funding* here is the demand for service. If consumer demand is insufficient, funding disappears and the program may be jeopardized or discontinued. Out-of-pocket payments for some services may be deductible from income tax obligations—day care, for example. *Mechanisms for holding and transferring funds* are unnecessary in that direct payment is made by the person receiving services. Because out-of-pocket payment for social welfare services typically is small, *distributional effects* are negligible here, except where we consider very expensive services like medical care. It must be noted that the medical care industry receives income transfers from the private-pay patient to the extent that its profitability (which is very high) is disproportional to the actual benefit received by that patient. Patients whose bills are paid by third-party payers may also benefit at the expense of the private payer. Often, public and private third-party payers, such as Medicaid and large insurance companies, limit what they will pay for hospital and long-term care services. However, hospitals and nursing homes typically are free to charge the private-pay patient more to make up for limits imposed by more powerful third-party payers.

Requiring direct payment for service clearly has *impact* on clients. When direct out-of-pocket payment for social services is required, persons who have social problems but little money may not apply for or continue to receive important services. However, policies can be developed that ameliorate this problem. For example, fees can be assessed using professional or administrative discretion so that the amount a client is expected to pay can be based on income. However, if the agency is to continue providing service, some other means of financing must make up the difference between what a client can pay and what it costs to provide the service.

Finally, service overutilization, especially in relation to public medical care, is a widely discussed problem. Belief is widespread that even a small charge operates to deter overutilization of nonaddictive prescription drugs and public dental services. Common wisdom among some psychotherapists is that direct out-of-pocket payment is an important test of motivation so that clients use the therapists' time more efficiently. The logic behind this stance is that most people are not inclined to waste their own money. (I am not aware of firm evidence for this popular hypothesis.) It is obvious that such hypotheses cannot be tested in relation to a population of poor people who do not have enough money to exercise a choice about whether to pay a fee.

Corporate/Employment-Based Funding of Benefits

The business community in the United States provides benefit packages for a large segment of workers. Public sector employees also receive employment-based benefit packages. These fringe benefits, which may include health care, day care, and employee assistance programs as well as retirement benefits, are often available for employees' dependents as well. Benefits and services made available through the workplace have assumed increased importance in this country. Early in the twentieth century, most employees received only direct wages for time worked.[28] Needs related to old age, poor health, and death were to be met by the employee or through the family. During the 1940s and 1950s, the use of employee benefits to compensate workers in addition to wages gained acceptance. The growth of employee-related benefits continues today as both private and public sector employers experiment with new types of benefits and expand existing ones.

Employers use a variety of benefit funding mechanisms. The traditional method is the group insurance contract with which the employer pays premiums to the insurance company in advance. Employees also must contribute for many benefits. The insurance company then has responsibility for administrative expenses related to claims if and when they occur, and for bearing the risk of claims being larger than anticipated. At the other extreme is the self-funded benefit package with which the employer assumes responsibility for administering the program, paying all claims, and bearing the risk that claims will exceed expectations. Of course, the company also keeps and earns interest on premiums paid in advance. Very few companies have turned to total self-funding. In fact, many companies use a combination of the two approaches.

When considering the *source of funding* for employment-related benefits, note that there is considerable interplay of function between the public and private sector. Public programs (such as OASDHI) discussed earlier in this chapter with regard to the insurance principle are work-related and financed through payroll taxes collected from employers and employees. Programs such as Workers Compensation are legally mandated but financed by employers that typically purchase Workers Compensation coverage from private profit-making insurance companies. Other benefits such as private health, life, and dental insurance also make use of the insurance principle. These insurance programs, pension plans, and other benefits such as day care centers and wellness programs, can be financed directly by the employers or by both the employee and employers. However, in many instances certain tax incentives provide these benefits; thus, tax dollars (in the form of tax expenditures, which are taxes deliberately uncollected) can be seen as an indirect source of financing for at least a portion of these benefits.

As Rein and Rainwater point out, this public/private interplay in the financing of social protection results in often-overlooked blurring of responsibility and function.[29] Although this blurring makes it difficult for social service workers to understand how programs are financed, it is crucial that they recognize these variations for the following reasons. First, they must help their clients make sense of their own package of social protection. Often a client in crisis is trying to piece together the resources needed to survive by using work-related and nonwork-related benefits that are financed publicly and privately. Unless practitioners are aware of variation in requirements and rights guaranteed under these different systems, they cannot help clients effectively. For example, the beleaguered parents of a severely disabled child may be trying desperately to sort out what is covered under employment health insurance, what publicly financed programs their child may be eligible for, and whether there are private charities that may help. All this must be contended with while they continue working, nurture their children, and find solace for themselves. Human service professionals who understand that help must be accessed through a variety of sources are sorely needed to help such families.

A second important reason for focusing on this blurring of sources of social protection is to help human service workers grasp the variety of possible financing arrangements in extending a social protection, such as health care, to the entire population. For

example, employers with a staff that exceeds a certain number could be mandated to provide health care insurance for all employees (just such a law was considered by Congress
in 1991). Private insurance companies could be mandated to provide insurance coverage
for uninsured people, and public funds could be used to pay portions of the premium on
a sliding scale based on individual ability to pay. Of course, in deciding whether to fun-
nel public funds through the insurance companies, the question of *how funds move from
point of collection to point of service provision, and at what cost*, becomes crucial. On the other
hand, all costs for health care could be shifted from the employer to the public sector. Policy makers must consider costs and benefits of different approaches. However, as
mentioned, before choices can be made it is important to grasp the variety of existing financing options.

Adequacy of employment-related benefits is a difficult issue to analyze because benefits vary from company to company based on the status of the worker and whether the
worker is full-time or part-time. *Adequacy* of pension plans is an especially troublesome
issue. Private pension reserves are currently worth more than $1 trillion.[30] However,
plan beneficiaries may lose benefits if they switch jobs or if their companies go bankrupt. Also, pension plans are attractive targets for corporate raiders, and benefits may be
terminated and pension plans mismanaged. Obviously, some pension programs are
more adequate than others; however, few private pensions provide automatic cost-of-
living adjustments (COLAs)—without which the adequacy of a pension can quickly de-
teriorate. Additionally, private pension plans cover only about one-third of all workers
and one-fourth of current workers.[31] Coverage under private pension plans appears to
be decreasing despite substantial federal subsidies.

Stability of private pension plans is also of concern. Social workers are all too familiar with the plight of the older worker whose company has shut down or has gone bankrupt and left the worker without the pension expected. A company can elect to develop
a "qualified" retirement plan that receives special federal tax benefits in return for being
designed in accordance with federal regulations. Tax law and labor law govern pensions.
The Employment Retirement Income Security Act of 1974 (ERISA) established the
Pension Benefit Guaranty Corporation (PBGC), which provides termination insurance
for qualified defined benefits plans. This insurance, which helps protect participants
from losing pension benefits if a plan terminates or an employer goes bankrupt, ensures
continuity of pension benefits.[32] However, some employers insist that new laws and regulations are so costly that they may have to terminate their plans. As Winifred Bell has
pointed out, the problems that beset private pension plans "make the social security system seem like the Rock of Ages."[33]

Additionally, it is important to examine how reimbursement strategies used by
private insurance companies paid to provide employee benefits *influence both social worker
and clients (impact)*. Examination of the effect of health insurance reimbursement on client
diagnosis can yield some insights into these influences. As Kirk and Kutchins point out,
reimbursement systems are a major factor in encouraging overdiagnosis.[34] For example,
more serious psychiatric diagnoses may be made simply because insurance companies
pay for therapy for those conditions whereas they may deny coverage for family problems. This practice may positively affect the social worker's economic well-being and also
may provide a way to pay for needed client services. However, the negative consequences

can be serious for the client, who may be stigmatized and later mistreated as a result of the misdiagnosis. Additionally, the social worker has behaved unethically. Social workers who are alert to incentives created by reimbursement systems can work to mitigate negative consequences for clients by reducing these incentives when possible and monitoring for misdiagnosis if such incentives cannot be reduced. As the number of social workers in private practice increases, pressure for such misdiagnosis may grow stronger. As pointed out earlier in this chapter, reimbursement based on diagnosis creates strong incentives that merit continuous scrutiny to safeguard clients.

It is also important to note that small-business employees and part-time workers may have minimal benefits packages or none at all (unemployed people obviously do not receive benefits). When this type of financing is used to provide for basic needs such as health care, people who lose their jobs also lose coverage when they are least able to pay for services out of pocket. Although it may *appear* that employee benefits result in redistribution of resources from employer to employee, benefits often are given in place of wage increases because of the attendant tax advantages.

Fringe benefit packages meet many of the health and welfare needs of large numbers of workers and their families. With the advent of employee assistance plans that provide a broad range of personal social services as part of the worker's fringe benefit packages, a greater variety of services are being offered, and human service professionals are becoming increasingly involved in service provision in the corporate sector. Coordinated public and private efforts that build on established private financing approaches may yield strategies that extend basic benefits to all citizens. One example is the inner-city day care center that is funded through a combination of corporate day care subsidies for workers, public day care subsidies for participants in AFDC-related work programs, and corporate-funded day care scholarships for working families who do not fit into either of the aforementioned categories but are unable to pay for day care. Such corporate investments, designed to meet the health and welfare needs of employees and their families as well as those of the community's children, help to produce a competent future workforce.

Public and Private Funding: Distinctions

When attempting to use the tools for analysis presented in this chapter to understand how a specific service is financed, and to consider other possible sources of funds, students often confuse how a service is financed with how it is provided. Figure 9.1 illustrates four basic combinations of public and private financing and service provision.[35]

Examples of case 1, in which services are both publicly funded and provided, include county welfare services, juvenile probation services, and services for the indigent in public residential facilities. Although much less common in the social services, an example of case 2, in which services are privately financed and publicly provided, might be a financially able parent who pays the full cost for an adult child with mental retardation to live in a public group home and to attend the county-run day activity center. If we step beyond social services and look at the public university, examples of private funds being used to provide public educational services are plentiful.

	Source of Funds	
Provision	Public	Private
Public	Case 1 Service publicly financed and provided	Case 2 Service privately financed/publicly provided
Private	Case 3 Service publicly financed/privately provided	Case 4 Service privately financed and provided

FIGURE 9.1   Service finance and provision.

Examples of case 3, in which services are publicly financed and privately provided, are becoming much more commonplace. As pointed out in the discussion of reimbursement methods, public health and welfare agencies increasingly contract with private for-profit and nonprofit agencies to provide residential and therapeutic services. An example of case 4 is a service provided by a private religious organizations and paid for with private contributions, or services of a for-profit agency to private-pay customers.

An additional element that must be remembered when sorting out public and private roles is that private financing of a service can be publicly mandated. Workers Compensation is an excellent example of a program that in some states is privately financed and privately provided; yet its provision is publicly mandated.[36] *Voluntary* and *private* are obviously not synonymous terms.

Once these distinctions are grasped, it is easier to understand how a private or public agency may provide services financed with public and private dollars. As Glennerster pointed out, in reality many agencies are not totally financed by either public or private funds, but rather draw on both sources.[37] Hopefully, heightened awareness of how sources of funds and public and private service provision blend will be the precursor to more creative thinking about integration of forms of financing and service provision to develop comprehensive social protection packages. However, as pointed out at the beginning of this chapter, the way in which a service is financed has a powerful impact on service provision. Different forms of financing are not simply interchangeable ways of funding the same service. The nature of the service will be shaped by the rules, regulations, or payer preferences that accompany the money to finance the service.

Summary

To provide effective service to clients, human service workers need to understand how social welfare benefits and services are financed and how providers are reimbursed. This chapter has provided a framework for understanding basic elements of social welfare financing. Five major types of financing were discussed:

1. Prepayments and other variations on the insurance principle
2. Voluntary contributions
3. General revenue appropriations
4. Direct out-of-pocket payment by consumer
5. Corporate/employment-based funding of benefits

So that the human service worker can judge the merit of a particular type of financing for a specific policy or program, eight basic questions should be considered:

1. What is the immediate source of funds?
2. Are funds adequate to pay for the cost of providing needed service?
3. How is fund security and year-to-year funding continuity ensured?
4. What mechanisms are used to ensure funding stability in the wake of economic and demographic changes?
5. What is the distributional effect of this method of financing?
6. How are funds transferred from point of collection to point of service or benefit provision, and at what cost?
7. What methodology is used to reimburse the service provider?
8. What is the impact of this method of funding and provider reimbursement on the client?

Basic elements of reimbursement were highlighted to heighten awareness of how reimbursement methods shape service provision of current and emerging structures. Practitioners need to understand how choice of unit of service and method of determining amount to be paid create incentives and disincentives for effective service delivery.

Distinctions between public and private funding and service provision were illustrated, along with possibilities for blending public and private financing. Throughout the chapter, the interplay of public mandates, public tax dollars, and other forms of funding were explored.

EXERCISES

1. Determine how services are funded in an agency where you might like to work. Specifically, what are the sources of funds? What reimbursement methodologies are used? Use the eight questions suggested at the beginning of the chapter to consider the advantages and drawbacks of this type of financing for both worker and client.

2. Compare and contrast the ways in which basic services and benefits are financed for the poor and the nonpoor in our society. How does the way we finance our schools and health care contribute to perpetuating poverty?

3. Determine what alternative results you can anticipate when the federal government mandates states to provide a service but does not increase federal funding sufficiently to pay for it. What are the implications for other services the state may already provide?

NOTES

1. The following list of financing types does not include attention to "privatization." Privatization is not actually a type of financing, rather, a specific method of *distributing* funds for social programs (see the section on "Reimbursement Mechanisms" in this chapter). Also students should not think of the move toward "state responsibility" in welfare reform legislation of Congress in the 1996–1998 period as a "new" type of financing. It is actually an increase in the use of federal "block grants," the most newsworthy of which is the conversion of the old AFDC programs to the new TANF program. Its main new features are fewer federal requirements for block grants, greater freedom of states to experiment with new policy, and fiscal incentives for states who set sharp limitations on the length of recipiency, increase recipient work/training requirements, and achieve federal goals for moving TANF recipients off welfare benefit income and into work income. However important is this development, it is not discussed here since most states are still in the process of developing their own policy, states are quite variable (the whole point) in setting beneficiary requirements, and only the most preliminary results on effectiveness are available. As good practical policy analysts, students should notice whether the large reductions in state welfare expenditures now being projected for this reform are actually achieved. To do so, states must meet sizeable targets for getting welfare recipients into jobs—a difficult and nearly unprecedented task for a *significant proportion* of welfare recipients, even in this period of economic boom. And students might profitably investigate how their own state has responded to this federal reform initiative and the results of same by making inquiries of legislators in their own and neighboring states. —Donald E. Chambers

2. B. T. Beam and J. J. McFadden, *Employee Benefits* (Homewood, IL: Irwin, 1988).

3. D. A. Hardcastle and D. E. Chambers, "O.A.S.I.: A Critical Review," *Journal of Social Welfare* 2(3) (1974): 19–26.

4. E. R. Kingson, "Misconceptions Distort Social Security Policy Discussions," *Social Work* (July 1989): 357–362.

5. A. Munnell, *The Future of Social Security* (Washington, DC: The Brookings Institution, 1977), pp. 130–132.

6. J. Brittain, *The Payroll Tax for Social Security* (Washington, DC: The Brookings Institution, 1972), pp. 60–81.

7. The Villers Foundation, *On the Other Side of Easy Street* (Washington, DC, 1987).

8. Ibid.

9. Robert Wood Johnson Foundation, *Challenges in Health Care* (Princeton, NJ, 1991).

10. Kingson, "Misconceptions Distort Social Security Discussion."

11. Ibid.

12. Beam and McFadden, *Employee Benefits*.

13. Ibid.

14. F. Horowitz and L. Paden, "The Effectiveness of Environmental Intervention Programs," in B. Caldwell and H. Riciutti (eds.), *Child Development and Social Policy* (Chicago: University of Chicago Press, 1973), p. 365.

15. United Way of America, *United Way of America Research Services Campaign Summary Survey* (Alexandria, VA: Author, 1991).

16. H. J. Karger and D. Stoesz, *America Social Welfare Policy: A Structural Approach* (White Plains, NY: Longman, 1990).

17. Social Security Administration, *SSI for the Aged, Blind and Disabled*, publication no. 05-11111, (Washington, DC: Author, 1982).

18. U.S. Department of Health and Human Services, Family Support Administration, Office of Family Assistance, *Characteristics of State Plans for Aid to Families and Dependent Children under Title IV-A of the Social Security Act* (Washington, DC: Author, 1989).

19. U.S. Congress, House Ways and Means Committee, *Green Book* (Washington, DC: U.S. House of Representatives, 1991).

20. Children's Defense Fund, *A Children's Defense Budget, F.Y. 1989* (New York: Author, 1989).

21. R. D. Plotnick, "Directions for Reducing Child Poverty," *Social Work* (1989): 523–530.

22. U.S. Congress, House Ways and Means Committee, *Green Book.*

23. Ibid.

24. U.S. Department of Health and Human Services, Administration for Children and Families, Office of Policy, Planning, and Legislation, *Social Services Block Grants, Summary of Pre-expenditure Reports, Fiscal Year 1990* (Washington, DC: U.S. Government Printing Office, 1991).

25. Committee on Ways and Means, *Green Book.*

26. R. Nathan, A. D. Manvel, and S. E. Calkins, *Monitoring Revenue Sharing* (Washington, DC: The Brookings Institute, 1977).

27. A. Kadushin, *Child Welfare Services*, 4th ed. (New York: Collier Macmillan, 1988).

28. Beam and McFadden, *Employee Benefits.*

29. M. Rein and L. Rainwater (eds.), *Public/Private Interplay in Social Protection* (New York: M. E. Sharpe, 1986).

30. Karger and Stoesz, *American Social Welfare Policy.*

31. Ibid.

32. Beam and McFadden, *Employee Benefits.*

33. W. Bell, *Contemporary Social Welfare*, 2nd ed. (New York: Macmillan, 1987), p. 187.

34. S. Kirk and H. Kutchins, "Deliberate Misdiagnosis in Mental Health Practice," *Social Service Review* (June 1988): 235.

35. For a full discussion of these and other contributions of public and private finance and provision, see Glennerster, cited in note 37.

36. Beam and McFadden, *Employee Benefits.*

37. H. Glennerster, *Paying for Welfare* (New York: Blackwell, 1985).

10 Analysis of Interactions among Policy Elements

Introduction

Policy elements, like entitlement rules and financing methods, are not singular and isolated; they are almost always interactive. So far, we've looked at policy elements one at a time and now we need to consider how they interact in live situations. They interact in sometimes surprising and unforeseen ways: intended or by accident; complex or simple; to others' advantage or to their serious disadvantage. Sometimes, the interaction is within a specific program; other times, it is within closely related policies and programs. A convenient way to speak of these interactions is to use the following simple classification of five interaction types:

1. *Coentitlement:* The use of one form of benefit automatically entitles a beneficiary to another.
2. *Disentitlement:* The use of one benefit automatically makes a beneficiary ineligible for another.
3. *Contrary Effects:* The operation of one policy or program feature cancels out the effect of another feature.
4. *Duplication:* An intended or unintended receipt of the same benefit form arises from more than one source for the same purpose.
5. *Government-Level Interaction:* Benefits or services administered or financed at one level of government affect those at another level of government (e.g., federal and state levels).

These classifications are neither mutually exclusive nor exhaustive, but they are believed to account for the main types. A discussion of each, along with a clarifying example, follows.

Coentitlement

In most child welfare programs that offer foster home care services, a child is also eligible to use the sponsoring agencies' resources for medical care or therapy. As a rule, foster care services come as a package even though there might be a separate price, a separate billing, and even a separate staff who administer them. Some social agencies that offer congregate meals for the elderly (nutritious main meals free or at low cost) also offer transportation services that are free or subsidized. Both are examples of *coentitlement* as an intentional policy. Simultaneous availability of two types of benefits is advantageous in that the benefit is more accessible or used more consistently by more people, or it increases the effectiveness of one benefit because of the simultaneous use of the other. Some coentitled benefit packages are very extensive. (Though it is now less extensive, the TANF program (the old AFDC program) is a good example of that.) Whereas full elaboration cannot be given because, as you may recall, TANF is state-administered and state-designed and therefore varies widely state by state, here is a partial list of the benefit types for which TANF children and their caretakers are most often eligible.

1. The cash benefit based on the number and age of children.
2. Medical care (under Medicaid) is paid in full on presentation of a medical card. Coverage includes prescription drugs, appliances, and immunizations.
3. Food stamps are benefits for which TANF families are automatically entitled in most states (because the income and asset rules for TANF are so much more stringent than for food stamps).
4. WIC benefits (Women, Infants and Children nutrition program), which supply extra food stamps for food believed especially appropriate for children under age three and for pregnant women. The intention is to ensure proper nutrition for families at the poverty level.
5. Vocational training. Note that all mothers of children over age five must either enroll or register for employment with the state employment service.
6. Supportive services (through Title XX) provided by vendor payments to personal counselors for fragile families, special education, or health services.
7. Family planning services: advice, medical care, birth-control appliances, or birth-control drugs by prescription. Abortion is included in many states.

Figure 10.1 is presented so that the full impact and complexity of social welfare benefit interactions can be appreciated. It was prepared by Lewis and Morrison in their attempt to understand interactions of the TANF program with the most obvious of common coentitled benefits: dependent care tax credit, day care expenses, earned income tax credit, Social Security contribution, federal income tax, food stamps, Medicaid, and excess shelter cost allowance (a part of benefit calculations for TANF).[1] Excepting the cash benefit, these benefits are given sometimes by administrative rules and regulations and sometimes at the administrative or professional discretion of the operating agency. Although coentitlement is automatic from a policy perspective, clients are not always informed of such coentitlement; to obtain the benefit or service, they sometimes must ask for it. One way practitioners can serve their clients is to have current and accurate information about these kinds of coentitlements. Other examples of coentitlement abound simply because most social problems require a number of services simultaneously. Most child abuse programs maintain temporary shelter care facilities, and most shelters for battered women

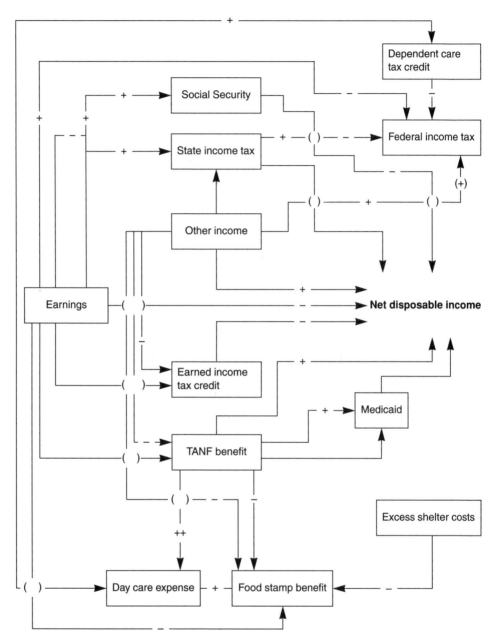

FIGURE 10.1   Relationships among social welfare tax and transfer programs.

Source: G. Lewis, and R. Morrison, *Interactions among Social Welfare Programs.* Discussion paper no. 866–88. (Madison: University of Wisconsin, Institute for Research on Poverty, 1988), p. 2. Copyright © 1988 by Sage Publications. Reprinted by permission of Sage Publications.

maintain counseling and medical services. Traditionally, Workers Compensation has not just a single goal but a whole set: income replacement, medical care, workplace safety, and rehabilitation. It must therefore have a diverse set of coentitlements: cash benefits, medical payments, rehabilitation counseling, prosthetics (e.g., artificial limbs and braces). A set of multiple goals will almost always imply the presence of coentitlements. Attention should also be called to instances where entitlement to multiple benefits is unintentional. That type of interaction will be referred to here as a "duplication" and will be discussed in what follows.

Disentitlement

When legislators, program designers, or administrators wish to avoid the added expense of one person receiving duplicate benefits for the same social problem, they will install an entitlement rule that specifically rules out receipt of one benefit while simultaneously receiving another. A disentitlement policy that probably affects more people than any other is the one Congress installed in the DI program. Any person receiving Social Security Disability benefits must report whether he or she also receives Workers Compensation; if so, then the dollar amount of the Workers Compensation benefit must be deducted from the disability benefit. Many workers totally disabled in a work-related accident are also covered under DI. Although it may seem unfair to disentitle a worker from a part of the DI benefits on the basis that the injury was work related and the person receives Workers Compensation, a reasonable case can be made for it under the present circumstances of both systems. First, workers do not pay for the full cost of Social Security Disability benefits, and they pay nothing at all for Workers Compensation insurance. Second, the Social Security system is in good shape now but may be under some strain after 2010 due to demographic change (more retirees, less workforce). (With a good economic recovery, Social Security trust funds might be *well off* by that year!) Third, Social Security DI benefits are not extravagant but they are generally more adequate than Workers Compensation *and* they continue beyond the eight- to ten-year limitation on Workers Compensation. Those facts suggest that there is a case for prohibiting two such simultaneous payments.

A different disentitlement is embedded in most Workers Compensation legislation. As mentioned, benefits are restricted to eight or ten years. The intent of Workers Compensation laws is to compensate workers for workplace injuries, thus placing the cost burden for that injury on industry, which is expected to pass it on to the consumer by incorporating the cost into the price of products or services. But, if Workers Compensation benefits cease in eight to ten years and the worker continues to be disabled, he or she will almost certainly apply for and receive Social Security Disability benefits. Consequently, the Social Security system is certain to be saddled with a cost the industry and its consumers should pay—an effect that no doubt contradicts the basic historical rationale behind Workers Compensation legislation. Clearly, this is a "welfare" benefit for industry.

Another classic instance of interaction among policy elements, in this case, between an entitlement rule and a program goal, produced very negative effects for people in need. Called the *relatives-responsibility* rule, it requires parents and children to exhaust their own resources on behalf of each other before any one could be eligible for public assistance benefits. This historical example (no longer in effect but still discussed as a possible solution to some problems) was nearly universal in the United States up to the mid-1950s. Relatives-responsibility policies, whatever merit they may have had, led to all kinds of mischief, chief among which was that they often disentitled those the program was most directly intended to benefit. Requirements were so strict in many places that unless both parents and their adult children could pass a means test for public assistance, neither family member was eligible. Some elderly parents simply went without, knowing than an application for assistance would be denied because their children were marginally able to give them money; but then their children (and perhaps their grandchildren) would be seriously deprived.

The relationship between parents and adult children can become painfully complicated when one is newly dependent on the other for regular financial support. These and other reasons complicate a relatives-responsibility policy. Much of the problem with relatives-responsibility policies vis-à-vis eligibility stems from the rise of the nuclear rather than the extended family as the paramount economic and social unit in modern Western industrial society. The relatives-responsibility policy arose in the context of multigenerational households that had few elderly. Such a norm made functional sense in the context of a more rural and agrarian economy.

Contrary Effects

Contrary effects produce both a negative and positive condition in which the effectiveness of at least one benefit characteristic is canceled out or seriously diminished. Recall that the ideal social welfare service-delivery system is characterized by integration, continuity, accessibility, and accountability. This section will consider two kinds of contrary effects. One is concerned with the unforeseen problem that an improvement in one of these ideal characteristics is likely to decrease performance in another ideal characteristic. Think about what happens when an administrator increases organizational integration. As discussed in Chapter 8, the common way to do that is to centralize authority over various program operations, for example, placing a single person in charge of many separate services to young mothers (health, family planning, nutrition) so that all clients are told about all services, and services are scheduled with attention to the need for simultaneous benefits. With one person "running the show," problems would be more easily resolved. Yet, however appealing such integration might be, it can create other problems; from the preceding example, integration redistributes (centralizes) authority by adding another layer of administration, which can mean a reduction in organizational accountability to consumers. That is, when (not if) the organization makes a mistake, there is one more layer of decision making through which the aggrieved consumer must pass before ultimately reaching a decision maker who might be the only person who can right the wrong. Note that the problem is made serious only if an organization fails to take accountability seriously. The point is that an organizational change like centralization always creates other problems, but those problems are serious or disabling only if the organization is unaware of the paradoxical nature of the enterprise it is tinkering with.

Is it possible for the opposite problem to occur—*for an increase in accountability to decrease accessibility?* Yes. Imagine the reaction of organizational employees to increased public criticism or a recent scandal. The most human reaction, most would agree, is to move more slowly, move with greater certainty, and reduce the occasion for taking risks in decision making and in the conduct of ordinary organizational affairs. That certainly slows the work of the organization and on that account decreases accessibility of benefits and services to those who need them.

A second contrary effect is an increase in the tendency toward organizational "paper trails," that is, copying all decisions made and referring constantly to written policy so that in the event of a demand to account for actions and decisions, the "evidence" of history and policy consistency is ready at hand. Does that mean that public criticism of organizations is unjustified? Not at all. Increased organizational attention to policy clarity and consistency generally has a positive effect for client/consumers. Do paper trails always signify bad outcomes? Again, no. Paper trails can protect an ethical professional who is legitimately opposing organizational leaders on behalf of needful clients. Life in an organization is not always simple; the best-intended changes can create unforeseen and sometimes negative effects. The prudent practitioner will want to anticipate these effects in order to circumvent (or minimize) them. Aside from these examples of interacting policies that produce contrary effects, there is the more straightforward type where one operating characteristic interferes seriously with another. For example, a particular entitlement rule might create difficulties for achieving a policy goal, or a particular service-delivery feature might create serious problems by inflating the demand for service and thus overwhelming the customary financing method. An easy example of the former (obstacles to goal attainment) are the Medicaid eligibility rules for achieving the program goal—best available medical care for the aged. No one seriously disputes the idea that, in general, the frail elderly get the best care in their own home with family. But until 1982 eligibility rules disallowed payment for any part of that cost for families to care for their elderly at home. Finally, Congress created an experimental program (called the Medicaid Waiver program) allowing states to use a limited part of their Medicaid funds for such a purpose.

The view of congress was that the entitlement rule restricting payments to licensed nursing homes was designed to ensure high-quality medical care for the aged; but in some unknown number of instances, it was producing poor care in miserable institutional or nursing home surroundings even though some relatives would have provided home care if they could have afforded to give up working so they could stay home and care for their elderly loved ones. The waiver program has expanded greatly. States had to show that each person who uses it would have occupied a nursing-home bed were it not for care received by relatives at home. The rub was that some states used the program so much that they ran into another policy feature that prohibited its expansion, a contrary effect. States were allotted Medicaid waiver money on the basis of a proportion of existing nursing-home beds. Some states used it to the maximum, but because they have (wisely) discouraged the provision of new nursing-home beds, the further use of the waiver program became impossible. This "contrary effect" was removed when Congress (sensibly) removed the limits on states use of Medicaid funds for services that kept the elderly at home, conditional only on states showing that such services were less costly than the nursing-home alternative.[2]

Other examples of the interaction of eligibility rules and goals come easily to mind. "Deinstitutionalization" of the mentally ill is just such an example. When mental institutions were first experimenting with it, there was often an "open-door" policy so that the facilities of the hospital were always available. It served many patients well. But, many believed that other patients became so comfortable with the sheltering arms of the hospital that it created an "institutional dependence" resulting in surprisingly high hospital admission rates alongside dramatic reductions in total hospital censuses. It was a type of (unexpected) contrary effect. And, of course, another contrary effect was that it took away the motivation of a community to provide general hospital care for its own mentally ill citizens.

One of the recent controversies about the Social Security system centered on the need to resolve an instance of a contrary effect. In this case it concerned the payment of a minimum benefit for the Old Age and Survivors Insurance (OASI) program. The original Social Security Act conceived of the minimum benefit as a temporary measure to provide benefits to retirees, but through no fault of their own, they had not yet worked long enough to build up an adequate benefit. That is always a problem when starting a new public retirement system, but it was not a major problem in the program's early years.[3] Currently, the majority of those receiving minimum benefits are not the workers for whom it was intended but for those who have *always* worked for very low wages, albeit over their entire lifetime. The original framers of the Social Security Act intended to cover those working full time in the primary workforce. This minimum benefit has placed Social Security in the position of making up for the low-wage features of the U.S. labor markets. The reason it became a problem is because the Social Security trust fund is now a bit pressed to meet its regular obligations—continuing the minimum benefit coverage creates even more obligations not paid for by contributions. This adds a fiscal threat to the trust fund and that is the contrary effect we are illustrating here: one policy (good thing in itself) creating substantial problems for another policy element—the trust funds financing method. The contrary effect was resolved in some measure by Congress in 1983 when it prohibited further *new* minimum benefit approvals. But, old minimum benefits will continue to be paid. Financing minimum benefits out of current Social Security contributions was always an idea full of potential mischief; far better to have financed relief of the problem of low wages out of general revenue since it is a problem of the whole society not just Social Security contributors. But notice that the elimination of minimum benefits in Social Security will take away an important source of income maintenance funds for the young, long-term disabled who presently use it extensively.

Duplication

The next interactive effect we will consider is duplication, specifically the *unintended* duplicate receipt of social welfare benefits or services as described in the earlier discussion on coentitlement. Coentitlement is in fact a form of duplication, but is distinguished by the fact that it is intentional. At one time a widely publicized instance of duplication was what the popular press has called *double dipping*, the simultaneous receipt of Social Security retirement benefits *and* federal civil service or armed service retirement benefits. That particular duplication was clearly unintended by Congress in the construction of any of the three federal retirement systems. Few, if any, anticipated early retirements from the civil or armed services such that a person could work for the next ten years and thus become entitled to Social Security retirement benefits. The result, of course, is a windfall for armed forces and civil service retirees and one with which the financing methods were not prepared to cope. In the mid-1980s Congress folded most federal retirement benefit systems into the Social Security system, as a general policy solution to the problem.

Notice that the most immediate reason why unintended duplication occurred in the preceding example is because the entitlement rules overlap in ways that were not anticipated. Such duplication occurs not only among programs that deliver material benefits, but actually are more frequent among programs that deliver social services. One of the most striking studies of social services delivery in the 1960s was reported as what was generally known as the "St. Paul Study." Among its many findings was that 10 percent of the midwestern metropolitan area study population received 95 percent of the social services. Of relevance here are the conclusions about the extensive duplication of services, even within this relatively small proportion of the population. Not only were the services strongly concentrated, they were unintentionally double-dosed. That situation was not unique to the 1960s. A brief glance at the usual organization of services in most metropolitan areas today would produce striking examples.

How many "counselors" does a child have who is adjudicated by almost any local juvenile court? First, there is the juvenile officer who nearly without exception is officially charged with advising and supervising the child. Then there is very likely to be the school counselor who also has official responsibility for counseling activities, albeit in relation to the child's life at school. Note, however, the few school counselors who would tell you that they only counsel about school problems. It is entirely likely that the same child will have a counselor at a local mental health clinic, and if the child's family receives welfare benefits (AFDC perhaps), there will be a social worker from the welfare department who has counseling duties. Nor is this necessarily the end of the list. Think of the family minister and the group leader of the local boy scouts or girl scouts who may (rightly enough) feel called on to serve this child in a counseling function. This catalogue of horrible examples is not intended to imply that none of the counselors have a legitimate role, only that such duplication is uncoordinated, unnecessarily expensive (at the least), and possibly destructive for the child.

Summary

Chapter 10 presented several important types of intended and unintended interactions between policies of closely related but separately administered policies and programs. The practical analyst should be alert to the presence of the consequences of at least four types of policy interactions:

1. Coentitlement
2. Disentitlement
3. Contrary effects
4. Unintentional duplication

Interactions between operating characteristics of social policy and programs can only be evaluated against their contribution or their detraction from the ability of the program or policy to contribute to the solution of the social problem of concern. In contrast to other operating characteristics, note that there is no inherently negative policy interaction; interactions are "good" or "bad" only insofar as they prevent some other operating characteristic from reaching its own ideal state.

NOTES

1. G. Lewis and R. Morrison, *Interactions among Social Welfare Programs.* Discussion Paper DP 866–88, (Madison: University of Wisconsin, Institute for Research on Poverty, 1988), p. 5.

2. Private communication with Mary Hillen, M.S.W., Program Consultant, Policy and Program Development Unit, Adult and Medical Services, Kansas Social and Rehabilitation Services, July 21, 1998.

3. E. Burns, *The American Social Security System* (Boston: Houghton Mifflin, 1949), p. 95.

PART THREE

Analysis of Social Policies and Social Programs Using Basic Concepts and Evaluation Criteria: An Example

Introduction

This final section of the book presents a demonstration of how the concepts discussed in Parts One and Two can be used in analyzing social policies and social programs. Note that they can also be used to design a new social policy or program. That will not be done here because, for most social workers or human service practitioners, the main problem is to understand the imperfect, day-to-day world of existing policies and programs. Included in the example will be some suggestions for policy or program (or legislative) changes that are implied by the analysis. Adventurous practical analysts may want to try their hand at using the results of a policy analysis to redesign a social policy or create a new program. Free rein can be given to the most utopian impulse; sometimes, it is just those idealistic conceptions that generate the best new ideas.

To demonstrate that this method has widespread usefulness, the example in this chapter will deal with a social problem (and its associated policies and programs) that is familiar to social work and human service practitioners: child abuse.

Remember that in Chapter 1, we concluded that the analysis of a social policy system cannot intelligently proceed without a clear understanding of the social problem that policies and program operations are intended to solve. Therefore, the demonstration analysis will begin with a serious study of the social problem viewpoints that were important in shaping the final legislation and program designs.

11 An Example of Social Policy and Social Program Analysis

Selected Features of Federal Child Welfare Legislation of the 1970–1998 Era Concerned with Child Abuse

The Social Problem Context

The first step in a social policy analysis is to analyze the underlying social problem, here the physical abuse of children. We will use various sources: government documents, reports of research on the topic from academic journals, and discussions of the policy implications of the legislation found in the journals and sometimes the quality media (e.g., *The New York Times*). Documentary sources such as legislative hearings and Senate and House Committee reports will give us a view of what Congress had in mind about the social problem of child abuse—definitions, causal explanations and the like. Major legislation here is (1) the Child Abuse Prevention and Treatment Act of 1974 (P.L. 93-247), (2) the Adoption Assistance and Child Welfare Act of 1980 (P.L. 96-272), (3) the Omnibus Budget Reconciliation Act of 1993 concerning its Family Preservation and Support Services sections and the Adoption and Safe Families Act of 1997. Committee Hearings and the Committee Reports can be found at government documents libraries of most universities or they can be obtained through the local office constituent staff of your Congresspersons or Senators (free). A second source for information and analysis of social problem issues are the human service, social work, and academic journals. They will contain data on the problem as well as causal explanations, but note that they will have their own ideological perspective. A computer search of a relevant database (e.g., ERL's WinSPIRS and WebSPIRS) is useful because it gives you access to very useful social research databases like MedLine and PsychLit and a social work literature data base as well. Of course, you can always do an old-fashioned review of annual journal indexes that will locate relevant titles of articles and research reports. Examples of journals of particular use for our immediate purposes are *Child Abuse and Neglect; Child Welfare; Children and*

Youth Services Review; Child Maltreatment; Social Work; Social Work Research and Abstracts; Journal of Social Service Research; Journal of Social Policy; and *Policy Studies Review.* Readers should never overlook British and Australian professional journals since they often contain useful and important research and intervention program reports.

It is useful to check reliable, reputable national newspapers on a topic because careful investigative journalism can be an excellent source of social problem data and policy history and status: e.g., the *Washington Post;* the *New York Times; The Wall Street Journal,* and some British newspapers, notably *The London Times* and *The Manchester Guardian.* Don't assume that the British and European press have inadequate coverage of U.S. issues. Some of the best policy and program commentary and empirical research have been done not at universities but by prestigious research institutes, prominent examples of which are The Brookings Institution, the Urban Institute, the Center for the Study of Democratic Institutions (Princeton University), and the Institute for Research on Poverty at the University of Wisconsin. An advance look at their research can be found in their publications, whose titles can be obtained by a search of your university library on-line catalog for holdings (most large universities get them all) or on each Institutes internet web pages. A major benefit from such reports is that they often contain excellent bibliographies. The institutes just listed are ideologically liberal. Conservative examples are The American Enterprise Institute and The Rand Institute.

Definition of the Social Problem

The first step in the social problem analysis is to sort out how the social problem is defined, find descriptions of major subtypes, and locate estimates of its magnitude. Most social problems present definitional problems and child abuse is no exception. Note the wild variation included under the term child abuse. Although it appeals to common sense since they all refer to harm to children, most experts agree that they differ in nature and consequences, and in how causation is understood.[1] Since it won't do to try to understand all of them, it is useful to simplify. We'll do that here by restricting our social problem focus to *physical* child abuse, the type of child abuse that is arguably the least ambiguous although the least frequent. And it will reduce the complexity when we begin to think of explanations and interventions. We need a definition to begin our analysis, so let's use Kempe's familiar term—*child battering, the intentional physical injury of a child by family members or their appointed caretakers, demonstrable by a licensed physicians diagnosis.* This definition is in common use and close to that used by the National Center for Child Abuse and Neglect (NCCAN) in their important study usually referred to as NIS-2.[2] Like all good definitions, it leaves out some things, for example, the abuse of children by institutional caretakers in day care and school rooms but such omissions don't create problems for our purposes here. Qualitative distinctions among types of physical abuse are ordinarily a matter of severity ranging from moderate to severe to fatal.

Having established a definition, the social problem analysis must now turn to the issue of incidence—how much physical child abuse is there? It is a vexed question since so much depends on the definitions used. The most recent data available show that *fatalities* among physically abused children in 1993 were 1,028, or 1.5 per thousand children under 18.[3] In particular, we must be careful to distinguish between incidence based on *reports* and incidence based on *substantiations* since, unsurprisingly, 65 percent of abuse reports are not "confirmed" nor is abuse "indicated."[4] On the basis of 1993 state-substantiated report data, physical child abuse occurred at a rate of about 3.5 per thousand children or roughly four-tenths of one percent of all children under the age of 18.[5] Reported/substantiated child abuse of *all kinds* occurs at a rate of about 15 per thousand children. Substantiated reports of physical abuse were not as frequent as substantiated reports of neglect (7.0/1,000 children under 18), but were more frequent than reported sexual child abuse (2.1/1,000 children under 18).[6] Thus, in 1993, there were substantiated nearly a quarter of a million (231,569) children who were physically abused, not a trivial figure by any standard. Thus, we can consider it an important social problem.[7] Most experts believe that these figures should be interpreted as minimal estimates since they are based on official reports, which cannot take account of large-scale *unreported* child abuse (e.g., middle- and upper-income households are unlikely to be reported for child abuse). The NCCAN figures are likely to be the best available since they improve on most earlier data based only on police reports, whereas the NCCAN data were taken from hospitals, schools and other major agencies as well. Still, as Pecora and colleagues observe, abusing parents can purposely avoid medical care, can obfuscate by switching physicians, and certainly medical recognition of physical child abuse is not a perfect art. Even with good practitioners, medical personnel can be reluctant to label middle- and upper-income parents as abusers of their children.[8] The reader should note that even the most recent data are not fresh, but rather from 1993.

The preceding data on national incidence obscure wild variability between states: Washington, Montana, and Kentucky have substantiated rates of physical abuse of around 8 per thousand children under 18, whereas in Kansas and Illinois, these rates less than 1 per thousand? Such variability is not only about cultural ideas of "right" child rearing: Rodwell noted a decade ago that what specific behaviors constitute child abuse or neglect also depend on the willingness of a locality to provide services, and it's tolerance for subcultural variation.[9]

The Ideological Perspective

The next step in the social problem analysis is to identify the underlying ideology. It is important since it will help the reader to understand differences in problem definitions and causation. Recall that ideology is a statement about what is preferred and how things "should" or "ought" to be—in this case, with respect to physical child abuse. It should be distinguished from statements asserting what actually "is." There are many sources for social problem ideology: major recent legislation of relevance (and documents like committee hearings and reports that constitute part of the legislative history), professional journals, publications of child advocacy organizations, and so on. Media statements by important political players and professional "experts" can be of special importance and in that context can be quite explicit about ideology. But, political figures and professionals working in child protection organizations usually have self-interests at stake, so their statements aren't always clear and forthcoming about ideological perspectives, perhaps out of concern that offending some audience or constituency may be costly. And, legislative acts are often intentionally vague. Capturing the ideology of a social problem often requires a good bit of inference. Following are examples of such inferences. Readers should keep in mind that our concern here is with *public policy*, beliefs embedded therein, not just private beliefs. Be forewarned, sometimes downright conflicting ideological positions can be inferred from legislative provisions, reports, and documents; there is no guarantee that legislation will be all neat and tidy, as the following analysis will show.

A good source for the understanding and identifying contemporary ideology about physical child abuse is the Adoption Assistance and Child Welfare Act of 1980 (P.L. 96-272). It is not enough just to say that in the act, the ideology is that parents oughtn't to physically harm their children. Though that certainly is the case, more detailed statements can be made. For example, since we can legitimately infer from the fact that this act continued funding for child abuse reporting systems, it affirms an ideological position that the state has a right to invade the privacy of the family in order to (as Garbarino says) "know what's going on" for children there.[10] Note that it is not an unqualified state right since there is strong indication of a counter-ideology in the provisions of P.L. 96-272 prohibiting the removal of children without judicial determination. Since it limits state invasions of the privacy of families, it is clearly a ideological position affirming citizen rights over administrative (but not judicial) power.[11]

And, since it requires services precisely to prevent placements outside families where possible, this act expresses a clear ideological preference for children remaining with kin wherever possible. That same ideological persuasion can also be inferred because the act requires a Least Restrictive Environment (LRE) feature of foster care placement, where "least restrictive" is defined as placement with own kin as first priority, extended family next and non-relative care last and least preferred.[12] Where blood kin are not available for children, permanent, adoptive families—fictional kin—*should* have a priority over long-term foster care with nonrelatives is implied in the act's provisions for subsidized adoption for some children. Permanency and kinship are the cultural/ideological preferences here.

It is also worth noticing that there are other ideological commitments expressed in the legislative history of the act. For example, the legislative history will clearly tell us that the provisions for subsidized adoption were passed over the objections of those whose ideology was that people should not be "paid for being parents." Note the act requires that subsidies be given only after ". . . reasonable search for adoptive placements which do not require a subsidy."[13]

With respect to the ideology, the Adoption and Safe Families Act of 1997 (P.L. 105-89) is substantively quite similar to the 1980 act, that is, although children should be protected from abuse, physical or otherwise, retention of kinship ties should be given very high priority. Barring that, permanent families for children should be the priority: Its provisions strengthen subsidies for adoption, give fiscal incentives to states for increasing adoptions of children in foster care, provide for the study of expanding and making permanent foster care with kin ("kinship-care") and attempt to promote state policies that avoid children remaining in foster care over long periods of time (foster-care "drift").[14]

The Indian Child Welfare Act of 1978 (ICWA) contains a clear departure from the ideological position discussed earlier concerning the right of the state to invade family privacy on behalf of children. *ICWA requires a higher standard of proof for removal of Native American children from their parents than for removal of non–Native American children—that is, "beyond a reasonable doubt."* The historical background of this provision is the forcible administrative removal of thousands of Native American children from their families and tribal communities for placement in government and private boarding schools (up through the early 1900s), on the theory that Native American children needed to learn farming and white customs and language. In the 1970s, it became clear that thousands of Native American children were still being placed in state-funded foster care with little probability of their return home to their families.[15] Worse, nearly 53 percent of Native American children were placed by their states in non–Native American homes.[16] The ideology of the ICWA can be inferred here in a straightforward way: Great caution should be exercised in removing Native American children from their parents and tribal community, and when they are, any kind of temporary or permanent placement should be within a Native American family or tribal community. Barth and others draw similar conclusions.[17] Another source for identifying the ideology underlying a social problem are professional publications on policy and practice. One example is a recent book by Christopher G. Petr, *Social Work With Children and Their Families*.[18] Petr's ". . . value based framework for practice . . ." has a great deal in common with the ideology implied in the legislation just discussed. For example, among the eight basic elements of Petr's framework is "family centered practice"; representing Petr's ideological commitment to the priority of the family and kin we found implied in the provisions of the Adoption Assistance and Child Welfare Act of 1980 (strong emphasis on family reunifications, placement prevention, and so on). But Petr does carry it a deal further, for in his hands, it means that families *control* intervention choices, outcomes, needs, and the sharing of information. There is not much in the act that implies that.[19] Petr's framework element "Least Restrictive Environment" shares the Act's definition of LRE: Any placement away from parents should give priority to kin first.[20] Readers will find other elements of Petr's framework familiar, for example, "respect for diversity and difference . . ."[21] However, Petr's element, ". . . achieving outcomes . . ." is, in one sense, contrary to the outcome focused provisions of the 1997 version of the act (Adoption and Safe Families . . .) since it turns out to be an argument *against* ultimate-outcome measures. Although Petr favors measuring the effects of practice, it is with short-term, intermediate "process" measures, quite different than establishing the worth of interventions by measures of *how it all turns out* for people in trouble. That would seem to put Petr with one but not both feet in the same ideological camp with the 1997 act.[22] He has respectable reasons for his position, of course.

There are ideological perspectives on child abuse quite contrary to those stated earlier. Here is Duncan Lindsey, Editor-in-Chief of *Children and Youth Services Review*, speaking of ". . . Child Abuse: The Red-Herring of Child Welfare":

> For in response to . . . the horrors of child abuse, public child welfare has been transformed from a system serving a broad range of disadvantaged children into one designed

primarily to protect children from battering and sexual assault . . . (so that most) children who come to the attention of . . . agencies . . . (as) the victims of neglect or inadequate care are (now) virtually excluded from receiving assistance.[23]

Lindsey's point is that the incidence of battering and sexual assault is small relative to other social problems that affect children. His opinion is supported in part by the data.[24] He concludes that intervention programs are not generally effective (true with exceptions). Lindsey then draws an (ideological) conclusion that, on these accounts, *basic child protection should be administered by the police* in order that the child welfare system can be freed to address the total well-being of a much larger number of children.[25]

Causal Analysis

The next step in analyzing the social problem of physical child abuse, child battering, is to identify causal explanations used to understand this problem. There are many; Tzeng, Jackson, and Karlson list twenty-four for physical child abuse alone.[26] Many experts think of these theories as in three types: (1) explanations focused on factors within individuals, (2) explanations focused on factors in the surrounding sociocultural and economic environment, (3) explanations focused on ecological factors occupying the interactional space between both of the preceding types of factors.[27] The reader should be clear that *no general theory of physical child abuse has been unequivocally confirmed and shown to be superior to competing theories*. The research reviewed here is often significantly compromised by small clinical samples and comparison groups with selection bias and differential attrition, among other problems.[28] Despite the recent, admirable growth in research on child abuse, it is quite clear that we are only beginning to understand a few of the basic issues.

The *individual focused theories* on child battering are concerned with the attributes of parents in the main—think here of the paradigmatic example, the 1960s studies of Henry Kempe, from whose research came the term "Battered Child Syndrome."[29] They range from focus on the characteristics of their personalities, their psychological states, their ability to bond with their infants to a focus on the presence of severe mental disorders of parents. Most of these studies show confirming evidence, interesting, perhaps potentially important, but so weak as to be altogether unpersuasive when it comes to use in practice. Here are some examples. Many studies find that abusing parents do indeed have unrealistic expectations for their children compared to nonabusers, though not all such parents abuse their children.[30] Some studies are useful in correcting long cherished but wrong generalizations, that is, that child batterers are psychotic or severely mentally ill. Actually, only a quite small proportion of battering adults have ever had such conditions at least as defined in standard psychiatric classification schemes such as the American Psychiatric Association's DSM-IV.[31] On the question of the relationship of race/ethnicity to child abuse, the research, as of now, is equivocal—some studies affirm the relationship, others don't. It is clear that the differences between races and ethnic groups are small in any case.[32] Of course, substance abuse is a major factor in all types of maltreatment.[33] Finally, there is now considerable doubt about whether the idea that those who have been abused as a child will then abuse their own children is generally true. Actually, research has always shown clearly that *most* parents who have such experiences don't, in fact, abuse their own children, and, more interesting, there is some support for the idea that when they don't, they seem to have had an emotionally supportive parent, partners, or friends.[34] Most people do.

Among other things, *sociocultural-type* theories focus on economic factors such as poverty, where the research consistently shows strong relationships to child battering. But notice that most poor people don't abuse or batter their children, so poverty by itself is not causal.[35] Some researchers think they have found a complicated link between the two: low-status employment emphasizing subordination to authority translates into authoritarian styles in child rearing. Unemployment and job loss creates crises (constants for families in poverty) that are themselves associated with increased parental irritability, arbitrary discipline, and physical punishment. A good many studies support their association with physical abuse.[36] And, of course, this explanatory type is concerned with cultural sanctions toward corporal punishment of children. Clearly, the U.S. population is more accepting of physical punishment for children than Canada or England and some Asian countries.[37] But although corporal punishment is somewhat politically incorrect among middle-class America these days, the respected Diana Baumrind's review of the research concludes that nonabusive corporal punishment is: ". . . not harmful when administered deliberately for disciplinary purposes and legitimately belongs in the disciplinary repertoire of parents."[38] She also reminds us of some findings that could be important in designing interventions: that the importance of singular maternal attachments is not supported by cross-cultural research; that personal "warmth" is good for children in other ways, but is *not* associated with secure attachment of children to mothers and may not even be necessary to same; that unconditional approval is *not* associated with preschool competence.[39]

Ecological explanations turn on complex interactions between persons, parental pairs, families, social networks, cultural influences, and environmental factors, all taken together. Here are some interesting interactional findings. Yes, some abused parents from poverty backgrounds do abuse their children but those who do are *also* in unstable, intimate relationships during the first four years of their child's life.[40] Violence between intimate partners is likely to be associated with violence to young children.[41] Abusive families display fewer social interactions, especially positive ones, with their children, larger families are susceptible to low levels of positive and high levels of negative interactions, all are heightened by crowded housing conditions.[42]

Sociobiological theory takes an evolutionary perspective on social behaviors and understands them as survival strategies for species. The important motivations are ultimately genetic—to continue the species gene pool. Sociobiology theory (following Tzeng, Johnson, and Karlson here) predicts that a parents' natural children are more likely to be abused than adopted children, disabled children are more likely to be abused than fully functioning children, and that stepfathers will direct more energy toward their own than toward their stepchildren.[43] Research studies find some but not strong support for these propositions.[44]

Learning theory considers observational learning, operant conditioning, and social context as crucial to explaining human behavior. As applied to child abuse and aggressive behavior, its principles have some obvious applications: people literally learn how to be aggressive, learning when and where aggression is appropriate to social norms, and learning the consequences of aggression. Indeed, studies show that children who observe their parents being aggressive or violent in the course of family interactions will probably include aggression in their own kit bags, for example.[45] Tzeng believes that learning theory can be used to ". . . re-educate parents about parenting and . . . taught new better stress coping skills and communications processes."[46] And recent research suggests that he may be correct.

Gainers and Losers

The obvious losers from this social problem are abused children, but, of course, society itself is a loser when its stock of human capital is degraded, abused, or disabled. There are few gainers who somehow profit from the abuse of a child. But there is no social problem without a sizable set of winners, and, clearly, one of the most obvious winners here is the abuse perpetrator: abuse reaffirms their power in the family and is a clear message to those who would dispute it—including spouses as well as other children. Indeed, in the United States there is considerable support for the rights of parents to be completely free of interference from official government in physically punishing their children. Were there a social consensus on corporal punishment or on the idea that injuring children is always a socially shameful act, could it be that physical child abuse would disappear? A primate biologist who has studied the abuse of young in primate groups in the wild has reviewed the human child abuse research and concluded that abuse among humans is a result of ". . . an unsocialized child and an inconsistent parent living in a social system where there is ambiguity about child rearing practices and discipline."[47]

The Judicial Context

Judicial decisions have framed child abuse policy on all sides. Constitutional questions concerning the right to be free from harm (Eighth Amendment) and the right not to be deprived of either property or liberty without due process (Fourteenth Amendment) are often potentially applicable to child protection where removal of children from biological parents are involved. But most judicial contests around child abuse are ordinarily the prerogative of state and local courts since most family law is left to the states. Here are several examples of important court decisions establishing or extending social policy about abused children. Investigations of complaints of child abuse must inevitably compromise the privacy of a family. But where workers harass parents by threats of prosecution, or initiate court actions where there is little evidence, the judiciary has created a potential for civil liability and damages against them.[48] Stein says, in general, social workers *don't* have to give "Miranda warnings" prior to interviews during child protection investigations if it is being conducted in the family home or the workers' office.[49] And, in at least one federal jurisdiction, in 1989, when social workers were being sued for failing to monitor a foster home placement of two girls who were sexually assaulted, a Federal

Circuit Court granted social workers nearly absolute immunity, Stein says, ". . . for all actions taken from the time dependency begins until dependency ends. . . ."[50] Administrators and practitioners need to take notice of the U.S. Supreme Court ruling on the rights of fathers in proceedings terminating parental rights: It cannot be assumed that fathers are unfit parents just because mothers have been so adjudged, says the U.S. Supreme Court. "These and other Supreme Court decisions make clear that the rights of unmarried fathers who have lived with and cared for their children and have legally established paternity cannot be terminated without notice to the father and a determination of his fitness as a parent.[51]

The Historical Context

The first statute concerned with child abuse and neglect was a timid 1735 law passed in Massachusetts when, under British Common Law, children were thought of as nonpersons with no standing or rights.[52] They were, literally, an adult possession. In the middle and late 1800s, organized "child saving" appeared. From its very beginning, this social movement understood children from a strongly "scientific," rationalistic view—natural beings who were to be understood from the perspective of whatever positivistic science (as opposed to theological ideas) had to say about them.[53] Children were the evolutionary future and thus to be "saved," not in the theological sense, but in the Darwinistic sense! And, unthinkable a century earlier, it was not necessarily or only a matter for private organizations since child savers thought it was quite all right for the government to interfere in private affairs for the public good, for the sake of children. These days, the best known child-saving agency from those turn-of-the-century times may be the Children's Aid Societies because of their sponsorship of "orphan trains," which sent eastern seaboard "street-corner" children (mostly full orphans) west for adoption by farm families. That was heady child saving indeed to think of these children sent to the healthy air of the virtuous west, where bad things didn't happen in the popular imagination of that age. In actual fact, the Children's Aid Societies were preceded in time by private organizations devoted solely to protecting children and animals from abuse: the Societies for the Prevention of Cruelty to Children and Animals (SPCCA). The first of same was the New York SPCCA, found in 1974, and they and others on the eastern seaboard brought the abuse of children in this newly urban and industrialized country to the consciousness of the American public.[54] There were nearly two hundred such Societies in the United States and Europe by 1910. The New York SPCCA program was devoted primarily to child protection in a law enforcement mode, in fact, many SPCCA field staff were sworn officers with certain police powers. Their child protection was pursued through coercive means: warnings, moral persuasion, surveillance, and imprisonment at hard labor on occasion. Its preferred mode of intervention was to remove children from families and place them more or less permanently in institutions.[55] Costin believes that ". . . the intent was to bring salvation to children by a permanent break from parents and substitute mass culture for an emigrant culture."[56] Costin quotes from a Report of the New York SPCCA: ". . . ignorant people must be compelled to do what is right by the strong arm of the law."[57] But the Massachusetts SPCCA branch developed along quite different lines. Cognizant of the problems of emigrants and different standards of child rearing and family life, the Massachusetts SPCCA thought that child abuse was partly a problem of cultural assimilation.[58] By 1907, they abandon policing to focus on remedial action and services to strengthen family life, child protection being only one part of their responsibility. SPCCAs the country over moved toward the Massachusetts SPCCA program idea rather than that of the New York Society. Early in its history, its practices focused on substitute and noninstitutional *family care* for abused children, provided citizenship classes in settlement houses, child care and the provision of kindergartens for emigrant children, and "friendly visiting," of course.[59] In the Progressive Era, after the turn of the century, the social problem of child abuse faded into the background. Costin believes that was due, in part, to the political focus of the Progressives on the external causes of social ills, on improving the quality of life not just for those considered "unfortunate" but through more or less "universalistic" programs that were directed at *all* the nation's children. Accordingly, the Progressives sponsored and passed legislation on maternal and child health for which almost all families were eligible.[60] In the social work profession, child abuse assumed a low profile as the profession became increasingly preoccupied with personal and counseling services.[61] That was followed by the economic disasters of the Great Depression in the 1930s when the professional perspectives were swept up in the situational disasters—unemployment, hunger, and housing—that were its consequences.[62]

The social problem of the physical abuse of children finally reappeared as a public issue in the 1960s with the discovery by radiologists of characteristic patterns in X-rays of the broken bones of battered children.[63] Following from that, Henry Kempe popularized the idea of the "battered child syndrome." Child abuse became a "child-saving" issue on the same basis that exploitative child labor and orphaned children had nearly a hundred years earlier: children, innocent victims, essentially helpless in terrible circumstances, were being exploited and injured at the hands of aggressive adults. Indeed, it took on the character of a social movement, just as had child labor a century earlier. When the Child Abuse and Prevention Act was passed in the 1970s, the country had long accepted the idea of public, rather than private initiatives to intervene in social problems and the child-saving movement had surely helped to prepare that ground. The policy initiatives were characteristic of the features that, in some ways, the child-saving movement had pioneered: not only federal leadership, but a preference for program designs influenced by the most recent research findings, strong roles for "experts" and professionals offering "treatment" interventions focused on families and individuals with much program implementation in the hands of the private sector. Notice, however, that the focus of the federal legislation is on individual children, clearly a legacy from the child-saving movement. There is a certain contradiction here because, as will be seen later, much of the research on child abuse implies that children are being abused because of unemployment, crowded housing, and cultural ambiguity about child rearing and corporal punishment in particular, not the ignorance and/or the neuroticisms of individual parents. History goes some way toward explaining that contradiction as a legacy from the child-saving movement. It is also a historical fact that the United States is a reluctant welfare state, unwilling as always to make public provision for secure employment and adequate housing stock for its citizens, even if there is good reason to think that a universal provision along those lines might go some way toward preventing an important proportion of child abuse. When the 1974 Child Abuse and Prevention Act was passed, its sponsor was shocked that there was not a single federal agency that had any legal responsibility for the problem. But states have, of course, always had first place when it came to matters of family law, so the act's sponsors perhaps should not have been so surprised.

The Social Program and Policy System

Introduction

Up to this point, the work of our policy analysis has been at a broad level, necessary so the reader can discover those vital things that explain how the program came to be and how its shape will have been influenced by history, ideology, and politics of the moment. Now our work turns to describing the details of how a specific program is supposed to work. Notice that there are always two general kinds of things for the policy analyst to do: (1) describe the program and (2) judge its worthwhileness.

Readers should be warned against their own ambition—don't try to analyze a whole piece of legislation, certainly not a whole social policy system or even large agencies. In fact, the readers' first attempt should be "bite-size," a small program or subprogram with homogeneous goals and objectives that can fit on a single page or two. That will probably be an administrative subunit in a social agency: for example, a food kitchen for the homeless, one small program unit serving, say, therapeutic foster care, or a case management unit for the chronically mentally ill.

Goals and Objectives

The first task is to describe goals and objectives. The program used throughout this chapter to demonstrate our policy and program analysis method is a child abuse prevention program roughly modeled on the work of Wolfe and colleagues, but that we shall call the Adolescent Relationships Program (ARP).[64] The basic program idea is to focus prevention on high school age students who have a high probability of becoming both teen parents and being violent toward their own children and those of intimates. Research shows that these are teenagers who (a) live in violent neighborhoods and (b) have either regularly witnessed family violence or experienced it themselves. Studies indicate these adolescents are very likely to engage in serious dating violence (both sexual and physical aggression) plus considerable difficulty in ending such relationships.[65] Studies also show that the developmental process for violence in teen dating seems to parallel that of violent families; that such violence appears at around 15 to 16 years of age, when, in a year or so, attachment relationships of longer duration will begin.[66] It is relevant to child battering because *research findings show clearly that abuse of intimates and child battering are very likely to occur together.*[67] In short, the program theory is that from their families and neighborhood, children learn that violence is normative, acceptable behavior and a useful way to resolve conflicts with others—reinforced of course by media and cultural models. The program theory assumes that coercive violence strategies are gender-specific and that peer and family apply socialization pressures to adopt them. The program goal is to reduce child battering by both male and female adolescents. Specific objectives of this program are for adolescents to

1. learn awareness of how their tendencies toward abusive behavior began (e.g., understanding power and control in relationships, victim/batterer gender socialization, sex-role stereotypes)
2. learn that violent attitudes and behaviors are not normative, rather the reverse (e.g., peer, media, and family role models)
3. learn specific skills for building nonviolent relationships and specific behavioral responses to abuse (or the tendency to abuse) in their own relationships (e.g., choosing partners, defining powerful relationships through equality, empathy, and emotional expressiveness)[68]

These are what are called *intermediate objectives*, that is, if these are achieved, it is logical to expect that the probability for child battering is significantly reduced. ARP is a program that could be funded under many of the broad and very loose legislative mandates for child abuse prevention in the United States, here let's assume it is funded by a state Children's Trust Fund. We'll take some liberties here—the program is actually Canadian. The fact is that from a policy perspective, the success of most "after-the-fact" intervention programs for child batterers is either not impressive or not enduring.[69] ARP is a preventive, "before-the-fact" program with all its obvious advantages. The ongoing research on the program we are about to study is encouraging.[70]

   Our next task is to make a judgment as to the merit of the goals and objectives: How good are they? In fact, they turn out to be good ones for the most part. First, they are clearly concerned with outcomes that can stand justified on their own merit, not just "means" to some distant end. Second, they are defined with sufficient clarity so that they can (potentially) be measured. Third, the terms of the objectives "fit" quite closely with the definitions of physical child abuse. The theory on which the program is based is a particular case of one of the causal explanations found in the social problem analysis. But, *performance standards* cannot be found anywhere in the program description, and that is a lack. Not stating them can be acceptable if the program is a *prototype* (never before implemented). It is important because if no specific expectations are set out for program success then it could be considered a success if only a single (or two or four) participant achieved the objectives. Doubtless, neither the program designers, the staff, nor those who supply program funds would be satisfied with that. When a program goes "public," performance standards ought to be public since that has the virtue of "keeping everybody honest." The temptation to adjust expectations to fit performance (and say "good job") is very strong when investment in program achievement is high. And, it almost always is.

   It is useful in any discussion of goals and objectives to notice the extent to which they concern social control issues. In this instance, that is very much the case: This program wants to change behaviors that are socially deviant to those that are normative. Clearly, this program is deeply committed to social control of the first order. In this case, is that right or wrong from the readers' own ideological perspective? Of this, more later in the upcoming section on "Administration and Service Delivery."

Eligibility Rules

Program participation is limited to the following:

- age between 14 to 16 years
- enrollment in a particular high school
- those from a family known to the local protective services office because violence has occurred. The participant might not have been abused, but must have witnessed family or neighborhood violence over a significant period of time.

For our present purposes, let us proceed as if these were the complete set of eligibility rules. Our first question is: What type of eligibility rules are these? The rule maker here is clearly the program administration—thus, we have *administrative rules* here. No staff member has the right to admit any people to this program, so there is no *administrative discretion* here. Other types of eligibility principles (rules) are ruled out by the fact that there is no exchange of money or reference to legislation or judicial decision.

Now, are these "good" eligibility rules? First, *do these rules "fit" the social problem analysis* to which this program intends to contribute at least a partial solution? The answer is yes, indeed they do, since these rules target those who research shows are at some documented risk of child battering. But it is also clear that they limit the program to a small sector of the target group. That is acceptable as long as that is all the program claims to do.

Another criterion on which we should judge eligibility rules concerns whether program participation *stigmatizes*. To be stigmatizing, program participation has to be known to the public, and the observing public must know that participation is associated with social deviancy. It seems hard to imagine that attending these program activities in the ordinary public high school could go unnoticed by other students. Aren't students immensely curious, not to mention observant, about what their peers are doing and why? It might be possible to obscure participation, but it would take some clever planning indeed. Public knowledge about participation seems likely to create stigmatization since the program itself is about a serious social deviancy (family violence). At any rate, it is a matter to which program staff should be alert: Left unattended, it could be the cause of program nonparticipation, high dropout rates, and so on.

Other criteria for eligibility rules are *off-targeting* and *over-* or *underutilization*. The former is not an issue here since these eligibility rules closely target potential participants. *Underutilization* is an issue since the small numbers allowed by funding don't come close to covering the numbers of potential abusers. Notice that readers should not expect every evaluative criteria to apply in every policy or program analysis. It is not intended that they should.

Form of Benefit and/or Service

The type of benefit this program offers is not a "hard" benefit (like cash or commodities) but a service. In this case, it is an *expert service*, sometimes called "psycho-education," that is, education and skill training in understanding and avoiding family violence. It is not a personal social service since the program design doesn't call for one-on-one tutoring in this educational venture (though it conceivably could). There is no attempt to individualize program participants and focus particular kinds of service and benefit packages on their unique problems. Since no money (or equivalents) change hands, this benefit form is not material goods, not credits or vouchers nor subsidies or loan guarantees, and so on. Although it concerns citizens who have been protective services clients, this program does not involve *protective regulation*, something very different from protective services for children. "Protective regulation" refers to government regulations protecting some businesses from competition from other businesses (often imports, or dairy subsidies), not protection from child abuse or neglect.

Now, how shall we evaluate this benefit form: Is it a "good" one with respect to this social problem? At the most obvious level, the benefit is a *good fit with what the social problem requires.* But we must also take a large-scale perspective here: How far could this program go in dealing with the child battering problem among the population in general; could this type of program be implemented in *every* high school in the nation? Would a public high school in a wealthy urban neighborhood tolerate a program whose very existence implies that child battering and family violence might occur among the wealthy? It does of course; it's just unlikely to be officially reported. Notice that this suggests the possibility of *political risk* for the supporters of this program should it be more widely implemented. And, of course, that raises the relevance of another evaluative criteria: *How adaptable is this program across users?* Those are serious issues.

Analysts need to realize that this program cannot reach child batterers who have not so far come to the attention of official child protective units—that is, who are never reported. That illustrates a problem in *target efficiency* for this benefit form: Although it does an excellent job of focusing services only on those who have the problem, it must overlook a significant number of them. Although this is not a reason to avoid implementing the program, the analyst should never lose sight of what is left over after program intervention has occurred.

Finally, the good practical policy analyst must always be conscious of the immense temptation to substitute services for hard benefits as a solution to social problems. The advantage is that social services often can be implemented on a relatively small scale and thus are less expensive than broad-scale hard benefits like income supplements or medical care. Although most of the poor do not batter children, there is no debate that the stresses and constant crises for those living in poverty may set the stage for child battering. The point is that we don't know how much battering would be reduced if income adequacy were the hard benefit delivered rather than services like counseling, psycho-education, and so on). Practical policy analysts need to keep in mind that the legislative motive for services may not be altogether altruistic: Social services are never cheap, but they are usually cheaper than universal income protections and health care for all citizens.

The costs of this service are less than the costs of some personal social services since its personnel serve groups of program participants rather than single subjects. Assuming this program design ultimately proves itself to be effective in reducing child battering, this form of benefit is most likely *cost-effective* (at least for those who receive it)—even as it ignores most of the social problem.

Does this program have a potential for serious *coerciveness* toward clients? That kind of inquiry should be made by the practical social policy analyst. The answer to the question turns on the extent to which teenagers from families known to protective services are free to refuse participation without retaliation. There is nothing in the program design itself that would prohibit teenagers from opting out when their participation is solicited or thereafter. But it could be just the opposite; the point is that we don't know until we ask program staff the questions. If so, it might produce high dropout rates or otherwise compromise participant characteristics. This program design doesn't appear to entail serious *intrusiveness* into program participants lives, although participants are asked to apply the concepts learned to their own life experience. The issue is whether those in charge of the group meetings do or do not use group pressure or the pressure of their own professional status to force participants to divulge personal information against their ordinary caution. That information must come from participants themselves.

Administration and Service Delivery

Program Theory.   Administration and service delivery must be in service of implementing the program design. Administration is means to an end, a vehicle for a purpose, not an end in itself. That is why we will begin with a discussion of program design for the ARP. It is derived from three general social science theories, and here applied to the goal of reducing violence toward family intimates and children. They are (1) social learning theory, (2) feminist theory, and (3) attachment theory.[71] *Social learning theory* explains how violence among intimates arises as intimate relationships develop in adolescence. As children, violent males are taught hostile beliefs about women, power-assertive behavior, and how power and control over women is a benefit by their families, culture, and subculture. *Feminist theory* explains the socialization process through which the power imbalance between genders occurs: Males are reared to be in charge, competitive, and "silent," whereas females are reared to be compliant, oriented to others' needs, and anger-denying. Thus, women are socialized to believe that the outcomes for and well-being of intimates are their task, where the point is "the other," not themselves. And, for males, rigid gender roles produce a perspective on females that is both demeaning to women and radically separates the functions females play in subroles—mother, cook, whore, and so on. Empowerment is an important concept in feminist perspectives and used in ARP program design with respect to working with adolescents and health promotion aspects of the program. *Attachment theory* explains how the choice of ". . . partners in dating relationship may be directly related to attachment experiences in childhood and early adolescence."[72] Readers should remember here the empirical fact that 70 to 80 percent of children who grow up in violent families don't abuse their children or intimates.[73] Many believe that it is being reared in a violent environment and in a culture that gives sanction to male violence toward women that makes the difference. For example, there is a research finding that the presence of a supportive intimate partner substantially reduces the probability of spousal and mother/child abuse.[74]

Program Design.   The program design for the ARP is drawn from the three general (social science) theories described before. This design (illustrated in Figure 11.1) assumes that child battering and violence to intimates by males is based on learned gender roles and reinforced by cultural and media-idealized models. There is nothing much ARP can do about the latter, but it might be able to help males "unlearn" gender roles and replace them with relationship skills that promote clear communication, avoid coercion, and reduce the drive toward power and control. And it may be able to help females "unlearn" gender roles that reward the problematic male gender roles described before: compliance, other orientations and anger repression. The program objectives are clearly reflected in the outcomes found in the program theory and outlined in Figure 11.1. They are unabashedly cognitive in that they assume that "knowing" a new gender role will translate into "doing" it, that is, playing it out in real life relationships.

Notice in Figure 11.1 that associated with each objective is a set of *program specifications* intended to achieve that objective. Here is the way this chart is to be read. The objective of "unlearning" male devaluation of women (left column) is intended to be accomplished by a program activity that has respected male models speaking in the discussion (right column) positively of women. And women model the obverse of female compliance, repression of anger and other orientedness. Program specifications are exactly the activities that the program staff will put into operation. That list could be more detailed, but what is there serves as an illustration. The practical policy analyst should work to obtain program activity descriptions at, at least, this level of detail. If the staff cannot provide those specifics, it should raise questions about whether they are clear about what they are implementing.

Type of Service-Delivery Organization.   The ARP program is intended for high school students, and although it could be administered in various organizations, let us assume that a public high school in the United States is the "host" organization providing financing, community sanction, and administrative accountability. It seems reasonable to assume that public high schools are a *centralized* type of organization in which classrooms and subprograms such as ARP are embedded in a hierarchical organization with authority concentrated at the top levels of an organizational pyramid. Even so, the practical policy analyst should be alert to whether the ARP program has more than one "boss," ordinarily a bad idea since it requires the administrator to constantly negotiate between each authority when decisions are made or when issues of refunding, evaluation, staff, facilities, equipment, and supplies are considered. That can happen if funding is from one source and direct administration is from another. The ARP program should have a single authority to whom it is responsible and the administrator should be clear on who that is.

Now let's consider whether the administrative arrangement is a good one for ARP. First, let's look at the evaluative criteria requiring an administration and service-delivery organization to have qualities of *integration and continuity* with other relevant social services. The practical policy analyst should consider that ARP's program participants are from families who are most vulnerable to being reported for child abuse: from families

Program Theory Elements (theory)	Program Specification (practice)
1. Learning that male violence *is not* normative (males unlearning male devaluation of women; females unlearning the devaluation of women) [from learning theory]	• Small group teaching/discussion on positive relationships in ordinary families
+	+
	• Modeling of nonviolent relationships; techniques of anger control by former abusers and victims
	+
2. Males unlearning myth and false facts underlying the devaluation of women [from feminist theory]	• Small group teaching/discussion on the female character
+	+
	• Modeling of positive/assertive women
3. Males learning relationship skills (empathy, equality, and expressiveness)	+
	• Teaching/modeling empathy, equality, and expressiveness
nonviolent, noncoercive, nonsexist intimate relationship	+
	• Rehearsing males on how to give compliments
reduction of probability for spousal abuse	• Rehearsing/mastering relationship skills above
+	+
4. Women learning how to identify power imbalances in society and in intimate relationships [from feminist theory]	• Modeling power imbalances between genders to women • Women rehearsing/role-playing power imbalances • Video demonstrating power imbalances • Teaching/modeling for women female noncompliance and anger expression
+	+
5. Learning a redefinition of intimate relationships based on empathy, expressiveness, and positive communication skills (both genders) [from attachment theory]	• Modeling the redefinition of intimate relationships based on empathy and expressiveness/positive communication skills by former abusers and victims
+	+

6. Learning the origins of gender role socialization as origin of coercive sex by males	• Group discussion of family/society cultural socialization processes
	  -group discussion of peer socialization
	  -role-playing scenarios
	  -teaching males how to ensure consent to sexual relationships
	  -teaching females to be clear about consent, assertive, and safe
	  -program participants assist in later programs as demonstrators/modelers and the teaching of others

[All of above taken together]	

[All of above program taken together]

Reduction of Probability for Child Battering (Program Goal)

FIGURE 11.1   How a program specification puts a theory into practice.

who are likely to live on the edge of poverty or worse, likely to have serious health problems because medical care is not easily come by, likely to be in crisis much of the time from illness and injury, unemployment, arrest, conflict in the schools, and so on. ARP should show evidence of having done advance organizational preparation so that referrals to community helping resources can be made easily and without delay when needed—medical care for health problems, personal counseling, remedial education, and so on. That means seeking out advance understandings with various service providers about how, to whom, and under what conditions ARP participants can be referred. Without advance preparation, it can be time-consuming, clumsy, and may not achieve its purposes. Humanitarian considerations aside, unless the program is prepared to do that, program participants can drop out and good program outcomes can be completely overwhelmed when participants become preoccupied with coping with the pressing and serious negative outcomes that happen to people in constant crisis. For ARP to be "integrated" with other community services means the participants know people in those organizations who can help ARP participants get services when they need them.

Another service-delivery criterion is *accessibility*. Geographic location and transportation are commonly an issue, although that is not the case here—the program is conducted at the high school attended by all program participants. But there are other things that can make a social program inaccessible to people who need it, for example, language. For those for whom English is not a first language, a program without staff who speaks the language of, say, a recent emigrant is inaccessible to that emigrant. The ARP program might fail that test if its potential participants were not competent English speakers. The *helper-therapy principle*—teaching others what you yourself have just learned—is one device by which to make learning certain things accessible to people. It has been been demonstrated to be a powerful educational strategy. This program includes it in its program specification: Program participants are enlisted to help teach other adolescents the same material.

If ARP is a good service-delivery organization, it should meet the criterion of having *accountability* features. Recall accountability is concerned with an organization's ability to establish who made decisions and a forum for appealing them when program consumers (or staff) feel that they have not been consistent with the organization's own policies. In Chapter 8 on the analysis of service delivery, we described what a rudimentary accountability system should contain. Since we have imagined ARP as existing in the context of a host agency, we should assume that program participants (and staff) have accountability features available to them. Many school systems have fair-hearing procedures and other accountability systems in place. ARP participants, for example, need recourse for appeal if they are dismissed from the program, and the same applies to ARP program staff.

Another evaluative criterion for service delivery systems is their ability to relate to *ethnic, gender, and racial diversity*. ARP is clearly relating to gender diversity, *but the program opposes cultural and ethnic tradition* whenever it is the origin of adolescent socialization to the acceptability of putting women at a power disadvantage with respect to men. Indeed, the program theory expects cultural differences to be an important source from which the conditions for male violence toward women and child battering originate. The objective of the program is to challenge such cultural perspectives and attempt to socialize program participants to quite the opposite perspective. It is a very large order since the program is entirely cognitive. That is, it takes no action with respect to changing cultural influences or peer group socialization factors—both powerful reinforcers of these attitudes. So, does the program "fail" on this criterion? Readers must examine their own ideological perspectives to decide where the limits are for "accepting and being sensitive to cultural diversity." It is important for the practical policy analyst to pursue policy issues beyond the obvious. One way to do that here might be to put the following question to the ARP program staff: How would they react to, say, a traditional Moslem adolescent who was clearly adopting the ARP perspective about gender power differentials they saw in their peer group and family, but who, in all other ways, responded from her religious perspective in the group discussion?[75] The answer that might save ARP from being a form of sectarian evangelism, is whether ARP group leaders would act to protect her right to change her own religious belief at her own pace and *only so far as she herself desires.* It is an interesting, difficult issue here, but it is a good illustration of the difference between various types of policy analyses. Remember, this is a value-critical analysis, but some would argue it must indeed be a value-committed policy analysis.

Financing

Let us assume here that the ARP program is funded from a Children's Trust Fund. These trust funds, enacted by state legislatures, first began in the early 1980s, and early on were funded from a tax on marriage licenses.[76] Usually, an appointed board administers the trust, including the responsibility for making decisions about disbursements to projects. Much of the initial motivation to establish these trust funds was out of a concern for funding prevention programs. Then or now, only a small proportion of all funds expended on the social problem of child abuse go for prevention.[77] This type of financing would seem to be a good fit with the social problem analysis because it focuses on a type of prevention. Also, the causal analysis found here suggests that developing knowledge of prevention is a serious need since after-the-fact treatment of child battering is not reliably successful in reducing subsequent incidents or healing the trauma. But, of course, the most important issue is whether the revenue generated by the trust fund strategy is sufficient to cover the "need." It isn't clear that trust funds have sufficient funds for all the projects they consider worthwhile. It must be observed that although a "marriage tax" is a clever way to fund research, it is not been tested to see whether it could produce sufficient amounts. No one ever expected it to be used as a method of funding for basic preventive services. It would raise the cost of marriage licenses.

This type of funding is unusual for social welfare programs and so let us use the term "special revenue" funding. That identifies it as coming from tax revenues, but sets it off as coming from a special source—*not* from general revenue funding whose sources are from taxes on, say, income and property and from the public at large. That isn't especially unusual—think of the special taxes on hunting licenses used to fund wildlife projects. Or on gasoline taxes used to conduct research on alternative fuels.

One of the recommended criterion for funding is its *dependability over time*. Compared to other financing methods, taxes on marriage licenses would appear to produce very dependable funds. The state legislature isn't likely to take the trouble to lower the amount of this small and seemingly uncontroversial tax. And its constancy is assured as long as marriage rates are reasonably constant over the short to medium term (*demographic change*). But notice that this type of funding fails another of the evaluative criterion: it cannot *respond quickly to economic change* (say, inflation). Program costs increase under inflation, but the tax is set in law as some absolute dollar amount per marriage license. Thus, any change requires a special action of the state legislature, which is never quick. Notice that indexing the tax rate to the rate of inflation, as for Social Security retirement benefits, would settle this problem.

Finally, let's consider the criterion that calls attention to whether financing provides *incentives or disincentives for obtaining specific client outcomes*. The answer for the Children's Trust Fund financing is "yes," since most trust funds require project proposals to specify preventive outcomes as a condition for consideration for funding.

Interactions between Basic Policy Elements and between This and Other Programs

This program necessarily interacts with the local Protective Services who identify and refer program participants and the local public high school, which is its host organization. But this program does not make participants either coeligible for other services nor make them ineligible either. It is unlikely to duplicate services, given its unusual psychoeducational design. It is conceivable that there is potential for what we've called *contrary policy/program effects* given that the type of changes the program seeks to make is in the participant's perspective on imbalanced power relationships among genders. For example, an ARP program participant might be simultaneously involved (at the initiative of Protective Services) in a family counseling program attempting to reduce internal family conflict. In contrast, ARP might well be creating family conflict around cultural and family traditions with respect to gender role issues.

NOTES

1. D. Cicchetti and R. Rizley, "Developmental Perspectives on the Etiology, Intergenerational Transmission and Sequelae of Child Maltreatment," in R. Rizley and D. Cicchetti (eds.), *New Directions For Child Development* (San Francisco: Jossey-Bass, 1981), p. 11.

2. A. J. Sedlak, *Study of the National Incidence and Prevalence of Child Abuse and Neglect: Report on Data and Analysis.* Technical Report. (Washington, DC: Department of Health and Human Services, National Center on Child Abuse and Neglect, 1987).

3. Patrick A. Curtis et al., *Child Abuse and Neglect: A Look at the States* (Washington, DC: CWLA Press, 1995), Table 1.11, p. 40. Data based on U.S. Department of Health and Human Services, National Center on Child Abuse and Neglect, *Child Maltreatment 1993: Reports from the States to the NCCAN* (Washington, DC: U.S. Government Printing Office, 1995).

4. Curtis et al., *Child Abuse and Neglect*, Table 1.8, p. 32.

5. Ibid.

6. Ibid.

7. Ibid.

8. P. J. Pecora et al., *The Child Welfare Challenge* (New York: Aldine de Gruyter, 1992), p. 99.

9. M. K. Rodwell, *Policy Implications of the Multiple Meanings of Neglect: A Naturalistic Study of Child Neglect.* Ph.D. diss., University of Kansas School of Social Welfare, Lawrence, 1988.

10. R. Wollons, *Children At Risk in America: History, Concepts and Public Policy* (Albany: State University of New York, 1993), p. 269.

11. Pecora et al., *The Child Welfare Challenge*, p. 23.

12. Ibid., pp. 22–24, 433.

13. E. Segal, "Adoption Assistance and the Law," in E. C. Segal (ed.), *Adoption of Children with Special Needs: Issues in Law and Policy* (Washington, DC: American Bar Association, 1995), pp. 127–134.

14. *Summary of the Adoption and Safe Families Act of 1997 (P.L. 105-89)* (Washington, DC: Child Welfare League of America, 1997).

15. L. Matheson, "The Politics of the Indian Child Welfare Act," *Social Work*, 41 (1996): 232.

16. M. Plantz, R. Hubbell, B. Barrett, and A. Dobrec, "The Indian Child Welfare Act: A Status Report," *Children Today*, 18(2) (1989): 27.

17. R. Barth, "Adoption," in P. J. Pecora et al., *The Child Welfare Challenge*, pp. 367–369.

18. Christopher G. Petr, *Social Work with Children and Their Families* (New York: Oxford University Press, 1998).

19. Ibid., p. 44.

20. Ibid., pp. 85–87.

21. Ibid., p. 167, quoting 42 USC 675 (5) (A).

22. Ibid., p. 111–113.

23. D. Lindsey, *The Welfare of Children* (New York: Oxford University, 1994), p. 161.

24. Ibid., quoting S. Kammerman and A. J. Kahn, "Social Services for Children, Youth and Families in the U.S.," *Children and Youth Services*, 12(1) (1995).

25. Lindsey, *The Welfare of Children*, pp. 173, 177.

26. O. Tzeng, J. Jackson, and H. Karlson, *Theories of Child Abuse and Neglect* (New York: Praeger, 1991), p. vi.

27. R. Ammerman and M. Hersen, *Children At Risk: An Evaluation of Factors Contributing to Child Abuse and Neglect* (New York: Plenum Press, 1995), pp. 201–203; O. Tzeng et al., *Theories of Child Abuse and Neglect*, pp. 31–108; Pecora et al., *The Child Welfare Challenge*, p. 133–136.

28. R. Chalk and P. King, *Violence in Families* (Washington, DC: National Academy Press, Commission on Behavioral Science, on Social Sciences, Committee on Education of the National Research Council and the National Institute on Medicine, 1998), p. 3.

29. C. H. Kempe, F. Silverman, B. Steele, and H. Silver, "The Battered Child Syndrome," *Journal of Marriage and the Family*, 18(2) (1962): 17–24.

30. R. Ammerman and M. Hersen, *Children At Risk: An Evaluation of Factors Contributing to Child Abuse and Neglect* (New York: Plenum Press, 1995), p. 90.

31. Chalk and King, *Violence in Families*. See also J. Garbarino, "Preventing Child Maltreatment," in R. Price et al., *Prevention in Mental Health: Research, Policy and Practice* (Beverly Hills, CA: Sage, 1980), pp. 63–80.

32. Chalk and King, *Violence in Families*, p. 44.

33. Tzeng et al., *Theories of Child Abuse and Neglect*, p. 35.

34. Chalk and King, *Violence in Families*, pp. 46–47. See also B. Egeland and K. Papatola, "Intergenerational Continuity of Abuse," in R. Gelles and J. Lancaster (eds.), *Child Abuse and Neglect: Biosocial Dimensions* (Hawthorne, NJ: Aldine de Gruyter, 1987).

35. L. Pelton, "The Role of Material Factors in Child Abuse and Neglect," in G. Melton and F. Barry (eds.), *Protecting Children from Abuse and Neglect* (New York: Guilford Press, 1994). See also Chalk and P. King, *Violence in Families*, p. 43.

36. J. Vondra, "Sociological and Ecological Risk Factors in Child Abuse," in R. Ammerman and M. Hersen (eds.), *Children At Risk: An Evaluation of Factors Contributing to Child Abuse and Neglect* (New York: Plenum Press, 1995), p. 162.

37. Tzeng et al., *Theories of Child Abuse and Neglect*, p. 111. See also Vondra, "Sociological and Ecological Risk Factors in Child Abuse," p. 162.

38. D. Baumrind, *Child Maltreatment and Optimal Caregiving in Social Contexts* (New York: Garland, 1995), p. 80.

39. Baumrind, *Child Maltreatment*, pp. 65, 71.

40. Vondra, "Sociological and Ecological Risk Factors," p. 157.

41. A. Rosenbaum and D. O'Leary, "Marital Violence: Characteristics of Abusive Couples," *Journal of Consulting and Clinical Psychology*, 49 (3) (1981): 63–71.

42. Tzeng et al., *Theories of Child Abuse and Neglect*, pp. 57–58.

43. Ibid., pp. 90–91.

44. Ibid., p. 92.

45. Ibid., p. 94.

46. Ibid., pp. 96, 97.

47. T. Field, "Child Abuse in Monkeys and Humans: A Comparative Perspective," Martin Reite and Nancy G. Caine (eds.), in *Child Abuse: The Nonhuman Primate Data* (New York: Alan R. Liss, 1983), p. 171.

48. D. Besharov, *Criminal and Civil Liability in Child Welfare Work: The Growing Trend*, 3rd ed. (Washington, DC: National Legal Resource Center for Child Advocacy and Protection, American Bar Association, 1986).

49. T. Stein, *Child Welfare and the Law* (New York: Longman, 1991), p. 62; and A. O'Connor, "Child Protection Investigations: Miranda Warnings," *Juvenile and Child Welfare Law Reporter*, 8(2) (April 1989): 29–30.

50. Stein, *Child Welfare and the Law*, p. 70.

51. *Stanley v. Illinois*, 405 U.S. 645 (1972). Stein, *Child Welfare and the Law*, p. 73; *Caban v. Mohammed*, 441 U.S. 380 (1979).

52. Richard P. Barth, "Abusive and Neglecting Parents and the Care of Their Children," in M. Moan, A. Skolnick, and S. Sugarman (eds.), *All Our Families* (New York: Oxford University Press, 1998), p. 217.

53. R. Wollons, *Children at Risk in America: History, Concepts and Public Policy* (Albany: State University of New York, 1993), p. 65.

54. Lela B. Costin, "Cruelty to Children: A Dormant Issue and Its Rediscovery, 1920–1960," *Social Service Review*, 66(2) (1992): 177–181.

55. Ibid., p. 179.

56. Ibid.

57. Ibid.

58. Ibid., p. 181.

59. Ibid.

60. Ibid., p. 182

61. Ibid., p. 183.

62. Ibid., p. 193.

63. Ibid., p. 194.

64. Wolfe's program is described in full in D. Wolfe et al., "Empowering Youth to Promote Healthy Relationships," in D. Wolfe, R. McMahon, and R. Peters (eds.), *Child Abuse: New Directions in Prevention and Treatment Across the Lifespan* (Thousand Oaks, CA: Sage, 1997), p. 114. The program design in the book you are now reading is my own work not Wolfe's and an invention for illustrative purposes, inspired by Wolfe's Youth Relationships Program as described in his article referenced at the beginning of this note. It is not intended to be an exact replica in any way.

65. Wolfe et al., "Empowering Youth," p. 111.

66. Ibid., p. 112.

67. J. Vondra, "Risk Factors Associated with Child Abuse and Neglect—Sociological and Ecological Factors," in R. Ammerman and M. Hersen (eds.), *Children At Risk* (New York: Plenum Press, 1990), p. 156.

68. Wolfe et al., "Empowering Youth," pp. 106–107.

69. Chalk and King, *Violence in Families*, pp. 118–119.

70. Wolfe et al., "Empowering Youth," pp. 121–123.

71. Ibid., pp. 106–107.

72. Ibid.

73. E. Zigler and N. Hall, "Physical Child Abuse in America: Past, Present and Future," in D. Cicchetti and V. Carlson (eds.), *Child Maltreatment: Theory and Research on the Causes and Consequences of Child Abuse and Neglect* (Cambridge: Cambridge University Press, 1989), pp. 52–53, 63–64.

74. Chalk and King, *Violence in Families*, p. 46.

75. It won't do to challenge this question on the basis that if a person actually did that they would be inconsistent in their beliefs—few people are entirely consistent with respect to their ideology.

76. J. Poertner, "The Kansas Family and Child Trust Fund: Five Year Report," *Child Welfare*, 66 (1987): 3–12.

77. Pecora et al., *The Child Welfare Challenge*, Table 1.4, p. 18.

BIBLIOGRAPHY

Aaron, H. (1982). *Economic effects of social security.* Washington, DC: The Brookings Institution.

Alderman, H. (1993). *Poverty, household food security and nutrition in rural Pakistan.* Washington, DC: International Food Policy Research Institute.

Ammerman, R, & Hersen, M. (1995). *Children at risk: An evaluation of factors contributing to child abuse and neglect.* New York: Plenum Press.

American Bar Association. (1982). *Joint AMA-ABA guidelines: Present status of serologic testing in problems of disputed parentage.* Washington, DC: Author.

Arnhoff, F. (1975). Social consequences of policy toward mental illness. *Science, 188,* 1277–1281.

Baker, J. (1978). *The neighborhood advice project in Camden.* London: Routledge and Kegan Paul.

Barth, R. (1998). Abusive and neglecting parents and the care of their children." In M. Moan, A. Skolnick, and S. Sugarman (eds.), *All Our Families.* New York: Oxford University Press.

Barth, R. (1992). Adoption. In P. J. Pecora et al. (Eds.), *The child welfare challenge* (pp. 367–369). New York: Aldine de Gruyter.

Baumheier, E. C. (1971). *Intergenerational dependency, a study of public assistance in successive generations.* Unpublished doctoral diss., Brandeis University, Waltham, MA.

Baumrind, D. (1995). *Child maltreatment and optimal caregiving in social contexts.* New York: Garland.

Beam, B. T., & McFadden, J. J. (1988). *Employee benefits.* Homewood, IL: Irwin.

Bebbington, A., & Davies, B. (1983). Equity and efficiency in allocating personal social services. *Journal of Social Policy, 3,* 309–330.

Bell, W. (1987). *Contemporary social welfare* (2nd ed.). New York: Macmillan.

Bellak, L., & Barton, H. (1975). *Progress in community mental health.* New York: Brunner/Mazel.

Bernstein, B., & Meezan, W. (1975). *The impact of welfare on family stability.* New York: Center for New York City Affairs.

Besharov, D. (1986). *Criminal and civil liability in child welfare work: The growing trend* (3rd ed.). Washington, DC: National Legal Resource Center for Child Advocacy and Protection, American Bar Association.

Best, F. (1981). *Work-sharing, issues, options and prospects.* Grand Rapids, MI: W. E. Upjohn Institute on Employment Research.

Bickman, L. (1987). The functions of program theory. In L. Bickman (Ed.), *Using program theory in evaluation* (pp. 5–18). New Directions for Program Evaluation Series. San Francisco: Jossey-Bass.

Biestek, F. (1977). *Client self-determination in social work.* Chicago: Loyola University Press.

Boulding, K. (1962). Social justice in social dynamics. In R. B. Brandt (Ed.), *Social justice.* New York: Prentice Hall.

Brager, G. (1965). The indigenous worker: A new approach to the social work technician. *Social Work, 10,* 33–40.

Brenner, R. (1956). *From the depths.* New York: New York University Press.

Brittain, J. (1972). *The payroll tax for Social Security.* Washington, DC: The Brookings Institution.

Brown, M. (1981). *Working the street: Police discretion and dilemmas of reform.* New York: Basic Books.

Brown v. Topeka Board of Education, 347 U.S. 483 (1954).

Burke, V., & Townsend, A. (1974). Public welfare and work incentives: Theory and practice. In *Studies in public welfare,* Paper No. 14, Subcommittee on Fiscal Policy, Joint Economic Committee, United States Congress, April 15, 1974.

Burns, E. (1949). *The American social security system.* New York: Houghton Mifflin.

Burns, E. (1968). Childhood poverty and the children's allowance. In E. Burns (Ed.), *Children's allowances and the economic welfare of children* (pp. 1–9). New York: Citizens Committee of New York.

Burt, M., & Blair, L. (1974). *Options for improving the care of neglected and dependent children.* Washington, DC: The Urban Institute.

Caban v. Mohammed, 441 U.S. 380 (1979).

Canon, B. C. (1982). A framework for the analysis of judicial activism. In S. C. Halpern & C. M. Lamb (Eds.), *Supreme court activism and restraint* (pp. 86–99). Lexington, MA: Lexington Books.

Cassetty, J. (1978). *Child support and public policy.* Toronto: Lexington Books.

Chalk, R., & King, P. (1998). *Violence in families.* Washington, DC: National Academy Press, Commission on Behavioral Science, on Social Sciences, Committee on Education of the National Research Council, and the National Institute on Medicine.

Chambers, D. E. (1971). Residence requirements for welfare benefits. *Social Work, 14,* 29–36.

Chambers, D. E. (1985). The Reagan administration's welfare retrenchment policy: Terminating Social Security benefits for the disabled. *Policy Studies Review, 5,* 207–215.

Chambers, D. E. (1987). Policy weaknesses and political opportunities. *Social Service Review, 42,* 87–99.

Chambers, D. E., & Rodwell, M. K. (1989). Promises, promises: Predicting child abuse. *Policy Studies Review, 4,* 66–77.

Chapin, R., & Chambers, D. E. (1991). *Targeting payment in community residential services providing social skills development.* Mimeographed manuscript, University of Kansas, Lawrence.

Children's Defense Fund. (1988). *A children's defense budget, F.Y. 1989.* New York: Author.

Cicchetti, D., & Rizley, R. (1981). Developmental perspectives on the etiology, intergenerational transmission and sequelae of child maltreatment. In R. Rizley & D. Cicchetti (Eds.), *New directions for child development* (pp. 1–29). San Francisco: Jossey-Bass.

Connecticut General Statutes §17–34a(b)1.

Conrad, K., & Miller, T. (1987). Measuring and testing program philosophy. In L. Bickman (Ed.), *Using program theory in evaluation* (pp. 19–42). New Directions for Program Evaluation Series. San Francisco: Jossey-Bass.

Costin, L. (1992). Cruelty to children: A dormant issue and its rediscovery, 1920–1960. *Social Service Review 66,* 177–181.

Costin, L., & Rapp, C. (1984). *Child welfare policies and practices.* New York: McGraw-Hill.

Curtis, P., et al. (1995). *Child abuse and neglect: A look at the states.* Washington, DC: CWLA Press.

Damer, S., & Hague, C. (1971). Public participation in planning: A review. *Town Planning Review, 42,* 224–228.

Danziger, S., & Portney, K. (1988). *The distributional impacts of public policies.* New York: St. Martin's Press.

Deitchman, W. (1980). How many case managers does it take to screw in a light bulb? *Hospital and Community Psychiatry, 31,* 788–789.

DeNitto, D. M. (1991). *Social welfare: Politics and public policy.* Englewood Cliffs, NJ: Prentice Hall.

Department of Health and Social Security (UK). (1971). *Child benefit.* Leaflet No. CH1. London: Her Majesty's Stationery Office.

Department of Health and Social Security (UK). (1977). *Social security benefit rates.* Leaflet No. NI 196. London: Her Majesty's Stationery Office.

Derthick, M. (1979). *Policy making for social security.* Washington, DC: The Brookings Institution.

DeSchweinitz, K. (1939). *England's road to social security.* New York: A. S. Barnes.

Doern, G. B., & Phidd, R. W. (1983). *Canadian public policy: Ideas, structure, process.* Toronto: Metheun.

Donison, D. (1979). *Power to the poor.* London: Blackwell.

Egeland, B., & Papatola, K. (1987). Intergenerational continuity of abuse. In R. Gelles & J. Lancaster (Eds.), *Child abuse and neglect: Biosocial dimensions*. Hawthorne, NJ: Aldine de Gruyter.

Ehrmann, H. W. (1976). *Comparative legal cultures*. Englewood Cliffs, NJ: Prentice Hall.

Fanshel, D., & Shinn, E. (1978). *Children in foster care: A longitudinal investigation*. New York: Columbia University Press.

Feagin, J. (1975). *Subordinating the poor*. Englewood Cliffs, NJ: Prentice Hall.

Federal Register, (1975). Vol. 40; No. 125, p. 27355. Concerning Section 228—Social Services Programs for Individuals and Families, Title XX of the Social Security Act.

Feldman, R., Wodarski, J., & Flax, N. (1973). Pro-social and anti-social boys together. *Social Work, 19*, 26–36.

Festinger, T. (1976). The impact of the New York court review of children in foster care: A follow-up report. *Child Welfare, 8*, 515–544.

Field, T. (1983). Child abuse in monkeys and humans: A comparative perspective. In M. Reite and N. G. Caine (Eds.), *Child abuse: The nonhuman primate data* (pp. 169–178). New York: Alan R. Liss.

Garbarino, J. (1980). Preventing child maltreatment. In R. Price et al., (Eds.), *Prevention in mental health: Research, policy and practice* (pp. 63–80). Beverly Hills, CA: Sage.

Geron, S. (1991). Regulating the behavior of nursing homes through positive incentives: An analysis of the Illinois Quality Incentive Program (QUIP). *The Gerontologist, 31*, 299–301.

Gilbert, N., & Specht, H. (1974). *Dimensions of social welfare policy*. Englewood Cliffs, NJ: Prentice Hall.

Gilbert, N., & Terrell, P. (1998). *Dimensions of Social Policy* (4th ed.). Boston: Allyn & Bacon.

Gilley, T. (1990). *Empowering poor people*. Sydney: Brotherhood of St. Laurence.

Ginzberg, E. (1975). What next in health policy? *Science, 188*, 1182–1186.

Glennerster, H. (1985). *Paying for welfare*. New York: Blackwell.

Goering, J., & Coe, R. (1970). Cultural versus situational explanations for the medical behavior of the poor. *Social Science Quarterly, 51*, 309–319.

Goldsborough, D., et al. (1963). *The Social Security Administration: An interdisciplinary study of disability evaluation*. Mimeographed manuscript, George Washington University Law Center, Washington, DC.

Goodwin, L. (1972). *Do the poor want to work?* Washington, DC: The Brookings Institution.

Gordon, K. (1975). Introduction. In J. Pechman & P. Timpane (Eds.), *Work incentives and work guarantees*. Washington, DC: The Brookings Institution.

Handler, J. (1979). *Protecting the social services client*. New York: Academic Press.

Hannan, M., Tuma, N., & Groeneveld, L. (1977). Income and marital evidence from the income maintenance experiment. *American Journal of Sociology, 82*, 345–367.

Hansen, W. L., & Byers, J. G. (Eds.). (1990). *Unemployment insurance*. Madison: University of Wisconsin Press.

Hardcastle, D. (1971). The indigenous nonprofessional in the social service bureaucracy: A critical examination. *Social Work, 16*, 56–64.

Hardcastle, D. A., & Chambers, D. E. (1974). O.A.S.I.: A critical review. *Journal of Social Welfare, 2*, 19–26.

Horowitz, D. (1977). *The courts and social policy*. Washington, DC: The Brookings Institution.

Horowitz, F., & Paden, L. (1973). The effectiveness of environmental intervention programs. In B. Caldwell & H. Riciutti (Eds.), *Child development and social policy* (pp. 362–368). Chicago: University of Chicago Press.

Hoshino, G. (1965). Simplifying the means test. *Social Work, 39*, 98–103.

Howlett, M. (1991). Policy instruments, policy styles and policy implementation: National approaches to theories of instrument choice. *Policy Studies Journal, 19*, 1–21.

Hunter, R. (1965). *Poverty*. New York: Harper & Row.

In re Shannon S., No. 562 A.2d 79 (Conn. Super. 1989).

In the Matter of the Adoption of Schoffstall, No. 368 S.E.2nd 720 (W. Va. 1988).

Jackson, D. (1990). A conceptual framework for the comparative analysis of judicial review. *Policy Studies review, 19*, 161–171.

Janson, B. S. (1990). *Social welfare policy: From theory to practice*. Belmont, CA: Wadsworth.

Jones, K., Brown, J., & Bradshaw, J. (1979). *Issues and social policy*. London: Routledge and Kegan Paul.

Jones, M. A. (1988). *The history of the Australian welfare state*. Sydney: Allen and Unwin.

Kadushin, A. (1986). *Child welfare*. New York: Macmillan.

Kahn, A. J. (1963). *Investments in people: A social work perspective*. New Brunswick, NJ: Rutgers University, Urban Studies Center.

Kahn, A. J., & Kammerman, S. (1980). *Social services in international perspective*. New Brunswick, NJ: Transaction Books.

Kammerman S., & Kahn, A. J. (1976). *Social services in the United States*. Philadelphia: Temple University Press.

Kammerman, S., & Kahn, A. (1995). Social services for children, youth and families in the U.S. *Children and Youth Services, 12*, 116.

Kansas Statutes Annotated, §59-2101(a)(1).

Karger, H. J., & Stoesz, D. (1990). *American social welfare policy: A structural approach*. White Plains, NY: Longman.

Katz, S., & Gallagher, U. (1976). Subsidized adoption in America. *Family Law Quarterly, 10*, 3–54.

Keith-Lucas, A. (1975). A critique of the principle of client self-determination. In F. E. McDermott (Ed.), *Self determination in social work* (pp. 43–53). London: Routledge and Kegan Paul.

Kempe, C., Silverman, F., Steele, B., & Silver, H. (1962). The battered child syndrome. *Journal of Marriage and the Family, 18*, 17–24.

Kingson, E. R. (1989, July). Misconceptions distort Social Security policy discussions. *Social Work*, 357–362.

Kirk, S., & Kutchins, H. (1988). Deliberate misdiagnosis in mental health practice. *Social Service Review, 43*, 230–235.

Kolata, G. (1991, September 30). Parents of tiny infants find care choices are not theirs. *New York Times*, pp. A1, A11.

Kollman, G. (1996). *How long does it take new retirees to recover the value of their Social Security taxes?* 94-149 EPW. Washington, DC: Congressional Research Service.

Kopolow, L. E. (1976). A review of major implications of the O'Connor v. Donaldson decision. *American Journal of Psychiatry, 133*, 379–383.

Kotz, N. (1979). *Hunger in America*. New York: The Field Foundation.

Krammer, R. (1970). *Community development in Israel and the Netherlands*. Berkeley: University of California Press.

Krause, H. D. (1981). *Child support in America*. Charlottesville, VA: The Mitchie Company.

Legal analysis: Infrequent contacts with the child, grounds to terminate parental rights in abandonment cases. (1989, December). *ABA Juvenile and Child Welfare Reporter, 8*, 157–158.

Levine, M. (1986). The role of special master in institutional reform litigation. *Law and Policy, 8*, 275–321.

Lewis, G., & Morrison, R. J. (1988). *Interactions among social welfare programs*. Discussion Paper No. 866–88. Madison, WI: University of Wisconsin, Institute for Research on Poverty.

Lewis, O. (1975). The culture of poverty. *Science, 188*, 865–880.

Linder, S. H., & Peters, B. G. (1989). Instruments of government: Perception and contexts. *Journal of Public Policy, 9*, 35–38.

Lindsey, D. (1994). *The welfare of children*. New York: Oxford University Press.

Lipsky, M. (1980). *Street level bureaucracy: Dilemmas of the individual in public services*. New York: Russell Sage Foundation.

MacDonald, M. (1975). *Food stamps and income maintenance*. New York: Academic Press.

Macias, C., Kinney, R., Farley, O. W., Jackson, R., & Vos, B. (1994). The role of case management within a community support system: Partnership with psychosocial rehabilitation. *Community Mental Health Journal, 30*, 323–339.

Marbury v. Madison, 1 Cranch 137 (1803).

Marmor, T. R. (1970). Public medical programs and cash assistance. In I. Lurie (Ed.), *Interpreting income maintenance programs* (pp. 271–278). New York: Academic Press.

Marshall, J. D. (1968). *The old poor law* (pp. 14–15). London: Macmillan.

Mashaw, J. (1983). *Bureaucratic justice*. New Haven: Yale University Press.

Matheson, L. (1996). The politics of the Indian Child Welfare Act. *Social Work, 41*, 232.

Matter of Adoption of B.C.S., 777 P.2d 776 (Kan. 1989).

McDermott, W., Deuschle, K., & Barnett, C. (1972). Health care experiment at many farms. *Science, 175*, 23–30.

Menefee, J., Edwards, B., & Scheiber, S. (1981). Analysis of non-participation in the SSI program. *Social Security Bulletin, 44*, 3–21.

Mental Health Association of Minnesota v. Schweiker, 5543 Fed. Suppl., 157 (D.C. Minn., 1983).

Merton, R. (1957). *Social theory and social structure*. Glencoe, IL: The Free Press of Glencoe.

Miller, W. (1962). The impact of a "total community" delinquency control project. *Social Problems, 10*, 168–191.

Modrcin, M., Rapp, C., & Poertner, J. (1988). The evaluation of case management services with the chronically mentally ill. *Evaluation and Program Planning, 11*, 307–314.

Morgan, J., et al. (1974). *Five thousand american families: Patterns of economic progress* (Vol. 1). Ann Arbor, MI: Institute for Social Research.

Morris, R. (1979). *Social policy of the American state*. New York: Harper & Row.

Mott, P. (1976). *Meeting human needs, a social and political History of Title XX*. Columbus, OH: National Conference on Social Welfare.

Munnell, A. (1977). *The future of Social Security*. Washington, DC: The Brookings Institution.

Murdrick, N. (1978). The use of AFDC by previously high and low income households. *Social Service Review, 52*, 107–115.

Musgrave, R. (1961). *The theory of public finance*. New York: McGraw-Hill.

Myrdal, A. (1968). *Nation and family*. Cambridge, MA: The MIT Press.

Nathan, R., Manvel, A. D., & Calkins, S. E. (1976). *Monitoring revenue sharing*. Washington, DC: The Brookings Institution. (1990).

Newton, K. (1976). *Second city politics*. London: Oxford University Press.

Notes, J. (1989). The least dangerous branch. *Revue de Droit de McGill, 4*, 1025–1028.

O'Connor, A. (1989). Child protection investigations: Miranda warnings. *Juvenile and Child Welfare Law Reporter, 8*, 29–30.

Orwell, G. (1937). *The road to Wigan Pier*. London: Golancz and Song.

Pechman, J. A., & Timpane, P. M. (Eds.). (1975). *Work incentives and income guarantees*. Washington, DC: The Brookings Institution.

Pecora, P., et al. (1992). *The child welfare challenge*. New York: Aldine de Gruyter.

Pelton, L. (1994). The role of material factors in child abuse and neglect. In G. Melton and F. Barry (Eds.), *Protecting children from abuse and neglect* (pp. 46–58). New York: Guilford Press.

Perlman, H. H. (1975). Self-determination: Reality or illusion. In F. E. McDermott (Ed.), *Self determination in social work* (pp. 65–80). London: Routledge and Kegan Paul.

Petr, C. (1998). *Social work with children and their families*. New York: Oxford University Press.

Pettigrew, T. (1980). Social psychology's contribution to an understanding of poverty. In Vincent T. Covello (Ed.), *Poverty and public policy* (pp. 198–224). Cambridge, MA: Shenkman.

Phillips, D. (1974). Community health councils. In K. Jones (Ed.), *The yearbook of social policy in Britain* (pp. 62–76). London: Routledge and Kegan Paul.

Pinstrup-Andersen, P. (1994). *World food trends and future food security.* Food Policy Statement Number 18. Washington, DC: International Food Policy Research Institute.

Piore, M. (1979). Qualitative research in economics. *Administrative Science Quarterly, 24,* 560–569.

Piven, F. F., & Cloward, R. (1971). *Regulating the poor.* New York: Pantheon Books.

Plantz, M., Hubbell, R., Barrett, B., & Dobrec, A. (1989). The Indian Child Welfare Act: A status report. *Children Today, 18,* 27.

Plotnick, R. D. (1989). Directions for reducing child poverty. *Social Work, 32,* 523–530.

Podell, L. (1968). *Families on welfare in New York City.* New York: The Center for Study of Urban Problems.

Poertner, J. (1987). The Kansas Family and Child Trust Fund: Five year report. *Child Welfare, 66,* 3–12.

Polyani, K. (1944). *The great transformation.* New York: Holt, Rinehart and Winston.

Prisons replace hospitals for the nation's mentally ill, *New York Times,* March 5, 1998, p. A1.

Rapp, C. (1998). *The Strengths Model.* Oxford: Oxford University Press.

Rapp, C., & Chamberlain, R. (1985). Case management services to the chronically mentally ill. *Social Work, 28,* 16–22.

Rapp, C., & Wintersteen, R. (1989). The Strengths Model of case management: Results from twelve demonstrations. *Psychosocial Rehabilitation Journal, 13,* 23–32.

Rein, M. (1983a). *From policy to practice.* Armonk, NY: M. E. Sharpe.

Rein, M. (1983b). Value-critical policy analysis. In D. Callahan & B. Jennings (Eds.), *Ethics, the social sciences and policy analysis* (pp. 83–112). New York: Plenum Press.

Rein, M., & Rainwater, L. (1978). Patterns of welfare use. *Social Service Review, 52,* 511–534.

Rein, M., & Rainwater, L. (Eds.). (1986). *Public/private interplay in social protection.* Armonk, NY: M. E. Sharpe.

Reynolds, B. C. (1942). *Learning and teaching in the practice of social work.* New York: Farrar and Rinehart.

Rodwell, M. (1988). *Policy implications of the multiple meanings of neglect: A naturalistic study of child neglect.* Ph.D. diss., University of Kansas School of Social Welfare, Lawrence.

Rosenbaum, A., & O'Leary, D. (1981). Marital violence: Characteristics of abusive couples. *Journal of Consulting and Clinical Psychology, 49,* 63–71.

Rossi, P. (1979). *Evaluation, a systematic approach.* Beverly Hills, CA: Sage.

Ryan, C., Sherman, P. S., & Judd, C. M. (1994). Accounting for case management effects in the evaluation of mental health services. *Journal of Consulting and Clinical Psychology, 62,* 965–974.

Saleeby, D. (1992). Building a strengths perspective for social work. In Dennis Saleeby (Ed.), *The strengths perspective in social work practice.* New York: Longman.

Sawhill, I. (1975). *Income transfers and family structure.* Washington, DC: The Urban Institute.

In re Schoffstall, No. 368 S. E. 2nd 720 (W. Va.) 1988).

Schorr, A. (1965). Income maintenance and the birth rate. *Social Security Bulletin, 28,* 2–3.

Schultz, T. (1962). Reflections on investment in man. *Journal of political economy, LXX* (Supplement), 2.

Sedlak, A. (1987). *Study of the national incidence and prevalence of child abuse and neglect: Report on data and analysis.* Technical Report. Washington, DC: Department of Health and Human Services, National Center on Child Abuse and Neglect.

Segal, E. (1995). Adoption assistance and the law. In E. C. Segal (Ed.), *Adoption of children with special needs: Issues in law and policy* (pp. 127–134). Washington, DC: American Bar Association.

In re Shannon S., No. 562 A. 2d 79 (Conn. Super. 1989).

Sharon, D. (1972). Eduardo the healer. *Natural History*, 32–49.

Sheehan, S. (1976). *A welfare mother.* New York: Signet Books.

Shyne, A., & Schroeder, A. (1978). *National study of social services for children.* Rockville, MD: Westat.

Social Security Administration. (1982a). *Social Security handbook.* Social Security Regulations No. 83-15, 16, 17. Washington, DC: U.S. Government Printing Office.

Social Security Administration. (1982b). *SSI for the aged, blind, and disabled.* Publication No. 05-11111. Washington, DC: U.S. Government Printing Office.

Spargo, J. (1968). *The bitter cry of the children.* New York: Quadrangle Books.

Stanford Research Institute and Mathematics Policy Research. (1978). *The Seattle-Denver Income Maintenance Experiment, midexperiment results and a generalization to the national population.* Menlo Park, CA: Author.

Stanley v. Illinois, 405 U.S. 645 (1972).

Stein, T. (1991). *Child welfare and the law.* New York: Longman.

Steiner, G. (1976). *The children's cause.* Washington, DC: The Brookings Institution.

Summary of the Adoption and Safe Families Act of 1997. (1997). Washington, DC: Child Welfare League of America.

Tarasoff vs. The Regents of University of California. Supreme Court of California July 1, 1976).

Tate, C. N. (1990). Introductory notes. *Policy Studies Review, 19,* 76–80.

Tax Reform Act of 1969, P.L. 91-972, H.R. 13270

Terkel, S. (1992). *Working.* New York: Avon.

Titmuss, R. (1968). Welfare state and welfare society. In *Commitment to welfare* (pp. 130–134). London: Allen and Unwin, Ltd.

Tucker, D. (1980). Coordination and citizen participation. *Social Service Review, 54,* 17–18.

Tzeng, O., Jackson, J., & Karlson, H. (1991). *Theories of child abuse and neglect.* New York: Praeger.

United Nations, Food and Agricultural Organization. (1977). *The fourth world food survey.* Statistics Series No. 11. Rome: Author.

United Way of America. (1991). *United Way of America research services campaign summary survey.* Alexandria, VA: Author.

U.S. Congress, House of Representatives. (1988). *Medicaid source book. Background data and analysis.* Washington, DC: U.S. Government Printing Office.

U.S. Congress, House Ways and Means Committee. (1991). *Green Book* (Washington, DC: U.S. House of Representatives, 1991).

U.S. Congress, House Ways and Means Committee. (1997). *The Green Book—1997.* 104th Congress, 2nd Session, Nov. 4, 1996, Print No. 104-14, Table 1-50. Washington, DC: U.S. Government Printing Office.

U.S. Congress, Senate Subcommittee on Oversight of Government Management of the Senate Committee on Governmental Affairs. (June 8, 1983). *SSDI reviews: The role of the administrative law judge.* Hearing Report (and Appendix), 98th Congress, 1st Session. Washington, DC: U.S. Government Printing Office.

U.S. Department of Health, Education and Welfare Office of the Secretary. (1980). *Annual report to the Congress on Title XX of the Social Security Act, Fiscal Year 1979.* Washington, DC: U.S. Government Printing Office.

U.S. Department of Health and Human Services, Administration for Children and Families, Office of Policy, Planning, and Legislation. (1991). *Social services block grants, summary of pre-expenditure reports, fiscal year 1990.* Washington, DC: U.S. Government Printing Office.

U.S. Department of Health and Human Services, Family Support Administration, Office of Family Assistance. (1989). *Characteristics of state plans for aid to families and dependent children under Title IV-A of the Social Security Act.* Washington, DC: U.S. Government Printing Office.

U.S. Department of Health and Human Services, National Center on Child Abuse and Neglect. *Child maltreatment 1993: Reports from the states to the NCCAN.* Washington, DC: U.S. Government Printing Office.

U.S. Department of Health and Human Services, Social Security Administration, Office of Family Assistance. *Characteristics of state plans for aid to families with dependent children—1984.* Washington, DC: U.S. Government Printing Office.

Villers Foundation. (1987). *On the other side of easy street.* Washington, DC: Author.

Vondra, J. (1990). Risk factors associated with child abuse and neglect—sociological and ecological factors. In R. Ammerman & M. Hersen (Eds.), *Children at risk* (p. 156). New York: Plenum Press.

Vondra, J. (1995). Sociological and ecological risk factors in child abuse. In R. Ammerman & M. Hersen (Eds.), *Children at risk: An evaluation of factors contributing to child abuse and neglect* (pp. 156–166). New York: Plenum Press.

Walker, H., & Cohen, B. (1985). Scope statements: Imperatives for evaluating theory. *American Sociological review, 50,* 288–301.

Webster, C. D. (1984). On gaining acceptance: Why the courts accept only reluctantly findings from experimental and social psychology. *International Journal of Law and Psychiatry, 7,* 407–414.

Wedel, K. (1991). Designing and implementing performance contracting. In R. L. Edwards & J. A. Yankee (Eds.), *Skills for effective service management* (pp. 106–118). Silver Spring, MD: NASW Press.

Wedel, K., & Colston, S. (1988). Performance contracting for human services: Issues and suggestions. *Administration in Social Work, 12,* 73–87.

Weick, A. (1987). Reconceptualizing the philosophical base of social work. *Social Service Review, 42,* 218–230.

Weick, A., & Pope, L. (1975). *Knowing what's best: A new look at self-determination.* Mimeographed manuscript. Lawrence: University of Kansas.

Weissman, H. (1970). *Community councils and community control.* Pittsburgh: University of Pittsburgh Press.

Wolfe, D., et al. (1997). Empowering youth to promote healthy relationships. In D. Wolfe, R. McMahon, & R. Peters (Eds.), *Child abuse: New directions in prevention and treatment across the lifespan* (pp. 112–118). Thousand Oaks, CA: Sage.

Wollons, R. (1993). *Children at risk in America: History, concepts and public policy.* Albany: State University of New York.

Wootton, B. (1959). *Social science and social pathology.* London: Allen and Unwin.

Zigler, E., & Hall, N. (1989). Physical child abuse in America: Past, present and future. In D. Cicchetti & V. Carlson (Eds.), *Child maltreatment: Theory and research on the causes and consequences of child abuse and neglect* (pp. 52–64). New York: Cambridge University Press.

INDEX

266